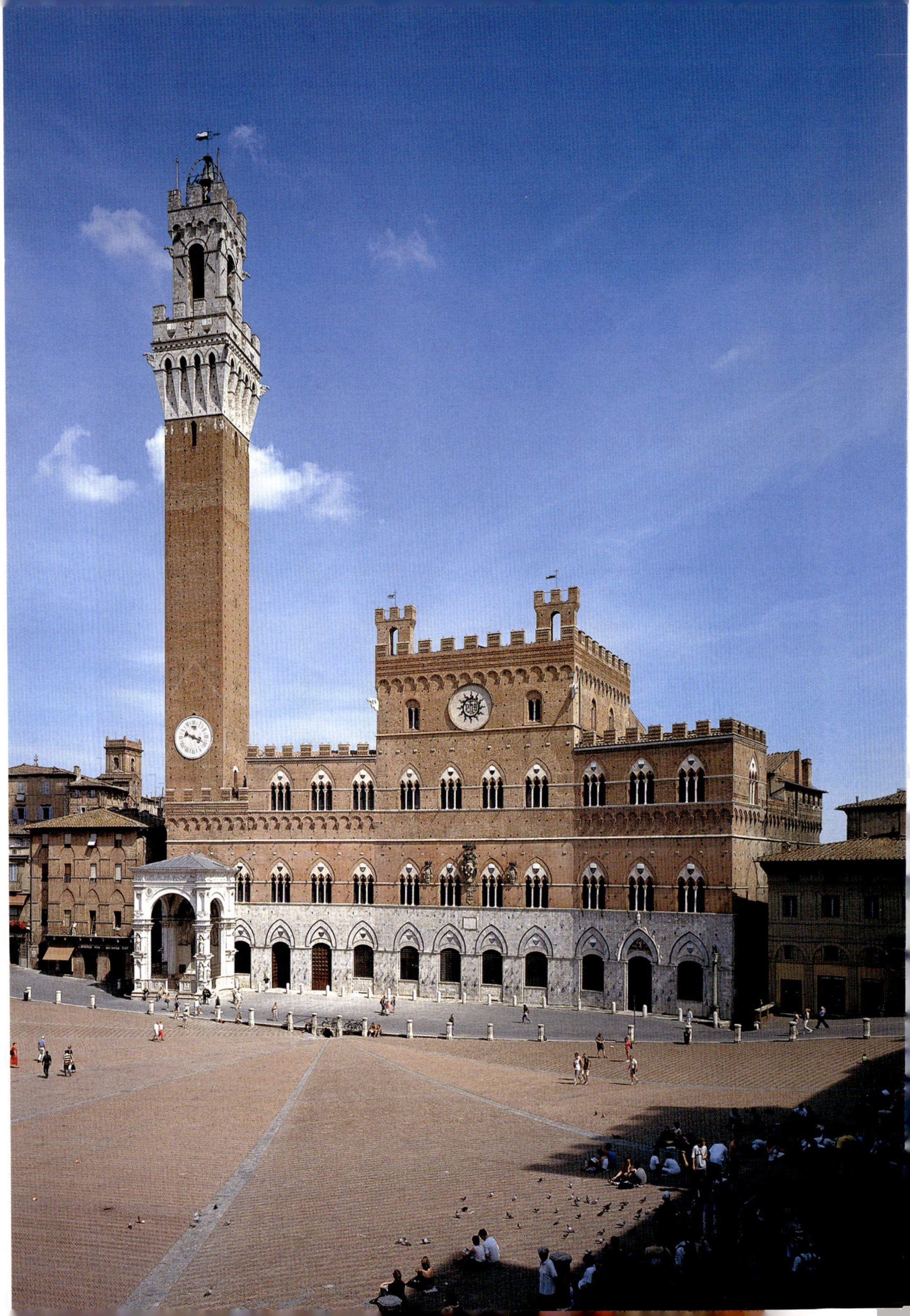

Introduction

One of the most emotional moments of Siena's world-famous Palio is when the historical parade enters the Campo (pl. 1). Marked by a fanfare of trumpets, this elaborate procession of men and women representing various aspects of Siena's past progresses slowly round the circumference of what shortly becomes the track for the horse race itself. As remarked by a number of modern scholars of the Palio, it is as if the independent Republic of Siena lives again – wiping out later centuries of political domination by others. Dating in its present form to 1879, the procession acts as a metaphor for how the Sienese wish to represent themselves and their history.[1] It also reflects a long and enduring historiographical tradition that celebrates Siena's identity as an independent city state and interprets that period of independence as the high point of the city's political, economic and cultural life.

Two events mark the beginning and end of this carefully constructed historiography. The first is the battle of Montaperti in 1260 when the Sienese, threatened by outside forces – principally those of their traditional enemy and close neighbour, Florence – won a decisive victory. This event quickly took on the status of a civic myth that was elaborated over the centuries and still features today in modern Sienese consciousness. Thus, a notice, spotted a few years ago at a bus stop on the outskirts of the city where supporters of Arezzo's visiting football team were likely to alight, warned the away-fans to 'remember Montaperti'. The second is the capitulation of Siena to the army of the Hapsburg emperor Charles V and his Florentine allies in 1555 after a long and agonising siege. Although the incorporation of Siena and its surrounding territories into the Medici state was only finally conceded in 1559, the entry of imperial and Florentine troops

1 Siena, the Piazza of the Campo, with the Palazzo Pubblico and the Cappella di Piazza.

Modern scholars, having interpreted the year 1221 to denote something other than the date of the painting's execution, have correctly assigned the painter's work to the 1260s and 1270s.[4] Nevertheless, it is notable that the histories of Sienese painting generally start with Guido da Siena – this painter being the only thirteenth-century Sienese artist who, to date, has had a full-length monograph devoted to him, despite the fact that there are other thirteenth-century Sienese painters for whom there exist signed works or documentary references.[5] Guido da Siena is thus conventionally seen as the predecessor of Duccio, celebrated in the history of Italian painting as a worthy rival of the Florentine painter Giotto. Thereafter, Sienese painting is securely associated with artists such as Simone Martini and Pietro and Ambrogio Lorenzetti, whose work is frequently characterised as the most innovative in fourteenth-century Italian painting. Sienese painters working in the second half of the fourteenth century, during a period of great political turmoil and economic hardship, have received less critical acclaim but a number of recently published monographs on Bartolo di Fredi, Luca di Tommè and Bartolommeo Bulgarini have attracted new interest in the painting of this period.[6]

Similarly, while fifteenth- and early sixteenth-century Sienese painting has generally been assigned a more peripheral role in the history of Italian art than that of other Italian cities such as Florence, Rome and Venice, several major exhibitions staged in the last two decades of the twentieth century highlighted the achievements of Sienese painters such as Sassetta, Giovanni di Paolo, Domenico di Bartolo, Sano di Pietro, Francesco di Giorgio and Domenico Beccafumi, as well as a variety of other artists.[7]

Beccafumi, whose documented working life spans the first half of the sixteenth century, and who gained a glowing testimonial from Giorgio Vasari in his influential *Lives of the Painters, Sculptors and Architects* (1568 edition), died in 1551. The year of his death thus occurred just before Siena's final defeat and loss of political autonomy. Although Sienese painting continued to flourish in later centuries, as seen by examples of seventeenth- and eighteenth-century Sienese painters' work in the city's principal art gallery, the Pinacoteca, it is striking that the majority of visitors rarely linger in these rooms. It appears that such is the power of the way in which the Sienese have constructed their history that it continues to cast a long shadow on how we view and appreciate their art.

* * *

Topography

A popular song still sung today by the Sienese ends with the refrain, 'Siena, the most beautiful city in the world'. Although entirely conventional in tone, this sentiment reflects the intense pride that the Sienese have for their city, a pride that dates back many centuries. Thus, from the thirteenth century, government directives relating to urban planning frequently refer to the desire of the civic officials to make the city a more beautiful and pleasant place.[8] And, indeed, Siena is still a strikingly beautiful city. Set on three hills, its winding streets follow the irregular contours of its natural site (pl. 4). Enclosed by long stretches of its original medieval walls, it is largely constructed in brick, the product of the reddish soil on which Siena is built and whose colour has entered the English language as 'burnt sienna'. This soil or *tufo* is sufficiently soft to allow the hilltop site to be easily excavated, creating an alternative, hidden city of subterranean passages, cellars and storehouses. Two major civic sites – both marked by tall *campanili* –

4 Aerial view of Siena.

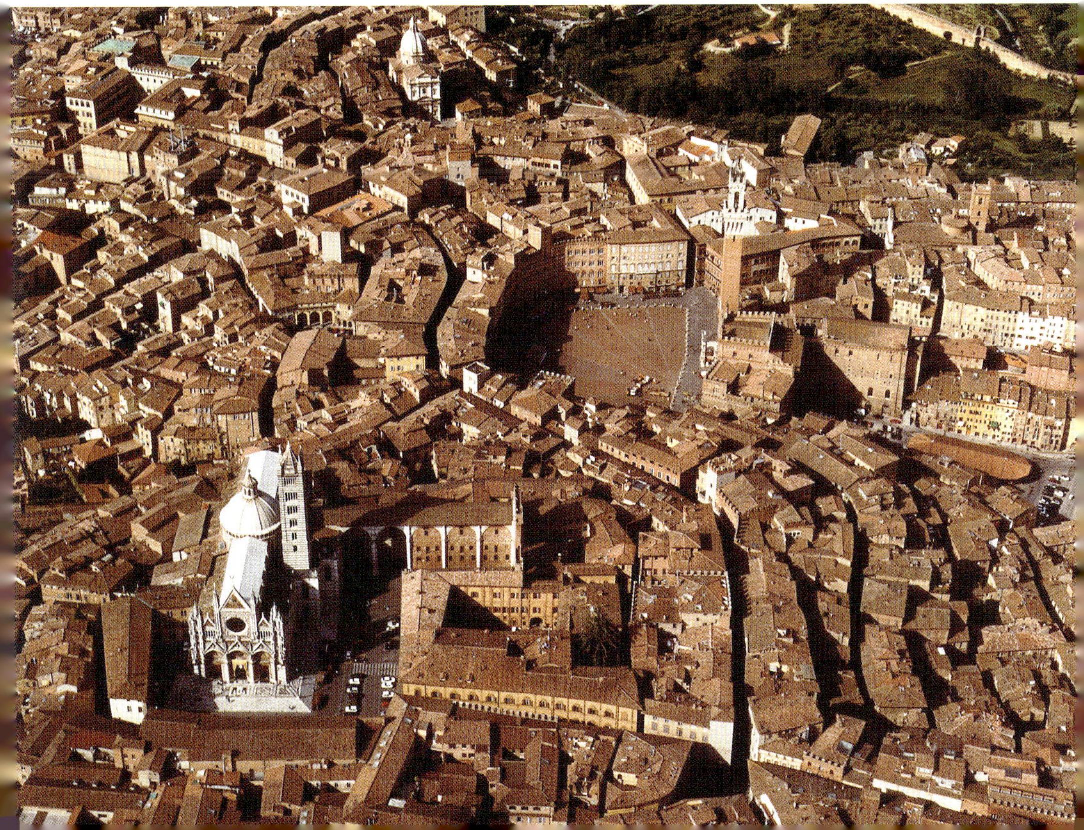

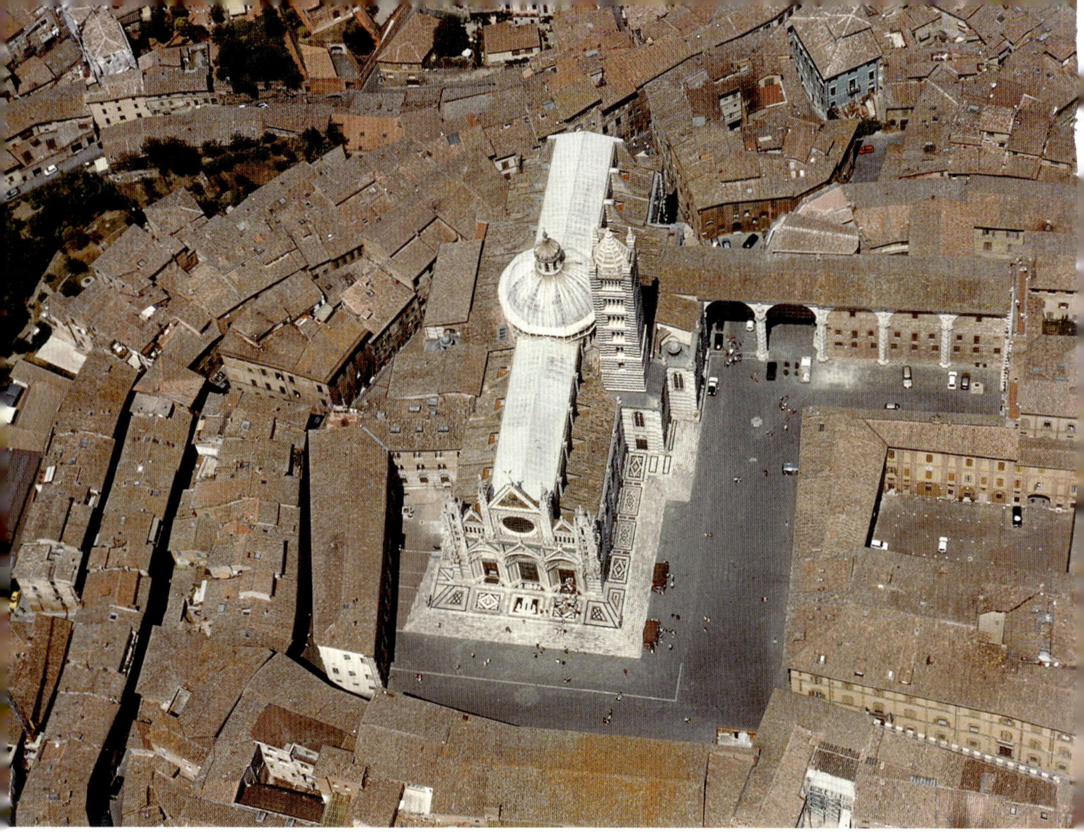

5 Aerial view of the cathedral.

stand out within the tightly packed urban fabric. The oldest of these belongs to the city's cathedral, built on the summit of a hill that was originally the site of a sixth-century fortress, part of which now acts as the foundations of the cathedral *campanile* (pl. 5).[9] Faced with dark green, pink and white marble and decorated with sculpture, the exterior of this monumental ecclesiastical building is strikingly different from that of the other major public buildings in the city. The result of several building campaigns dating from the thirteenth and fourteenth centuries, the cathedral and its baptistery (built below the chancel as an integral part of the building) was and still is the principal religious building of the city. The original bishop's palace stood adjacent to the south of the cathedral.[10] The residence of the cathedral clergy, meanwhile, was situated on the north side of the cathedral. As indicated, the cathedral was a place that witnessed rituals that were not only religious but also overtly political (see pls 2–3); and it housed images that were deeply venerated by the Sienese (see, for example, pl. 20). It was thus a building invested with enormous significance and its embellishment was a constant cause of concern not only to the bishop and his clergy but also to the Sienese government itself who delegated this particular task to a special board of civic officials, the Opera del Duomo.

Facing the cathedral is another important civic building, the Spedale di Santa Maria della Scala (the Hospital of Saint Mary of the Stairs).[11] The product of centuries of building and re-fashioning – of which the present scheme to turn it into an extensive civic museum is the latest stage – the hospital grew from a simple loggia to shelter pilgrims to a huge complex of buildings built along one side of the cathedral square (pl. 6) and down the steep slope of the hillside leading up to it (see pls 67, 96). Housing a church, oratories, meeting rooms, offices, lodgings for pilgrims, hospital wards, an orphanage, residential quarters for the rector and the religious community serving the hospital, granaries, storerooms and stables, the monumental scale of this building demonstrates both the variety of charitable functions that the hospital performed for the city and also its importance for Siena's government. Like the cathedral, it too became a location for paintings that supported the diverse religious, social and political activities that took place within its walls.

The second major civic site of Siena is the Campo itself – situated a short distance from the cathedral and comprising a harmonious semi-circle of open space (see pls 1, 4). For centuries it has represented the civic heart of the city and the place where the Sienese naturally congregate both for official public spectacles, such as the Palio, or for private recreational enjoyment, such as the evening stroll or *passeggiata*. Paved as long ago as the 1330s, its design was further enhanced early in the fifteenth century by the erection of an ornate marble fountain known as the Fonte Gaia – the 'fountain of joy' (see pl. 65). A nineteenth-century copy replaces it and is positioned slightly to the left of the original site, in order to make it a more central feature of the Campo; the original sculptures are now exhibited in the museum of the Spedale di Santa Maria della Scala.

Directly opposite the Fonte Gaia, along the south side of the Campo, stands the town hall or Palazzo Pubblico (see pl. 1), begun in the late thirteenth century by amalgamating several earlier buildings and incorporating a narrow medieval alleyway into its design. Its scale, its towering *campanile* – known as the Torre del Mangia – and its crenellations give the building an air of strength and security appropriate for the seat of civic government. The stone facing of the ground floor and the elegant design of the windows on the upper floors also invest the building with an air of ele-

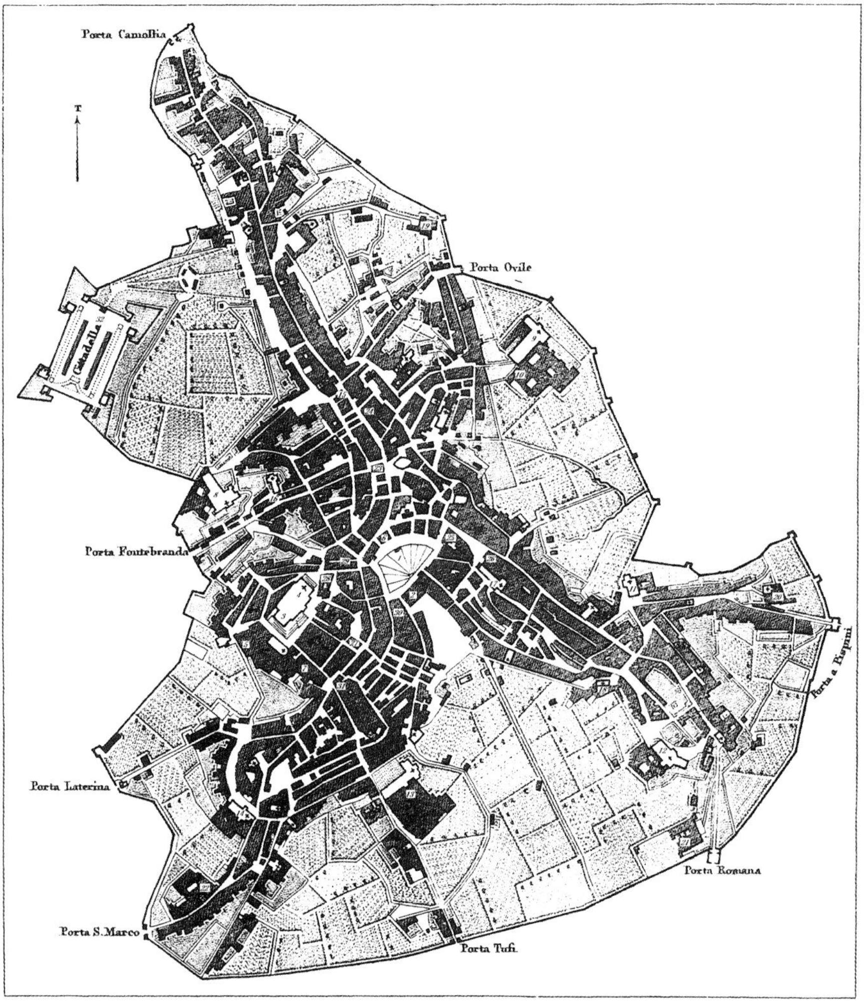

6 Plan of Siena.

1 Campo
2 Palazzo Pubblico
3 Cathedral
4 Baptistery
5 Spedale di Santa Maria della Scala
6 Loggia of the Mercanzia
7 Palazzo del Capitano della Guerra
8 San Domenico
9 San Francesco
10 Oratory of San Bernardino
11 Santo Spirito
12 Santa Maria dei Servi
13 Sant'Agostino
14 San Niccolò al Carmine
15 Santa Maria delle Nevi
16 Santa Caterina in Fontebranda
17 San Martino
18 San Girolamo
19 San Lorenzo
20 Santa Chiara (after 1555)
21 San Niccolò
22 Santa Marta
23 Palazzo Tolomei
24 Palazzo Spannocchi
25 Palazzo Piccolomini
26 Loggia of Pius II
27 Palazzo Piccolomini (delle Papesse)
28 Palazzo Petrucci
29 Palazzo Venturi
30 Palazzo Chigi
31 Palazzo Borghesi
32 Fortress

gance and civility. Designed to house the residential quarters of the city's judge – the Podestà – and of leading members of government, together with council rooms, chapels, offices, prison cells and storerooms, the Palazzo Pubblico fulfilled a wide range of functions.[12]

Like the Spedale, it too was enlarged during its history. A fifteenth-century painting of Saint Bernardino preaching outside the Palazzo Pubblico gives a sense of its original design with a tall tower-like building at its centre and two wings comprising only two storeys on either side (see pl. 95). This painting also shows the original form of the external chapel, known as the Cappella di Piazza (the Chapel of the Piazza), built between 1352 and 1376 as an expression of thanks for the cessation of plague that decimated the city in 1348. Originally built as a single-storey loggia with a simple pitched roof, the chapel's classicising upper storey was added in the 1460s (see pl. 1). As the seat of the city government, the Palazzo Pubblico was also a building invested with huge significance both for the government of Siena and the Sienese people. Its painted decoration had to reflect this – particularly by exemplifying certain political ideologies designed to inspire those in charge of Siena's government and to impress visiting dignitaries.

These three major civic buildings, therefore, had enormous prestige, a prestige that was reflected in their constant embellishment over the centuries by the city's leading painters. Thus in 1302 Duccio was commissioned to execute an altarpiece for a chapel in the Palazzo Pubblico. Nine years later, in 1311, his magnificent double-sided altarpiece, popularly known as the *Maestà* (see pls 35, 36, 38), was placed over the high altar of the cathedral. And at about the same time, a multi-tiered altarpiece of the Virgin and Child with saints, now in the Pinacoteca, was commissioned from Duccio for the high altar of the hospital church of Santa Maria della Scala.[13] Similarly, towards the end of the period covered in this book, one of Beccafumi's earliest commissions in the second decade of the sixteenth century was for an altarpiece and frescoes for a chapel on the ground floor of the rector's palace in the Spedale. Then between 1529 and 1535 he executed a high sophisticated painted scheme for the ceiling of one of the principal council rooms in the Palazzo Pubblico (see pls 146–9), and at the very end of his life, in the 1540s, he received commissions to embellish the chancel of the cathedral in a variety of media (see pl. 117).[14] Such continuity is a striking feature both of Sienese culture in general and of Sienese painting in particular. In the following chapters, therefore, there will be good reasons for returning frequently to these three major civic sites in order to discuss the paintings commissioned for them.

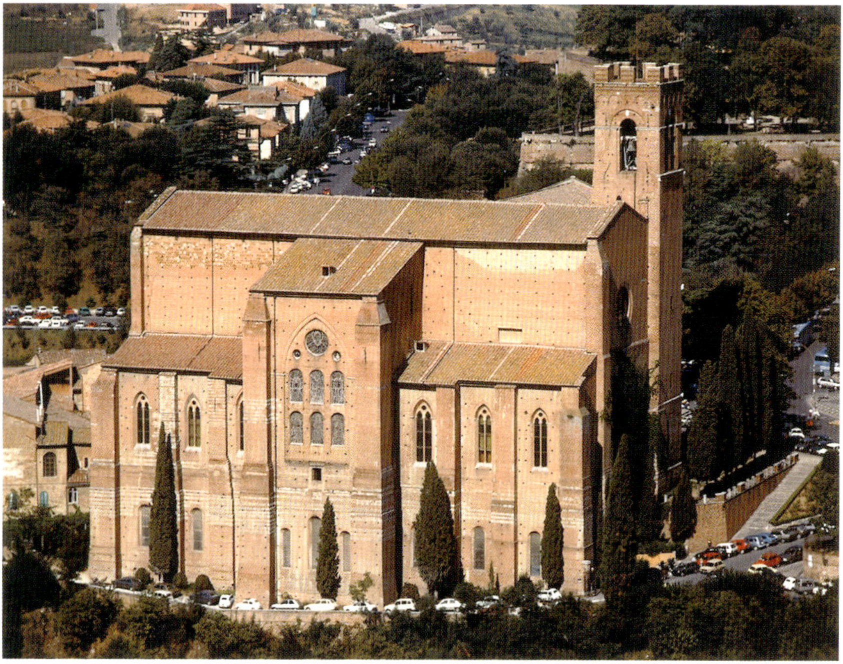

7 Siena, San Domenico.

Other focal points in the fabric of Siena are provided by the large churches and friaries belonging to the mendicant orders, who were particularly successful in serving the religious needs of urban populations in the thirteenth and fourteenth centuries. Monumental in scale and fronted by squares used for preaching (see pl. 94), the churches of San Domenico, San Francesco, Santa Maria dei Servi, Sant'Agostino and San Niccolò al Carmine[15] are all set at a distance from the city centre, as defined by the cathedral, Spedale and Palazzo Pubblico (see pl. 6), and utilise land that, at the time of their construction, was still outside the city walls. Their imposing edifices soon became the centres of new urban districts: thus the Dominican church of San Domenico became the centre of a part of the city known as Camporegio and the object of the patronage not only of the city government, who regularly gave financial support for its development, but also of powerful local families, such as the Malavolti (pl. 7). During the fifteenth century, reformed branches of the Dominican and Franciscan orders,

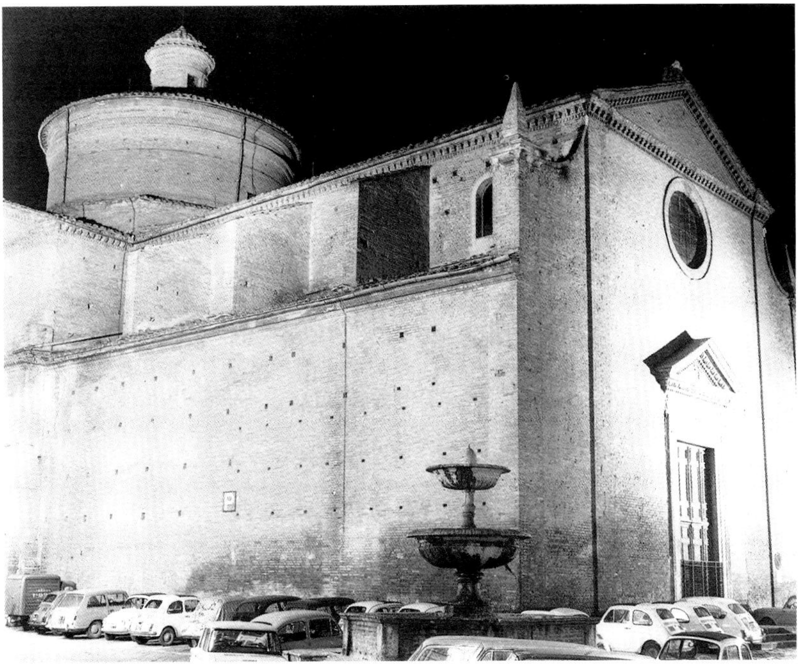

8 Siena, Santo Spirito.

known as the Observants, then built new churches. While the Franciscan Observants chose a rural site outside the city for their new church of the Osservanza, it was still financed by both the government and the Petrucci family. The new Dominican Observant church of Santo Spirito, meanwhile, was constructed round an earlier church that stood within the city walls, near the Porta Pispini, again associating the church with a particular urban locality (pls 6, 8).[16] Although they reflected contemporary architectural fashion, all Siena's mendicant churches were built largely in brick and on much simpler lines than the cathedral (see pl. 5). The scale of these buildings, however, advertised the prestige of the orders and also facilitated their aim of preaching to large congregations gathered inside their churches. The religious order in question generally kept control over how both the church and the adjacent conventual buildings were embellished, but it was also dependent on the financial support of the laity. This principally took the form of local families founding altars and chapels in the churches where

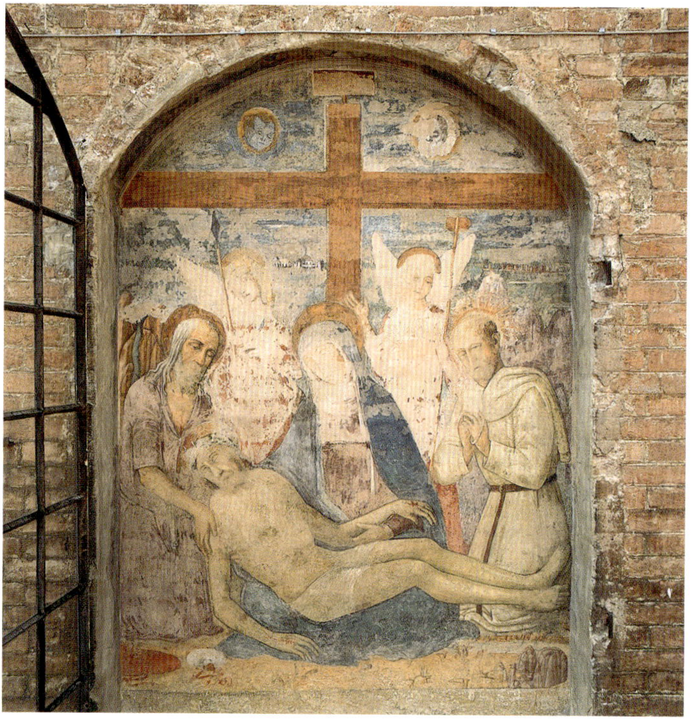

Guerra, the city's military commander (see pl. 6). The city guilds also had their own palaces where they conducted their meetings and administrative business. One of the most impressive of these was the guild hall belonging to the Mercanzia, an official body representing the political, legal and economic interests of the city's merchants, particularly those engaged in international trade. Such was the importance of the Mercanzia that it was represented on one of the city's principal governing councils, the Consistory. Its status was also reflected in the location of its hall, begun in 1309, facing onto the Campo directly opposite the Palazzo Pubblico and elevated above a row of shops. The other side of the building faced the main intersection of the city, the Croce al Travaglio (see pl. 6). In the fifteenth century, a grand loggia was added to this side of the building that – in terms of its scale and sculpted decoration – boldly advertised the identity of the Mercanzia as an important civic institution and still strikingly dominates one of the city's main thoroughfares (pl. 11).[19]

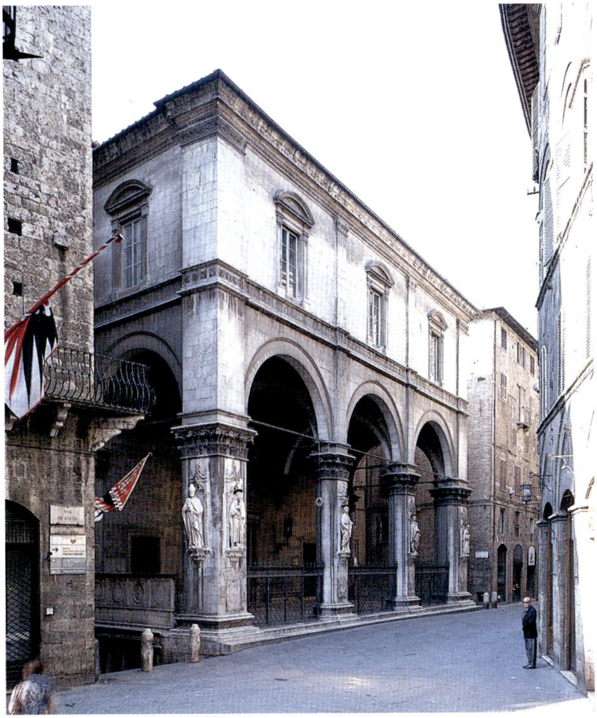

10 (*facing page*) Guidoccio Cozzarelli, *Lamentation over the Dead Christ by the Virgin and Saint Jerome and the Blessed Giovanni Colombini* (*c.* 1450–1516). Fresco, 210 × 150 cm. Siena, via San Girolamo, 8.

11 Siena, Loggia of the Mercanzia.

The city government was also concerned to provide an adequate water supply, which took the form of an elaborate network of underground aqueducts and an impressive series of monumental fountains. The latter were strictly functional and – apart from the Fonte Gaia (see pl. 65) – not embellished by painting or sculpture. This, however, was not true of the city gateways (see pl. 6). These imposing fortified entry points into the city were frequently painted with frescoed images protected under projecting stone canopies. It is still possible to see the traces of a late thirteenth-century painting of the Virgin and Child with saints that ornamented the outer face of the double gateway known as the Due Porte that provided entry into the city from the south west, through the city's first circle of walls. The principal gateway from the south, the Porta Romana, constructed in the early fourteenth century, was likewise decorated – from the fifteenth century at least – with a large-scale painting of the Coronation of the Virgin. On the northern and more heavily defended side of the city the Antiporto, begun

13 (*facing page*) Siena, Loggia of Pius II.

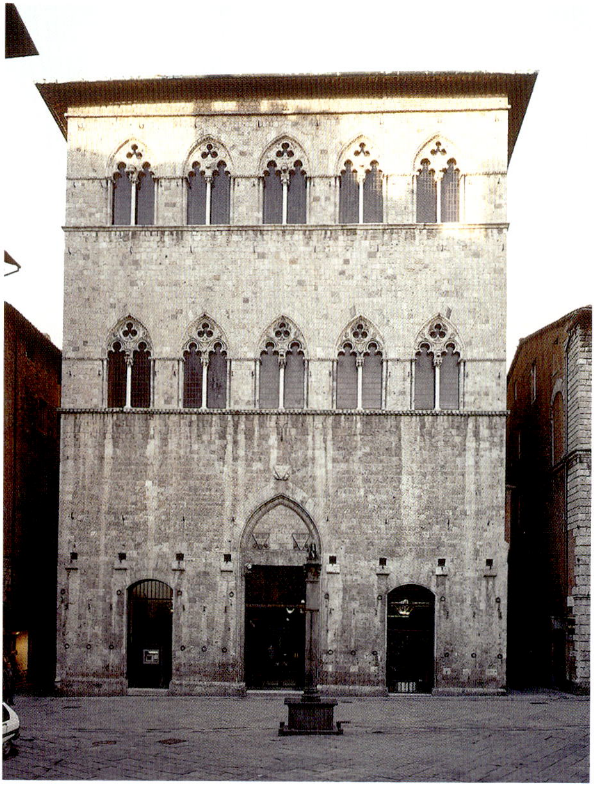

12 Siena, Palazzo Tolomei.

around 1270, provided a first line of defence before the actual city gateway of the Porta di Camollia. The Antiporto was probably also adorned with a painting of the Virgin of the Assumption that may have dated from the first decade of the fourteenth century. Certainly, by the date of Giovanni di Lorenzo's painting of the Virgin protecting the city at the battle of Camollia in 1528, such an image was clearly present (see pl. 114).[20] Thus visitors approaching the city would be under no illusion that Siena regarded itself as the city of the Virgin and – as the heavily fortified walls and gateways demonstrated – under her protection.

While much of Sienese painters' work came from the various religious and civic authorities in charge of the buildings and edifices described so far, some of it was also commissioned by people wishing to decorate their own homes. Although quite modest urban dwellings might have boasted a few images, such as a panel painting of the Virgin and Christ Child or a painted coffer, the large town houses, known in Italy as *palazzi* and owned by the city's wealthier families, were likely to be furnished with a wide variety of paintings. If one walks through Siena's streets, the façades of these *palazzi*, now belonging to the city's archives, museums and banks, are still an eye-catching feature of the urban fabric. Many of the earlier *palazzi* dating from the thirteenth and fourteenth centuries were extended and heavily restored in later centuries but they still retain something of their original fortified, castle-like structure – a relic of the period when a family would occupy and defend a part of the city from other rival families. The early thirteenth-century Palazzo Tolomei provides a particularly striking example of the solidity and scale of these early Sienese *palazzi* (pl. 12).

In the fifteenth century the city's leading families built new *palazzi* that, in terms of their design and architectural style, reflected a prevailing taste in Italy for buildings that were reminiscent of Italy's classical past. Thus, the Palazzo delle Papesse, facing onto one of the city's principal streets leading from the Campo to the cathedral and built largely by papal funds for Caterina Piccolomini, sister to the Sienese pope Pius II, is generally viewed as one of the most distinguished examples of renaissance architec-

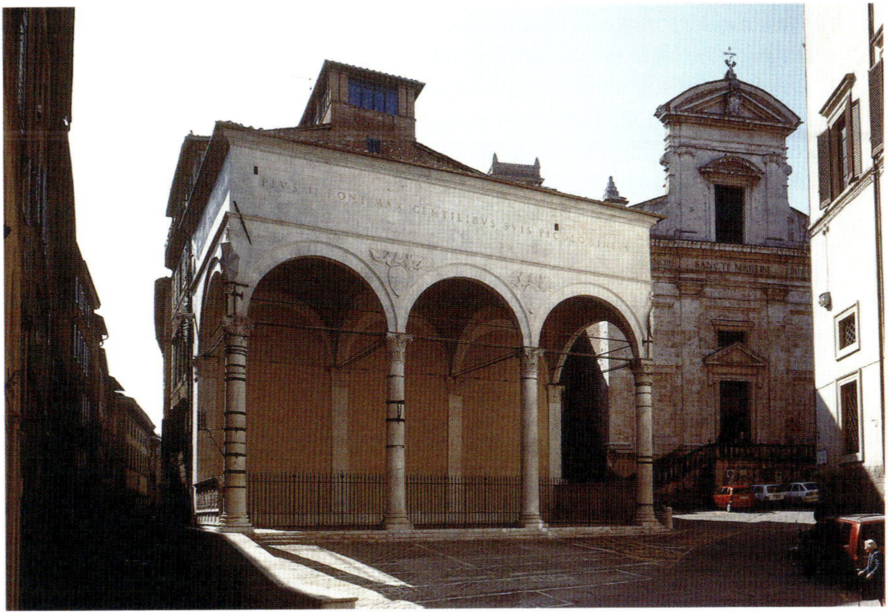

observance and sexual abstinence. Although the community comprised both men and women, it was the male half, headed by the rector, which took the major decisions regarding the administration and embellishment of the hospital. The rector was originally elected by his fellow-tertiaries but such was the political and economic power of the office that the Sienese government insisted on controlling his appointment. Rectors therefore characteristically belonged to the city's lay political elite and their patronage of art in the hospital frequently reflected family interests and those of close political associates. And, since the hospital housed one of the city's principal churches and a number of oratories belonging to the city confraternities, several other kinds of patron also actively commissioned paintings for their altars and chapels.

The painted embellishment of the Palazzo Pubblico was the concern of the various city magistracies who either lived or worked in the building. This kind of patronage extended to the painted decoration of other civic monuments, such as the Cappella di Piazza and the city gateways. Although on occasion the city's principal legislative committee – the Council of the Bell – was asked to ratify work of this kind, it appears that responsibility for its initiation was usually undertaken by the Consistory or by one of the other magistracies such as the city treasury, known as the Biccherna. Since the Palazzo Pubblico was also the residence of the Podestà during his six-month term of office, and of the city's principal governors during their two-month terms of office, it is likely that these important officials exerted some influence over the painting commissioned for their council rooms, chapels and private quarters.

Elsewhere in the city, the collective membership of confraternities and guilds acted as patrons of art for their oratories and guildhalls, while other city officials such as the Capitano della Guerra commissioned paintings for their official residences in a broadly similar manner to the city's wealthiest families. In the sphere of private familial patronage, the city's churches offered regular opportunities to individuals to purchase paintings for their family altars and chapels. Other chances lay in the decoration of privately owned houses.

When studying the patronage of painting in late medieval and renaissance Siena, it is therefore essential to keep in mind its diversity and flexibility. Broad distinctions can be made, with qualification. One such distinction might be that between commissions initiated by the clergy and those initiated by the laity. But the distinction between the ecclesiastical and secular spheres is not always clear, particularly in the commissioning of art. Committees of lay officials, for example, administered the city's churches.

The city's hospitals and confraternities present another example of such blurring between the religious and lay. Thus, at the Spedale di Santa Maria della Scala, the responsibility for the hospital's embellishment lay primarily with the rector, a government appointee but also the head of a religious community.

Another broad distinction might be made between the patronage of art by men and that by women. Men commissioned the majority of Sienese paintings studied in this book – be they clerics, government magistrates or the men of a family. Two groups of late medieval and renaissance women in Siena apparently, however, had the legal status and economic means to commission paintings, namely nuns and widows. The number of surviving fourteenth- and early fifteenth-century frescoes in the church and cloister of the convent of Santa Marta suggests that the Augustinian nuns there were active in commissioning painters to work for them (albeit through the mediation of a male procurator). Several altarpieces and illuminated manuscripts, dating from the fourteenth, fifteenth and sixteenth centuries and originating from churches and convents belonging to Siena's female religious communities (see pl. 42), similarly indicate the regular employment offered to painters by these female communities. Another popular and socially acceptable form of art patronage by women took the form of altarpieces commissioned by widows in memory of their deceased husbands. Thus in 1430 Ludovica, the widow of Turino di Matteo (a former cathedral *operaio*) commissioned the *Madonna of the Snows* (see pl. 92) for an altar in the cathedral; and in the 1520s Anastasia, widow of Ugolino Ugolini, commissioned a *Nativity* from Beccafumi for an altar in the church of San Martino (see pl. 143).

A further distinction might be made between public and private patronage of art. The paintings commissioned for such buildings as the cathedral, Palazzo Pubblico, churches, guildhalls, hospitals and confraternity buildings were arguably public commissions, accessible to the population of the city as a whole. Within the palatial residences of Siena's principal families, meanwhile, were painted schemes and images designed for private use. But even here the distinctions are not always easy to maintain. The liturgical east end of the cathedral and of the city churches belonging to the religious orders was generally divided from the rest of the church by a choir screen and therefore only accessible to the resident clergy and to a few lay persons of high status such as the governing magistrates of the city. All lay women were expected to remain outside the choir screen and to keep to their area of the church, usually the north aisle. The family chapels and altars that characteristically lined the aisles and transepts of the churches were also frequently marked out as exclusive and privately owned areas of the church by metal screens. And such were the restrictions imposed on the enclosed orders of nuns that very few persons other than the nuns themselves would have been allowed to view the paintings commissioned for their churches and convents.

Similarly, although the fifteenth-century Sienese saint Bernardino, when preaching in the Campo in 1427, referred his audience to paintings by Ambrogio Lorenzetti in the Palazzo Pubblico (see pls 51–3) in such a way as to suggest that they all had easy access to the town hall's meeting rooms and offices,[24] much of the painted imagery inside the building was devised for a more select audience – the governors and magistrates of the city itself and important visitors. This also appears to have been the case for many of the paintings commissioned for privately owned *palazzi*. Nevertheless, from the end of the fifteenth century there was a marked increase in the number of paintings commissioned for such venues. Some of these commissions resulted in painted schemes that were as ambitious as those for the city's churches, civic palaces, hospitals and confraternity buildings (see pls 123–6, 133). As will be demonstrated in later chapters, this shift from the public, civic patronage of art to private, familial patronage reflected, to a degree, shifts in the power bases and ideologies of the city's political and social elite, which in turn reflected wider political and social developments in the rest of Italy.

Types of Painting

Like other Italian patrons, the Sienese commissioned a range of paintings, executed in different media. The walls of churches, oratories, chapels, hospital and confraternity buildings, civic and private *palazzi*, gateways and street tabernacles were frequently decorated with fresco paintings – a technique that required painters to paint quickly and surely on the surface of newly applied plaster.[25] Generally painted in the summer months when the plaster could dry easily, fresco painting might involve a single image such as Guidoccio Cozzarelli's tabernacle painting (see pl. 10) or a whole series of paintings whose subjects were intended to be viewed sequentially as a story or narrative (see pls 77, 120). Such paintings – depending on their location and original audience – might have been designed primarily for religious and devotional purposes (see pls 77, 134) or for political and propaganda reasons (see pls 51, 97) or for private enjoyment and education (see pls 133).

Another popular genre was the painted altarpiece, designed to stand over consecrated altars in churches or other types of building. Imagery on altarpieces conventionally alluded to the saint or saints to whom the altar was dedicated and to the celebration of mass that regularly took place before it (pl. 14). In addition, it frequently advertised the identity and status of those who had commissioned it, as well as demonstrating the skills of its painter. While the religious function of the altarpiece remained substantially unchanged over the centuries, as a highly favoured type of religious image it witnessed dramatic changes in its format and style. Fourteenth- and early fifteenth-century altarpieces were comprised of wooden panels held together by elaborate Gothic frames (see pls 35, 71, 93), whereas from the 1460s altarpieces tended to be single panels (or less often single canvases) set in classicising frames (see pls 110, 140, 142).[26] Similarly, while the earlier altarpieces with their gold backgrounds and representation of holy figures have a formal, visionary appearance, reminiscent of Byzantine icons (see pls 36, 43), later altarpieces, with their detailed description of the

14 Sassetta, *A Miracle of the Eucharist* (*c.* 1423–6). Tempera on panel, 24 × 38 cm. Durham, the Bowes Museum, Barnard Castle. This painting probably reflects the interior appearance of Sienese churches at that date.

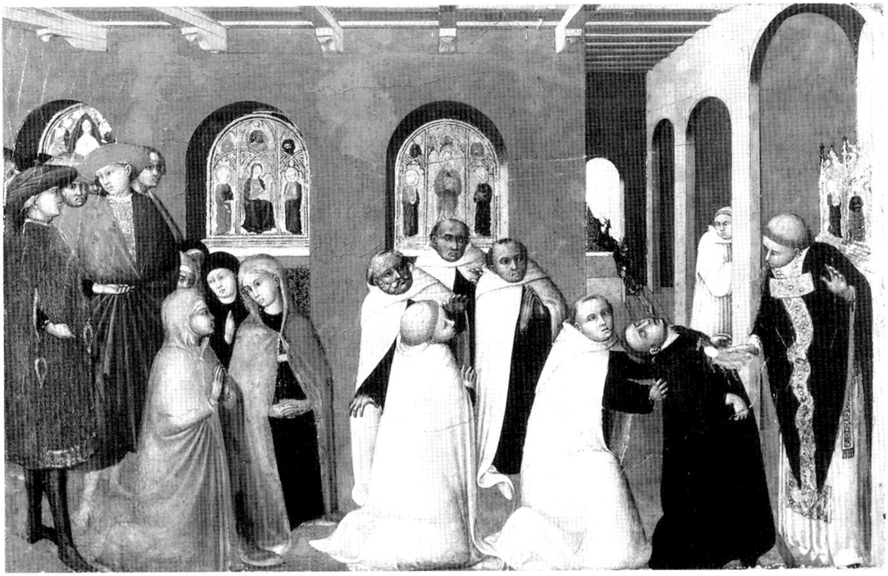

holy figures and their environment, have a more literal, worldly feel to them (see pls 139, 143).

Wood as the surface on which to paint was used in a huge variety of works produced by Sienese painters. In this study are examples of paintings designed to act as covers to official, government records (see pls 3, 32), wooden chests or *cassoni* (see pl. 111) and *spallieri*, paintings designed as wall panelling or the backs to seats and benches (see pl. 128–31). Portraits – a genre that became much more popular in the fifteenth and sixteenth centuries – might also be painted on wooden panels (see pl. 127), although there are relatively few surviving examples in Sienese painting of the period up to 1555. The panels on cupboards designed to house religious relics in churches and sacristies were also embellished with painted figures and narrative events (see pls 76, 100, 101). Other such items were painted bier heads – frequently commissioned by confraternities in charge of ensuring that their members received a decent burial – and birth trays, painted objects that were presented as gifts to women who were either pregnant or had just given birth.[27] Another lucrative sideline was the painting of objects produced by other kinds of craftworkers. Sienese painters were frequently employed to paint wooden sculptures – full-length figures of the saints (see pls 86, 118) or busts designed to house the skulls of saints.[28] They might also be commissioned to paint objects fashioned in metal, leather or glass (see pl. 85b). Particularly in the fourteenth century, Sienese goldsmiths enjoyed great prestige for their intricate and costly work that was valued far beyond Siena itself. Painters, in their turn, were clearly inspired by the work of their fellow sculptors (see pls 47, 68).

Linen and canvas were also occasionally used. An early example is a thirteenth-century painting of narrative scenes executed on linen (see pl. 28) that was probably designed to cover the front of an altar during Lent. Another popular use for these lighter materials was for the production of *palii* or banners that were used primarily for processional purposes. These might be commissioned by the clergy or by confraternities for their religious processions. They might also be commissioned for political purposes – like the *palii* customarily brought annually to the cathedral at the feast of the Assumption by representatives of Siena's subject territories or the *palii* awarded to the victor of the horse races run through the city streets on certain feast days and holidays.

Parchment and paper were other surfaces on which Sienese painters often worked. Many of them were engaged in the specialised task of illuminating manuscripts – particularly the large initials that allowed sufficient space to represent complex figural groupings and narrative scenes (pl. 15).

Although a majority of these manuscripts were designed for liturgical use, particularly by the cathedral clergy, painters might also decorate books of a more secular kind (see pl. 83).

15 Lippo Vanni, *The Birth of the Virgin* (1345). Illuminated initial of a choir book, 15 × 13 cm. Siena, Museo dell'Opera del Duomo, MS 98–4, fol. 14r.

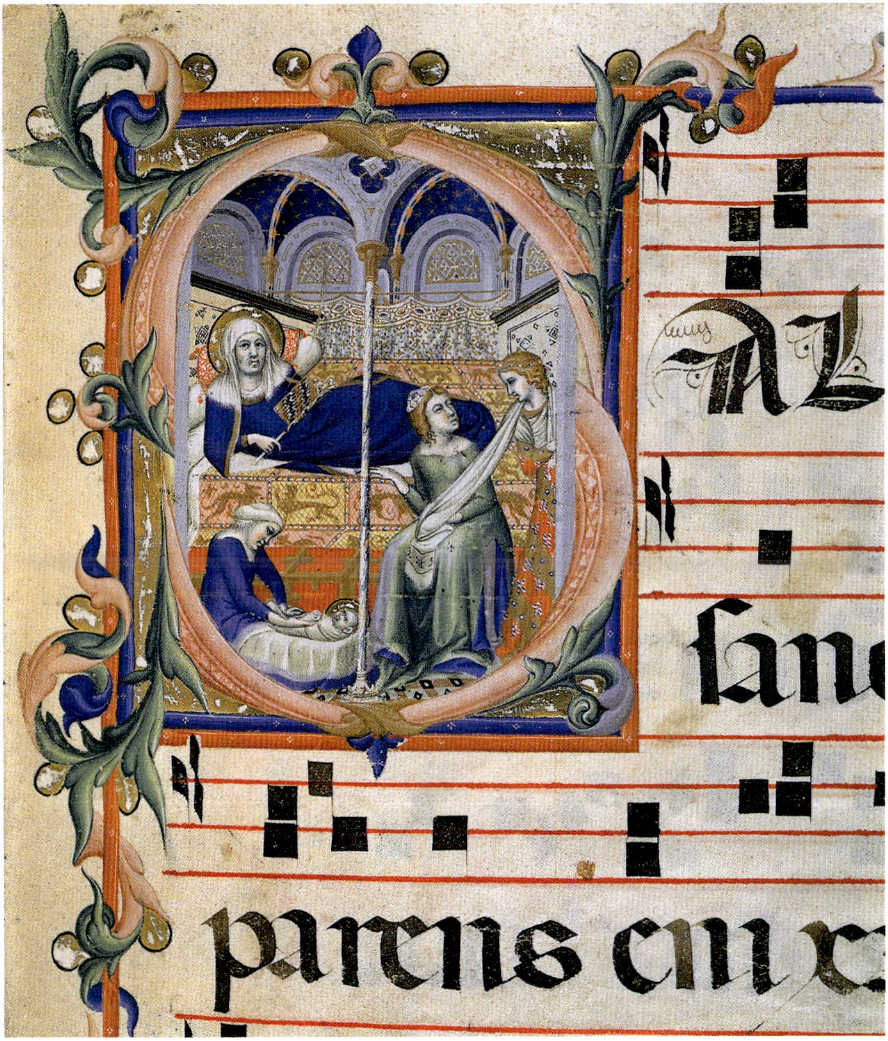

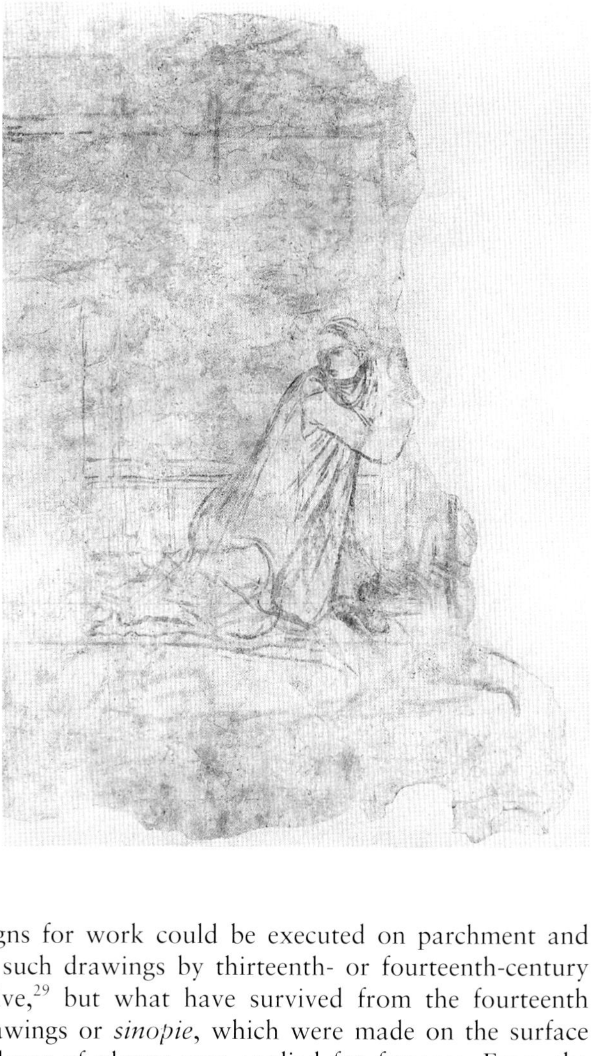

16 Ambrogio Lorenzetti, *Virgin of the Annunciation* (*c.* 1344). Part of the under drawing of a fresco of the *The Annunciation.* Montesiepi, Oratory of San Galgano.

Drawings and designs for work could be executed on parchment and paper also. Very few such drawings by thirteenth- or fourteenth-century Sienese painters survive,[29] but what have survived from the fourteenth century are under drawings or *sinopie*, which were made on the surface of a wall before the layer of plaster was applied for frescoes. From the evidence of the *sinopia* of the *Virgin of the Annunciation* in the Oratory of San Galgano at Montesiepi, south-west of Siena, which is generally attributed to Ambrogio Lorenzetti, it appears that Sienese painters of the time not only practised the art of drawing but were also capable of an assured and expressive touch (pl. 16). Many more drawings from the fifteenth and sixteenth centuries have survived. These range from sketches to carefully worked drawings where a painter used the medium to investigate how drapery might be represented through the use of light and shade (pl. 17).[30] As the profession of painting came over the centuries to be viewed not merely as a form of manual labour but as an artistic vocation, drawings became increasingly elaborate and valued in their own right as works of art. It is probably for this reason that the preparatory drawings made by Beccafumi in the 1520s, as part of the design process for the execution of the cathedral pavement, were carefully preserved by his executors as part of his artistic legacy.

The Profession of Painter

In terms of their artistic practice, therefore, Sienese painters had to be highly versatile. Duccio may not have worked in fresco but this celebrated early fourteenth-century Sienese painter produced panel paintings on a range of religious subjects (see pls 25, 35, 36, 38–41, 62) and is documented as painting wooden covers for the financial accounts of the city treasury. Other early fourteenth-century painters, such as Simone Martini and the Lorenzetti brothers, produced frescoed murals, altarpiece panels and manuscript illuminations (see pls 43–5, 47, 51–6, 58, 59, 61), and in the case of the former, also painted two *palii* for the Angevin prince Charles of Calabria and his wife, Mary of Valois, when they visited Siena in 1328.[31] In the second half of the fourteenth century, this diversity appears if anything to have increased, probably as a result of the changed conditions for painters' work caused by successive outbreaks of the plague during this period. For example, one of the leading practitioners of the period, Bartolo di Fredi, not only produced a large number of altarpieces (see pls 71–3) and frescoes but also collaborated with other artists on mural and altarpiece paintings and polychromed sculptures.

A similar degree of versatility continued in the fifteenth century. Sano di Pietro produced frescoes for the Palazzo Pubblico (see pl. 105) and the Porta Romana; altarpieces for the chapel of the Palazzo Pubblico, the monastery of San Girolamo (see pl. 93) and the confraternity of the Virgin that met in the Spedale di Santa Maria della Scala (see pl. 94); and manuscript illuminations for the Franciscan convent of Santa Chiara (see pl. 6). Vecchietta, meanwhile, in addition to producing frescoes and panel paintings for such venues as the Spedale di Santa Maria della Scala, the cathedral baptistery and the Palazzo Pubblico (see pls 98, 100–02, 104, 106), produced bronze and marble sculptures and an architectural design

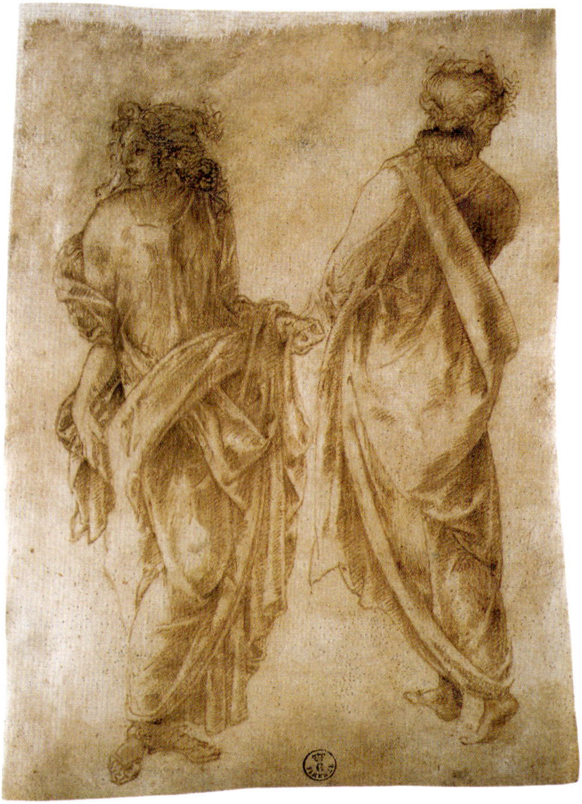

17 Francesco di Giorgio, *Two Draped Female Figures* (*c.* 1475–80). Pen on parchment, 19.6 × 14.6 cm. Florence, Uffizi, Gabinetto Disegni e Stampe, inv. 396E.

for the Loggia of Pius II (see pl. 13). He also served as a fortification expert for the Sienese government.

Such a range of artistic skills was extended further by Francesco di Giorgio Martini in the last decades of the fifteenth century and by Baldassare Peruzzi in the first half of the sixteenth century. Francesco di Giorgio was a painter, an illuminator, a draughtsman (pl. 17), a sculptor, medallist, architect, engineer, theorist and writer. Baldassare Peruzzi, while confining his painting principally to frescoes executed for a variety of patrons in Rome, was also a highly skilled draughtsman and one of Italy's leading architects. Other late fifteenth- and early sixteenth-century Sienese artists who confined their activities more narrowly to the art of painting were still capable of broadening their repertoire beyond altarpieces and frescoes for churches, civic buildings and privately owned palaces to more specialised items, such as bier heads and Biccherna covers – and, in the case of Beccafumi, engravings, woodcuts and designs for other media (see pls 113, 117).

As a result of the specialised nature of the training and the expense – in terms of materials and equipment – of setting up a workshop, painting often ran in families, although apparently strictly among the men of such families. None of Siena's well-known painters were women, although women may have been employed in a minor capacity in painters' workshops. A few women in religious orders also appear to have worked as manuscript illuminators.[32] The fourteenth century boasts the striking example of two brothers, Pietro and Ambrogio Lorenzetti, both highly successful painters in their own right but also collaborators with each other on several major commissions of fresco painting.[33] From the kinds of decorative tooling on the gold-leaf backgrounds of a number of panel paintings by the two painters, it appears that they also shared their tools, such as punches.[34] Closely contemporary with the Lorenzetti was the family clan of Memmo di Filippuccio, his sons Lippo and Tederigo Memmi and his famous son-in-law, Simone Martini. Simone Martini, in turn, had a brother, Donato, who was also a painter. Later in the century, Bartolo di Fredi apparently worked on many of his most important commissions with his son, Andrea di Bartolo (see pl. 71). Andrea in turn secured a number of commissions independently of his father (see pl. 88), and passed on his skills to his sons, Giovanni and Ansano. In the early decades of the fifteenth century, Taddeo di Bartolo collaborated on a number of his later commissions with his adopted son, Gregorio di Cecco (see pl. 86), who married the daughter of the Sienese sculptor Domenico di Niccolò dei Cori. Such family relationships continued into the fifteenth and sixteenth centuries with examples such as the painter Priamo della Quercia and his brother, the well-known sculptor Jacopo della Quercia; and the painter–sculptor Vecchietta and his sculptor son Giovanni di Stefano.

In addition to family members working together on specific commissions, a striking feature of Sienese painting practice was the degree to which painters frequently collaborated with one another or with other kinds of artist. Sometimes the collaboration was put on a formal, legal footing. Thus in 1353 the painters Bartolo di Fredi and Andrea Vanni agreed to rent a workshop together for two years, and in the 1470s Neroccio dei Landi and Francesco di Giorgio had a temporary but formal partnership.[35] This kind of close collaboration naturally arose from the way young painters were trained to emulate the techniques and repertoire of the 'master painter' heading the workshop. It was also a logical way to work on large-scale projects such as a cycle of frescoes, for a church or a meeting room in the Palazzo Pubblico, in order to get the work done on time. So, it was quite common for several fully trained painters to work alongside one another while the less experienced members of the workshop would be allocated more menial tasks such as mixing the plaster or grinding the pigments. Such was their skill at adopting a house style that it is often impossible to discern with confidence different hands working on fresco schemes – unless, as in the case of the frescoes for the mid-fifteenth-century Pellegrinaio in the Spedale di Santa Maria dell Scala or the early sixteenth-century Oratory of San Bernardino, it is obvious either from painted inscriptions or the deliberately distinctive styles of specific paintings that individual master painters had taken prime responsibility for single paintings (see pls 134–7).

A similar degree of collaboration could also occur on panel paintings. Technical investigation of some of the narrative panels from Duccio's *Maestà* (see pls 36, 38–40) clearly shows that even on relatively small paintings several members of a workshop would work together, individual painters with specialised skills (such as representing architecture) being allocated particular tasks.[36] The primary evidence for such collaboration is the presence on the art itself of a number of different names, or references in documents to joint commissions. As early as 1333, Simone Martini and his brother-in-law Lippo Memmi both had their names placed upon an altarpiece for the cathedral (see pl. 58). As in the case of fresco painting, it is difficult to determine which painter was responsible for which part of the painting. The list of payments by the Opera suggests, however, that Lippo Memmi took responsibility for the execution of the gilded ornament on this altarpiece.[37] This may also have been the responsibility of Niccolò di Ser Sozzo when he and Luca di Tommè worked together on an altarpiece, dated 1362, probably for the church of San Tommaso (see pl. 82).

Whereas in the fifteenth and sixteenth centuries this degree of overt collaboration does not seem to have happened so often, some examples are recorded or known. It appears that when painting altarpieces and frescoes for several Sienese churches, Francesco di Giorgio frequently collaborated with another talented painter whose identity is now no longer known (see pl. 119). The striking stylistic differences within a number of fifteenth- and early sixteenth-century altarpieces also suggest that their main panel had been painted by one painter and their subsidiary panels by others.[38]

Sculptors were frequent collaborators. Payments dating from 1395, 1397 and 1400, for example, indicate that the painter Paolo di Giovanni Fei was responsible for polychroming a wooden statue of Saint Savino carved by the wood sculptor Fra Guido di Giovanni for the choirstalls of the cathedral.[39] A number of payments to Bartolo di Fredi indicate that he also painted sculptures. It has been plausibly suggested that both the pose and the richly ornate polychromy on the early fifteenth-century statue of the Virgin and Child – popularly known as the *Madonna of the Magnificat* – strongly indicate that Taddeo di Bartolo and his adopted son Gregorio di Cecco collaborated with the sculptor Giovanni di Turino on this sculpture (see pl. 86).[40] Such collaborations continued into the later part of the fifteenth century and into the sixteenth, as attested by an altarpiece for the chapel of the Bichi family in the south transept of Sant'Agostino that combined a polychromed wooden statue of Saint Christopher and the Christ Child, carved by Francesco di Giorgio, with painted panels by Signorelli, a visiting painter from Cortona (see pl. 118).

This sustained pattern of collaboration indicates the flexibility of Sienese painting practice and is also a corrective to the modern notion that a painting should be more highly valued if completed by a single painter. It is clear from surviving contracts that late medieval and renaissance patrons wanted to ensure that the work was of a high standard and bore evidence of 'the hand' or the work of the painter whose skill they were buying. But it is also clear that – rather like many modern builders today – Sienese painters ran fairly small businesses made up of only a few permanent members of the workshop. As the pattern of work demanded, they either sub-contracted work to other specialised artisans, such as beaters of gold leaf, or made temporary arrangements to work with other fully trained painters and other kinds of artist as the demands of a particular commission dictated.

Most artistic training was received within the workshop and from first-hand experience of working on a variety of commissions, but certain aspects of Sienese painters' work came under the jurisdiction of the painters' guild, the Arte dei Pittori. The surviving records of membership lists for the Arte dei Pittori, dating from the mid-fourteenth century to the late eighteenth century,[41] reveal that most of the city's principal painters joined this guild. Unlike Florence, however, where painters belonged to the powerful guild of apothecaries and spice merchants that was represented on the city's principal government committees, the Sienese Arte dei Pittori was a relatively modest civic institution. Nevertheless, it is clear from the earliest surviving statutes that the guild imposed various rules on its members, regulating relations among fully trained painters, apprentices and workmen, restricting the activities of painters from outside the city, and also making stipulations on the religious ceremonies in which the members were required to participate.[42] The Arte dei Pittori also provided painters with legal means of redress should disputes over their work arise and ensured that they received a decent burial and financial aid for their dependants.

While Sienese painters' workshops may have occasionally produced ready-made objects for sale – such as small, portable, devotional images or painted household furniture – most of their output was the result of commissions. The workshop also remained the primary unit of painting production in Siena throughout the period studied in this book, although certain painters – such as Simone Martini, Ambrogio Lorenzetti, Lippo Vanni and Bartolo di Fredi in the fourteenth century; Taddeo di Bartolo, Sano di Pietro in the fifteenth; and Sodoma in the sixteenth – also seem to have acquired the status of semi-official painters to the government. This did not exclude them from working for other kinds of patron. In the early decades of the sixteenth century, however, the pattern of commissioning presents a stronger sense of certain painters becoming more dependent on the patronage of the city's leading families. Thus Sodoma, a Lombard in origin, was probably encouraged to come to Siena by the Spannocchi family who had extensive banking concerns in Milan.[43] Once working in Siena, the painter obtained a variety of commissions from a wide range of patrons. He seems to have secured particularly favourable commissions from the Chigi family, providing paintings for their *palazzo* just behind the Campo and also for Agostino Chigi's suburban villa in Rome.

Likewise, according to Vasari, Beccafumi, the son of a poor farmer from a village outside Siena, became the protégé of Lorenzo Beccafumi, a rich Sienese citizen whose name the painter subsequently adopted.[44] He also worked for the powerful Petrucci family and their close political associates in the early stages of his career. Nevertheless, once both Sodoma and Beccafumi were established in Siena, they obtained commissions from a variety of patrons including such collective bodies as the government, the cathedral Opera and the lay confraternity of San Bernardino – which indicates that Sienese painters did not become permanently attached to a single family or household, preferring instead to retain their professional autonomy and economic flexibility.

* * *

Social Status and Reputation

In the main, the social origins of Sienese painters were relatively humble, apart from those painters who were the sons of other painters: Taddeo di Bartolo was the son of a barber, Benvenuto di Giovanni the son of a bricklayer and Sodoma the son of a shoemaker. Francesco di Giorgio, although the grandson of a poultry farmer, was the son of a civil servant. It was probably through his father, therefore, that the young artist met the Sienese notary Mariano Taccola, whose studies on mechanics influenced Francesco's later theoretical writings.[45] Neroccio dei Landi, as a member of the noble Landi del Poggio family, was a marked exception to the rule.[46]

As citizens of Siena, the painters could act as representatives of their neighbourhood on one of the city's councils or as emissaries on diplomatic missions for the government. Instances of this are relatively rare in the first half of the fourteenth century – a famous example being the record of Ambrogio Lorenzetti's contribution to a government debate in 1347[47] – they became much more common in the second half of the century. There is good evidence of painters such as Bartolo di Fredi, Andrea Vanni, Luca di Tommè and Paolo di Giovanni Fei acting as members of various city councils and as government agents – a situation brought about by the more popular tenor of the governments at that period and by the substantial decrease in the city's population as a result of successive outbreaks of plague. In the fifteenth and sixteenth centuries there are even instances of painters taking on diplomatic roles on behalf of the Sienese republic, such as Francesco di Giorgio's presence at the courts of Urbino and Naples. But the increasingly narrow powerbase of Sienese politics during the fifteenth and sixteenth centuries meant that matters of government were more commonly left in the hands of specially trained civil servants.

By 1555, the year that marks the fall of Siena to Florence and the end of the period surveyed by this book, claims for the social standing of painters had markedly changed across Italy. Painters were no longer viewed as mere craftworkers but as artists whose professional skills afforded them a greater degree of social status and respect. On the one hand, there was an increasing value placed upon art – particularly if it appeared to conform to recommendations made by such writers as Leon Battista Alberti and Giorgio Vasari. On the other hand, painters increasingly found employment at the princely courts of Italy. Sienese painters were certainly not immune to this trend. Francesco di Giorgio, for example, worked extensively for the courts of Naples, Milan and Urbino and also wrote a number of detailed treatises on the practice of architecture. Baldassare Peruzzi worked in Rome for the papal court, and Beccafumi very briefly worked for the Doria court in Genoa. In Siena Vecchietta designed an elaborate funerary chapel for himself in the church of the Spedale di Santa Maria della Scala – a monument that in terms of its public location, inscriptions and highly personalised imagery made an assertive claim about his identity and status as both painter and sculptor.

Even thirteenth- and fourteenth-century Sienese painters were not averse to displaying their names prominently on their work. As early as the 1270s, Guido da Siena proudly appended his name to one of his major paintings (see pl. 22).[48] An inscription along the edge of the step of the Virgin's throne in Duccio's *Virgin and Christ Child with Saints and Angels* makes an even more assertive claim (see pl. 36). Reading 'Holy mother of God, be the cause of repose for Siena, and, because he painted you thus, of life for Duccio', this painted text now appears as a form of conventional religious vow. In the context of the painting's original and sacred ecclesiastical setting, it would also once have boldly proclaimed the identity of Duccio himself and the value of his painterly skills.

By the late fifteenth and early sixteenth century, paintings were particularly esteemed if they displayed the painter's knowledge of the art of antiquity. Writers such as Alberti and Vasari deemed that paintings – particularly those identified as history paintings or *istorie* – lent themselves to the expression of high ideals. They also challenged painters to represent large numbers of figures in elaborate architectural or landscape settings. Sienese renaissance art furnishes many examples of such paintings, one of the most striking being Beccafumi's scheme for the ceiling of the Sala del Concistoro in the Palazzo Pubblico (see pls 146, 148, 149). With their highly erudite references to obscure events in the history of the Roman Republic and their virtuoso display of foreshortening and other types of pictorial illusion, these paintings were precisely the kind of art valued by renaissance patrons. At the same time, however, Beccafumi's painted scheme represents one in a long series of similarly ambitious schemes commissioned by the Sienese government for the Palazzo Pubblico from the beginning of the fourteenth century. These earlier schemes – although apparently much more easily accessible in terms of their form and content – also relied on specialised knowledge and understanding (see pls 51–3, 80, 81).

Sienese painters also worked outside the city. There is some evidence to suggest that younger painters – before they had acquired the experience and reputation to secure a steady flow of commissions within the city itself – travelled to find work elsewhere. In his early career, Duccio secured altarpiece commissions for Dominican churches in Florence (see pl. 25) and Perugia. Taddeo di Bartolo too spent the early years of his profession as a painter working on commissions for towns in Tuscany, Umbria and Liguria. Once fully established in Siena itself, however, painters also continued to receive a large number of commissions from other towns and cities. Sometimes these were situated within the *contado* (the surrounding territories to which Siena laid claim) and therefore in communities that enjoyed close political and cultural ties to Siena.[49] Indeed, it is possible to find numerous examples across the entire period covered by this book of Sienese painters producing paintings destined for such locations. The painters were also highly successful in obtaining work in neighbouring towns and cities in Tuscany and Umbria, and even as far afield as the southern kingdom of Naples. This was particularly the case in the fourteenth century when Sienese painting seems to have been particularly in demand. Simone Martini worked on commissions for Naples, Assisi, Pisa, Orvieto, Perugia and San Gimignano, before leaving Siena in the mid-1330s to work at the papal court in Avignon. Apart from supplying frescoes and altarpieces to a number of churches in the Sienese territories, Pietro Lorenzetti received commissions for churches in Assisi, Florence, Pistoia, and Cortona. In the fifteenth century, Vecchietta worked in Castiglione d'Olona in Lombardy, and Francesco di Giorgio in Naples, Milan, Urbino and Cortona. In the sixteenth century Beccafumi, while apparently preferring to work in his own city, nevertheless also received commissions for work in Pisa and Genoa and probably Rome as well.

A distinction needs to be made, however, between painters who physically travelled to other places to work (sometimes for many years, as in the case of Francesco di Giorgio), and those who received commissions for work that could be executed at the painter's workshop in Siena and then transported elsewhere. Fresco painting necessarily required the painter to remove himself and his team of apprentices and fellow painters to the place in question. This would have necessitated finding accommodation, local suppliers and contacts, and possibly permission from the local guild authorities to work in the town. Panel paintings, however, could be manufactured and painted in the painter's workshop in Siena and transported to their intended location. A notable instance of this occurred in 1437 when Sassetta agreed with the Franciscan friars of San Francesco in Borgo San Sepolchro that he would paint numerous panels for a double-sided altarpiece for them in Siena itself. It is also likely, however, that Sassetta supervised the installation of the altarpiece in Borgo San Sepolchro before the end of June 1444.[50]

By visiting other places either to work or – as increasingly became true of late fifteenth- and early sixteenth-century Rome – to study the work of others, Sienese painters were naturally open to various artistic stimuli. They encountered the works of artists from other localities and learnt about the latest trends and fashions in Italian painting. In the last decades of the thirteenth century and the first decades of the fourteenth, the Upper and Lower Churches at San Francesco in Assisi became an important venue for many painters drawn from various parts of Italy who shared and exchanged new ideas regarding painting sacred narrative. Two such painters were Pietro Lorenzetti and Simone Martini (see pl. 55). Pietro's brother Ambrogio, meanwhile, benefited from working in Florence in the 1320s. This kind of experience was repeated throughout the remainder of the fourteenth century and the fifteenth and sixteenth centuries. At the beginning of the fifteenth century, Taddeo di Bartolo apparently utilised his knowledge of schemes of painting that he had seen in Pisa, Florence and Padua while painting in the Palazzo Pubblico (see pls 77, 78, 80, 81). Sassetta's altarpiece of the *Madonna of the Snows* of 1432, for an altar in the south transept of the cathedral, not only demonstrates a debt to Duccio's *Maestà* but also shows that he was keenly aware of the kinds of artistic experimentation taking place in Florence at that time (see pl. 92). The work of Domenico di Bartolo in the 1440s displays a similar familiarity with contemporary Florentine art (see pls 89, 99), while Vecchietta's experience of working at Castiglione d'Olona apparently influenced his later painting for the Pellegrinaio of the Spedale di Santa Maria della Scala (see pl. 98). In the early sixteenth century both Sodoma and Beccafumi introduced into their Sienese paintings details drawn directly from contemporary art being produced in Rome at a time when both Raphael and Michelangelo were engaged on a number of major projects in the Vatican palace (see pls 132, 136, 137).

In addition to travelling themselves, Sienese painters were also stimulated by the work of 'foreign' painters visiting their city. As early as 1261, it appears that a Florentine painter, Coppo di Marcovaldo, who may have been taken prisoner at the battle of Montaperti in 1260, produced an altarpiece for one of Siena's major churches that was destined to be highly influential for other later Sienese versions of this subject (see pl. 23). During the fourteenth century, major painting commissions in Siena seem to have been awarded almost exclusively to Sienese painters, but from the early decades of the fifteenth century there appears to have been a significant shift with a number of important commissions being given to outsiders. Thus in 1408

facing page Sassetta, *The Virgin and Christ Child with Saints Peter, Paul, John the Baptist and Francis*, showing Saint Francis (detail of pl. 92).

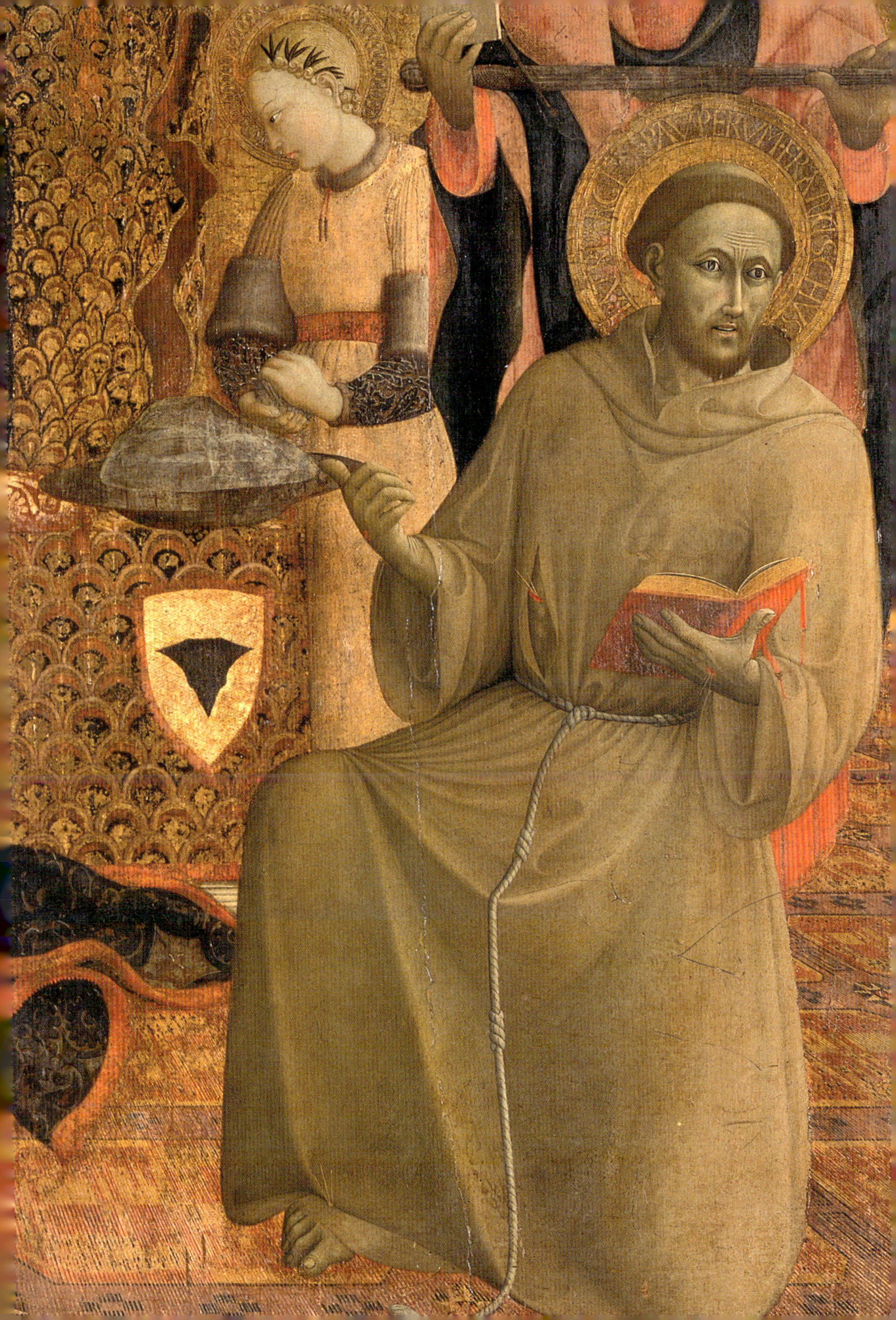

the Aretine painter Spinello Aretino was commissioned to fresco the walls of a meeting room – now known as the Sala di Balìa – in the Palazzo Pubblico (see pl. 79).

Other influential commissions of outsiders followed, most notably the employment of the Florentine sculptors Ghiberti and Donatello to produce large narrative panels in bronze for the baptistery font (see pl. 90). Later in the century Donatello was again employed to produce sculptures for the cathedral. In the mid-fifteenth century, two manuscript illuminators, Liberale da Verona and Girolamo da Cremona, were employed by the Opera to produce magnificent illuminations for choir books for the cathedral (see pl. 112). The ornate decoration of these manuscript illuminations introduced Sienese painters to stylistic conventions current in the courts of northern Italy.

In the later fifteenth and early sixteenth century a number of Siena's more influential patrons again commissioned work from non-Sienese painters. Prominent among these were the Piccolomini who employed the Umbrian painter Pintoricchio to paint the Piccolomini Library (see pls 120–22). Fresh from his experience of working in Rome for the pope and other Roman families, Pintoricchio introduced into Siena many of the latest trends of contemporary painting. In a similar manner, Pandolfo Petrucci employed foreign painters – Pintoricchio, Girolamo Genga (from Urbino) and Luca Signorelli (from Cortona) – to execute the decoration of one of the principal rooms in his palace (see pls 123–6). Signorelli had earlier collaborated with Francesco di Giorgio to decorate the family chapel of the Bichi family, who were close allies of Pandolfo Petrucci (see pls 118, 119). Finally, Sodoma, although one of the most prolific painters in Siena in the first half of the sixteenth century, was strictly speaking non-Sienese. He introduced into his adopted city stylistic conventions and modes of expression that belonged to the Milanese art of Leonardo da Vinci and the Roman art of Raphael (see pls 136, 138).

Sienese painters thus worked beyond the confines of their city and were subject to a variety of artistic stimuli and influences emanating not only from various parts of Italy but on occasion from Europe as a whole. While recognising this, the present study will focus primarily upon paintings produced in Siena for locations in the city and for the city's major patrons. This approach will allow a full appreciation of the value placed upon continuity in Sienese painting. Thus, when reviewing paintings executed for the principal buildings of the city, it is striking how often these paintings acknowledge – both in content and form – earlier paintings designed for the very same buildings or for other equally prestigious civic sites in Siena.

In part, such continuity can be explained by the fact that the majority of surviving Sienese paintings from 1260 to 1555 is religious in content. They were therefore designed with conventional expectations in mind – to teach the faithful the lessons of Christian doctrine. Among such religious paintings, the figure of the Virgin features most prominently. This popularity was mainly owing to the fact that the Virgin was revered as the city's principal patron saint and protector. But other saints also featured in Sienese popular devotion and art. Within the paintings in the cathedral and the Palazzo Pubblico, the city's four other early patron saints, Ansano (the saint who reputedly brought Christianity to Siena), Savino, Crescenzio and Victor, were particularly celebrated (see pls 36, 47, 49, 58, 60).

Within the city's mendicant churches, meanwhile, the official and popular veneration of various local holy men and women who attained the status of *beati* was supported and given greater intensity by the presence of paintings of them (see pl. 54). This trend increased strongly in the fifteenth century with the canonisation of two local saints, the Franciscan Bernardino and the Dominican Catherine. Once again, Sienese painters furnished the laity with compelling portrayals of these revered local figures and the dramatic events associated with their lives that brought about their canonisation.

What is most striking here is that the majority of the city's principal painters were engaged in the common task of representing these holy figures. In so doing, they both acknowledged the efforts of earlier predecessors and also strove to introduce into their work the latest artistic fashions and stylistic trends. And, as will be argued in the following chapters, it is precisely this tension between an intense respect for continuity and tradition, and a capacity for change and innovation that constitutes the enduring fascination of Sienese painting.

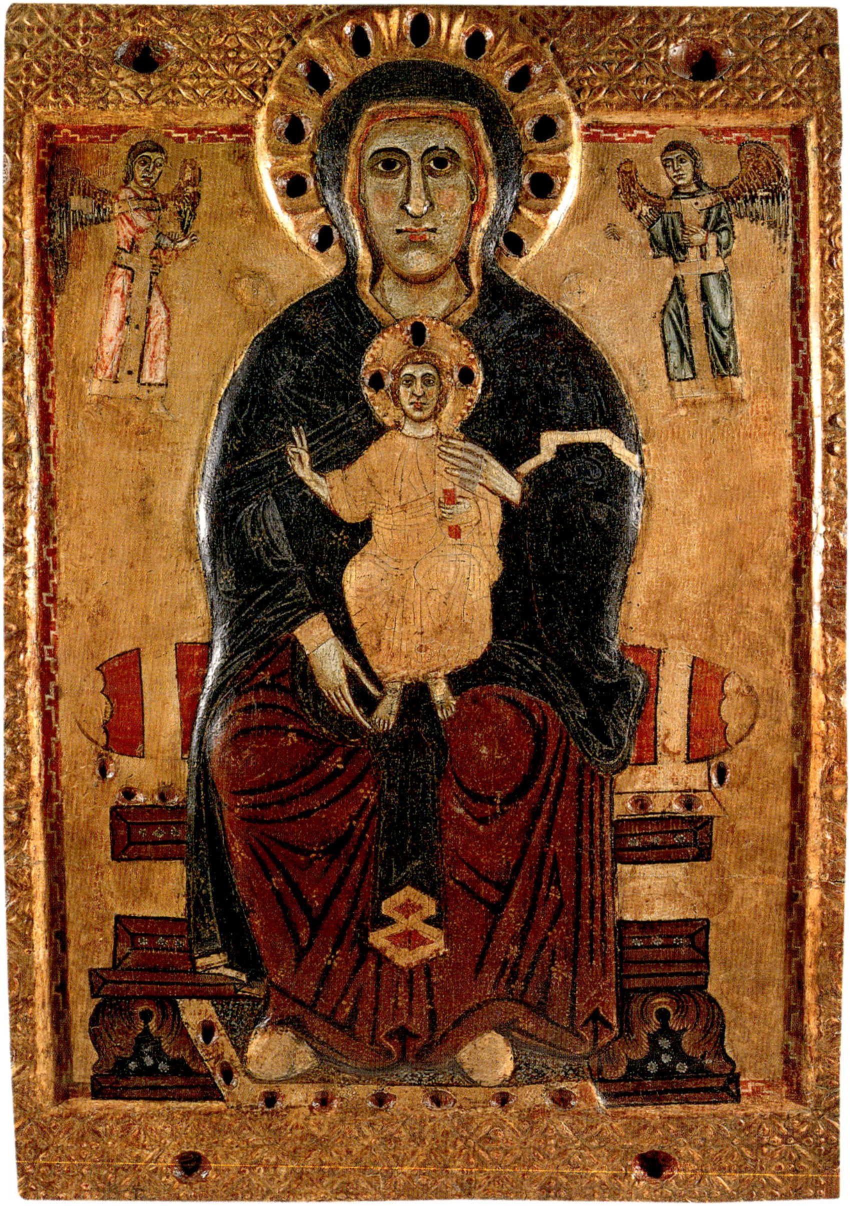

18 *Madonna degli occhi grossi* (mid-thirteenth century). Tempera on panel, 97 × 67 cm. Siena, Museo dell'Opera del Duomo.

I

Early Sienese Painting (1260–1300)

Siena's decisive victory over Florence in 1260 was naturally a cause for celebration and commemoration but, as noted in the introduction, such celebration was intimately linked to the belief that the Sienese had dedicated their city to the Virgin on the eve of the battle.[1] From an illustrated chronicle compiled in the 1440s[2] it appears that the vow of dedication took place before an image of the Virgin located over the high altar of the cathedral. An early thirteenth-century painting of this type – now housed in the cathedral museum and known popularly as the *Madonna degli occhi grossi* (the 'Madonna of the big eyes') – is likely to have been that image (pl. 18).[3] It was cut down at some point in its history, probably in order to carry it in procession in the manner shown in one of the drawings in the 1440s chronicle (see pl. 2). In its original state, the painting would have been a rectangular panel depicting the Virgin and Christ Child and a series of smaller narrative paintings on either side of the central image. Other contemporary or slightly later examples (see pl. 30) provide evidence for this format.

Any painted inscription that might once have indicated who was responsible for its execution has now been lost,[4] but in terms of style it is likely that the painting was executed about twenty years before the act of dedication took place. By the 1440s, when Niccolò di Ventura was writing his chronicle, this painting may have been twice replaced on the high altar of the cathedral by subsequent images of the Virgin (see pls 20, 36). The first replacement is likely to have been an image of the *Virgin and Christ Child* that is known to the Sienese as the *Madonna del Voto* (Our Lady of the Vow) and is the centrepiece of an elaborate chapel built in the mid-seventeenth century. Now appearing like an icon, it too has been cut down and embellished with a number of precious objects.[5] The painting probably took the form of a gabled panel displaying a three-quarter-length image of the Virgin and Christ Child with a pair of saints on either side (see pl. 29).[6] The surviving painting has traditionally been attributed to Guido da Siena who, as noted earlier, was a successful Sienese painter during the 1270s. Recently, however, it has been suggested that the artist could have been Dietisalvi di Speme, another thirteenth-century painter for whom documented work survives (see pl. 32).[7] Although the earliest documentary references to the painting date to the fifteenth century – by which time it had been placed in a specially constructed chapel off the south aisle of the cathedral (see pls 3, 57) – they clearly state that it was originally commissioned for the high altar as a form of thanks for the Virgin's perceived intervention at the battle of Montaperti.[8] By 1265, the cathedral Opera had already initiated not only the commission for the cathedral's magnificent pulpit (see pl. 21) but also a new high altar and enclosed choir for the cathedral canons.[9] The addition of a new high altarpiece in the late 1260s or early 1270s would thus be entirely logical – as well as an appropriate expression of gratitude to the Virgin.

At the time of Montaperti, primary responsibility for Siena's government lay in the hands of a committee of twenty-four citizens who held office for only two months before passing it onto another twenty-four elected men. It was they who initiated government policy, which was then debated and passed into law by a larger council of 300 citizens – the Council of the Bell – under the chairmanship of the city's principal judge, the Podestà. As representatives of a prosperous city state with widespread international contacts through banking and trade, the Twenty-Four made common cause with other Italian cities that were Ghibelline in their political sympathies. This meant that at this date the Sienese saw the German Hohenstaufen rulers of southern Italy as their natural allies. Indeed, the support they received from German troops enabled them to win at Montaperti. Such political allegiance brought them into conflict, however, with the Guelph league, which included both Florence and the papacy.[10]

With the defeat and deaths of the last of the Hohenstaufen rulers of southern Italy in 1266 and 1268, the political fortunes of the Guelphs in Tuscany rallied and in 1269, on the plain to the north of Siena between Colle Val d'Elsa and Monteriggioni, they inflicted defeat on the Sienese. This, together with the success of Charles of Anjou in establishing himself as the ruler of southern Italy and leader of the Guelph league in northern and central Italy, meant that the pro-Ghibelline government of the Twenty-Four gradually fell out of favour in Siena. In 1280 a new governing regime, now comprising thirty-six members who were supporters of the Guelph cause, came into power. Subsequently the power base of Siena's governing executive narrowed first to a committee of fifteen men (1280–87) and then to a committee of nine. Composed of the most prosperous and well-established of Siena's merchant and banking families, and generally seeking pragmatic political alliances with Florence, the papacy and the new Angevin kings of Naples, the magistracy of the Nine proved to be a particularly successful and long-lasting political institution, remaining in power until 1355.[11] During their period of office, the Nine initiated policies that resulted in the city and its subject territories enjoying a period of economic prosperity and political stability. They were also – as this chapter and the next will show – responsible for a remarkable series of artistic projects that still dominate and shape the fabric of Siena today.

All Siena's governing regimes offered their support through both close consultation and generous funding to the construction of the cathedral (pl. 19). Although the history of the thirteenth-century building programme is difficult to reconstruct in detail, it is possible to outline its principal stages.[12] During the first half of the century the crossing and east end were in the process of construction – but on a smaller scale than that of the present building. The imposing dome and hexagonal crossing were part of this scheme but the chancel extended only as far as the steps of the present chancel and the north and south transepts as far as the entrances to the present chapels of Saint John the Baptist and the *Madonna del Voto* (see pl. 34). Between 1258 and 1265 the canons' choir, high altar and pulpit (pl. 21) were commissioned from Nicola Pisano and his skilled assistants. In 1264 the wooden outer covering of the dome was leaded and completed. Over the next two decades work proceeded on the nave working westwards and in 1284 the façade was begun, probably under the direction of Nicola's son, Giovanni Pisano, although he features in the documents as the master of works only in 1297. While the later stages of the construction and embellishment of the sculpted façade are a matter of intense scholarly debate,[13] it is uncontroversial that in the last decades of the thirteenth century Siena cathedral became the site of a talented sculpture workshop whose members co-operated to produce an elaborate programme of sculpted figures, reliefs and decorative detail, all designed to glorify the Virgin and to bring honour and prestige to Siena and its cathedral.

Once the main body of the cathedral including the bishop's place to the south and the canonry to the north had been built, the square between the cathedral and the Spedale di Santa Maria della Scala was cleared. The hospital was already a civic institution of some importance but its scale was still relatively modest, comprising a simple church with its longitudinal axis parallel to the cathedral square and a number of other buildings grouped

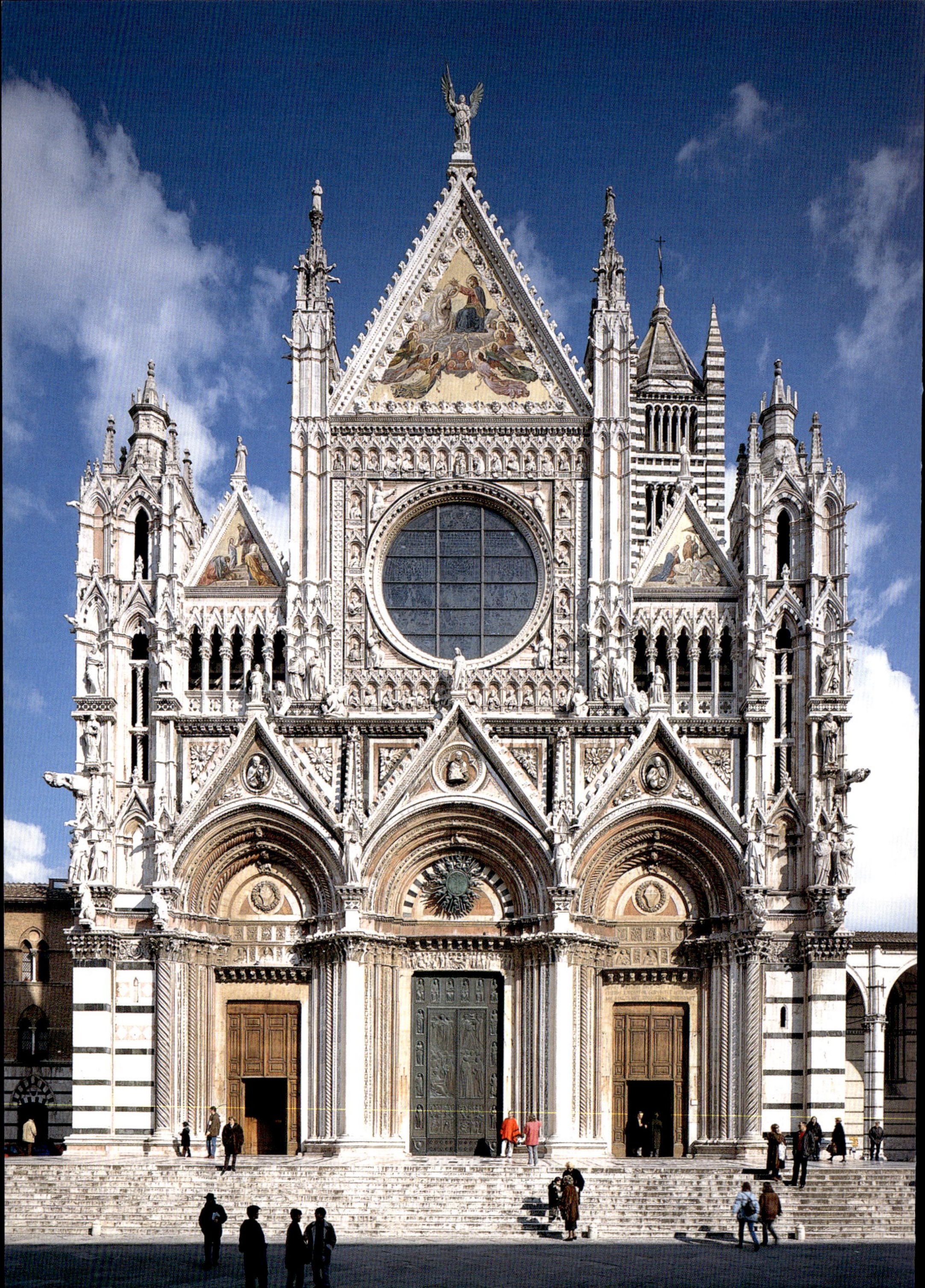

19 (*facing page*) Siena, façade of the cathedral.

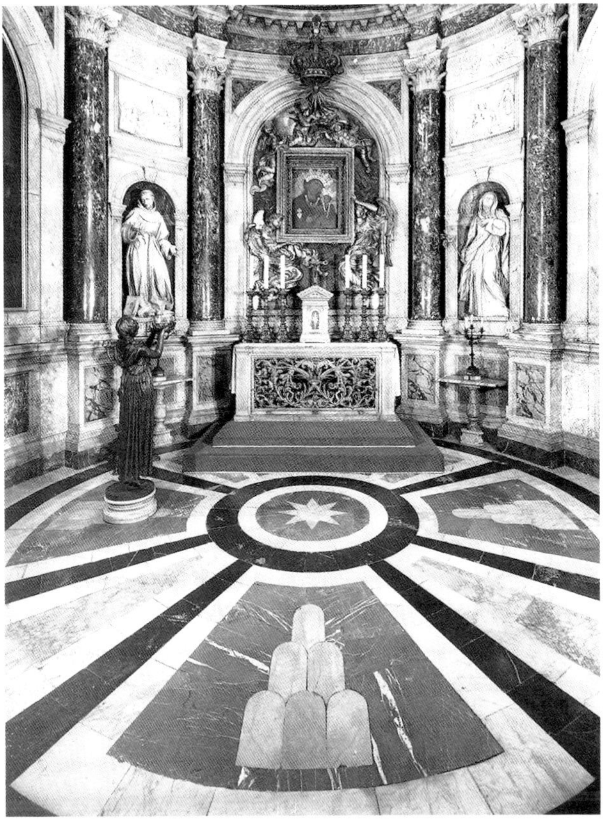

20 Siena, cathedral, view of the chapel of the *Madonna del Voto*.

about it. In the last decade of the thirteenth century, however, the hospital's principal façade on the cathedral square was made more impressive by the construction of two new buildings (see pl. 67). Built in brick and further dignified by series of arched windows, that to the right of the church was designed as the residence of the hospital's rector and that to the left as an orphanage for young girls.[14]

Before the 1290s the government's official buildings had been as modest as those of the Spedale. The city councils had met in various churches and privately owned houses in Siena. On the south side of the Campo, meanwhile, was located a building that functioned variously as the city mint, customs house and meeting place. From two entries in the treasury accounts, dated 1289 and 1291, it appears that one of the rooms in

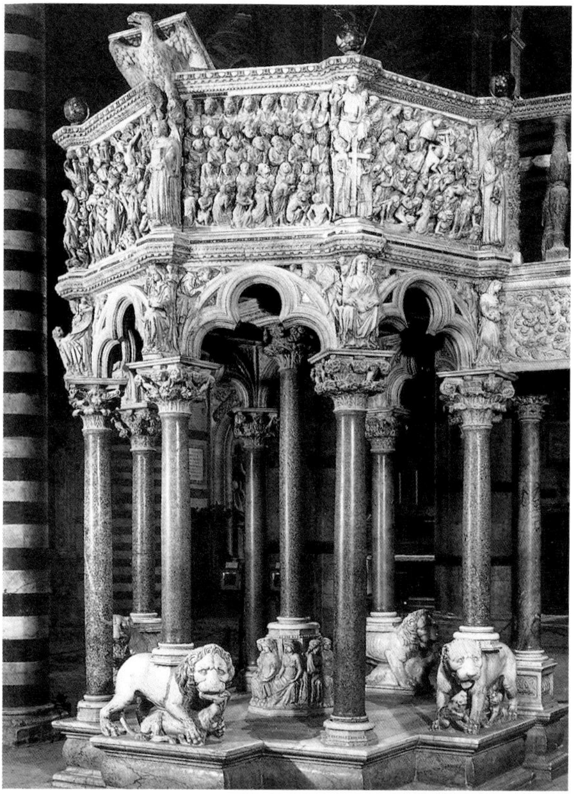

21 Nicola Pisano, pulpit (1265–8). Marble, 460 cm. Siena, cathedral.

this building had already been decorated with a mural painting of the Virgin and saints.[15] Other historical sources indicate that in the 1280s the Podestà and the Nine were assigned houses in the vicinity of this building. In 1297, however, the Council of the Bell instructed the Nine that they should appoint twelve men who should take responsibility for beginning the process of designing and constructing a new palace 'for the utility and honour of the Sienese Commune'.[16] Work on the Palazzo Pubblico (see pl. 1) took place principally in the fourteenth century and thus discussion of its painted embellishment belongs to a later chapter. Nevertheless, it is significant that once the cathedral had reached the stage of the west façade, the government turned its attention and energies towards the construction of this imposing civic palace – a building destined in its final form to rival other civic palaces in northern and central Italy.

Early Maestà

In addition to the support given by the government to the construction of the cathedral, Spedale and Palazzo Pubblico, the religious orders throughout the city received generous financial subsidies for the building and upkeep of their churches. This was particularly the case for the mendicant orders. For example, in 1298, the government granted 600 *lire* to the Augustinian Hermits who were in the process of constructing a new church – Sant'Agostino – on the south side of the city (see pl. 6).[17] One of the reasons the mendicants were favoured was their important role in serving and nurturing the spiritual life of the urban laity. By the second half of the thirteenth century the friars had encouraged and facilitated the participation of the laity in a more active style of religious devotion – saying prayers, going on pilgrimages, fasting, taking part in processions, giving alms, attending sermons and performing other acts of piety.

One way in which laymen and women were able to achieve this was by joining one of Siena's confraternities – lay organisations whose members regularly attended masses, participated in religious processions, prayed together and sang hymns or *laude*.[18] Such confraternities were usually of two kinds – the Disciplinati who practised flagellation as an act of religious penitence, and the Laudesi who took their name from their custom of singing *laude*. These were frequently written in honour of the Virgin and Laudesi companies therefore often used a painted image of the Virgin and Christ Child as a focal point for their collective act of singing. Since the Virgin already had a special role in Sienese religious and civic life, it is not surprising that Laudesi companies became increasingly popular in Siena during the thirteenth century and that several of the most imposing examples of thirteenth-century Sienese paintings that survive today have been associated with them, including Guido da Siena's panel painting of the *Virgin and Christ Child enthroned* (pl. 22).

As noted in the introduction, the year 1221 is inscribed on Guido da Siena's painting and, if it was indeed painted at that date, it would be by far the earliest of such paintings for Laudesi companies. By comparing it, however, with the *Madonna degli occhi grossi*, which was certainly painted in the early decades of the thirteenth century, it is easy to see how much more sophisticated Guido's painting is in terms of pictorial illusionism (see pl. 18). In place of the rigid frontality of the figures and objects in the earlier painting, Guido's Virgin, Christ Child and throne all appear as three-dimensional forms. The two principal figures also seem to be related to one another in a more subtle and emotive way. Moreover, another large

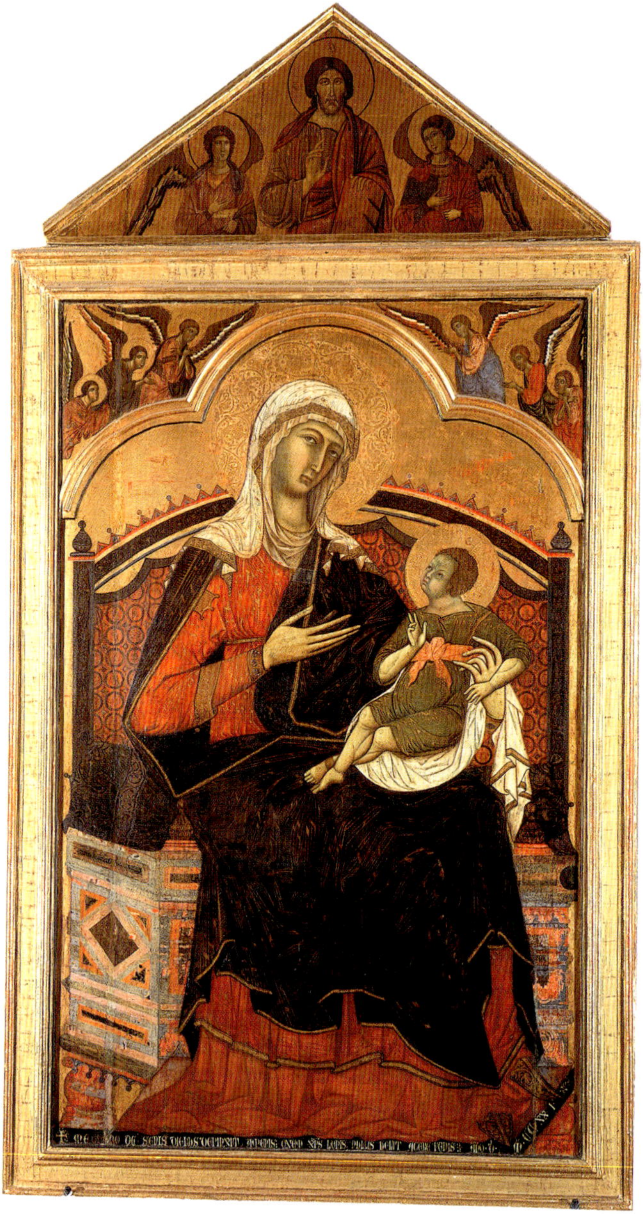

22 Guido da Siena, *The Virgin and Christ Child enthroned*, with *Christ blessing and Two Angels* above (1270s). Tempera on panel, 283 × 194 cm. Siena, San Domenico.

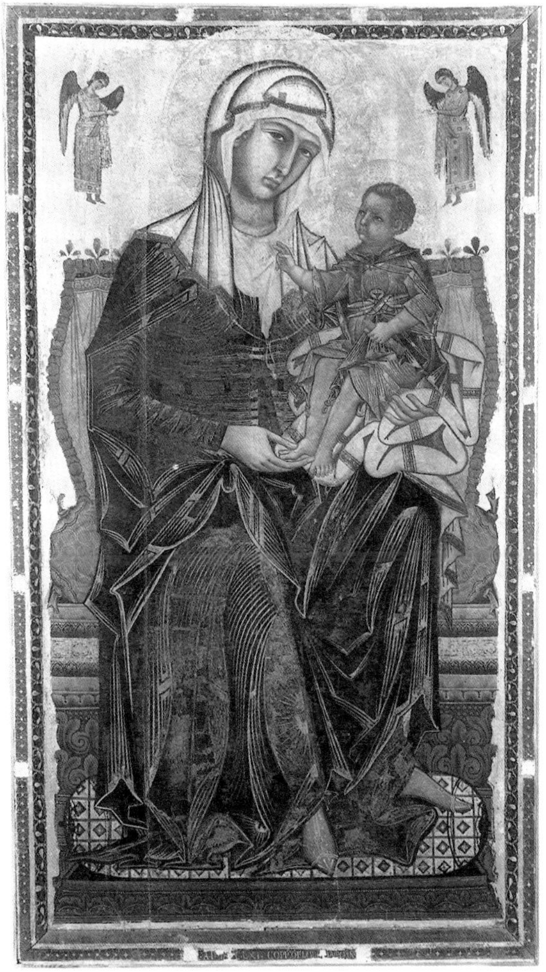

23 Coppo di Marcovaldo, *The Madonna del Bordone* (1261). Tempera on panel, 220 × 125 cm. Siena, Santa Maria dei Servi.

24 *The Virgin and Christ Child enthroned* (1262). Tempera on panel, 142 × 100 cm. Siena, Pinacoteca Nazionale.

25 (*facing page*) Duccio, *The Rucellai Madonna* (1285). Tempera on panel, 450 × 293 cm. Florence, Uffizi.

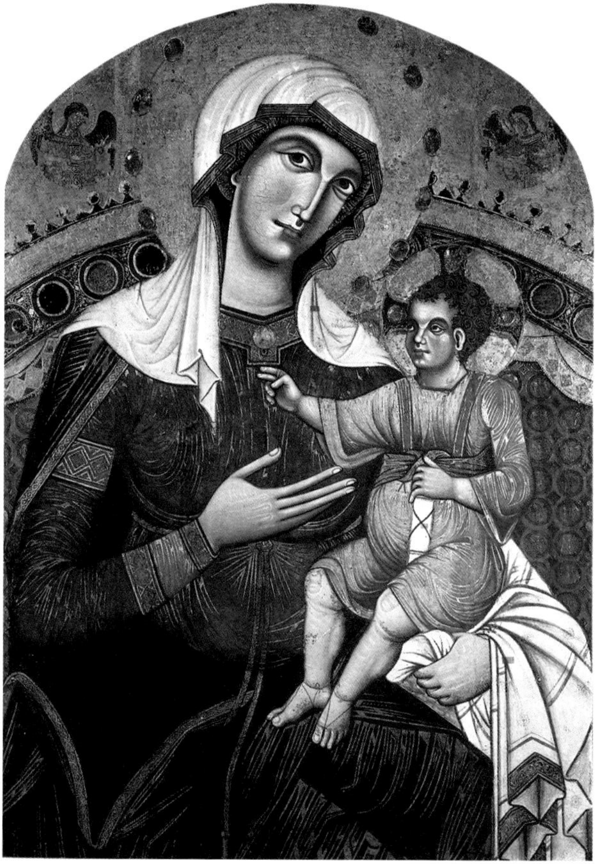

painting, known as the *Madonna del Bordone*, may provide a point of transition between the two paintings in terms of its painter's treatment of the Virgin and Christ Child and the throne on which they are seated (pl. 23). On the lower frame of this painting is an original inscription, executed in gold leaf, that gives the name of the painter as Coppo and the date 1261.[19] On grounds of style, therefore, Guido da Siena's *Virgin and Christ Child*, despite its painted date of 1221, was probably executed in the 1270s.

Why then does the date of 1221 appear on this painting? As with most paintings of this period, the original circumstances of the commission are

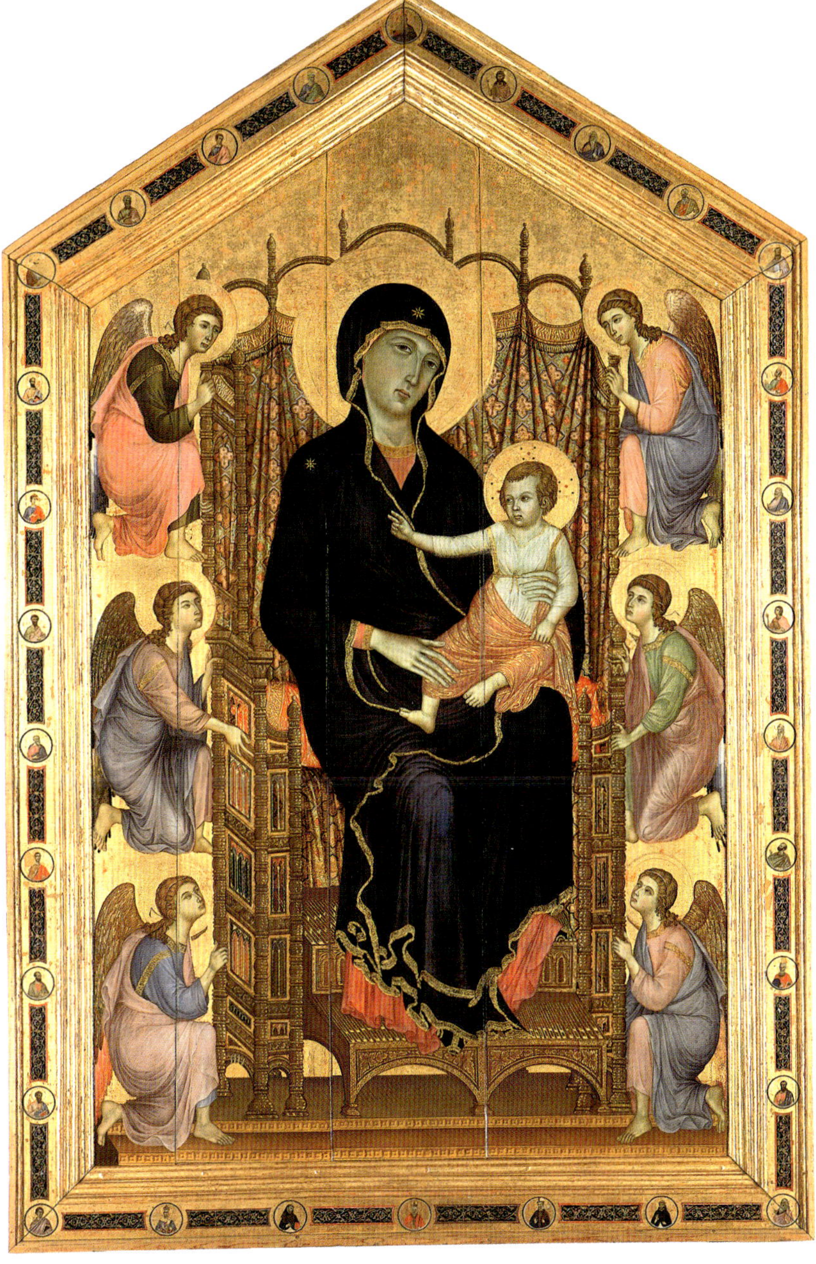

now lost and only by carefully collecting various kinds of historical evidence can a hypothesis be put forward. The painting now stands in a chapel in the north transept of the church of San Domenico, to the left of the chancel and high altar.[20] An elaborate stucco frame, with an inscription dated 1705, indicates that both the painting of the Virgin and Christ Child and its gable panel of *Christ blessing and Two Angels* were located there at that time. Given this, it is not unreasonable to assume that the painting was originally executed for San Domenico – a much smaller church in the 1270s than the present one, which is largely the result of late thirteenth- and fourteenth-century building campaigns. A further complicating factor regarding the history of the painting is that parts of it – notably the faces of the Virgin and Child – have been repainted.[21] The style of modelling the faces is, in fact, similar to that of Duccio (see pl. 36) and it has therefore been argued that this thirteenth-century painting was of sufficient importance to be updated in the second or third decade of the fourteenth century. This, however, raises again the issue of the painting's original location and devotional function.

The painting is an imposing object, much larger in scale than other surviving paintings from the first half of the thirteenth century. In terms of its lavish use of gold, intricately patterned surface and vivid colours, it must have made a considerable visual impression in its original setting. Although it shows indebtedness to Byzantine art, it provides evidence of a marked interest on the part of the painter in making the presence of the Virgin and Christ Child seem more palpable and 'real'. It also involves the spectator in a chain of relationships that begins with the Virgin looking directly outwards while gesturing towards her son who in turn gazes intently at his mother. The six adoring angels in the spandrels of the painting also prompt an emotional involvement with the two holy figures. Thus the painter has taken a standard image from Byzantine art, designed to honour the Virgin as the mother of God, and treated it in such a way as to underline the Virgin's fundamental role of interceding with her son on humanity's behalf. In addition, he has adopted other formulae taken from Byzantine icons, such as the angels and the elaborately worked throne, cushion and hanging, in order to convey another of the Virgin's epithets, that of the queen of heaven. For this reason, this type of early painting of the Virgin is generally known in Italy as a *Maestà* – the word for 'majesty' in Italian.

Given its subject and Guido's distinctive treatment of the figures of the Virgin and Christ Child, the painting would have served the devotional needs and requirements of a Laudesi company particularly well. The Dominican Order was particularly anxious to promote lay piety through the foundation of confraternities and they frequently encouraged such confraternities to meet in their churches.[22] Thus, two of the earliest Sienese confraternities for which there are historical records met in San Domenico. One of these was the Laudesi Company of the Virgin and Saint Dominic that included both men and women and for which there are statutes dating from 1267. The other was the Disciplinati Company of the Holy Cross that was founded in about 1261 and which, some nine years later, was given formal statutes and the new name of the Company of Saint Dominic by a local Dominican Ambrogio Sansedoni.[23] Both companies appear to have been closely linked to this eminent Sienese Dominican who, in 1273, persuaded Pope Gregory X to lift a papal interdict placed upon Siena. After his death in 1286, Ambrogio Sansedoni duly took his place in the pantheon of revered Sienese saints, being honoured by a state funeral and, a year later, by the construction of an elaborate reliquary tomb inside San Domenico.[24]

It may be, therefore, that Guido da Siena's *Maestà* was not executed for a specific altar – such as the high altar[25] – but was placed on the choir screen or a wall of the church in a location that would be easily accessible to members of the two confraternities. Given its subject matter it is likely to have been commissioned by the Laudesi Company of the Virgin and Saint Dominic. Gathering around it regularly, the members of the company would have used the imposing painting as a means by which to focus on the holy figure of their principal patron, the Virgin, and to direct their *laude* sung in honour of her and her son. It is clear from the texts of surviving *laude* that the descriptions of the Virgin as a tender mother and celestial queen would have directly echoed the imagery of the painting itself. As for the date of 1221, the decision to place it on the painting probably reflected a moment of doubly historic importance for the Laudesi themselves and for the Dominican Order in whose church they met. Saint Dominic, the founder of the Order, had died in 1221, while in Siena this was the year when the Order first took possession of a church of their own.[26]

The proposal that Guido da Siena's *Virgin and Christ Child* was commissioned as a devotional image for a Laudesi confraternity in San Domenico receives support from two other thirteenth-century Sienese *Maestà*. As already noted, the *Madonna del Bordone* (pl. 23), still situated in the Servite church of Santa Maria dei Servi on the south-eastern side of the city (see pl. 6), was painted in 1261. It too was selectively repainted in the early fourteenth century but it was originally painted by the thirteenth-century Florentine painter Coppo di Marcovaldo. He is believed to have fought at Montaperti and been captured by the Sienese. It has further been suggested that the motif of the two-headed eagle – a Hohenstaufen symbol – that appears along the edges of the Virgin's headdress might have been intended to allude to Siena's Ghibelline political allegiance at that time.[27] The Sienese government had been active in supporting the Servite Order by giving them financial support to adapt the church of San Clemente (which later became Santa Maria dei Servi) to their needs, and may therefore have been influential in the commissioning of this painting and the choice of its imagery in the wake of Montaperti. However, the Servites were a mendicant order that had been founded specifically to promote the veneration of the Virgin. The commissioning of such a large and striking panel of the Virgin in majesty would thus have been entirely logical. It may have been painted for the main altar of their newly acquired church, but San Clemente had also become the meeting place for a number of Laudesi confraternities. Moreover, the inclusion of *bordone*, meaning a type of melody in Italian, as part of the popular title of this painting could well have been derived from the practice of singing *laude* in front of it.[28] It seems highly likely, therefore, that the Servites had already introduced such paintings as a focus for Laudesi devotions as early as 1261.

The immediate impact of Coppo's panel can be judged by a third Sienese painting of the *Maestà* theme (pl. 24). This painting was drastically cut down on all four sides, not as an act of vandalism but in order for it to continue to play an important role in the devotional lives of the Sienese. As a result the painted text recording the painting's commission in 1262 by the Company of the Virgin Mary was destroyed – but fortunately its content was carefully transcribed in a legal document of 1655.[29] This confraternity was under the spiritual guidance of the Franciscans and was therefore located in the church of San Francesco on the north-eastern side of the city (see pl. 6).[30] The faces of the main figures of this particular painting have not, however, been repainted and therefore provide an indication of the way in which the faces of the Virgin and Christ Child on the *Maestà* of Coppo di Marcovaldo and Guido da Siena are likely to have appeared originally (see pls 22, 23). At the same time, however, this *Maestà* – painted in all likelihood by a Sienese painter[31] – suggests the immediate impact that the *Madonna del Bordone* apparently had upon local painters and their patrons.

In 1285, and thus some ten years after the commissioning of Guido da Siena's *Maestà* for San Domenico, another Laudesi confraternity contracted a painter to execute an impressive painting of the Virgin (pl. 25). On this occasion, however, the commission involved the Laudesi confraternity of the Virgin Mary based in Santa Maria Novella, the principal Dominican church in Florence, and the Sienese painter, Duccio.[32] There is a pleasing reversal here. In the 1260s, the Sienese relied on the expertise of a Florentine painter, Coppo di Marcovaldo, to execute a new type of religious painting commemorating and celebrating the Virgin (see pl. 23). Sienese painters subsequently took up the challenge thus posed and produced their own highly individual versions of this subject (see pls 22, 24). Then a Florentine confraternity – probably learning of Guido da Siena's impressive rendition of this subject from their contacts with the Dominican house in Siena – turned to a Sienese painter to produce a painting for them that was highly innovative in its approach to this traditional theme.

Duccio's painting is now known as the *Rucellai Madonna* because – before its removal to the Uffizi gallery in 1948 – it was located in a chapel under the patronage of the Rucellai family in Santa Maria Novella. As in the case of its prototypes, it is not known precisely where in the church it was originally located. The presence of several sturdy metal rings on the back of the panel suggests that it was hung on a wall of the church and since it had been commissioned by the Laudesi, it was presumably placed in a part of the church to which its members had access. It seems most likely, therefore, that it was originally hung on the end wall of the south transept close to both a chapel under the patronage of the Laudesi and to the Rucellai chapel where it was first reported in the eighteenth century.[33]

In certain respects the *Rucellai Madonna* is entirely conventional, showing the familiar repertoire of the Virgin indicating the identity and importance of the Christ Child by the angle of her head and her steady outward gaze. However, in his treatment of the two principal figures, Duccio went much further than earlier painters in making the implied presence of the Virgin and Christ Child strongly felt. The expanse of dark blue used on the Virgin's mantle is painstakingly modelled in order to convey the fall of the fabric and form of the body beneath – in particular the outline of the Virgin's left breast and the projection of her left knee. The Christ Child likewise appears to be sitting in a convincing pose upon his mother's lap. Immensely fine gradations of paint give an impression of the softness of the child's flesh and the rotundity of his head. Duccio's use of colour is highly effective: the wide expanse of deep blue serves to emphasise the Virgin, while the contrasting tones of white, pink, pale blue, green and mauve subtly draw attention to the Christ Child and angels. Despite these self-consciously naturalistic features, the painting still retains the otherworldly qualities of its Byzantine models. This is achieved partly by the extensive use of gold on the background of the painting and such details as the intricate edge of the Virgin's mantle and the stars on her head and shoulder. The positioning of the six angels contributes to this effect. While conceived as far more substantial beings than their earlier thirteenth-century counterparts, four of them appear as if suspended in the air while effortlessly supporting the Virgin's elaborately worked throne. In its original state, with the gold-leaf background burnished so that it reflected the light of the candles placed around it, the imagery of the painting must have taken on an almost visionary quality – giving the faithful gathered below an impression that they were indeed witnessing the Virgin and Christ Child enthroned in heaven.

This extraordinarily sophisticated balance between tradition and innovation continues in the embellishment of the broad wooden frame of the painting. The device of painting a series of roundels containing half-length figures of saints had already occurred on the frame of another mid-thirteenth-century painting of Saint Francis surrounded by scenes from his life.[34] Duccio introduced it to the *Maestà* type and – by representing Christ, the apostles, prophets and five saints of particular importance to the Dominicans and Laudesi[35] – skilfully used it to extend his repertoire of painted imagery for his confraternity clients.

Sienese painters continued to produce this type of *Maestà* painting in the early decades of the fourteenth century[36] but in many respects the *Rucellai Madonna* represented the apogee of this type of Marian painting. Produced on panels of a substantial scale and retaining many of the conventional features of Byzantine icons, these paintings were designed to celebrate the Virgin Mary in her role as mother of God, queen of heaven and divine mediatrix. Given Siena's commitment to the Virgin as the city's principal patron and protector, it is not surprising that thirteenth-century Sienese painters were resourceful in producing and developing paintings of this type. It is no more surprising that the city's lay confraternities – particularly those dedicated to the Virgin and to singing *laude* – appear to have been instrumental in encouraging painters to develop such skills.

Other Sacred Art

A fresco from the famous series depicting the life of Saint Francis in the Upper Church at Assisi offers an insight into how paintings like the *Rucellai Madonna* might once have been displayed in a late medieval church (pl. 26). It shows a large crowd gathered round the bier of Saint Francis, which has been set up in front of the choir screen that separates the

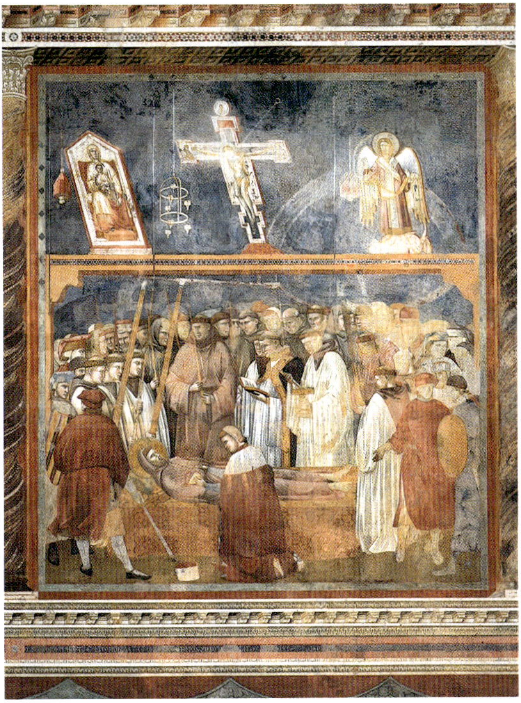

26 *The Funeral of Saint Francis* (*c.* 1291–1305). Fresco, 270 × 230 cm. Assisi, San Francesco, Upper Church.

main body of the church from the choir. The choir screen was a common feature of medieval churches, dividing the space of the church into those parts to which the clergy and the laity had access. Attached to this screen in the Assisi fresco appear three painted objects. On the extreme left is a large *Maestà* panel, next to it a painted panel of Christ on the Cross and to the right the figure of an angel. In the case of the last two paintings, their shape corresponds to that of a Cross and a figure of an angel. The line between painting and sculpture is thus somewhat blurred and indeed many of the earliest surviving examples of Italian painting incorporate sculpted detail (see pl. 18). While the lack of surviving painted panels in the shape of angels or saints may indicate that this was not a favoured type of religious image, the large number of extant panels of Christ on the Cross suggests that they by contrast definitely were favoured. As paintings that decisively commemorated and celebrated Christ's death on the Cross – and therefore mirrored in a direct way the rite of mass – such images became a popular and revered form in thirteenth-century Italian religious art.

Moreover, their status was enhanced by the frequency with which they were associated with visions experienced by newly sanctified saints and *beati* such as Francis, Margaret of Cortona and Catherine of Siena. By the second half of the century – as a direct result of the more emotive piety that the Franciscans had promoted with regard to the cult of Christ crucified – painted crucifixes had undergone a dramatic change in their mode of representation. In place of the older portrayal of Christ as an upright figure looking directly out towards the spectator as if to emphasise his triumph over death, there appeared an image that emphasised the experience of death and suffering that Christ had undergone.

Among the painted crucifixes in the Pinacoteca of Siena is a powerful example of the earlier type, where Christ is represented as a steadfast figure triumphing over death. On grounds of style, it has been dated to the early decades of the thirteenth century and, since it came from the Franciscan convent of Santa Chiara in Siena, it has also been assumed that a Sienese painter executed it.[37] The other crucifixes on display in this gallery all date to the fourteenth century – a clear indication of the continuing popularity of this type of religious image. In order to form an impression of later thirteenth-century painted crucifixes it is necessary, therefore, to look further afield. The civic gallery of San Gimignano preserves a particularly fine crucifix that has been attributed plausibly to the Florentine painter Coppo di Marcovaldo (pl. 27). Its provenance is a Franciscan convent in San Gimignano, also dedicated to Saint Claire.[38] It is possible, therefore, that the Franciscan nuns of this convent wished to emulate their sisters in Siena by acquiring a painted crucifix. However, by employing Coppo di Marcovaldo who (as already seen) was a particularly innovative mid-thirteenth-century painter, they secured a highly emotive rendition of this traditional subject. Christ's face and body are portrayed in such a way as to emphasise both his death and his suffering on the Cross, an impression that is enhanced by the expressive presence of the group of mourning saints depicted on the terminals of the arms of the Cross. Looking again at the painting in the Upper Church at Assisi, it is instructive to note how the painted crucifix has been represented not standing upright on the top of the choir screen but at an angle. If Coppo di Marcovaldo's painted crucifix were originally hung in a similar way, the impression of the body being lowered towards the congregation would have made the dramatic, visual impact of the dead Christ even greater.

Another noticeable feature of this painted crucifix is the six narrative scenes situated on either side of Christ's body. These show a series of events taken from the Passion of Christ, beginning with the betrayal of Christ by

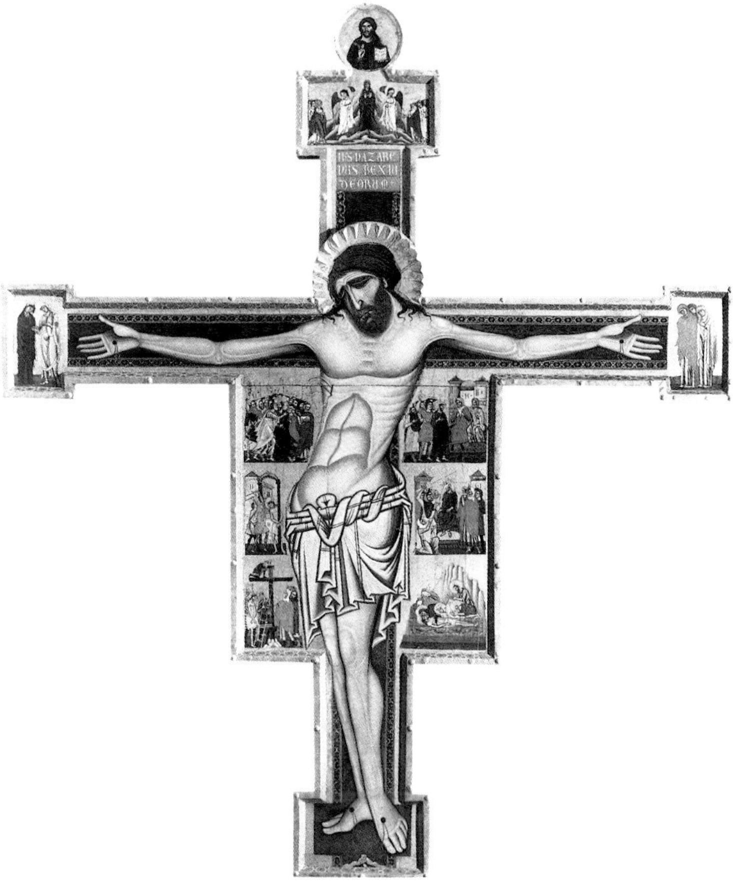

27 Coppo di Marcovaldo, *Crucifix* (1260s). Tempera on panel. San Gimignano, Palazzo Comunale, Pinacoteca Civica.

Judas and ending with his entombment. Their function was therefore to remind the devotee of the events surrounding Christ's crucifixion. They also, however, provide a vivid example of the painter's ability to portray narrative events and situations. Several paintings of narrative subjects that have been attributed to Guido da Siena on grounds of style indicate that Coppo's Sienese counterpart possessed a similar talent for this particular artistic task. Arguably the most impressive of these is a painting showing

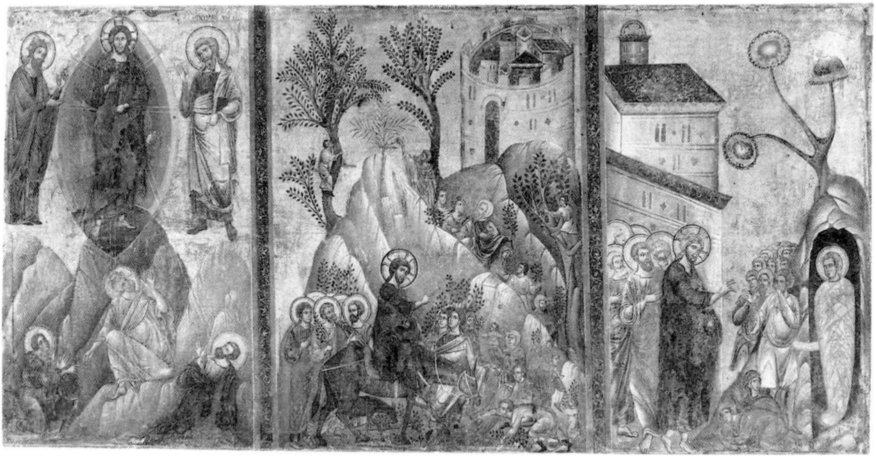

28 Guido da Siena, *The Transfiguration, the Entry into Jerusalem, and the Raising of Lazurus* (mid-1270s). Tempera on linen, 90 × 186 cm. Siena, Pinacoteca Nazionale.

three important events preceding Christ's crucifixion – the transfiguration, entry into Jerusalem and the raising of Lazurus from his tomb (pl. 28). Significantly, the order of these three scenes has been changed from that of the gospel accounts of Christ's ministry and Passion. Thus, the entry into Jerusalem has been placed before the raising of Lazurus – presumably to accord the first public event leading up to Christ's crucifixion greater prominence by making it the central image of the painting.

Probably executed in the 1270s, the painting is surprisingly simple in format for its date. The fact that it was painted on linen, rather than on the customary wood, suggests that it was designed as a covering for an altarpiece during the period of Lent.[39] Clearly, its subject would have made such a function appropriate. However, it was more generally the case that such Lenten coverings were painted in monochrome to complement the Church's teaching on abstinence during this liturgical period. It seems more likely, therefore, that it was designed as a cover for the front of an altar.

Earlier examples of such altar frontals had been sculpted and were often costly in terms of the materials from which they were made. It may be, therefore, that the commissioners of Guido da Siena's painting wished to purchase a cheaper substitute. But it might also have become the case that instead of expensive materials a premium was placed on the artistic skills

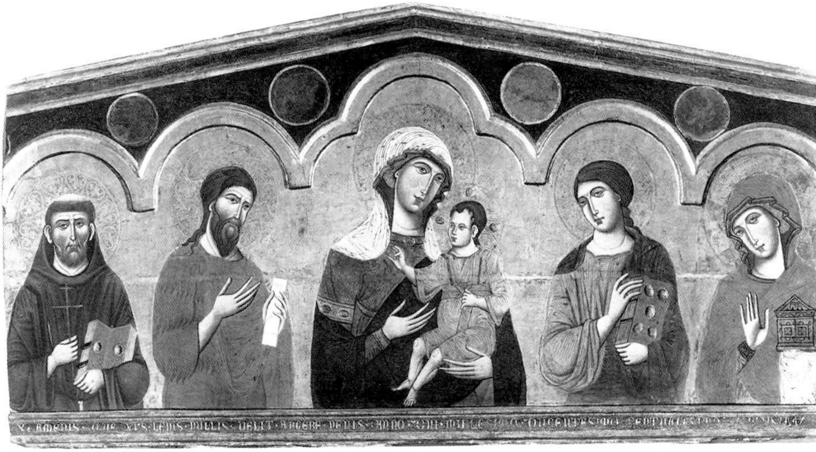

29 Guido da Siena, *The Virgin and Christ Child and Saints Francis, John the Baptist, John the Evangelist and Mary Magdalen* (1270s). Tempera on panel, 96 × 186 cm. Siena, Pinacoteca Nazionale.

of the painter. It is certainly striking how lively the expressions of the various figures are – including such engaging details as a woman holding her baby up to Christ in the *Entry into Jerusalem* and a figure beside the tomb in the *Raising of Lazurus* covering his mouth and nose in order to avoid the smell. While the forms of the buildings and contours of the land are largely schematic in their representation, they also provide broadly recognisable settings for the figures and events portrayed. Even at this early date, there is therefore a sense of how Sienese painters were striving to represent events, drawn from the bible and other kinds of religious text, in a sufficiently vivid way to meet the Church's expectation that painted images should educate, be memorable and fire religious devotion.

As well as his abilities as a painter of narrative, Guido da Siena may have introduced to Siena a new type of panel painting whose horizontal format made it ideal for the embellishment of altars. His *Virgin and Christ Child* with four saints, which carries a painted date indicating that it was produced at some point in the 1270s, offers an instructive example (pl. 29).[40] Unlike the *Maestà* for San Domenico (see pl. 22), it represents the Virgin as a half-length figure accompanied by half-length figures of saints placed on either side of her. The low gable used for the upper contour of the panel enabled the painter to depict the major cult figure of the Virgin on a larger scale than for the other figures. Like the Virgin on the 1262 *Maestà* (see pl. 24), she again indicates the status and significance of the Christ Child by the angle of her head and the gesture of her right hand. The Christ Child, meanwhile, has been portrayed in the guise of a priest in the act of blessing the faithful and a judge holding a tightly rolled scroll.

The identities of the saints offer an insight into the circumstances of the painting's commission. Medieval church legislation directed that on every altar there should be an inscription or a sculpture or a painting, and these should act as an indication of the dedication of the altar.[41] In the case of this altarpiece, the prominent presence of Saint Francis, who had been canonised only in 1228, suggests that this altarpiece was intended for an altar dedicated to Saint Francis – a hypothesis that is strengthened by the fact that the provenance of this painting was the church of San Francesco in Colle Val d'Elsa. In addition, the other three saints represented on the painting – John the Baptist, John the Evangelist and Mary Magdalen – were all venerated by the Franciscan Order.

These saints are portrayed in a relatively formal manner but Guido da Siena has also skilfully introduced a number of subtle variations of pose. Thus, the outer figures of Saints Francis and Mary Magdalen appear as if facing directly outwards and thus engaging with the painting's original audience.[42] Saints John the Baptist and John the Evangelist, meanwhile, appear at a slight angle to the lower frame and as if turning towards the two central cult figures – thus indicating to potential devotees where they should direct their attention and piety. This type of altarpiece painting, with its central focus upon the Virgin and Christ Child and its versatile complement of accompanying saints (who could be chosen to reflect not only the dedication of the altar but also the identities of the commissioners themselves), became a highly successful genre of religious painting and, as will be demonstrated in later chapters, a staple item in Sienese painters' artistic repertoire.

At first sight, the thirteenth-century panel painting of *Saint Peter enthroned* that hangs on the wall opposite Guido da Siena's painting in the Pinacoteca of Siena appears a much more old-fashioned type of altarpiece (pl. 30). Originally painted for the now destroyed parish church of San Pietro in Banchi in Siena, in terms of its shape and composition it conforms to a number of painted panels that can be dated to the first half of the thirteenth century. Yet, in terms of the confident representation of Saint Peter seated on a throne – the design of which is broadly similar to that of the San Domenico *Maestà* (see pl. 22) – and the lively pictorial narration of the painted scenes grouped on either side of the saint, it seems much more like-

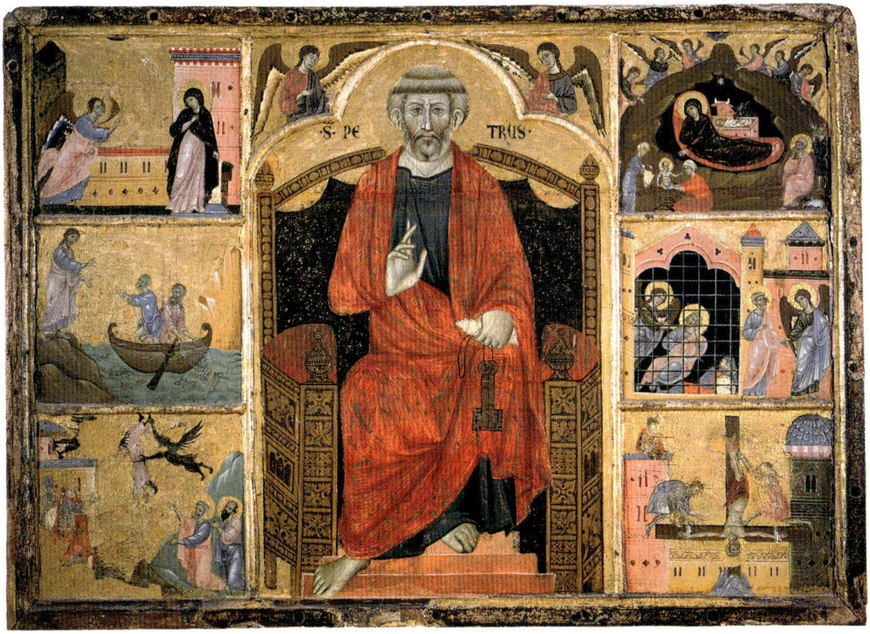

30 *Saint Peter enthroned with Scenes of his Life and the Annunciation and Nativity* (1280s). Tempera on panel, 100.5 × 141 cm. Siena, Pinacoteca Nazionale.

ly that this painting was executed in the 1280s by a painter who was aware of Guido da Siena's style of painting and yet retained a marked originality of his own.[43]

While adhering to a number of conventions favoured by Guido, this unknown painter was clearly capable of a high degree of pictorial invention, as seen in such details as the different species of fish portrayed in the Sea of Galilee in the middle scene on the left, and the extraordinarily dynamic devil tormenting Simon Magus in the lower scene on the left. It has been suggested that this painter might have been Guido di Graziano; who features in a number of payments for paintings commissioned by the city treasury.[44] Whether or not this is correct, the painting provides clear evidence of how, even in the later decades of the thirteenth century, such simple rectangular panel paintings were still being commissioned for the city's churches. Even within their traditional format, however, local painters were experimenting with new forms of pictorial expression in

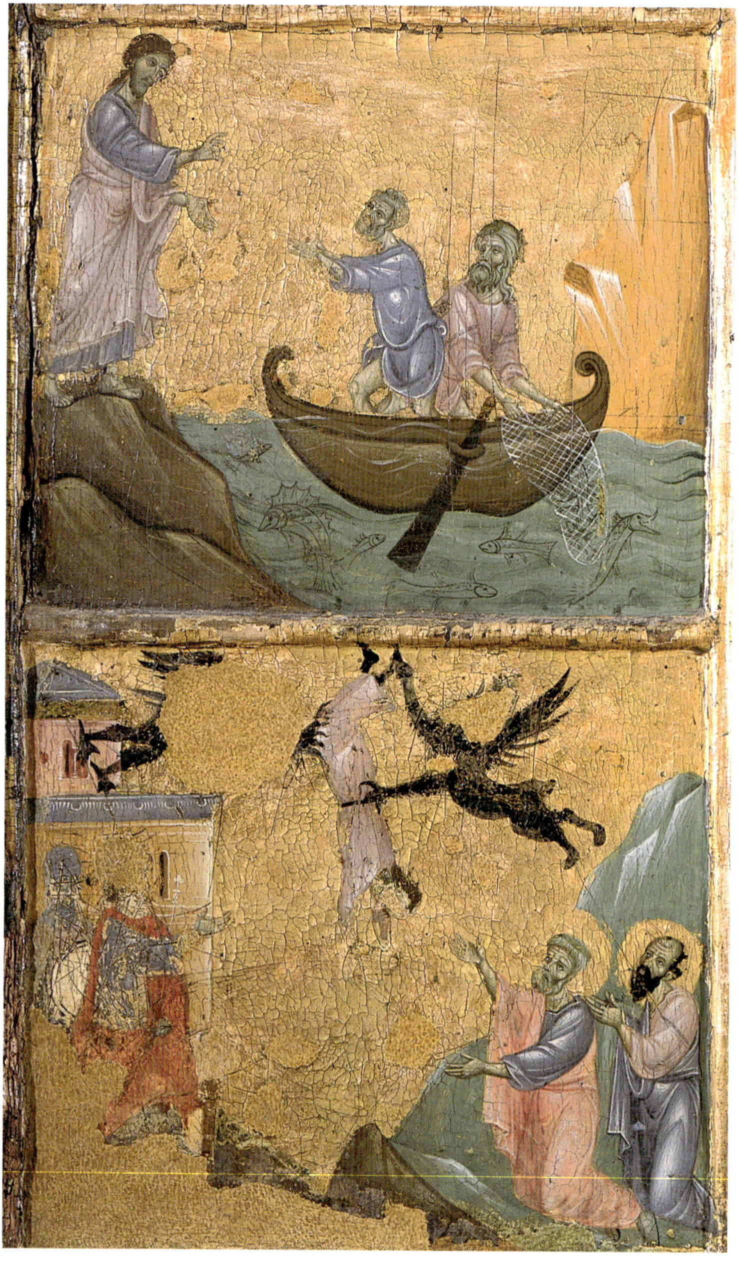

Scenes of the Life of Saint Peter (detail of pl. 30).

order to make the story of the conception and birth of Christ and the life and death of Saint Peter more immediate and 'real' to the parishioners of San Pietro in Banchi.

Narrative painting was not confined to panel painting at this date. Mural painting was a common type of decoration throughout Italy that readily lent itself to the representation of narrative. Relatively few thirteenth-century wall paintings survive in Siena and those that do are not in good condition. However, the remains of an extensive cycle of mural paintings dating to the 1270s have recently been discovered.[45] Hidden for centuries behind piles of rubble in a disused oratory beneath the chancel of the cathedral and covering an area of 180 square metres, they depict scenes from the Old and New Testaments. Still retaining the rich colours of the original painting and apparently carried out by more than one painter, these frescoes are currently not on public view but undergoing extensive consolidation and investigation.

They appear to correspond in dating to another series of thirteenth-century murals that have long been visible in a small crypt beneath the south transept of the cathedral. Now partially obscured by brick vaulting, constructed at a later date, these frescoes were clearly once part of a larger series depicting scenes from the Passion of Christ. The fresco depicting the betrayal of Christ by Judas suggests that the style of these paintings, in the modelling of the faces, hands and drapery folds, adheres closely to the conventions adopted by Guido da Siena (pl. 31). Given the lack of signed fresco paintings by Guido, it is difficult to gauge whether this Sienese painter would also have painted with the bold outlines and expressive brushstrokes still visible in the *Kiss of Judas*. If Guido da Siena was not the painter responsible for these frescoes, however, they may have been painted by one of the other Sienese painters for whom there are brief written records but no signed paintings.[46]

Secular Art

The main sources for the activities of painters other than Guido da Siena occur in the records of the Sienese treasury (the Biccherna). Here a number of named painters are cited as receiving payment for work, generally for painting wooden panels that were used as the covers of the Biccherna's account books. Many of these painted panels still survive today and have been separated from the account books themselves and displayed in a

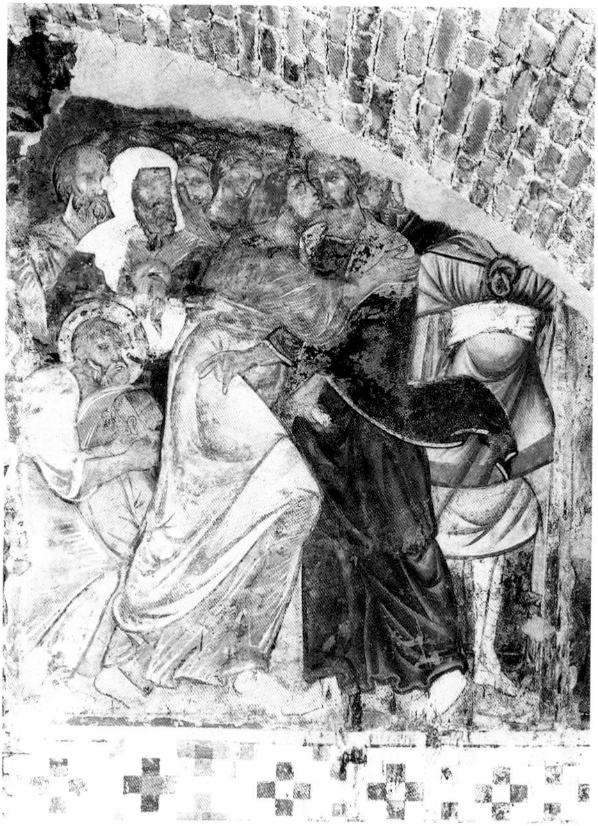

31 *The Kiss of Judas* (end of thirteenth century). Remains of a fresco. Siena, cathedral, crypt of the statues.

museum within the Archivio di Stato in Siena.[47] Beginning in 1258, most of the earliest examples incorporate the names and coats-of-arms of the chief officials of either the Biccherna or the customs office (the Gabella) together with the dates that the accounts in question were kept, which was a six-month period. They also frequently include painted imagery of a more descriptive kind. Of the fourteen surviving thirteenth-century panels, seven depict the chief treasurer or chancellor of the Biccherna working at his desk, either with an open account book or counting out money. In all seven cases, the chancellor is portrayed as a monk – thus presenting an accurate record of the religious profession of these officials, who at that date were regularly recruited from one of the religious orders. The Biccherna panel for July to December 1264, for which the painter Dietisalvi di Speme received

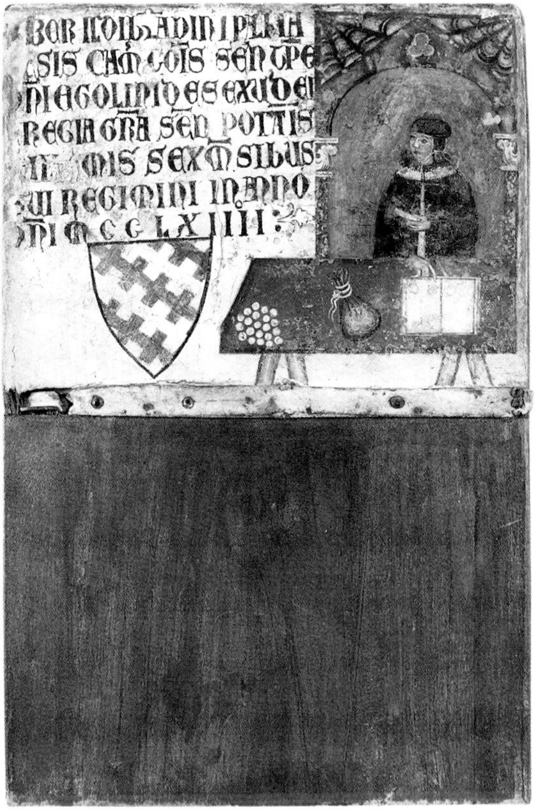

32 Dietisalvi di Speme, *Idilbrandino Pagliaresi, the Chancellor of Siena* (1264). Tempera on panel, 36.4 × 24.2 cm. Siena, Archivio di Stato, Museo delle Tavolette di Biccherna.

payment,[48] presents an unusual example of the chancellor portrayed in the costume of a lay person of some social standing (pl. 32). The coat-of-arms is that of the Pagliaresi family and the painted inscription beside it confirms that the chancellor for that period was Idilbrandino Pagliaresi. This painted image of an identifiable person, surrounded by the tools of his profession, thus offers a rare example of a thirteenth-century Sienese painting of a purely secular subject. Although the setting in which Idilbrandino Pagliaresi is placed is fairly rudimentary, it nevertheless represents him standing behind a trestle table and in front of a tiled portico supported on marble columns with ornate capitals. There is a sense, therefore, that the painter wanted to communicate something about the character and social standing of this civic official.

Privately owned houses in Siena at this date must have been furnished with wooden objects such as beds, settles and chests, and some of these may have been decorated with painted imagery. Similarly the walls and wooden rafters of rooms may have been painted but, unlike such decoration from later centuries, none of this privately commissioned, secular art appears to have survived.[49] The collection of thirteenth-century Biccherna panels thus provides the principal surviving evidence that thirteenth-century Sienese painters were not invariably employed to paint religious imagery but were occasionally asked to use their pictorial skills to record the secular activities of their fellow citizens.

Whatever the limits to modern knowledge of their secular work, it is clear that in the second half of the thirteenth-century Sienese painters were frequently commissioned to produce religious paintings that were destined for the city's principal churches and, more occasionally, for churches in outlying towns (for example, pls 25, 27). While indebted to the types of religious imagery and stylistic conventions common in Byzantine art that had been communicated to them through the presence of eastern artists in Italy, trade between Siena and the Levant, and the example of earlier Tuscan painters who had absorbed this stylistic idiom,[50] mid- and late thirteenth-century Sienese painters began to experiment with new formats and new ways of representing holy figures and events. Thus, while painters such as Guido da Siena represented the Virgin in a characteristically formal pose and applied paint and gold leaf in a similar manner to painters of Byzantine icons, they also appear to have been stimulated by the example of locally produced sculpture (such as the relief panels on Nicola Pisano's pulpit, see pl. 21). Their representation of holy figures and events thus became increasingly more accessible to worshippers who used them as an aid to their religious practice and devotion, whether it be singing *laude* in praise of the Virgin or focussing more fully upon the implications of the sacrament of Mass.

The rate of survival of thirteenth-century Sienese paintings, however, is very uneven. What tend to have been preserved are panel paintings that later became cult objects in their own right (see pls 18, 22–4), while other kinds of religious art – such as wall paintings and painted textiles – have survived less well (see pls 28, 31). A number of fine thirteenth-century illuminations also survive among the city's collections of religious manuscripts, but again the authorship of these lively images is no longer known.[51] What is true for religious painting is even more so for secular painting, almost nothing of which – other than the Biccherna panels – survives.

Moreover, quite apart from the problem of survival, there is the further difficulty of attributing what does survive to painters whose names are known. One of the reasons Guido da Siena emerges as painter with an identity and a group of paintings associated with him is precisely that he placed his name prominently on a large-scale painting that had been assiduously preserved by the Dominicans down through the centuries (see pl. 22). His fellow painters – Dietisalvi di Speme, Rinaldo da Siena and Guido di Graziano – were not so fortunate and it is only because of the ingenuity of modern art historians that these names have been recovered and surviving works of art attributed to them on stylistic grounds.[52]

By the last decades of the thirteenth century, however, one Sienese painter began to feature regularly in documents, both as a citizen of Siena liable for taxation and militia duty, and as a practising painter receiving commissions from the government and the Opera del Duomo.[53] This was Duccio di Buoninsegna who, as already seen, secured the prestigious commission of painting the *Rucellai Madonna* for a Florentine Laudesi company in 1285. In 1311 a local chronicler recorded the installation of Duccio's *Maestà* over the high altar of Siena cathedral, a painting that like Guido da Siena's *Maestà* carries the painter's name prominently upon it. From that point onwards the history of Sienese painting can be tied more confidently to the talents and careers of individual painters.

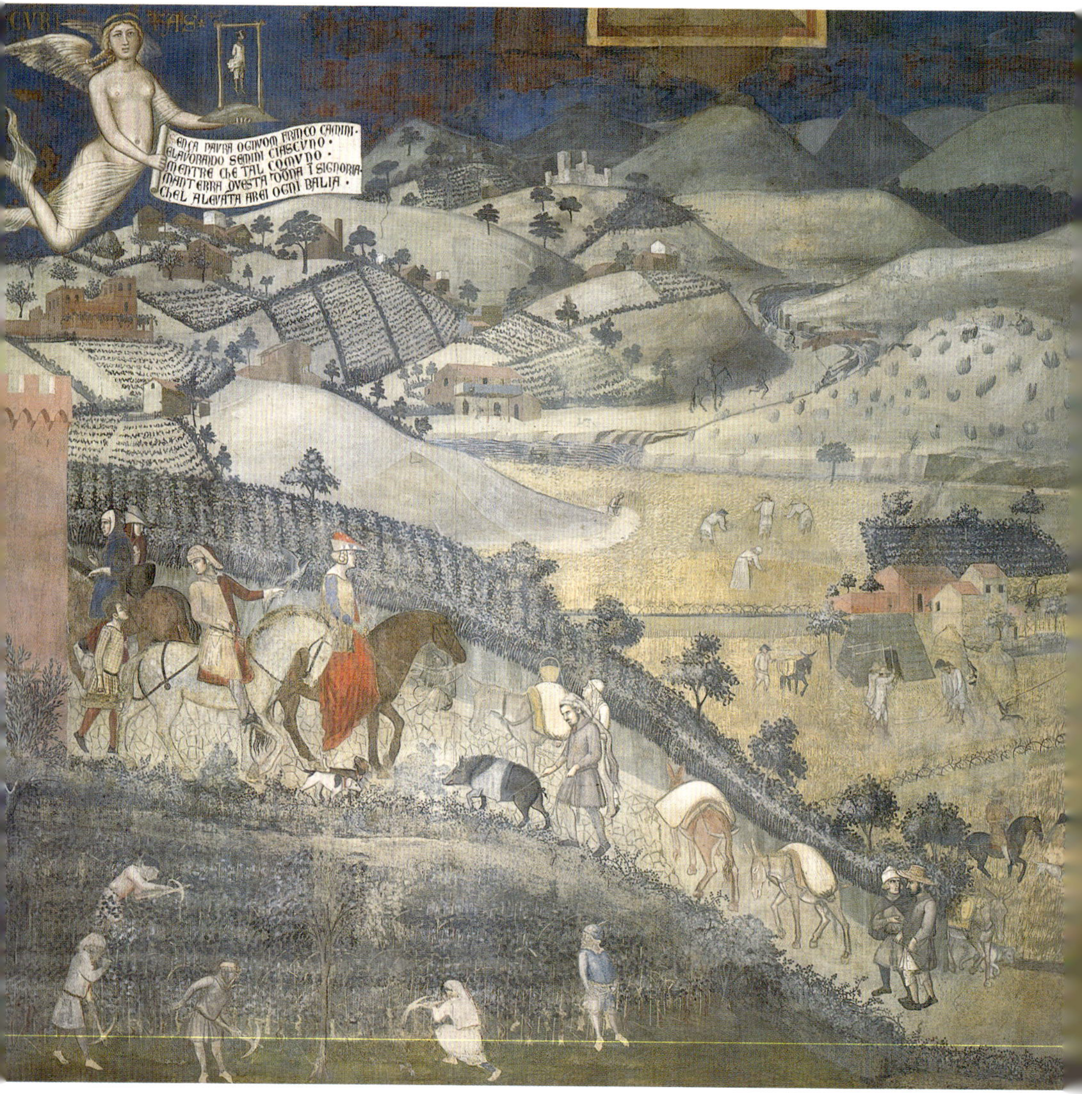

33 Ambrogio Lorenzetti, *The Good Countryside* (1338–9). Detail of east wall fresco of the Sala della Pace. Siena, Palazzo Pubblico.

2

The 'Golden Age' of Sienese Painting (1300–1355)

Writing at the very end of the fourteenth century, the Augustinian Hermit Fra Filippo Agazzari characterised the 1320s as a time when 'there was great peace and great abundance of all earthly goods for the city of Siena'.[1] This perception of the period between 1287 and 1355 as one of political stability and economic prosperity for Siena still continues in modern scholarship.[2] It is also generally recognised that the ruling magistracy of the Nine represented the interests of a tightly knit oligarchy drawn principally from the most prosperous merchant families of the city. Other sections of society were excluded from political power – notably the Tolomei, Piccolomini, Malavolti and Salimbeni families whose wealth and status had been attained through banking and international trade but who were deemed 'noble' and therefore denied membership of the Nine. Members of these families frequently obtained other kinds of lucrative government post, however. In the meantime, yet other sections of Sienese society, such as the notaries and the butchers, felt that their commercial interests were ill-served by the policies of the Nine. These sections of Sienese society periodically rebelled against the regime, as in the insurrections of 1311, 1318, 1328 and, finally, the insurrection of 1355 that brought about the overthrow of the Nine.

Throughout their long period of office, the Nine also had to weather a variety of external threats. In the early years of the fourteenth century they were engaged in a hard-fought military campaign against the powerful Aldobrandeschi and Pannocchieschi d'Elci families who – through their ownership of a large number of castles in southern Tuscany – were a constant impediment to the Nine extending Sienese rule over the *contado* and maintaining peace and security there. At the same time, as a member of the Guelph league, the Nine were expected to provide contingents of knights and foot soldiers to fight the armies of German princes, such as Henry of Luxemburg and Ludwig of Bavaria, who as claimants to the imperial crown offered military support to Ghibelline towns in Tuscany, such as Pisa and Lucca. The long campaign conducted by the Nine to wrest the southern Tuscan town of Massa Marittima from its political allegiance to Pisa and finally, in 1335, make it a subject city of Siena offers a particularly powerful example of this aspect of fourteenth-century Sienese politics.[3]

In addition the Nine had to deal with a number of major social and economic disasters, especially the failure of the Bonsignori and Tolomei banks in 1298 and 1313,[4] the drought, food shortages and riots of 1326 and, most seriously of all, the outbreak of the Black Death in 1348. It has been estimated that in that crisis Siena lost at least half its population.[5] The Sienese chronicler and civil servant Agnolo di Tura recorded with great poignancy that he buried five of his children with his own hands.[6] The social and economic effects of the Black Death were gravely disruptive for the stability of the city. Added to this, moreover, was a new threat of foreign mercenary companies who preyed upon the city and *contado* and had to be bought off with large sums of money.[7] The arrival in Siena of the emperor-elect, Charles IV, in 1355 provided the excuse for discontented elements within the city to unite, storm the Palazzo Pubblico and force the Nine and their allies to relinquish control of the government. Thereafter, government became more popular, in terms of social representation, but also much more unstable.

One of the most remarkable achievements of the Nine was their ambitious programme to beautify the city, summed up by the decree issued in 1297 that any new buildings facing the Campo were to be of uniform design.[8] The Campo itself was paved and provided with a fountain, fed by a complicated system of underground aqueducts. The Nine were also responsible for initiating the paving, widening and straightening of many of the city streets, for rebuilding the monumental Porta Romana, and for creating a public park between the Porta Camollia and the Antiporto.[9] Their most important act of artistic patronage, however, was the construction of the Palazzo Pubblico, a building that became the enduring symbol of the city and its civic identity (see pl. 1). Built on the foundations of a number of earlier buildings on the south side of the Campo and incorporating a former alleyway, the principal sections of the building were completed by 1310. The tall and imposing Torre del Mangia, the highest tower in the city, was built between 1325 and 1344. Between 1330 and 1342, a major addi-

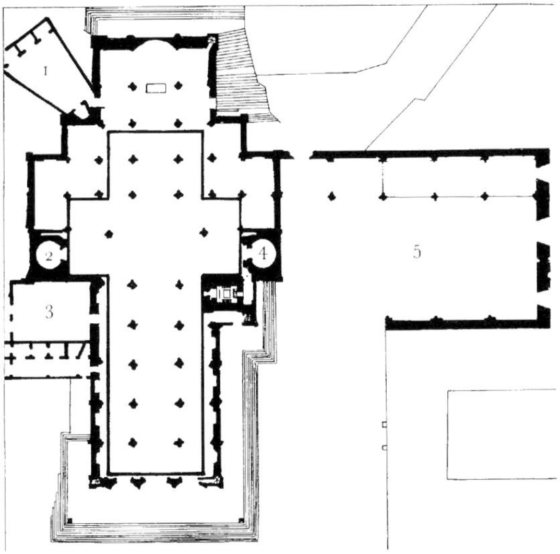

34 Siena cathedral. Ground plan of the thirteenth-century cathedral superimposed on the present church.
1 Sacristy
2 Chapel of Saint John the Baptist
3 Piccolomini Library
4 Chapel of the *Madonna del Voto*
5 Duomo Nuovo

tion to the rear of the building was built to accommodate the city prison and above it a large meeting hall for the city's principal council. Finally, as a mark of gratitude for the cessation of the Black Death, an elegant, open-sided chapel was begun in 1352.[10]

An ambitious programme of building and embellishment at the cathedral also took place in the first half of the fourteenth century. Beginning in the first decade, with the commission given to Duccio to paint a monumental double-sided altarpiece for the high altar, the campaign continued with the construction of a new baptistery that was literally dug out of the steep hill-side below the east end of the cathedral (see pl. 103).[11] In 1339, Bishop Donusdeo Malavolti of Siena laid the foundation stone for the proposed 'Duomo Nuovo'. This was to be a huge extension built beyond the south transept of the existing cathedral to form the nave and aisles of a new cathedral (pl. 34). This highly ambitious programme of construction continued throughout the final years of the Nine, only to be abandoned by their successors in 1357 who contented themselves with more modest extensions to the cathedral itself.[12] While the Duomo Nuovo now exists only as one vaulted aisle and the shell of its tall and imposing entrance façade, it still offers a powerful sense of the ambition of Siena's early fourteenth-century civic authorities who, under the leadership of the Nine, tried to build the largest and most magnificent cathedral in Tuscany.

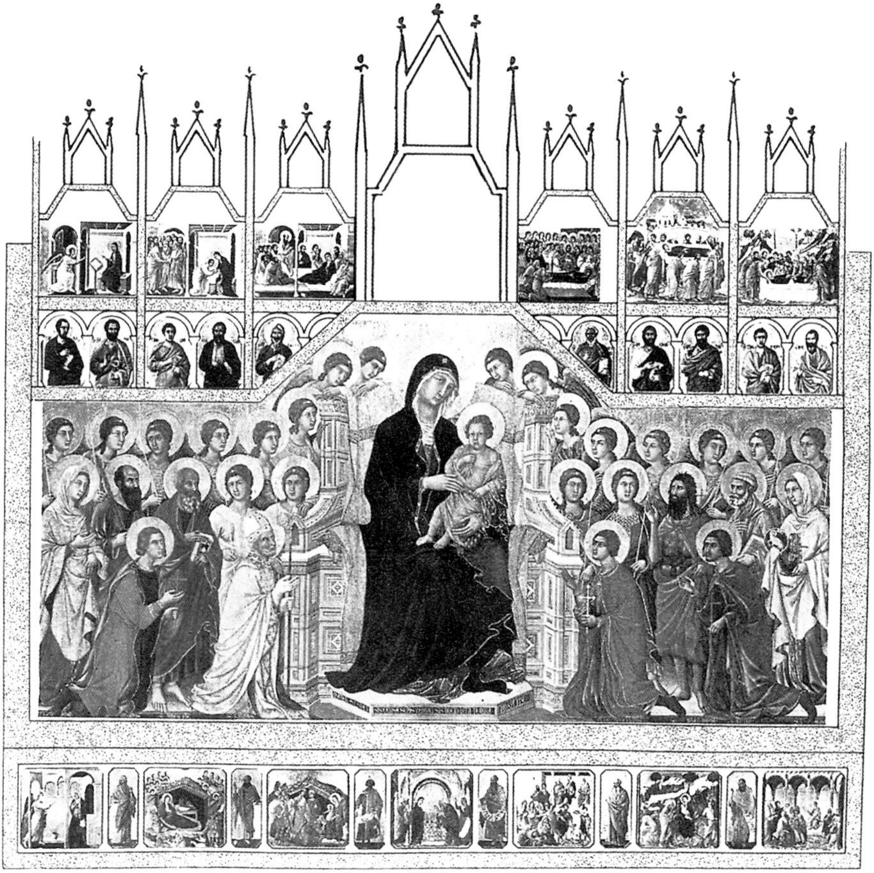

35 Reconstruction of the front face of the *Maestà* (by John White with modifications by Christa Gardner von Teuffel and the author).

Duccio's Maestà

In 1311, in a ceremony led by the Nine themselves, Duccio's famous painting of the *Maestà* was placed over the high altar of the cathedral.[13] Possibly replacing an earlier thirteenth-century altarpiece (see pl. 20), it too was removed from the high altar in the sixteenth century, and in the eighteenth century brutally cut up. Modern reconstructions of the altarpiece as a whole reveal, however, that in terms of its scale, architectonic form and

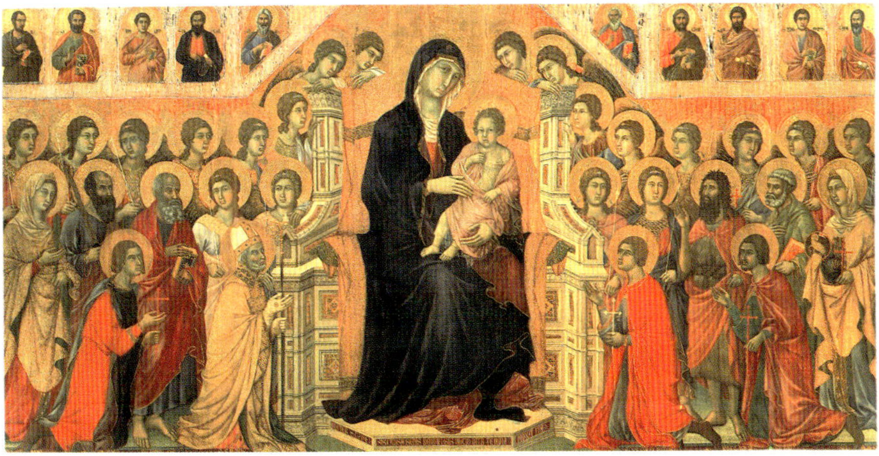

36 Duccio, *Virgin and Christ Child Enthroned with Saints and Angels* (*c.* 1308–11), the *Maestà*. Tempera on panel, 211 × 425 cm. Siena, Museo del Opera del Duomo.

complexity of design, it must have exerted a remarkable presence in the cathedral interior (pl. 35).[14] Even today, in its present museum setting, the jewel-like colours and burnished gold leaf of *The Virgin and Christ Child enthroned* still evoke something akin to reverence on the part of many modern viewers (pl. 36).

Duccio's innovatory design for a multi-tiered, double-sided altarpiece was highly ambitious for its time, far exceeding anything produced by his thirteenth-century predecessors. Features of its design (such as the sturdy side piers and clusters of pinnacles) were undoubtedly derived from contemporary church architecture (see pl. 19). The principal painting on the front of the altarpiece representing a large number of figures gathered together in an unified space around the Virgin's throne may have been inspired by early Christian mosaics and frescoes of this subject.[15] The back of the altarpiece, however, presents a strikingly different appearance (pl. 38). Comprising an extensive series of small-scale narrative paintings, it has the appearance of an iconostasis, the screen in a Byzantine church that closes off the sanctuary from the rest of the church and on which a large number of painted icons are hung.

Such a comparison is also a convenient reminder of the original liturgical location and function of Duccio's *Maestà*. Designed to embellish the high altar of Siena cathedral, this double-sided altarpiece clearly had two audiences in mind – those who worshipped in front of it and those who worshipped behind it. On the front of the altarpiece, facing towards the main body of the church, was the monumental representation of the *Maestà* theme, a well-established and popular subject in Sienese painting (see pls 22–5). How widely accessible this painting would have been to the public is, however, a debatable point. The chancel of the thirteenth-century cathedral might have been closed off from the rest of the building by a metalwork screen – although the earliest secure documentary evidence for such an arrangement dates to the second half of the fourteenth century.[16] Or the chancel might have been elevated above the rest of the cathedral pavement – thus making the high altar and its altarpiece easily visible to the congregation as a whole.[17]

What is certain is that by 1311 the high altar had become the location of a civic cult based on Siena's dedication to the Virgin. A painted inscription along the edge of the step of the Virgin's throne on the *Maestà* begins with the appeal: 'Holy mother of God, be the cause of repose for Siena'.[18] This strongly suggests that Duccio's painting was intended to continue the already venerable Sienese tradition of using art as a means of appealing in a direct and emotive way to the Virgin herself. Above the altarpiece would have been the magnificent stained-glass oculus, also attributed to Duccio, commissioned in 1287 and still located on the east wall of the cathedral directly behind the high altar (pl. 37).[19] Showing as its centrepiece the entombment, assumption and coronation of the Virgin, the imagery of this stained glass would have been directly reiterated by the pinnacle panels on the *Maestà* that once again represented – in more extended form – the events associated in Catholic belief with the death of the Virgin (see pl. 35). These, in turn, would have provided visual support for the annual celebrations that took place in Siena on the feast of the assumption and which culminated in the presentation of symbolic tributes to the Virgin in the cathedral.

In short, one of the major achievements of this altarpiece was that, in addition to its overtly religious content, its imagery had marked civic and political dimensions. These were emphasised by the inclusion of four kneeling saints in the foreground of the painting who – as the painted titles on the lower border indicate – represent the early Christian saints Ansano, Savino, Crescenzio and Victor. Figuring prominently in the early history of the Sienese church, these saints were venerated in the cathedral as patron saints of the city. They were already represented (with the exception of Victor) on the stained-glass oculus, but Duccio's altarpiece was the first instance of their inclusion in a *Maestà* painting, portrayed as saintly advo-

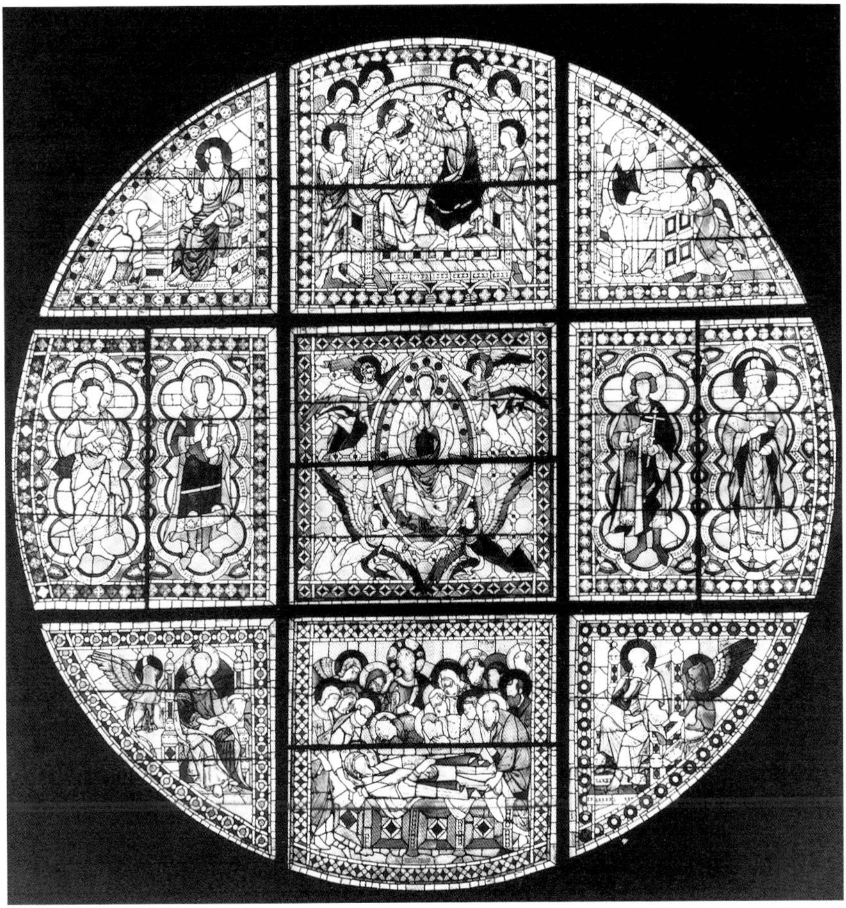

37 *The Burial, Assumption and Coronation of the Virgin with the Evangelists and Patron Saints of Siena* (1287). Stained-glass window in the choir of Siena cathedral.

cates for the Sienese, appealing on their behalf to their principal patron, the Virgin.

Contrasting with the Marian imagery on the front face of the altarpiece, the narrative paintings on the back of the altarpiece focus on the ministry and Passion of Christ. The design of the altarpiece also enabled Duccio to divide this narrative into three parts: on the predella, an 'introduction' of seven scenes from Christ's ministry; on the principal panel, twenty-six

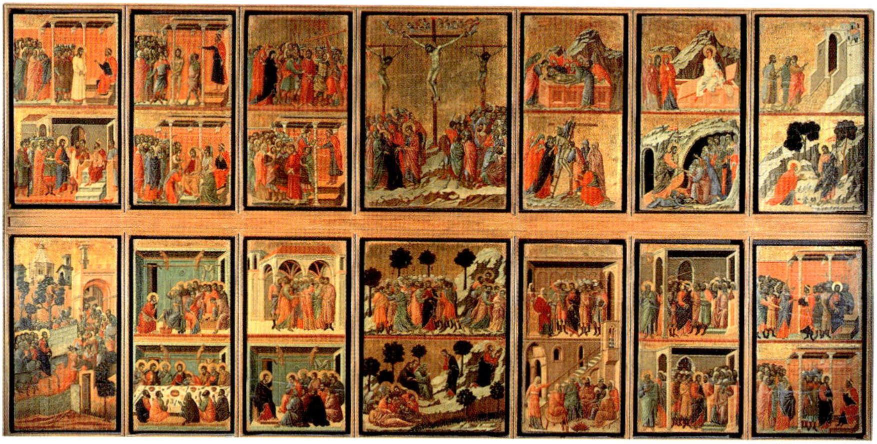

38 Duccio, *The Passion of Christ* (*c.* 1308–11). Tempera on panel, 217 × 425 cm. Siena, Museo del Opera del Duomo.

scenes from the Passion of Christ (pl. 38); and on the pinnacle panels, a 'finale' of seven scenes that took place after Christ's resurrection. The nature of this subject matter – with its strong emphasis on Christ's death on the Cross and, by association, with the liturgy of the mass – strongly suggests that a specific audience was intended for this part of the altarpiece. This is likely to have been the cathedral canons, gathered in their choirstalls behind the high altar. It is not hard to imagine how the sight of Duccio's richly varied imagery would have enlivened and supported the canons' daily acts of worship and religious meditation.

The inscription on the Virgin's throne ends: 'and because he painted you thus, of life for Duccio'. Reiterating the sentiment of the inscription on Guido da Siena's San Domenico painting (see pl. 22),[20] these words emphasise both the belief in the Virgin's power as a spiritual advocate and the painter's awareness of his own artistic skills. As noted in the previous chapter, by the time the *Maestà* was commissioned, Duccio had already been working as a painter for some thirty years, securing prestigious commissions both within Siena and further afield (see pl. 25).[21] The altarpiece for the cathedral, nevertheless, represented an extraordinary artistic achievement. Not only did the scale and complexity of this panel painting far exceed anything previously produced by Sienese painters but also the treatment of the *Maestà* theme itself was far more sophisticated than those

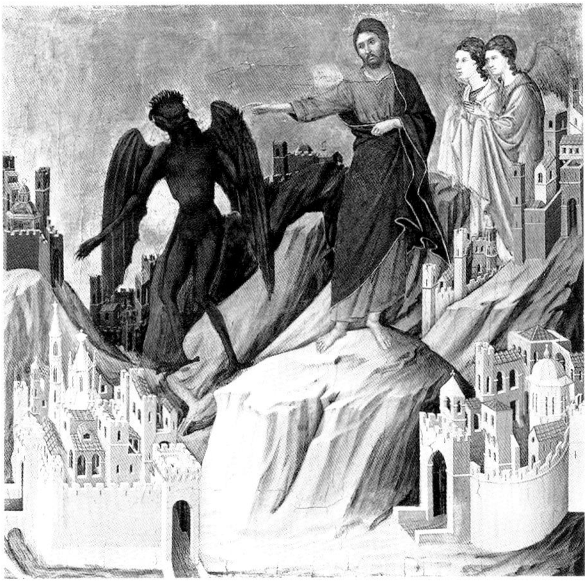

39 Duccio, *The Temptation of Christ*, predella panel from the rear face of the *Maestà* (*c.* 1308–11). Tempera on panel, 43.2 × 46 cm. New York, Frick Collection.

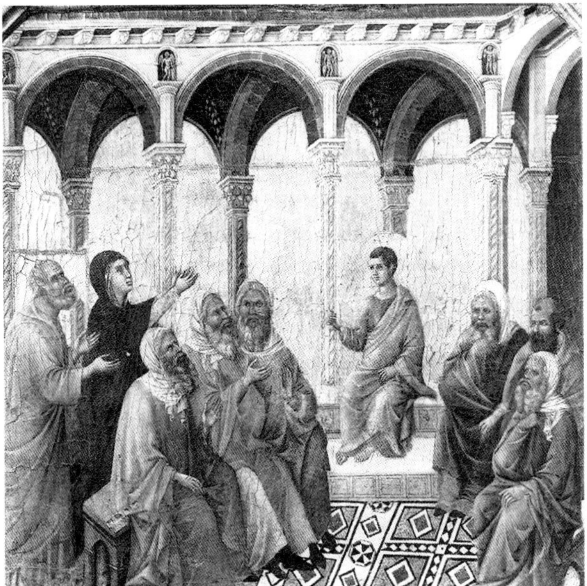

40 Duccio, *Christ with the Elders in the Temple*, predella panel from the front face of the *Maestà* (*c.* 1308–11). Tempera on panel, 48 × 48 cm. Siena, Museo dell'Opera del Duomo.

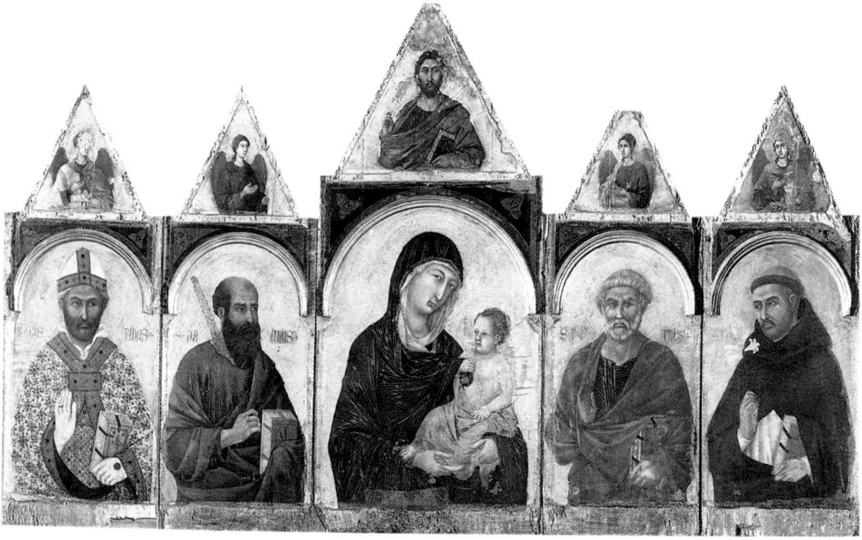

41 Duccio, *The Virgin and Christ Child with Saints Augustine, Paul, Peter and Dominic* (*c.* 1305–8). Tempera on panel, 139 × 241 cm. Siena, Pinacoteca Nazionale.

Damage over the centuries – to the extent of the green underpainting used for the painting of flesh tones on the face of the Virgin being clearly visible – still has not obscured the confident representation of the volume of the figures and the softness of the fabrics of their garments; these details strongly suggest that Duccio himself was involved in the design and painting of this altarpiece. On the ground of its relative simplicity of design, it is generally considered to be a slightly earlier painting than the *Maestà* altarpiece. Another altarpiece attributed to Duccio, also in the Pinacoteca and known as Polyptych 47, more closely approaches the ambition of the front face of the *Maestà*. Comprising three tiers and showing a company of twenty-six figures in all, this altarpiece was probably painted for the high altar of the church within the Spedale di Santa Maria della Scala.[26]

In 1319, eight years after the installation of Duccio's *Maestà* altarpiece, Simone Martini produced a polyptych for the high altar of the Dominican church of Santa Caterina in Pisa. Comprising seven principal panels and four tiers of figures of saints, prophets and angels, it was even more complex than Duccio's altarpiece for the Spedale in Siena. It was also support-

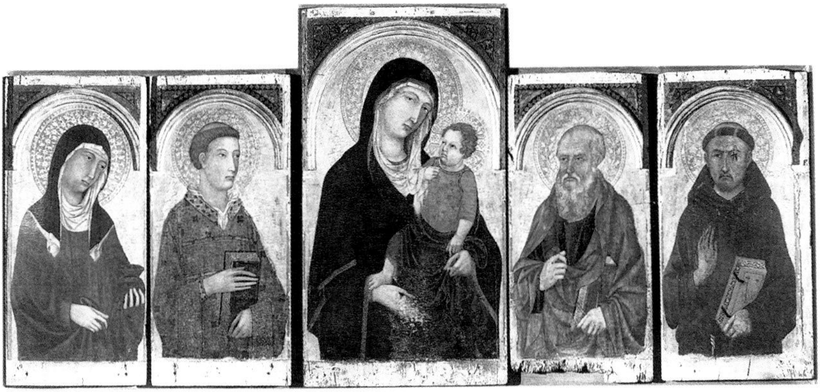

42 Ugolino di Nerio, *The Virgin and Christ Child with Saints Claire, Lawrence, John the Evangelist and Francis* (*c.* 1310–15). Tempera on panel, 84 × 189 cm. Siena, Pinacoteca Nazionale.

ed by a predella, which subsequently became a standard feature on Sienese altarpieces. In 1320, Pietro Lorenzetti painted a similar altarpiece for the high altar of the principal parish church of Arezzo. Although reverting to five panels on the main tier, he adopted from the *Maestà* the series of truncated gable panels for the second tier of the altarpiece. He also painted a predella for this altarpiece that is now lost. In the early 1320s Ugolino di Nerio painted a Marian altarpiece of a similar design for the high altar of Santa Croce in Florence, but with a predella of seven narrative paintings of the Passion.[27]

Not all Sienese altarpieces produced in the first half of the fourteenth century followed such complex designs, as several much more modestly conceived examples in Siena's Pinacoteca demonstrate. The *Virgin and Christ Child with Saints Claire, Lawrence, John the Evangelist and Francis* (pl. 42), now divested of its framing elements and pinnacle panels, would once have appeared similar in design to Duccio's altarpiece for San Domenico (see pl. 41). Attributed to Ugolino di Nerio and dated shortly after his ambitious altarpiece for the high altar of Santa Croce, the provenance of

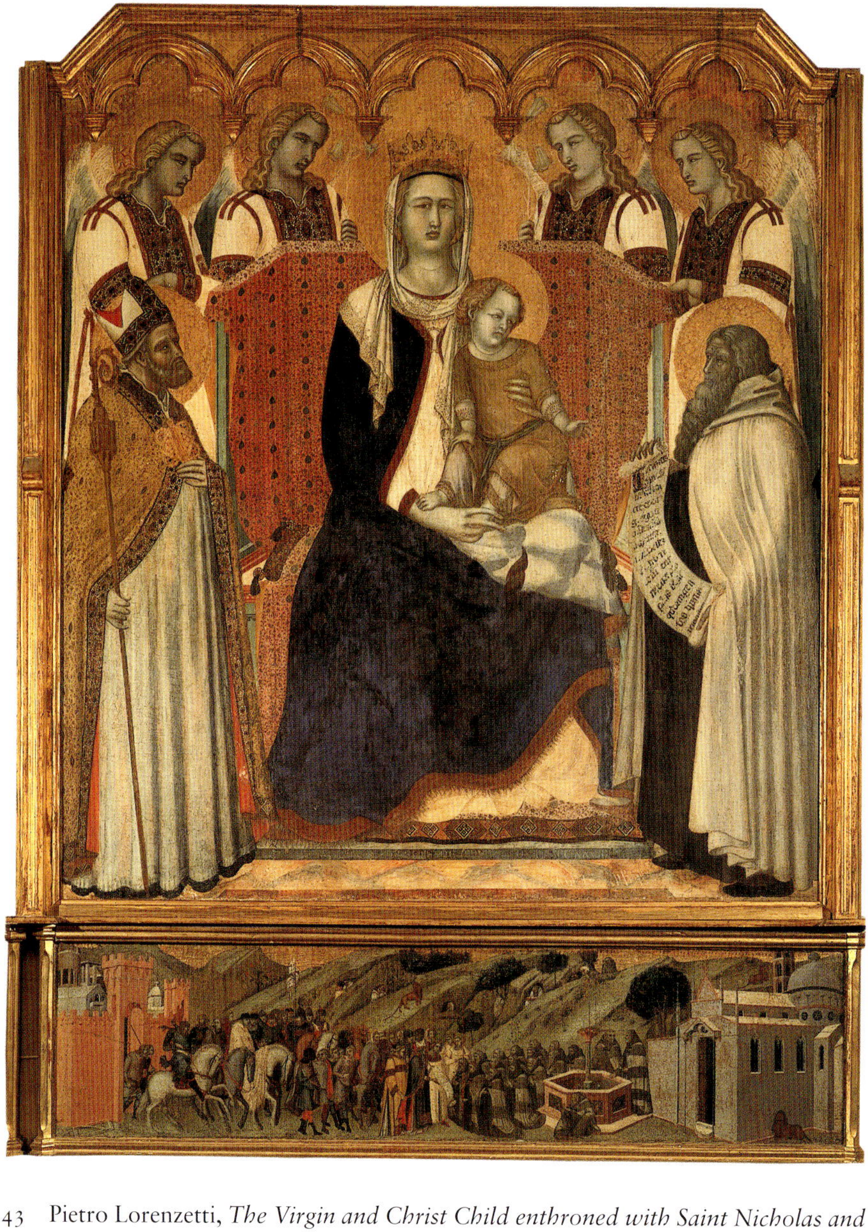

43 Pietro Lorenzetti, *The Virgin and Christ Child enthroned with Saint Nicholas and the Prophet Elijah* (1329), the Carmelite Altarpiece. Tempera on panel, 169 × 148 cm. Siena, Pinacoteca Nazionale.

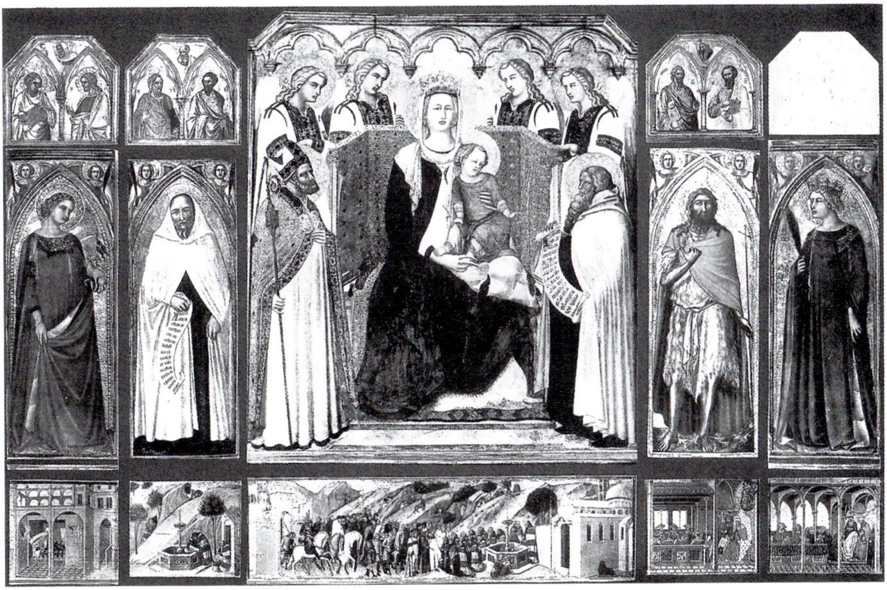

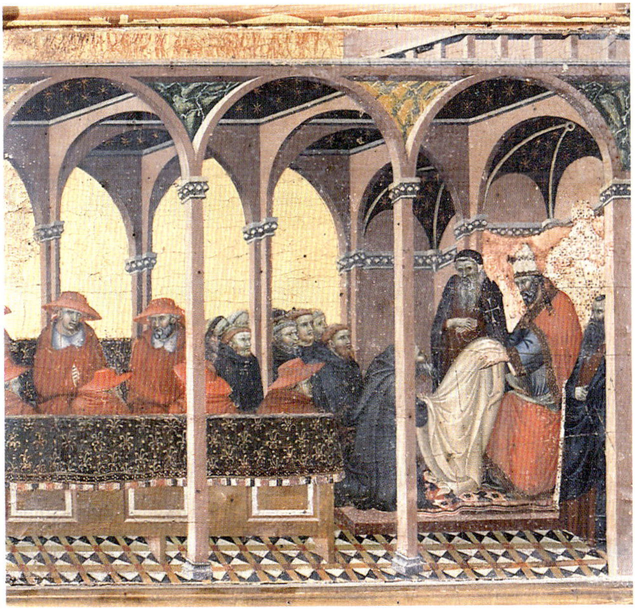

44 (*above*) Reconstruction of the Carmelite Altarpiece (by Hayden Maginnis).

45 Pietro Lorenzetti, *Pope Honorius IV awarding the White Habit to the Carmelite Order*, predella panel from the Carmelite Altarpiece (1329). Tempera on panel, 37.5 × 46 cm. Siena, Pinacoteca Nazionale.

this panel painting was the Franciscan Sienese convent of Santa Chiara (see pl. 6). The prominent presence of Saints Claire and Francis suggests that the nuns of Santa Chiara may have commissioned the altarpiece.[28] More importantly, it shows that well-established Sienese painters such as Ugolino, while responding in a highly innovative fashion to prestigious commissions like the high altarpiece for Santa Croce in Florence, nevertheless still produced modestly conceived altarpieces for communities of nuns who presumably lacked the economic resources of their Franciscan brothers.

By contrast, an altarpiece for the Carmelite church of San Niccolò in Siena perhaps rivalled the scale and sophistication of at least the front face of Duccio's *Maestà* for the cathedral. On 26 October 1329 the Council of the Bell debated a request to the Nine by the prior and brothers of the priory of San Niccolò for financial assistance to complete a 'renowned' and 'very beautiful' painting of the Virgin, saints and angels that they had commissioned from the Sienese painter Pietro Lorenzetti. The Council voted to grant the Carmelites 50 *lire* towards the total cost of the painting of 150 *lire*. On 29 November this money was handed to the painter, who then completed the altarpiece, placing his name and the date 1329 upon it. Taken from the high altar of San Niccolò two centuries later, the central panel of the altarpiece (pl. 43) and its predella panel were removed to a country church and repainted in order to reflect their new situation. Restored in 1936, the painting was subsequently taken to the Pinacoteca and re-united with two of the side panels of the altarpiece and the rest of the predella. Other parts of the altarpiece have now been identified in two North American art collections.

Modern reconstruction of the Carmelite altarpiece indicates that in its original form it comprised a large central painting of the Virgin and Christ Child enthroned in the company of Saint Nicholas of Bari, the Prophet Elijah and four angels (pl. 44). Like Duccio's *Maestà*, all the figures were shown full-length and gathered in a unified setting (see pl. 35). Framing this large central painting were four side panels showing, from left to right, Saint Agnes, the Prophet Elisha, Saint John the Baptist and Saint Catherine of Alexandria – all on the same scale as the saints on the central panel. Above these side panels were gabled pinnacle panels portraying pairs of apostles – thus again broadly emulating the design of Duccio's *Maestà* (see pls 35, 36). Above these was a further series of six smaller pinnacle panels, each depicting the standing figure of a saint. The predella, meanwhile, comprised a series of five narrative paintings. Instead of taking their subjects from the bible, these five paintings show events from the history of the Carmelite Order. A striking feature of the overall design of this altarpiece is the very wide central panel on the predella that allowed the painter to depict the consignment of the Carmelite rule in the early thirteenth century in a particularly detailed manner.[29]

Other mendicant orders, such as the Dominicans at Santa Caterina in Pisa and the Franciscans at Santa Croce in Florence, as already noted, had utilised the talents of Sienese painters to provide a form of visual propaganda for the embellishment of their high altars, but the Carmelites at San Niccolò appear to have been particularly ambitious in this respect.[30] Pietro Lorenzetti's representation of the Virgin as a crowned queen eminently reflected the Carmelites' long tradition of veneration of the Virgin. The vivaciously portrayed Christ Child, meanwhile, is shown actively gesturing towards the Prophet Elijah: both Elijah and Elisha are portrayed as Carmelite saints, thus emphasising their status as the perceived founders of the Order. Opposite Elijah stands Saint Nicholas of Bari, the titular saint of the church for which the altarpiece was painted. Saint John the Baptist was probably included both as the last of the prophets to foresee the coming of Christ and as the holy man who preached in the wilderness near the river Jordan, where the Carmelites first established themselves as a community of hermits. The two female saints, Agnes and Catherine of Alexandria, were revered as early Christian martyrs and as patron saints of the wool industry, whose powerful guild had close associations with the Carmelite Order and the church of San Niccolò.[31]

The predella offers an extraordinarily detailed and lively representation of the Carmelite Order's foundation legend, as it was being constructed at the time the altarpiece was painted. The order was founded in the mid-twelfth century by a group of Crusaders on Mount Carmel, near to what was believed to be the fountain of Elijah. Here they built a church to the Virgin and – like the Sienese in 1260 – made her their patron and protector. Albert, Patriarch of Jerusalem, gave the first official approval of the order some time between 1206 and 1214. This was followed by papal approval from Honorius III in 1226. After the fall of the Latin Empire in 1261, the Carmelites were forced to move to the west. In 1286, Honorius IV changed the Carmelite habit to a plain white cloak – it had previously been striped in memory of Elijah's cloak that, according to the biblical account, had been charred by flames as he was taken into heaven by the fiery chariot. The first predella scene illustrates an apocryphal subject that occurs only in Carmelite literature, that of Sobac, the legendary father of Elijah, dreaming of his son's future association with 'men clad in white raiment'. The second scene portrays the early eremetical life of the Carmelites beside the fountain of Elijah. The central and two final predella scenes show the awarding and confirming of the rule by Albert, Honorius III and Honorius IV. Much circumstantial detail has been included in these later scenes, such as the city gateway of Acre, the fountain of Elijah and the church of the Virgin on Mount Carmel in the central scene, and the careful distinction made between the striped cloaks of the Carmelites in the second, third and fourth scenes and the white cloak assigned by the pope in the last scene.

In its original state, Pietro Lorenzetti's altarpiece must have constituted an unusually self-confident statement about the Carmelite Order, their identity and their spiritual concerns. The skill of the painter contributed greatly to this effect. A well-established painter, notably of tender images of the Virgin and Christ Child for churches in the Sienese *contado* and further afield, Pietro Lorenzetti had also had the experience of working on at least one and perhaps two large-scale fresco cycles for the Franciscan Order.[32] In the principal painting of the Carmelite altarpiece, he furnished his patrons with a series of composed figures who appear as if gathered within a credible space marked out by the marble pavement and the draped throne. The extensive use of white – which, as indicated, was a particularly significant colour for the Carmelites – added a striking luminosity to the painting's appearance. The predella scenes likewise show great assurance in the way the figures were disposed in depth, within a range of architectural and landscape settings. In a scene such as *Pope Honorius IV awarding the White Habit* (pl. 45) the sophisticated treatment of the architecture is, for example, reminiscent of the *Christ with the Elders* from the front predella of the *Maestà* altarpiece (see pl. 40) but, in terms of its figural composition, it is more ambitious. The predella also provides clear evidence of the painter's interest in conveying a range of human emotions and a variety of naturalistic details. Thus the quiet, contemplative activities of the early Carmelites around Elijah's well in the second scene provide a striking contrast to the energy and curiosity of the crowd issuing out of the gateway of Acre to witness Albert's consignment of the rule in the central scene. Similarly, in the *Dream of Sobac* a black and white towel hangs over a rail to the right of the bed alcove, while in the *Fountain of Elijah*, two delicate glasses of water stand on the rim of the basin and draw attention to the water splashing down from the fountain into the basin itself.

* * *

Civic Art in the Palazzo Pubblico

In his Carmelite altarpiece Pietro Lorenzetti approached something of the grandeur and narrative inventiveness of Duccio's *Maestà* altarpiece. For his representation of the Virgin as the crowned Queen of Heaven he may have found inspiration in another imposing early fourteenth-century Sienese painting of the *Maestà* theme. Painted by Simone Martini in fresco on the east wall of the principal council hall of the Palazzo Pubblico (pl. 46), this *Maestà* painting provides a striking example of the adaptation of the principal subject of Duccio's altarpiece for an ostensibly secular setting. While copying the subject matter of the earlier *Maestà* – to the extent of showing Saints Ansano, Savino, Crescenzio and Victor as kneeling petitioners before the Virgin's throne – Simone Martini introduced other details

46 The Sala del Mappamondo (formerly known as the Sala del Consiglio). Siena, Palazzo Pubblico.

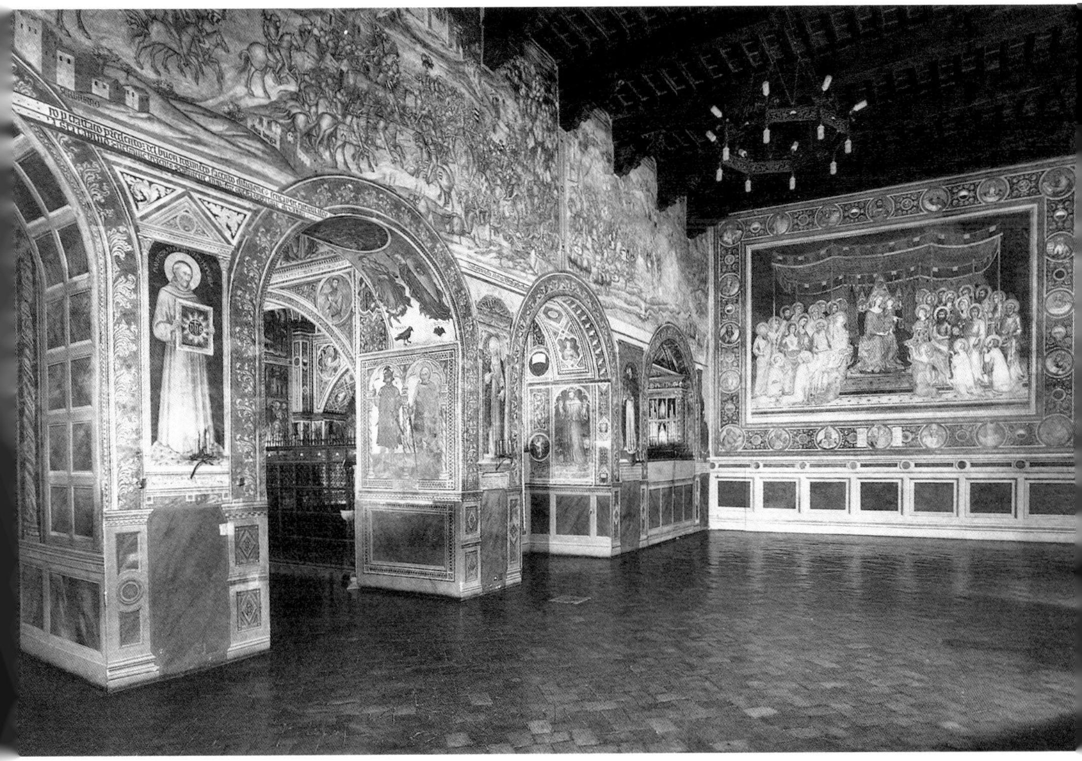

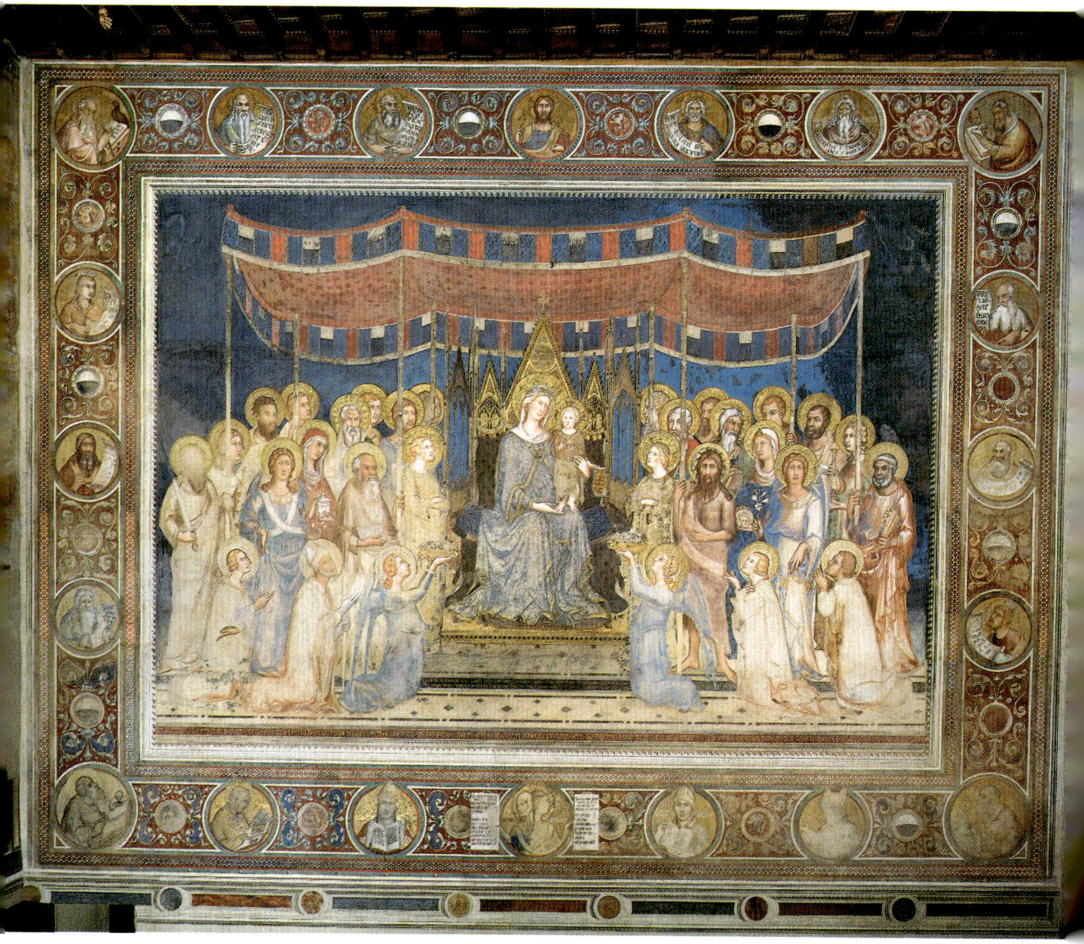

47 Simone Martini, *The Maestà* (*c.* 1315). Fresco, 836 × 977 cm. East wall of the Sala del Mappamondo. Siena, Palazzo Pubblico.

that gave the painting a much more worldly and courtly air (pl. 47, and see pl. 36). Overall, the impression given by the painting is of an intricately worked textile hanging on the wall. The expansive canopy held by four of the saints over the Virgin and assembled company is strongly reminiscent of those used for ceremonial entries and processions in honour of illustrious visitors to Siena at that time.[33] Duccio's solid, architectonic marble throne has been transformed into an intricately worked, gilded throne that owed its inspiration to contemporary architecture and metalwork. In order to convey the magnificence and splendour of the court of heaven, Simone Martini added other kinds of ornamentation such as a piece of glass for the brooch pinning together the edges of the Virgin's mantle and moulded, gilded plasterwork on the haloes of the saints.[34]

THE SALA DEL CONSIGLIO

This highly imaginative and essentially 'courtly' re-working of the *Maestà* theme raises several interesting questions regarding Simone Martini's early training, not least whether he might previously have worked at the south Italian court of the King of Naples.[35] Undoubtedly, however, the location and original function of the painting also influenced his treatment of the subject. The painting takes up the whole of the east wall of what was then known as the Sala del Consiglio (the 'room of the council', pl. 48). It was called this because it was the meeting room for the city's principal legislative body of the Council of the Bell. Under the chairmanship of the Podestà, this council made up of some 300 citizens met weekly to debate and vote on government business brought to the council's attention by the Nine and other groups of magistrates. Attendants would thus have been acutely aware of Simone's majestic image of the Virgin, the city's principal patron saint and protector, presiding over them and over their collective proceedings. Indeed, it appears that the Podestà was seated directly below the painting, thus replicating the ceremonial position of the Virgin herself, who faced the members of the Council.

Several details in the painting confirm that this *Maestà* was intended to inspire Siena's councillors. Firstly, the Christ Child is portrayed not as a baby – as in Duccio's *Maestà* (see pl. 36) – but as a child, standing on his mother's knee (pl. 47). With his right hand he blesses the assembled company and in his left he holds a scroll that is made of real paper stuck to the surface of the wall – just as many official Sienese government documents were then beginning to be written on paper rather than on parchment. On it is written the biblical text: 'Love justice, you who rule the earth', an

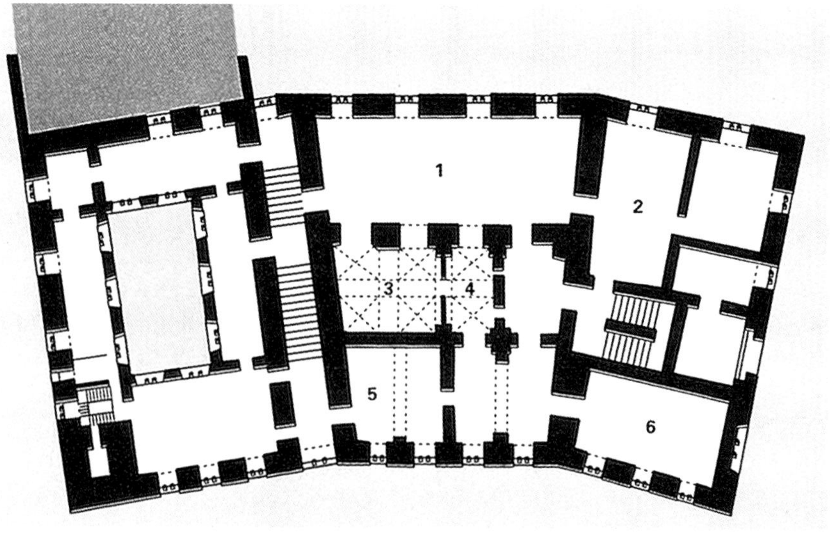

Plate 48 Plan of the first floor of the Palazzo Pubblico
1 Sala del Mappamondo (formerly known as the Sala del Consiglio)
2 Sala della Pace (formerly known as the Sala dei Nove)
3 Cappella dei Signori
4 Anticappella (formerly an ante-chamber to an earlier Sala del Concistoro)
5 Sala di Balìa
6 Sala del Concistoro

appropriate injunction to the painting's original audience of the Council of the Bell.

Simone's painting also includes in the foreground the four patron saints of Siena. Painted inscriptions along the edges of the steps leading to the Virgin's throne strongly re-iterate the impression given by the pose of the figures that they are meant to be seen as involved in a dialogue with the Virgin. The inscription begins with the words: 'My beloved ones, take heed that I will make the devotees of your honest prayers content as you desire'. This opening suggests that the Virgin is responding to a collective petition to her made by the four saints, which was probably once written on the scrolls held by the figures, the words of which are now lost but whose faint outlines can be seen on some of the scrolls.[36] The rest of the Virgin's response indicates clearly that although she delights in 'good counsel' – an apt sentiment for this setting – she will not support or favour those who despise or deceive her land. The use of the word *terra* (land) twice is particularly significant because it emphasises the idea of territorial ownership and the Virgin's close links with this political concept in the minds of the Sienese.

The political tenor of the painting's imagery is continued in more overt fashion in the painted embellishment that frames the *Maestà* and in the detail of the canopy within the painting. The restoration of the 1980s has revealed that the edges of the canopy were decorated with a sequence of heraldic devices: the civic insignia of the black and white shield of the Sienese Commune (the *balzana*) and the gold lion on a red field of the Popolo (the party of the people) alternate with the coat-of-arms of the Angevin dynasties of Naples and France. The close political association of Siena (under the leadership of the Nine) with the Guelph party (under the leadership of Robert of Anjou, King of Naples) was thus made explicit. On the broad painted borders the decoration similarly combines religious imagery of saints and prophets with the civic emblems of the *balzana* and the lion of the Popolo. The large number of sacred texts displayed by the prophets, evangelists and doctors of the Church, together with the Janus-like personification of the old and new law, further validated the council's principal task of making written records of the city's laws. Finally, embedded in the wall below the wide, lower border are painted replicas of the city's principal seal – depicting, appropriately, the enthroned Virgin and Christ Child flanked by two angels – and that of the seal of the Capitano del Popolo (Captain of the People).

Directly opposite Simone Martini's highly inventive and politicised treatment of the popular *Maestà* theme are the remains of two more paintings that arguably belong to the fourteenth-century embellishment of the Sala del Consiglio (pl. 49). Situated above and between two sixteenth-century paintings of Saints Ansano and Victor, these paintings are known as *Guidoriccio da Fogliano at the Siege of Montemassi* – a painting that extends the entire width of the upper part of the wall – and the *Submission of a Castle* – much smaller and located below it. The surface of the latter bears the scars of gouges caused by the rotation of a large painting, probably on canvas, depicting a map of the world – thus earning the room its later name of the Sala del Mappamondo. Until 1981 only the *Guidoriccio* had been visible, the *Submission* having been hidden under layers of whitewash. The *Guidoriccio* was conventionally attributed to Simone Martini and the date of 1328 painted on the lower border regarded as close to the date of the painting's execution.[37] Based on Sienese sources dating from the sixteenth century onwards, the subject of the painting had been

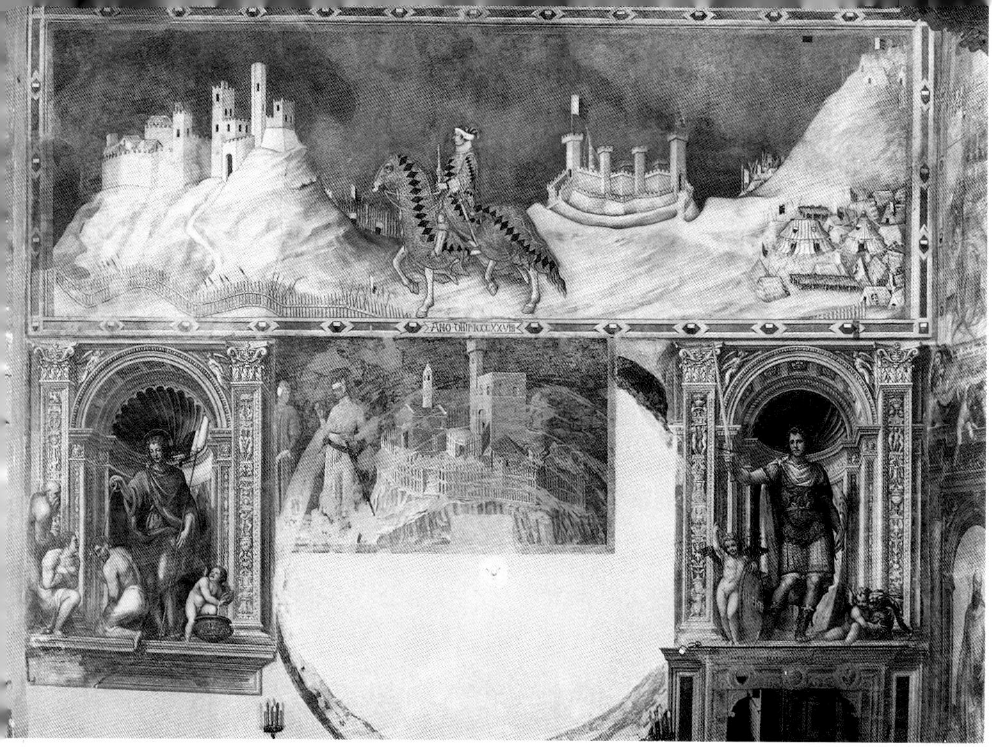

49 West wall of the Sala del Mappamondo showing the frescoes of *Guidoriccio da Fogliano at the Siege of Montemassi, The Submission of a Castle, Saint Ansano* and *Saint Victor*. Siena, Palazzo Pubblico.

identified as a commemoration of Guidoriccio da Fogliano, who as the leader of the Sienese army captured the fortress of Montemassi in 1328 for the Sienese. There appeared therefore to be persuasive symmetry in the early fourteenth-century decoration of the Sala del Consiglio. On one wall was represented the Virgin, the city's principal patron, 'queen' and governor, and on the other appeared the embodiment of the city's military power and prowess.[38] The two paintings also suggested that Simone Martini's talents as a painter extended beyond depicting holy figures in a particularly elegant and refined manner to include the portrayal of the distinctive appearance of Guidoriccio himself, together with details of late medieval warfare, such as the military camp on the extreme right of the painting.

In 1977, however, an American art historian raised a number of questions about the traditional attribution and dating of this painting. Intense and often controversial debate ensued and continues – it has been argued that this painting is not in fact by Simone Martini or, indeed, fourteenth-

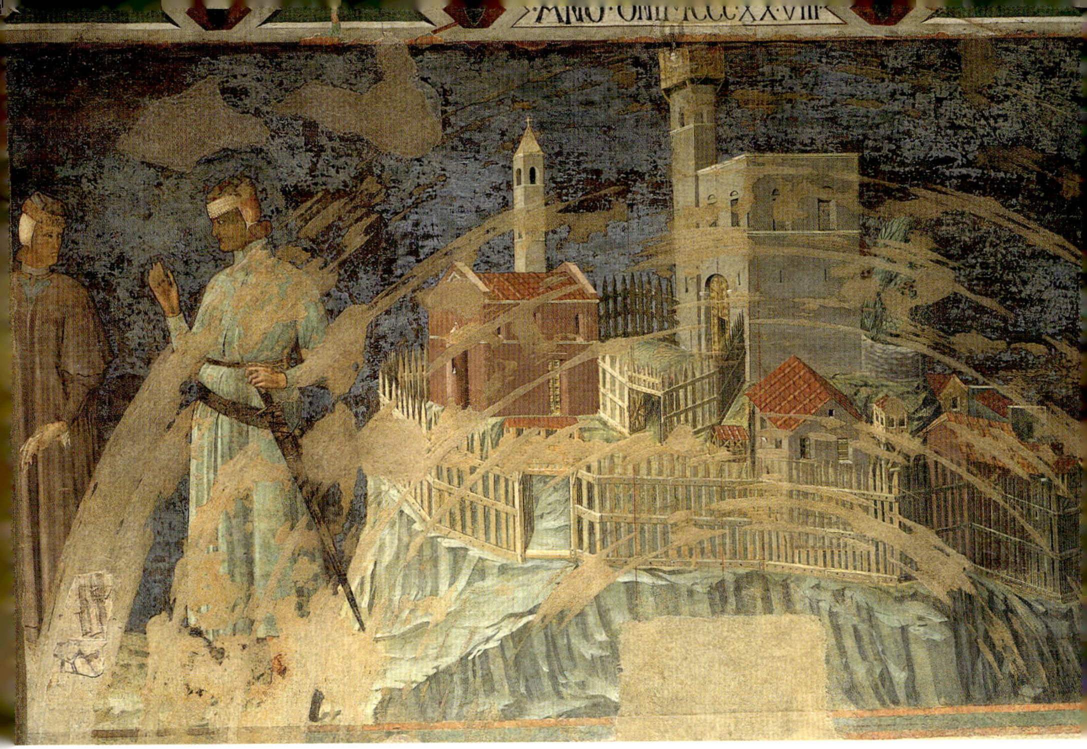

50 *The Submission of a Castle* (*c.* 1314–33). Fresco, 223 × 378 cm. West wall of the Sala del Mappamondo. Siena, Palazzo Pubblico.

century at all.[39] The controversy has been further complicated by the discovery of the painting of the *Submission of a Castle* (pl. 50). Recovered as a direct result of the detailed physical investigation of the west wall prompted by the speculation surrounding the *Guidoriccio*, the original dimensions of the painting have clearly been reduced both by the painting of the *Guidoriccio* and, to the left, by the early sixteenth-century *Saint Ansano*. Its date, authorship and precise subject have also been the subject of a wide range of views.[40] Scholars who wish to maintain the 1328 date for the *Guidoriccio* tend to date the *Submission of a Castle* to the second decade of the fourteenth century and attribute it to Duccio or to another Sienese painter, Memmo di Filippuccio, or even to Simone Martini himself. Proponents of this early dating suggest that it portrays the submission to Siena of another southern Tuscan town, Giuncarico, in 1314. By contrast, scholars who challenge the conventional attribution and dating of the *Guidoriccio* tend to propose a later dating for the painting of the

Submission of a Castle, linking it with payments made in 1331 by the Sienese treasury to Simone Martini for visiting and executing a painting of Arcidosso, yet another recently conquered town in southern Tuscany.

The evidence for the existence of the *Mappamondo* has also been drawn into this debate.[41] The fourteenth-century chronicle by Agnolo di Tura reports the commission of this painting from Ambrogio Lorenzetti in 1345, and in 1393 the treasury paid three painters for its restoration. What is not clear is the precise nature of this painting's imagery. Generally described in written accounts of it as a 'map of the world', it could have represented any one of a range of types of maps used by medieval cartographers. Intriguingly, however, three eighteenth-century Sienese historians described the painting as by then in a fragmentary state but as representing a topographical map of 'the state of Siena'. If this were the case, the *Mappamondo* would have continued the theme of the *Submission of a Castle* already painted on the west wall of the Sala del Consiglio. It would also have acted as a highly effective piece of civic propaganda for Siena and its political identity as a territorial state.[42]

With these uncertainties surrounding the dating and authorship of these paintings, what sense can be made of the decoration of this important hall between its completion in about 1305 and 1345 when the *Mappamondo* was installed on its west wall? A resolution by the Council of the Bell in 1314 that Giuncarico (a small town in southern Tuscany taken from the Pannocchieschi d'Elci that year) be painted as part of an existing series of castles suggests that the intention of the government was that the walls of the council hall should be painted with commemorations of Siena's conquest and rule over its subject territories. Given the subject of the *Submission of a Castle*, it is likely that this recently recovered fresco was part of this series.[43] The two open gateways provide a strong visual clue to this effect. The two figures to the left of the painting – both dressed in costumes denoting high social status – appear to be negotiating this change of control, just as government appointees were entrusted by the Nine to accept the ownership of newly acquired subject towns and castles.

Two inscriptions, one painted in the lower outer border of the *Maestà* and the other incised into the wall just below it, strongly suggest that 'Symone' (presumably Simone Martini) was responsible for painting the *Maestà* and that it was completed by June 1315 (see pl. 47). This date is supported by payments to Simone in June, October and December 1315. Another payment in 1321 provides evidence that the same painter, his assistants and apprentices, were paid for materials and work on 'repairing' the painting; and technical examination of the *Maestà* has revealed that several of the heads of key figures in the painting have been repainted and their haloes made more elaborate.[44] Thus, by the second decade of the fourteenth century the Sala del Consiglio had been graced with this painted celebration of Siena's spiritual patron and protector. The painted dialogue in the painting, with its expression of concern about those who 'harm the weak' and who 'despise' and 'deceive' the Virgin's 'land', continues and further validates the theme of territorial acquisition already begun in the earlier paintings of subject castles. The introduction of Ambrogio Lorenzetti's *Mappamondo* in 1345 would then have offered an elaboration of this theme – particularly if it did indeed focus on Siena and its surrounding towns and castles.

Whether the *Guidoriccio* painting was also part of this programme remains a matter of debate. Its subject – the commemoration of a famous victory over a town acquired as part of the Nine's systematic policy of territorial acquisition in southern Tuscany – would have complemented the documented paintings of subject castles. Payments made to a 'master Simone' between 1330 and 1331 for paintings of Montemassi, Sassoforte, Arcidosso and Castel del Piano, provide further circumstantial evidence that a painting of Montemassi could have been executed by Simone Martini, albeit some years after the date of the conquest of Montemassi in 1328.[45] Certain technical and stylistic details of the painting itself bear comparison with other paintings attributed to Simone (see pls 54, 55).[46] Yet in other respects the quality of the *Guidoriccio* compares unfavourably with these.[47] The painting could, however, have been painted by another fourteenth-century painter, such as Simone Martini's brother-in-law, Lippo Memmi, who as a close collaborator (see pl. 58) exhibited many of the characteristics of Simone's style and technique.[48]

On the other hand, there remain a number of unresolved questions concerning possible anachronisms in the use of heraldry and the type of costume and fortification portrayed in the painting. The most recent technical reports on the painting provide contradictory evidence regarding the precise date of its execution.[49] Whether these can both be accounted for by the long history of the *Guidoriccio* and the various repairs it has undergone over the centuries is difficult to say. Only by removing it from the wall and determining whether or not there are earlier paintings beneath it can such questions really be answered.[50] If such an investigation were able to prove the *Guidoriccio* a genuine example of a fourteenth-century painting, executed during the rule of the Nine, then it would be possible to claim that this monumental fresco – particularly when viewed in close conjunction to the *Mappamondo* – once presented a powerful image of Siena's claims to military might and control over the surrounding countryside.

THE SALA DEI NOVE

Some years before executing the *Mappamondo* for the Sala del Consiglio, Ambrogio Lorenzetti had been commissioned to paint a much more extensive scheme of decoration for the adjacent council room (pl. 51). Now known as the Sala della Pace (the Room of Peace, after one of its painted figures), at the time of the commission it was called the Sala dei Nove, after the Nine themselves, who used it as their meeting room (see pl. 48). The painted decoration should therefore be understood both as an expression of Siena's civic ideals for the members of the city magistracy who met there to formulate government policy and as a means of impressing the numerous foreign dignitaries who were received in this room.[51]

Payments by the city treasury to Ambrogio Lorenzetti between February 1338 and May 1339[52] suggest a sustained, well-organised campaign of painting in the Sala dei Nove, an impression borne out by the paintings themselves. Each wall (other than the south window wall) displays a large painting framed by broad painted borders that contain coats-of-arms, allegorical figures and long, detailed inscriptions that describe and explain the painting's subject matter. These texts, written in Italian, together with the numerous Latin names given to many of the painted figures, clearly show that the pictorial scheme was intended to have a serious, didactic purpose for those who originally used the room. Since the text below the painting on the east wall begins with the instruction: 'turn your eyes to behold her, you who are governing . . .', it is reasonable to conclude that it was primarily addressed to the Nine themselves.

On the north wall is a large mural painting composed entirely of figures (pl. 52). Rather in the manner of a family tree that identifies individual members and plots their relationship to one another, this painting was intended to demonstrate what to the late medieval mind, at least, constituted good government. As the inscriptions below the painting, and the Latin titles within it, indicate, on the left-hand side of the painting are grouped Wisdom, Justice and Concord and, on the right appear the nine Christian Virtues of peace, fortitude, prudence, magnanimity, temperance, justice, faith, hope and charity – all of which were regarded in late medieval political thought as desirable qualities for the practice of good government. While these figures express broad political ideals, other details in the

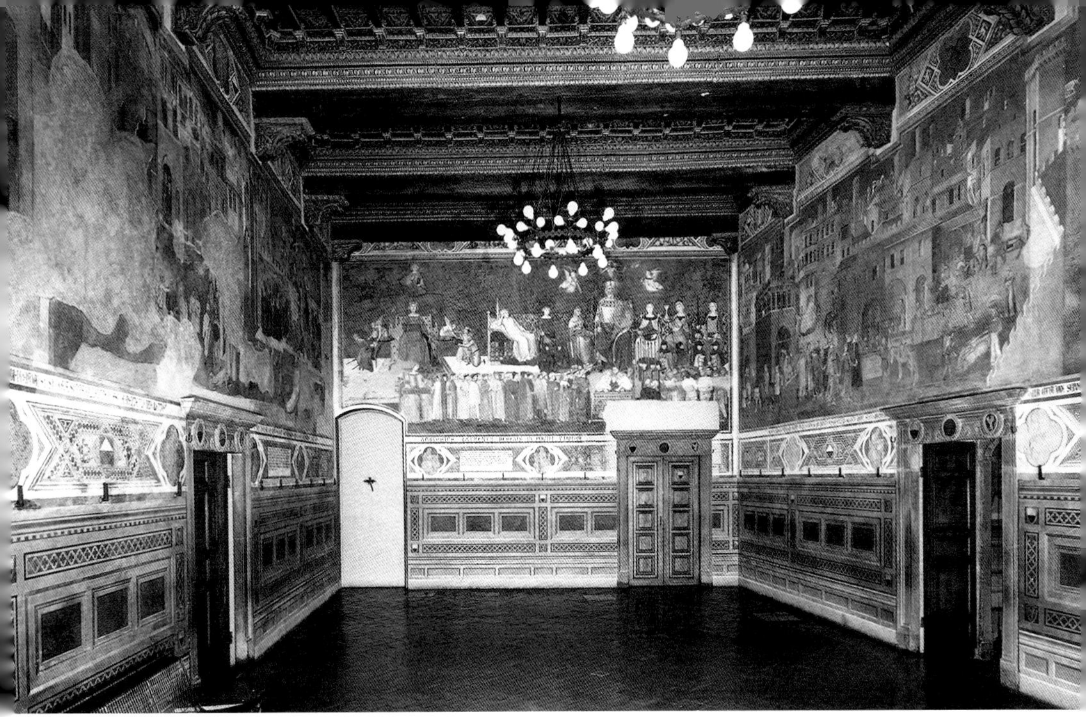

51 The Sala della Pace (formerly known as the Sala dei Nove). Siena, Palazzo Pubblico.

painting refer to specific aspects of Siena's own government. Thus, the nine Virtues are grouped about a bearded figure whose black and white robes represent the colour and design of the Sienese *balzana*. The imagery on his gold shield once replicated that of the city's civic seal, while the initials around his head and the wolf and suckling twins at his feet add further weight to the interpretation that he is intended to embody the communal government of Siena. Given a quasi-religious appearance by virtue of his close association with the Christian Virtues, this embodiment of the commune is also surrounded with details that allude to the more practical aspects of government – for example, although now somewhat obscured by a patch of damage, two knights present him with a miniature castle, a magistrate offers the keys of a city, and soldiers on horseback supervise several bound captives. The theme of territorial conquest begun in the paintings in the Sala del Consiglio (see pls 49, 50) was thus reiterated in this more erudite painting for the Sala dei Nove.

Linking the two sides of the painting is a procession of twenty-four men who carry a rope from the figure of Concord to the figure of Commune, thus relating the qualities of wisdom, justice and concord directly with this

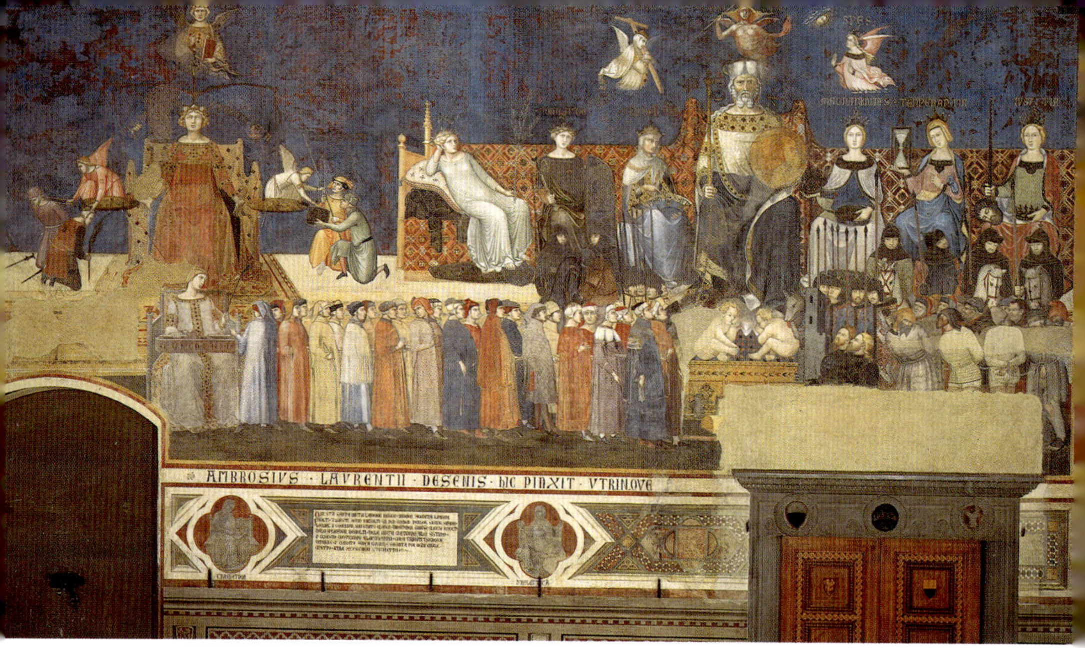

52 Ambrogio Lorenzetti, *The Good Government* (1338–9). Fresco, width 774 cm. North wall of the Sala della Pace. Siena, Palazzo Pubblico.

embodiment of Sienese government. While the identity of these figures is a matter of debate,[53] they act as a striking demonstration of Ambrogio Lorenzetti's remarkable capacity to portray a range of ages and different facial characteristics. They also convey vividly that Siena's government was not merely a matter of abstract, universal values but involved the active participation of the citizens themselves – even if only those drawn from a particular social group.

On the east wall of the room, to the right of the *Good Government*, is a painting that appears at first sight to be much less complex in meaning and content. Painted across the entire expanse of a wall measuring a little over fourteen metres in length, it shows a hilltop city and a panoramic view of the countryside surrounding it (pls 51, 53, 33). Hailed as one of the earliest landscape paintings in western art, it has been suggested that the painting represents an accurate impression of fourteenth-century Siena itself and the countryside lying to the south and west of the city. A number of details, such as the she-wolf over the city gateway, the striped bell-tower of the domed church on the extreme left and the name of the Sienese port of Talamone by the expanse of water on the extreme right, all provide circumstantial evidence that such an association was intended. However, just as in the case of the *Good Government* on the north wall, this painting was intended to have a wider application and meaning. Over the gateway of the city appears a figure representing Security whose text and miniature gallows clearly allude to the practice of justice – a sentiment given added support by the text below the painting. It is also clear from the latter text that this painting should be understood as a demonstration of the concrete benefits of just and peaceful government.

The sheer range of human activity that Ambrogio Lorenzetti incorporated into this painting has fascinated generations of viewers.[54] Within the city it is possible to identify a wedding procession, a game of dice in a tavern, a purchase being made at a shoemaker's shop, a lecture being given by a teacher and, high on the skyline, builders working on scaffolding. In the countryside, meanwhile, are scenes of ploughing, sowing and threshing, hunting and fishing. While thus appearing to offer a compellingly realistic view of Siena and its *contado*, the painting contains certain illogicalities, however. The agricultural activities associated with the months of spring, summer and autumn – such as sowing, threshing and hunting – have

53 Ambrogio Lorenzetti, *The Well-governed City* (1338–9). Detail of the east wall fresco of *The Well-governed City and Countryside* in the Sala della Pace. Siena, Palazzo Pubblico.

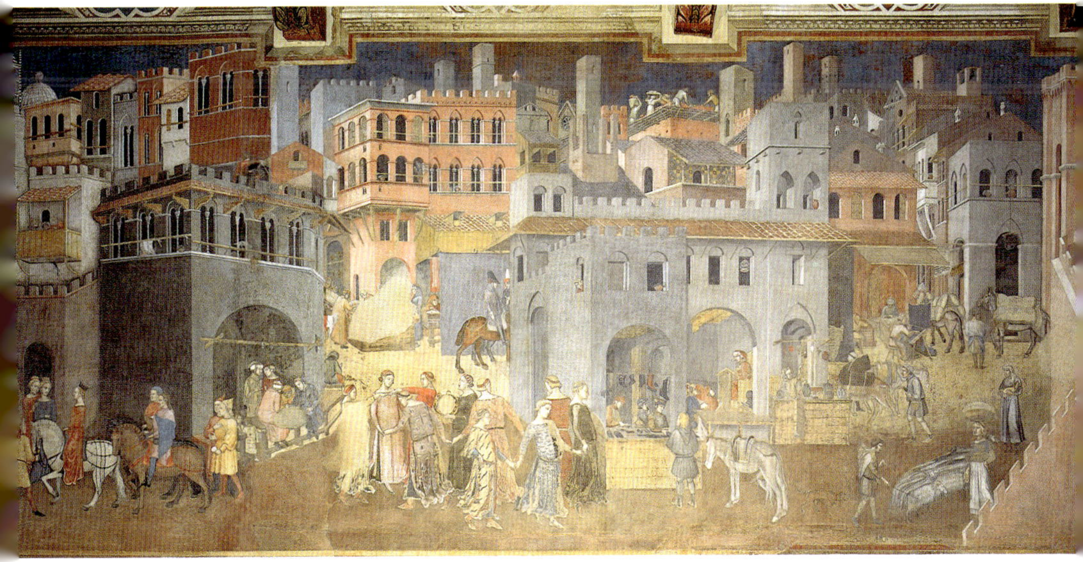

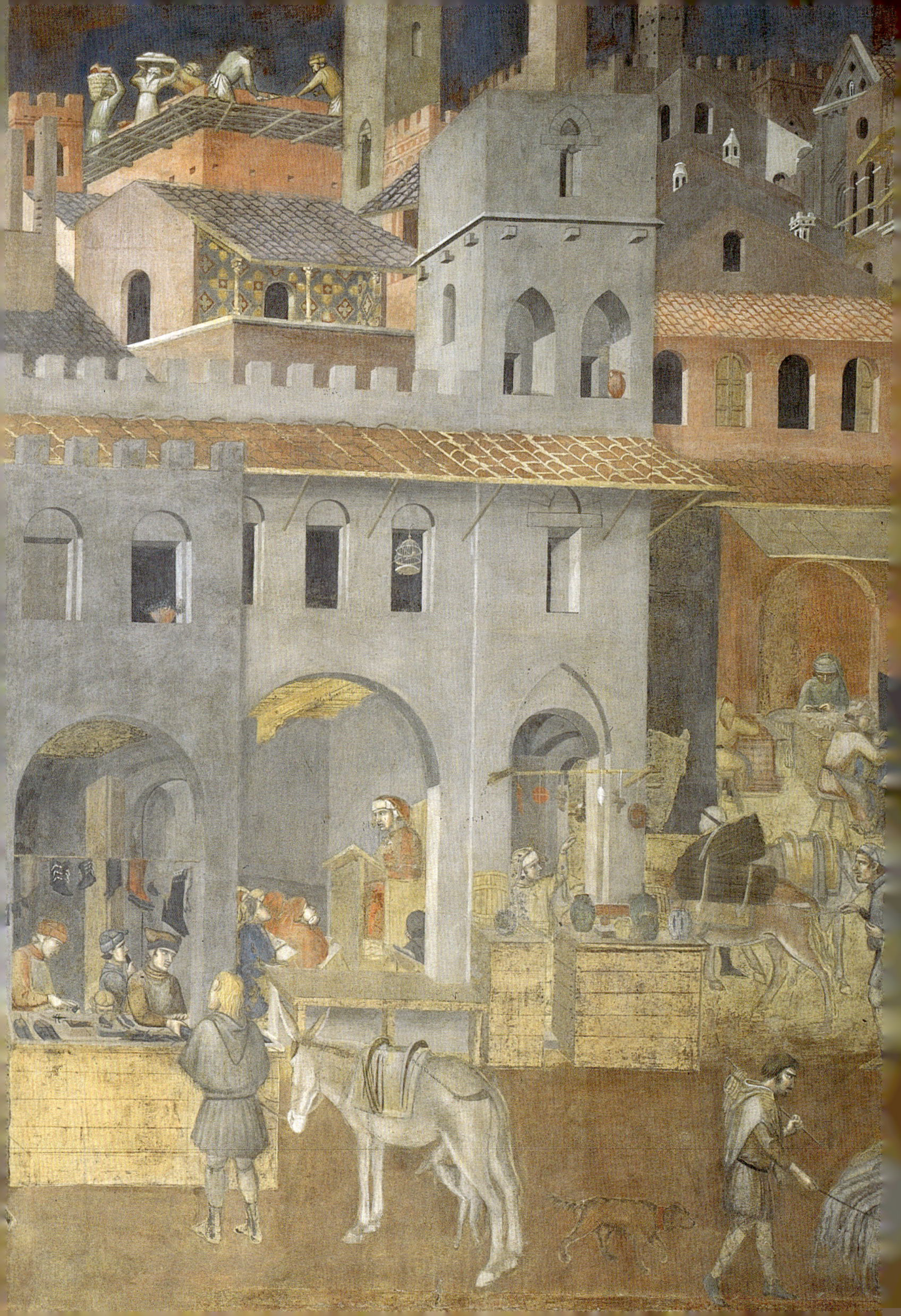

all been represented simultaneously in the countryside (see pl. 33). The painting thus has a symbolic dimension as well – a point which is made clear in the painted border that displays a sequence of personifications of the annual seasons, the planets and branches of late medieval scholarship.

Ambrogio Lorenzetti's treatment of space and light added a further layer of symbolic meaning to the painting. The open space in the city, where the dancers gracefully perform, acts as the centre of the pictorial space for the entire painting – every detail of the buildings and the natural features in the countryside appearing to recede from that point. Similarly, the distribution of the shadows in the painting suggests that the principal source of light for the scene is the city itself.[55] Elsewhere in the room, by contrast, the paintings appear as if lit by the window on the south wall. Since there was a well-developed Sienese tradition of equating Siena with Jerusalem – and therefore interpreting it as a divinely blessed city – it may well be that Ambrogio Lorenzetti deliberately sought to convey precisely this message in his idealised depiction of Siena and its *contado*.

The painting on the opposite west wall is now in very poor condition having once been an exterior wall and thus prone to damp. Its subject provides the antithesis of the paintings on the north and east walls and depicts the consequences of bad government. On the right appears a sequence of seated figures who mirror Commune and the Virtues on the north wall. Now representing Tyranny surrounded by the Vices and presiding over a bound figure of Justice, they act as a compelling demonstration of the vicious behaviour associated with tyrannical government. The pertinence of the imagery for the Sienese themselves is conveyed by such telling details as the robe of Division being in the black and white colours of the *balzana* and the warning tone of the message in the inscription below the painting. On the left appears a city in a state of disrepair and anarchy that contains only scenes of violence and preparation for war. The countryside, presided over by a personification of Fear, presents a barren landscape of ruin and devastation. Further contributing to the strong sense of contrast between this badly governed city and its prosperous counterpart on the opposite wall, the space within the badly governed city appears cramped and confined with abrupt shifts between light and shade.

In many respects the paintings of the Sala dei Nove sum up the achievements and aspirations of the Nine as a ruling magistracy. Their painted imagery presents a sophisticated pictorial argument for the benefits of legitimate government by a recognised council rather than the tyrannical rule of a single individual. Many of the details within the paintings arguably had particular pertinence to the Nine themselves. It is significant, for example,

Ambrogio Lorenzetti, *The Well-governed City* (detail of pl. 53).

that the traditional number of seven Christian Virtues has been increased by two to make nine. Many of the details in the *Well-governed City and Countryside* relate to the civic legislation of the Nine for facilitating trade and commerce in the city, encouraging the production of food in the countryside and maintaining roads and bridges there. The bleak picture of civic unrest on the west wall would also have had a particular relevance for the Nine, who during their period of government were confronted with threats to their political authority both from factions within Siena itself and from outside powers such as Ghibelline Pisa, which in 1332 laid waste to Sienese territory to within a few kilometres of Siena itself.[56]

Below the painting on the north wall, Ambrogio Lorenzetti proudly placed his name in Roman capitals, thus drawing attention to his responsibility for the extraordinary achievement involved (see pl. 52). Although relying on well-established pictorial conventions for portraying the sophisticated concepts that his paintings were designed to convey, he introduced a dazzling array of details and features that went beyond what had been achieved before in Sienese art. A notable example of this occurs in his portrayal of Peace in the *Good Government*, where the contours of her body are visible beneath the folds of her robe – a highly imaginative representation of the female form that probably owed its inspiration to Ambrogio's awareness of antique sculpted reliefs. Elsewhere in the room, he portrayed many well-observed naturalistic details, such as the caged bird and terracotta pots of herbs and flowers at the open windows of the well-governed city (see detail of pl. 53, p. 102) and, in a medallion on the west wall, snowflakes and a snowball.[57] By such means, a programmatic depiction of a late medieval understanding of what constituted the best form of government was given an immediacy and veracity that must have been deeply compelling for the paintings' original audience of the magistracy of the Nine and their close political associates.

Paintings for the Friars

A painting that is often cited in the debate over Simone Martini's role in the *Submission of a Castle* and the *Guidoriccio* is the arresting image of the Blessed Agostino Novello surrounded by four of his posthumous miracles (pl. 54).[58] This unusual panel painting originally came from Sant'Agostino, the principal church of the mendicant order of Augustinian Hermits in Siena (see pl. 6). Once assumed to be a conventional altarpiece, it appears in fact to have been part of the painted embellishment of the

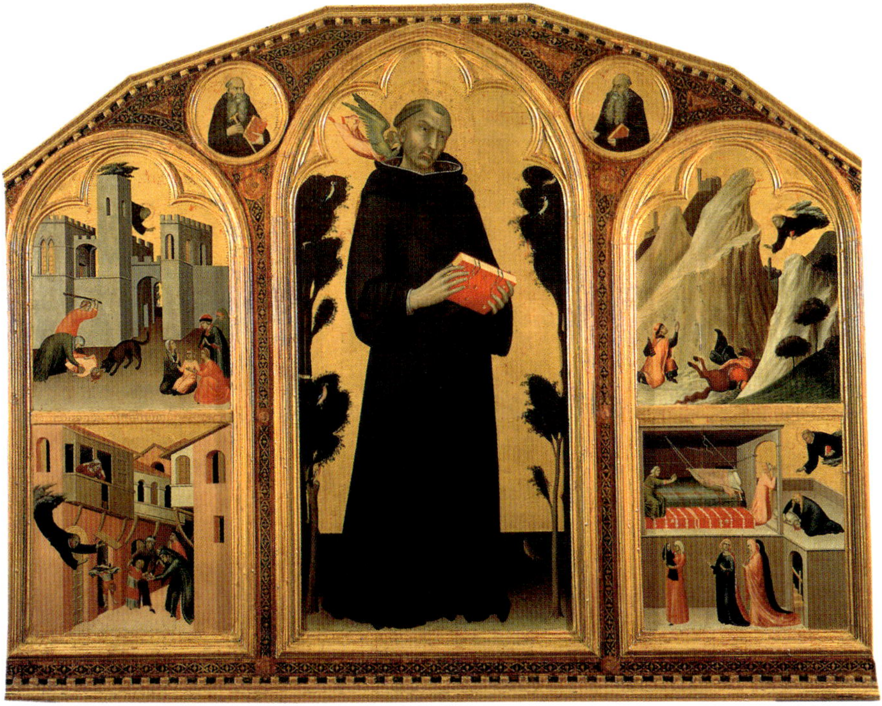

54 Simone Martini, *The Blessed Agostino Novello and Scenes of his Miracles* (1320s). Tempera on panel, 200 × 256 cm. Siena, Pinacoteca Nazionale.

shrine of this revered local man. It was designed to stand behind Agostino Novello's tomb chest – which was itself painted with scenes from his life – and the entire edifice was probably located at the end of the north aisle of the church, just in front of the choir screen and therefore in an easily accessible part of the church.

Agostino Novello was an important contemporary figure for the fourteenth-century Augustinian Hermits of Siena. An able jurist and Prior General, in 1300 he chose to retire to the rural Augustinian hermitage of San Leonardo al Lago, a few kilometres west of Siena. After his death and burial there in 1309, the Augustinian Hermits were clearly determined to honour the memory of their former Prior General – just as the Dominicans had with Ambrogio Sansedoni in 1287. They therefore translated his remains to Sant'Agostino and made him the centre of an intensely observed local cult. An entry in a fourteenth-century chronicle suggests that as early as 1310 the anniversary of his death was celebrated in Siena as a feast day. By the 1320s the Augustinian Hermits were petitioning the Council of the Bell to agree that the city's major officials would attend this annual celebration and give it financial support.[59]

Clearly the construction of the shrine was an integral part of the Augustinian Hermits' plans to honour this venerated member of their order, and for this reason the single painting that survives from this monument has been dated to the mid-1320s. On grounds of style it has been attributed to Simone Martini, not least because of its similarity to other works of his dating from this decade. Derived from a much older type of thirteenth-century painting showing the saint in a rigid frontal pose with narrative scenes grouped symmetrically on either side of the figure, the *Blessed Agostino Novello and Scenes of his Miracles* introduces an innovative and lively naturalism to this traditional format. The central figure of the Blessed Agostino Novello, silhouetted dramatically against a gleaming gold background, appears as a familiar, accessible figure, dressed in the black habit of his order. The tiny angel at his ear acts as visual confirmation of the claim made by the Augustinian Hermits that he received angelic visitations while at the hermitage of San Leonardo. The trees and the exquisite studies of birds in them similarly act as a reminder of his years at the rural hermitage and also recall the Augustinian Hermits' early history as an order living in the countryside.

The four narrative scenes, meanwhile, grouped in pairs on either side of the central painting, provide graphic evidence of Simone's abilities as a painter of narrative and genre detail. They show four posthumous miracles attributed to Agostino Novello – events that would have had great significance for the Augustinian Hermits in their campaign to secure his canonisation as a saint. In the two lower scenes, he is represented as a heavenly apparition intervening to restore life, firstly to a child who has fallen from a balcony and secondly to a baby that has fallen from his or her cradle: in gratitude the baby is then taken to church, clad in the black habit of the Augustinian Hermits, and holds a child-sized candle. Both paintings offer descriptive details of urban dwellings and contemporary fashion and furnishings.

The two upper scenes are set beyond the city walls, thus skilfully alluding once again to the Augustinian Hermits' association with the surrounding countryside. Here Agostino Novello is shown healing a child savaged by a dog and a man injured by a fall from his horse. Reminiscent of the

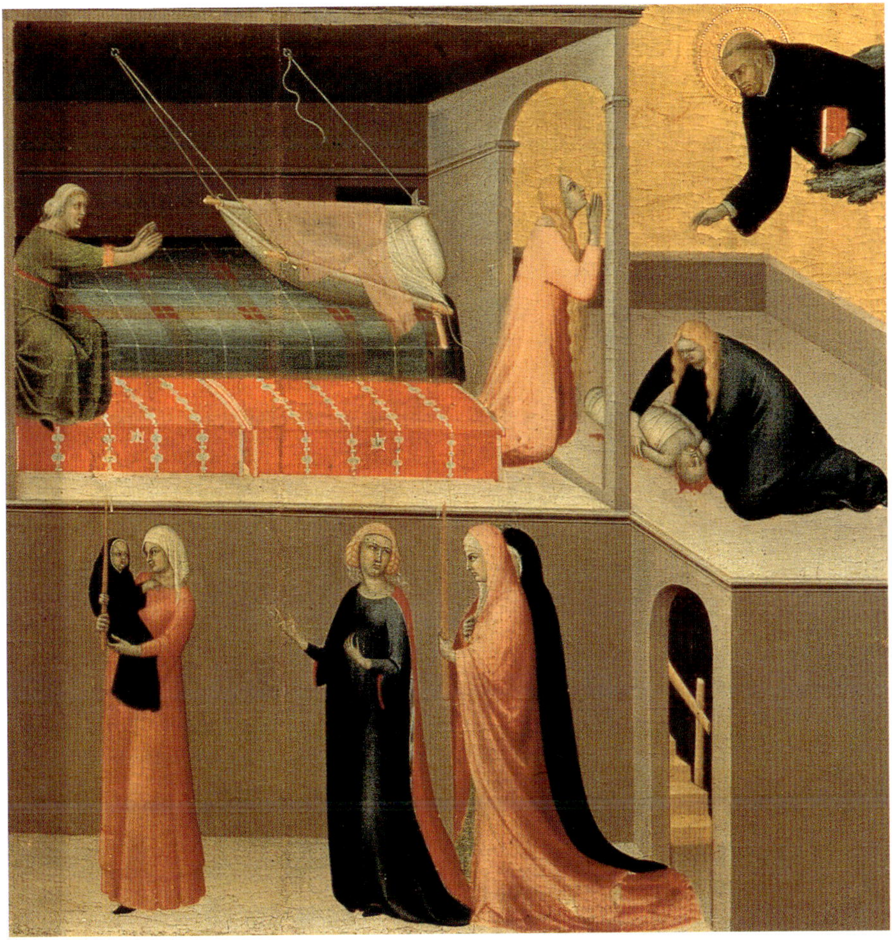

Simone Martini, *A Miracle of the Blessed Agostino Novello* (detail of pl. 54).

repertoire of lively narrative detail in the extensive series on Duccio's *Maestà* (see pls 35, 38–40), Simone Martini's painted propaganda for the reputation and sanctity of the Blessed Agostino Novello emulates the visual impact and descriptive power of Pietro Lorenzetti's predella scenes for the Carmelite altarpiece (see pls 44–5) – another painting that had a distinctive role as propaganda for its mendicant patrons.

Both Simone Martini and Pietro Lorenzetti had already gained valuable experience in painting narrative before they received their commissions from the Augustinian Hermits and the Carmelites of Siena. They had been involved in executing frescoes for the Lower Church at San Francesco in Assisi and were therefore able to study the extraordinary range of narrative painting that had been completed on the walls of this prestigious church (see, pl. 26). Although the dating of their work at Assisi is not certain, it is generally agreed that both painters worked there before 1319, when a period of civic strife began in Assisi. Thus, in about 1315, in a single campaign of painting, Pietro Lorenzetti and a number of assistants painted the walls of the left transept of the Lower Church with a series of emotive scenes depicting the events of the Passion and the stigmatisation of Saint Francis.[60] In one of the side chapels Simone Martini, meanwhile, executed lively paintings depicting the life of Saint Martin, with a number of subsidiary figures of Franciscan saints and a votive portrait of the chapel's founder, Cardinal Gentile Partino da Montefiore. The most likely date for the execution of this scheme is between 1315, the probable date of completion for the original version of the *Maestà* in the Palazzo Pubblico, and 1321, the date of its refurbishment (see pl. 47).[61] As in his Sienese fresco, it appears that Simone Martini greatly enjoyed introducing the colour and pageantry of secular life into his depictions of ostensibly religious subject matter (pl. 55).

Perhaps as a result of his work at Assisi, Pietro Lorenzetti also received an important commission from the Franciscans of Siena.[62] On this occasion, however, he shared the work with his brother Ambrogio. Painted for the chapterhouse of the friary at San Francesco in Siena, the scheme comprised the *Crucifixion* and the *Resurrected Christ* (attributed to Pietro) and scenes from the history of the Order (attributed to Ambrogio). The paintings fell out of fashion in later centuries and were removed from the chapterhouse in 1857 – three of them being set into the walls of two of the chapels in the north transept of San Francesco and the rest ending up in various art collections. *Saint Louis of Toulouse before Pope Boniface VIII* by Ambrogio Lorenzetti demonstrates the quality of this painted scheme and once again shows how fourteenth-century Sienese painters recorded and celebrated important events in the institutional life of their mendicant patrons (pl. 56). The fresco portrays what was then a relatively recent event: in December 1296 the future Franciscan saint Louis, son of King Charles II of Naples, having taken his Franciscan vows, received the bishopric of Toulouse from Pope Boniface VIII, thus forfeiting any claim to the throne of Naples.

55 Simone Martini, *The Knighting of Saint Martin* (*c.* 1315–19). Fresco, 265 × 200 cm. Assisi, San Francesco, Lower Church, Chapel of Saint Martin.

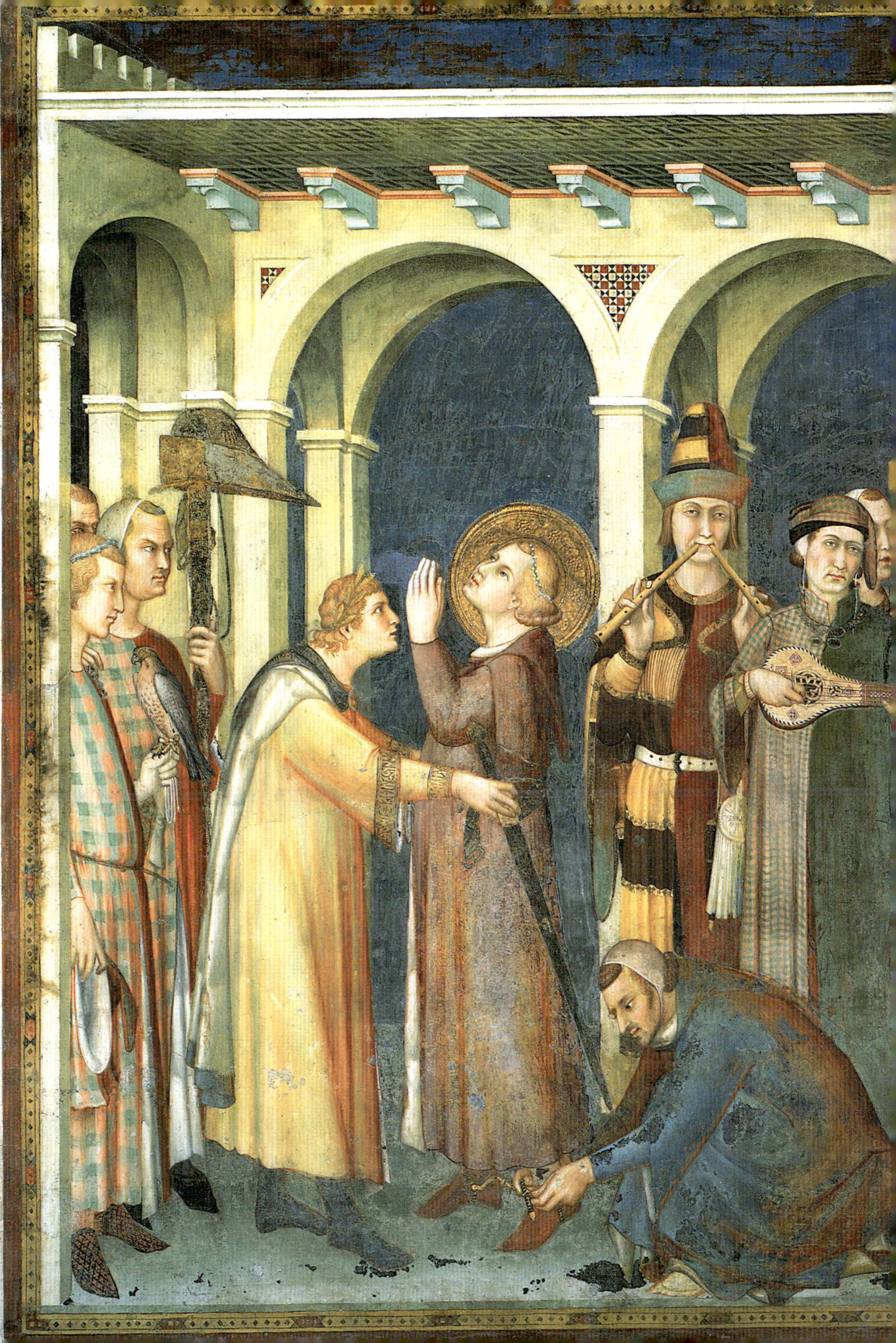

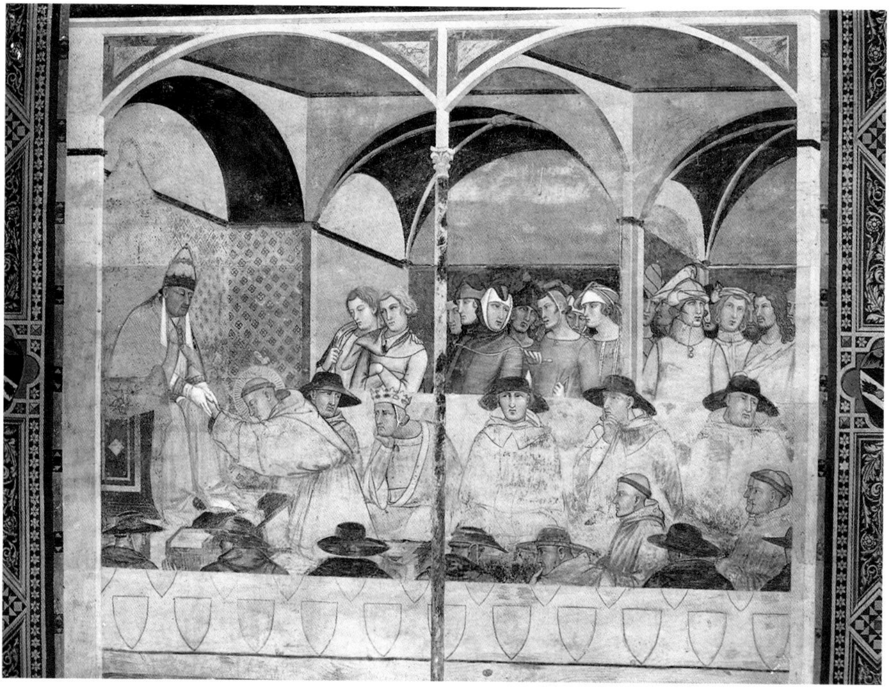

56 Ambrogio Lorenzetti, *Saint Louis of Toulouse before Pope Boniface VIII* (1340s). Fresco, width 403 cm. Siena, San Francesco, Bandini Piccolomini Chapel.

Canonised in 1317 – owing to the powerful influence of the Angevin monarchs of Naples – Louis of Toulouse was a saint of considerable importance to the Franciscan Order and it is not surprising that a commemoration of his sanctity should be included in the newly painted chapterhouse. This painting displays a similar compositional format to that used by Pietro on his predella panels for the Carmelite altarpiece (see pl. 45), thus demonstrating the cross-fertilisation of artistic ideas between the brothers. The subject also allowed Ambrogio to exploit his considerable powers of human characterisation and well-observed detail, seen most vividly in the impressive array of fashionable headgear worn by the lay figures in the background and the facial expression of King Charles which vividly conveys the monarch's concern regarding his son's decision to relinquish his rights and status as a secular prince.

The other painting by Ambrogio Lorenzetti from this series depicts another important event in the history of the Franciscan Order. Showing in all likelihood the martyrdom of six friars in 1339 at Almalyz in central Asia, this painting allowed Ambrogio to portray an array of different kinds of human emotion and ethnic types.[63] The theme of martyrdom was also addressed in a series of frescoes, probably painted shortly after 1336, for the cloister that connected the church with the chapterhouse. Attributed by the fifteenth-century Florentine sculptor Lorenzo Ghiberti to Ambrogio Lorenzetti, one of the paintings apparently depicted the martyrdom of three Franciscan friars in 1321 at Tana, near Bombay. A further fresco in this lost series probably showed the martyrdom of a local friar, Pietro da Siena. According to Ghiberti's description, this series of paintings again showed an unusually wide range of human emotions and weather conditions – including a 'storm with much hail, flashes of lightning, and thundering earthquakes'.[64] A few fragments recently recovered from this lost scheme provide partial confirmation of Ghiberti's account and suggest that it must once have provided the Franciscans with a powerful evocation of the drama surrounding the deaths of their fellow friars.

Altarpieces for the Cathedral

The pictorial skills of Simone Martini and Pietro and Ambrogio Lorenzetti, each of whom had provided powerful visual propaganda for the city's mendicant orders, were also utilised by the cathedral Opera for a project undertaken during the 1330s and 1340s.[65] As noted earlier, it was at precisely this time that the cathedral authorities embarked on an ambitious scheme to enlarge the cathedral by beginning to build the Duomo Nuovo (see pl. 34). One of the results of this new project was the provision of new altars at the east end of the cathedral, four of which were to be in honour of the four lesser patron saints of Siena: Ansano, Savino, Crescenzio and Victor.[66] Owing to the abandonment of the new cathedral project, these altars were eventually placed in the newly enlarged east end of the cathedral (pl. 57). To the immediate left of the high altar was the altar of Saint Ansano (no. 1); to the right of the high altar, the altar of Saint Victor (no. 2); at the head of the north transept, the altar of Saint Savino (no. 3); and opposite it, at the head of the south transept, the altar of Saint Crescenzio (no. 4).

Between 1333 and 1351, altarpieces were completed for all these altars, each one depicting as its central image an event from the life of the Virgin,

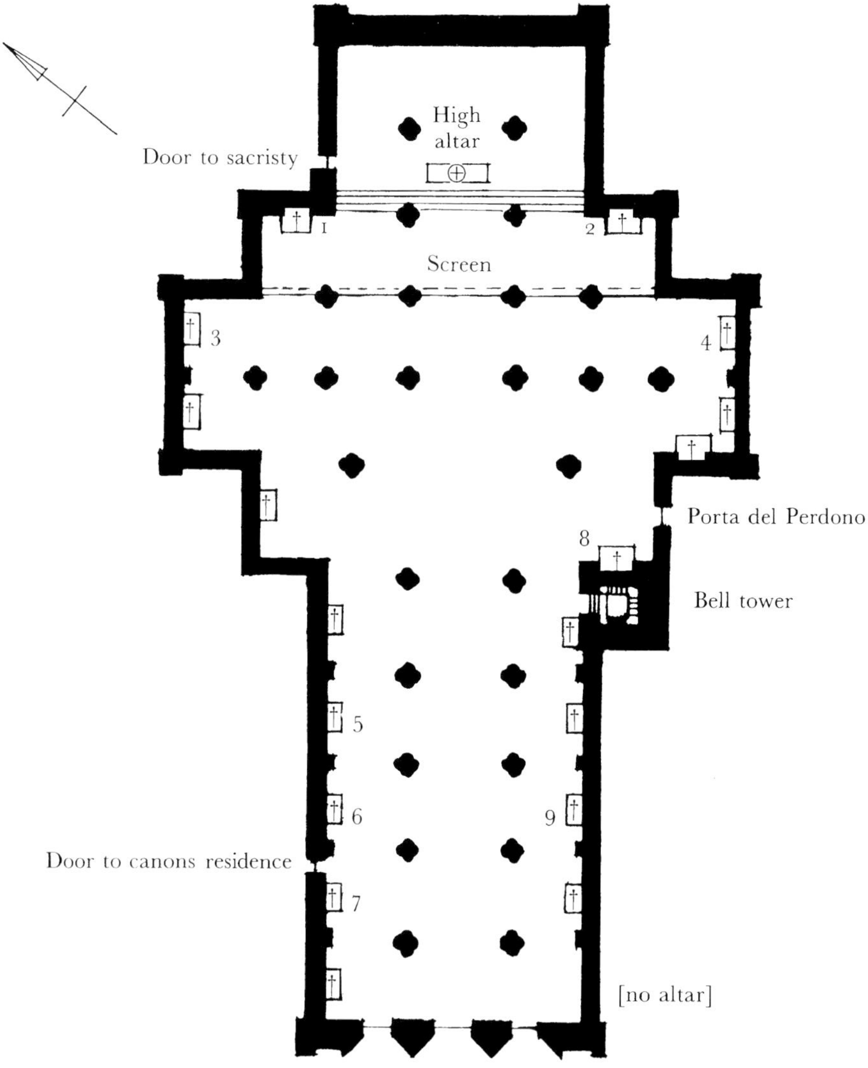

Plate 57 Plan of altars in Siena cathedral and their dedications.

1 Saint Ansano (original site of pl. 58)
2 Saint Victor (original site of pl. 60)
3 Saint Savino (original site of pl. 59)
4 Saint Crescenzio (original site of pl. 61)
5 Shoemakers' Guild
6 Magi (original site of pl. 73)
7 Saint Peter (original site of pl. 74)
8 Santa Maria delle Nevi (original site of pl. 92)
9 Santa Maria delle Grazie (see pl. 3)

thus continuing and extending the celebration of the Virgin initiated on the front face of Duccio's *Maestà* altarpiece (see pls 35–36).[67] The particular events from the life of the Virgin chosen for the four altarpieces all corresponded to major Marian feasts in the liturgical calendar of the medieval Church. Thus, the altar of Saint Savino was embellished with the *Birth of the Virgin* (pl. 59) by Pietro Lorenzetti; the altar of Saint Ansano with the *Annunciation* (pl. 58) by Simone Martini and Lippo Memmi; the altar of Saint Victor with the *Nativity and Adoration of the Shepherds* (pl. 60), attributed to Bartolommeo Bulgarini (of which only about two thirds of the original painting survives); and the altar of Saint Crescenzio with the *Presentation of the Christ Child in the Temple* (pl. 61, also known as the *Purification of the Virgin*) by Ambrogio Lorenzetti.

With the exception of the *Annunciation*, these altarpiece paintings have now been separated from their side panels, but on the basis of brief descriptions of them in fifteenth-century cathedral inventories, it appears that in each case the main painting was framed by, on the left, the saint to whom the altar was dedicated and, on the right, another saint who was either a close associate of the patron saint or was greatly venerated within the cathedral. Thus, for example, Bulgarini's *Nativity and Adoration of the Shepherds* was originally framed by paintings of *Saint Victor* and his fellow martyr *Saint Corona*.[68] All the altarpieces have lost their original framework and been separated from their predellas. Four small paintings, however, have been identified as predella panels from three of these altarpieces.[69] Together they provide evidence that each altarpiece had a predella with a wide central painting of a scene relating to Christ's Passion, framed by smaller scenes of the life of the patron saint to whom the altar was dedicated. The overall design would have been broadly similar, therefore, to that of Pietro Lorenzetti's 1329 Carmelite altarpiece (see pl. 44).

Despite the unified nature of their design, the four altarpieces appear to have been produced over a period of some eighteen years. The earliest secure date for the beginning of the project is that of 1333 on the gilded inscription on the lower edge of the *Annunciation*, together with a final payment made by the Opera that year for the completion of the altarpiece of 'San Sano'. In 1335, the Opera paid Pietro Lorenzetti for work on the altarpiece of Saint Savino and paid also a grammar teacher for translating the story of Saint Savino from Latin into Italian for the painter. In 1339, Ambrogio Lorenzetti was paid for work on the altarpiece of Saint Crescenzio. Three years later, Pietro and Ambrogio Lorenzetti each placed their name and the date of 1342 on their respective altarpieces. Much later,

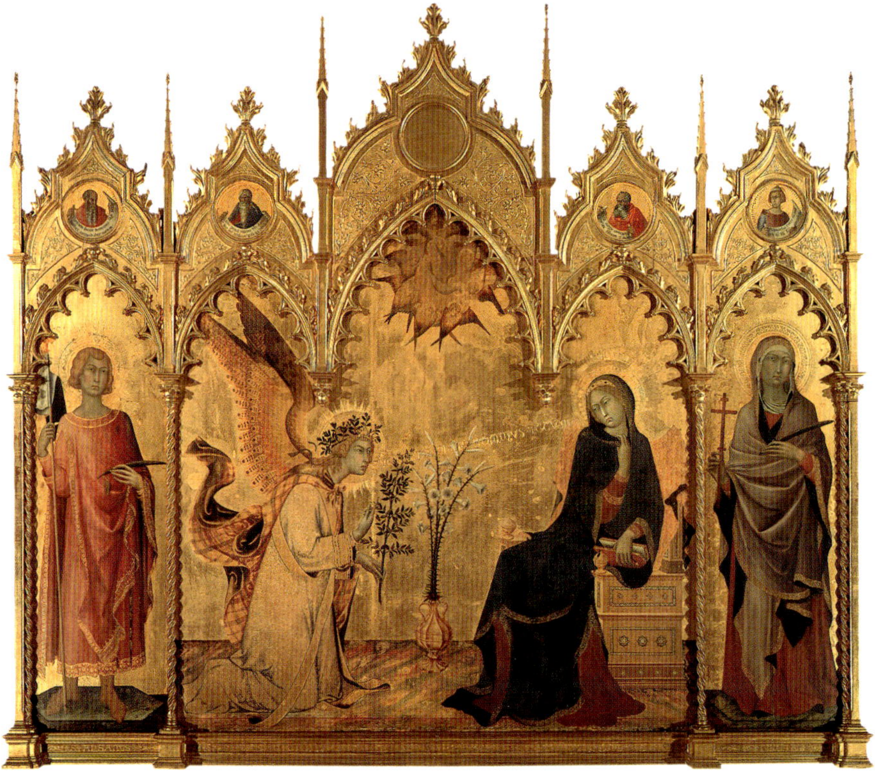

58 Simone Martini and Lippo Memmi, *The Annunciation with Saints Ansano and Massima* (1333). Tempera on panel, 260 × 305 cm. Florence, Uffizi.

in 1351, woodworkers were paid for the final decorative details on the altarpiece of Saint Victor. The ambition and uncertainties surrounding the project for the Duomo Nuovo can account for the drawn out nature of the project. It is, moreover, relevant that, between 1335, when Pietro began work on the Saint Savino altarpiece, and 1342, when he and Ambrogio completed their altarpieces for the cathedral, they may both have worked together in Cortona on an elaborate cycle of narrative paintings celebrating the life and miracles of Saint Margaret of Cortona.[70] Ambrogio Lorenzetti may also have painted in the chapterhouse and cloister of San Francesco during this period, and he had certainly completed the Sala dei Nove frescoes (see pls 33, 51–3).

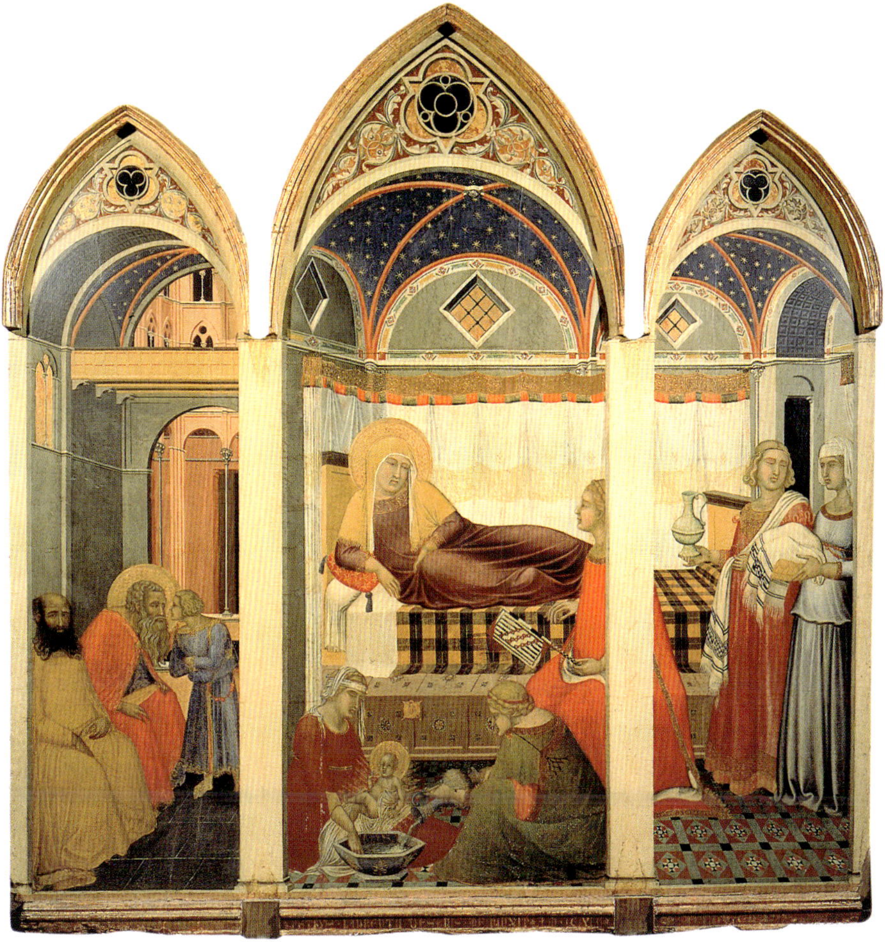

59 Pietro Lorenzetti, *The Birth of the Virgin* (1342). Tempera on panel, 187 × 182 cm. Siena, Museo dell'Opera del Duomo.

The four altarpieces were thus produced over a relatively long period of time, but appear to have had a number of features in common in terms of their subjects and design. Although the *Annunciation* and the *Nativity* were the first and last paintings to be completed, they both have a much more formal appearance than the *Birth* and *Presentation* – an effect achieved by a far greater use of gold leaf and by the representation of heavenly appari-

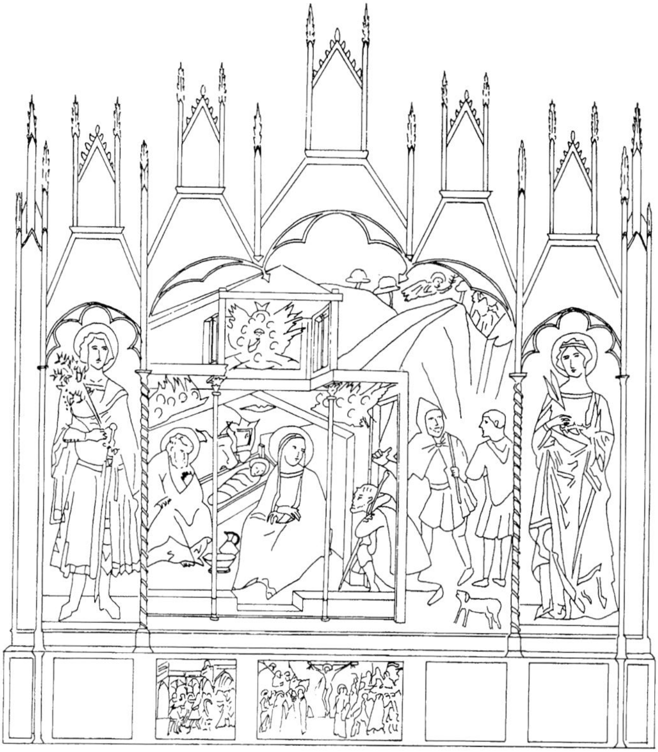

60 Reconstruction of *The Nativity and Adoration of the Shepherds with Saints Victor and Corona* (by Norman Muller).

tions in the form of angels and seraphim. This can partly be accounted for by their religious subject matter, which would have made them peculiarly fitting companions to Duccio's *Maestà*, located over the high altar and thus in relative proximity to them (see pls 35–36). Pietro Lorenzetti's *Birth* and Ambrogio Lorenzetti's *Presentation* are, by contrast, much more descriptive in terms of their appearance and design. Both, however, include extraordinarily inventive representations of interiors – one domestic, the other ecclesiastical. Pietro provided an interesting insight into the furnishings of a fourteenth-century bedroom and the social rituals surrounding the birth of a child to a woman from a wealthy family (pl. 59). He also used the framework of the panel painting itself in an inventive way, simultaneously

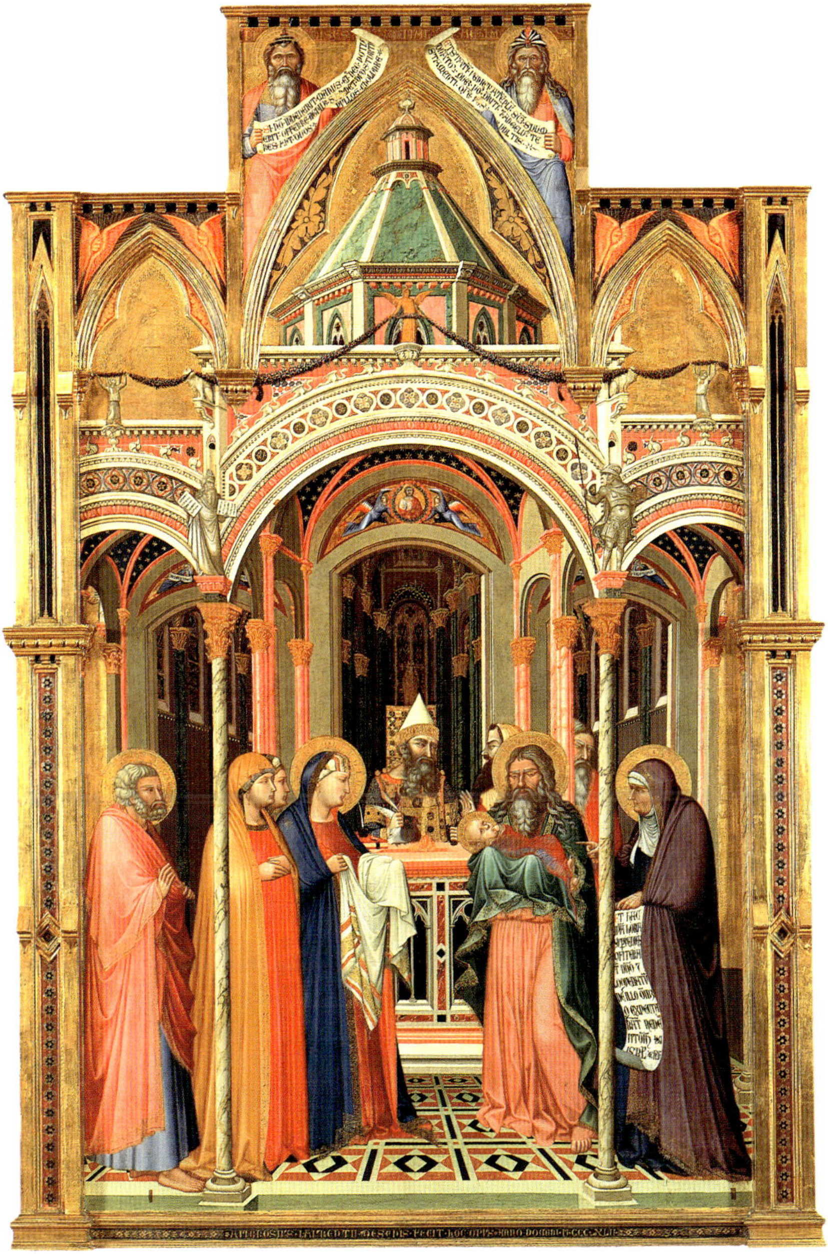

61 Ambrogio Lorenzetti, *The Presentation of the Christ Child in the Temple* (1342). Tempera on panel, 257 × 168 cm. Florence, Uffizi.

deploying it as part of the painted architecture and as a means of increasing the illusion of seeing into a spacious interior marked out by the bold perspective of the tiled floor, chequered bed cover and ribbed vaults. Ambrogio, in a similar way, offered a tour-de-force of dazzling pictorial effects to conjure both the magnificence of the Temple in which his scene was set and also the depth of the building's space (pl. 61). Taking his cue from the architecture of Siena cathedral itself (see pl. 19), he thus introduced into the design of this painted altarpiece a bold pictorial statement that Siena and its principal ecclesiastical building could be equated with that of Jerusalem itself.[71]

Private Art

As well as this impressive array of painting executed for the public venues of the cathedral, the city's churches and its town hall, a modest amount of painting executed for private use survives from the first half of the fourteenth century. A number of small-scale devotional works have been attributed to Sienese painters including Duccio, Simone Martini and both Pietro and Ambrogio Lorenzetti. A particularly well-preserved example of this genre of art is the triptych of the *Virgin and Christ Child with Saints Dominic and Aurea* (pl. 62). Designed as a triptych, in which the central panel is framed by two side panels on hinges that can be folded over the central image, it was thus portable: its original owner could easily carry it with him or her, set it up in a variety of venues and use it as an aid to his or her private devotions. The half-length figures of the Virgin and Christ Child, giving a close and intimate viewpoint of the holy figures, complement such a function. The standing figures of Saint Dominic and the virgin-martyr saint Aurea – who was the object of particular devotion in Ostia – have led art historians to speculate that this preciously crafted object was produced for Niccolò da Prato, a Dominican friar and Cardinal Bishop of Ostia, who as a high-ranking papal legate had diplomatic contacts with Siena.[72]

In addition to offering a compelling example of the scale and intimacy of such objects produced for private consumption, the triptych also provides evidence of the collaboration undertaken by painters in order to produce them. Technical investigation has revealed that – as in the case of the *Maestà* altarpiece – several painters worked together on different parts of the triptych.[73] This is particularly evident in the strikingly different styles of the figures on the side panels when compared to those on the central panel.

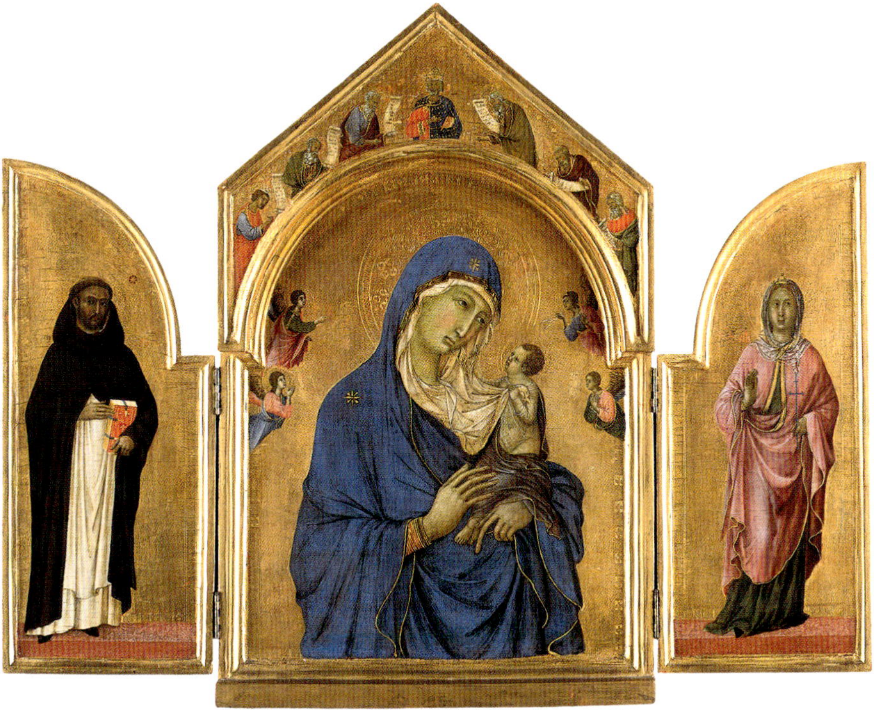

62 Duccio, *The Virgin and Christ Child with Saints Dominic and Aurea* (c. 1300–05). Tempera on panel, central panel 61.5 × 39 cm, left panel 45 × 20.5 cm, right panel 45 × 18 cm. London, National Gallery.

Appearing rather like sculpted figures of saints, they compare closely to Saints Ansano and Massima on the *Annunciation* altarpiece, signed and dated by Simone Martini and Lippo Memmi in 1333 (see pl. 58). It may be, therefore, that one or both of these painters had collaborated with Duccio on the great enterprise of the *Maestà* altarpiece and continued to do so in the second decade of the fourteenth century. Although this exquisitely crafted object has the appearance of a specially commissioned work for a wealthy patron, it is possible that Duccio's workshop also routinely produced small-scale devotional paintings of this type for a wider clientele.

Nothing of the equivalent survives in Siena itself but the nearby town of San Gimignano contains an example of the kind of mural painting that originally decorated the walls of privately owned houses. Probably painted

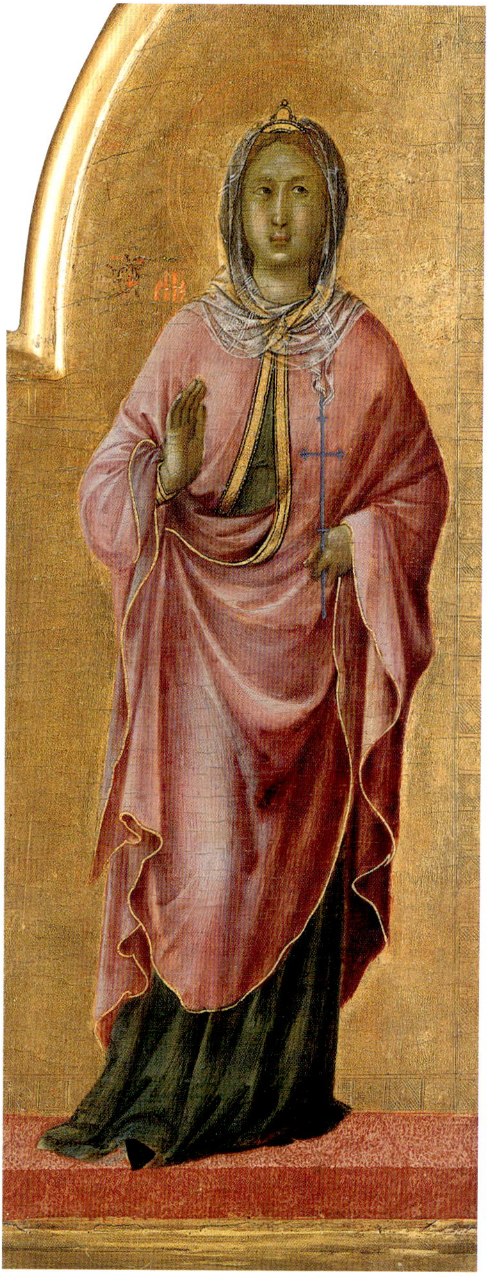

Duccio, *The Virgin and Christ Child with Saints Dominic and Aurea* (detail of pl. 62, showing Saint Aurea).

by the Sienese Memmo di Filippuccio, this fourteenth-century scheme survives because it was painted inside the Palazzo Comunale, San Gimignano's equivalent of the Palazzo Pubblico. Located in a tower on the floor above the city's council hall (which was itself embellished with a close replica of Simone Martini's *Maestà*, painted in 1319 by Memmo di Filippuccio's son, Lippo Memmi[74]), the room probably originally functioned as the Podestà's bedroom.[75] In the first decade of the fourteenth century, it appears to have been painted with a series of frescoes whose subject matter – though obscure – is whole-heartedly secular in content. Drawing on the rich range of popular stories about the snares and temptations of a worldly life, it shows a number of scenes that are explicitly sexual in content.[76] Thus on the entrance wall are a pair of frescoes that show a man and woman, first in a bathtub together and then sharing a bed. Another woman, dressed in a striking parti-coloured dress, is shown in attendance upon them (pl. 63). While probably designed as a warning about the kinds of activity commonly associated with local public baths, these paintings, in terms of their colour and pattern, also convey a sense of amusement and pleasure, suitable for the private quarters of this important San Gimignanese official.

63 Memmo di Filippuccio (attrib.), *Bath Scene* (*c.* 1313–15). Fresco. East wall of the Camera del Podestà. San Gimignano, Palazzo Comunale.

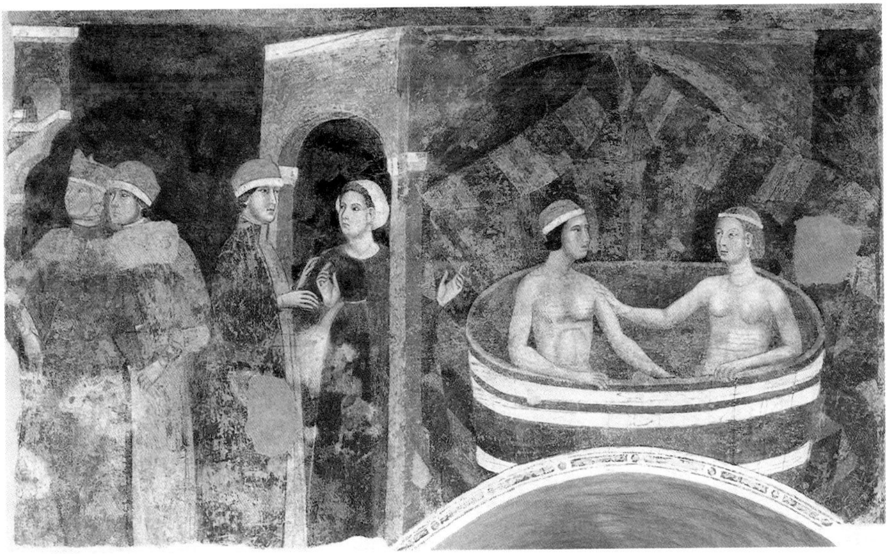

Like the episodes illustrating the participation of the saints in the daily lives of people (see, pl. 54), the demands of this particular commission clearly stimulated the painter to record in a particularly lively way certain aspects of his own culture and experience.

The idea of a 'Golden Age' of Sienese painting in the first half of the fourteenth century is by no means unfounded. Facilitated by the widespread building programme sponsored by the Nine and the city's religious orders, two generations of painters worked on a steady flow of varied commissions. Although still conforming broadly to the types of painting executed by their thirteenth-century predecessors, they pushed the boundaries of pictorial representation in a number of exciting directions. Duccio's ambitious portrayal of the *Maestà* theme on the front face of the cathedral high altarpiece was taken up by other painters, such as Simone Martini and the Lorenzetti, and explored in different ways – sometimes with greater emphasis on the Virgin's role as queen (see pls 43, 47), at other times with the focus on her role as a tender-hearted mother, ready to intercede on humanity's behalf (see pl. 42). What was achieved overall, however, was an increasingly assured depiction of the holy figures as lifelike people who related to one another and, by extension, with the spectator.

Duccio's rich array of narrative imagery on the *Maestà* altarpiece (see pls 35, 38–40) similarly inspired younger Sienese painters to explore an extraordinary variety of subjects. In many ways, it is in the field of narrative painting that the greatest artistic experimentation appears to have taken place. Painting narrative, whether drawn from the bible, the legends of the saints or more recent political and historical events, required an ability on the part of the painter to create an illusion of recognisable events and situations – precisely what this generation of Sienese painters achieved. Thus, Simone Martini in his painting for the shrine of the Blessed Agostino Novello effectively conveyed not only the ascetic character of his famous contemporary but also the specific nature of his alleged miraculous interventions in the daily lives of the Sienese themselves (see pl. 54). Similarly, Pietro and Ambrogio Lorenzetti portrayed canonical religious subjects on their cathedral altarpieces, but set them in familiar surroundings (see pls 59, 61) – just as local preachers urged their congregations to envisage holy stories taking place in their own neighbourhoods and homes.

Within the ostensibly secular setting of the Palazzo Pubblico, this pictorial inventiveness was maintained and extended in the painted embellishment of its two principal council halls. While the commissions for the *Submission of a Castle* (see pl. 50) and the *Mappamondo* arguably required of their painters an ability to portray features of local topography in a particularly graphic way, the Sala dei Nove scheme inspired its painter,

Ambrogio Lorenzetti, to deploy a dazzling range of pictorial skills in order to portray expansive landscape settings, contrasting city topographies, an array of human characterisation and activities and different sorts of weather condition (see pls 33, 51–3). It is not for nothing that in his memoirs Lorenzo Ghiberti identified this particular Sienese painter as especially worthy of his praise.[77]

In terms of their training and professional practice, it is likely that fourteenth-century painters did not differ greatly from their thirteenth-century predecessors. More documentary evidence for their activities survives – although it, too, is full of frustrating gaps and tantalising uncertainties. These later painters seem to have been particularly assiduous about appending their names to their more important commissions (see pls 36, 43, 52, 58, 59, 61); indeed, it is when they neglected to do so that problems occur for art historians – such as the hotly contested authorship of the *Guidoriccio* (see pl. 49). It also appears that, even when they were fully trained master-painters, they readily collaborated with one another on the execution of commissions – a natural consequence of the way that apprentice painters were trained in the workshop. What is remarkable, however, is that in such cases as the *Annunciation* altarpiece by Simone Martini and Lippo Memmi, where the signature makes it clear that the painting was executed by both painters (see pl. 58), it is almost impossible to distinguish who painted which part of the painting – despite the best efforts of modern art historians to do so. Thus, to their already formidable list of achievements can be added the skill of working collaboratively in a consistent and harmonious style.

A final indication of the skill and talent of this generation of Sienese painters is the extent of the demand for their work in other towns in Tuscany and Umbria. All the best-known Sienese painters of the period were involved in producing altarpieces for churches in neighbouring cities and towns. Simone Martini, Lippo Memmi and Pietro and Ambrogio Lorenzetti all travelled to such places as Assisi (see pl. 55), Arezzo,Cortona, Florence and San Gimignano to work on large-scale fresco schemes. Indeed, Simone Martini ended his days working at the papal court in Avignon, dying there in 1344.[78] Four years later the Black Death struck Siena, probably killing, among thousands of others, the highly innovative Ambrogio Lorenzetti.[79] As a result of the devastating social and economic consquences of the plague, conditions for the practice of painting changed markedly in the second half of the fourteenth century. Sienese painters then had to evolve new methods and techniques in order to adapt to changed circumstances.

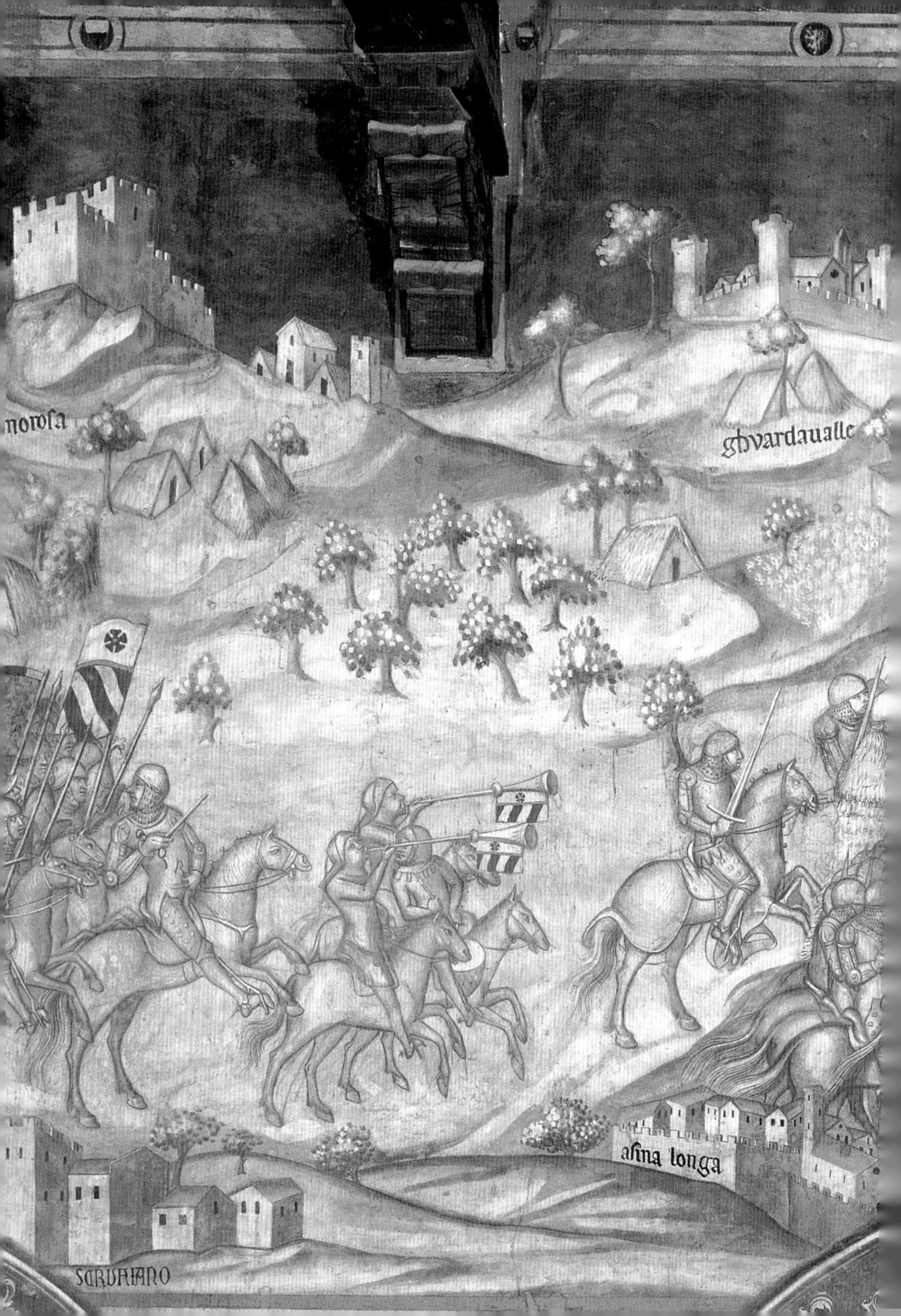

morosa
ghvardavalle
asina longa
SCRVDIANO

3

Crises, Changes and Continuities: Sienese Painting (1355–1420)

The second half of the fourteenth century was not a happy period for Siena and the Sienese. In 1348, the Black Death decimated the population of the city and outbreaks of the plague recurred frequently.[1] Meanwhile, the crops failed often and in consequence there were periods of famine of varying intensity. The Nine were unable to deal effectively with these crises and on the occasion of the Emperor Charles IV's visit to the city in 1355 they were overthrown by a coalition of nobles and artisans. For a few months Siena was ruled by this coalition and then by a new regime – the Twelve – whose members were recruited from the 'little people', a class of society just below that of the Nine.[2] In 1368 the Twelve in turn lost their precarious hold over the government, an event that was again precipitated by the entry of Charles IV into the city. The reputation of the Twelve has suffered greatly from comparison with the Nine, but it should be remembered that they inherited problems from the earlier regime and, although ostensibly more popular in their membership, always suffered from the political ambitions of their noble allies.

More seriously, the Twelve were in power during a period when Siena and its *contado* were constantly subject to the depredations of mercenary companies. These companies were private armies, made up of professional soldiers from all over Europe who hired out their services during wartime and conducted disastrous raids during peacetime. Between 1342 and 1399, Siena experienced some thirty-seven raids at the hands of such mercenary companies, who subjected the countryside to systematic campaigns of arson, plunder and looting.[3] To persuade the companies to leave its territo-

64 Lippo Vanni, detail of *The Battle in the Val di Chiana* (*c.* 1363) Fresco, 400 × 1250cm. North arcade of the Sala del Mappamondo. Siena, Palazzo Pubblico.

ry, the Sienese government had to pay out huge sums of money, which it was frequently forced to borrow from its citizens. This already difficult situation was made even worse by the devastating effects of recurrent outbreaks of plague and famine, which often coincided with the timing of the mercenary raids.

A measure of the impact of the mercenary companies upon Siena can be seen in the Sala del Mappamondo of the Palazzo Pubblico where on the north-west arcade is a fresco commemorating a rare victory against one of these mercenary bands (see pl. 46). Painted by Lippo Vanni, primarily in shades of ochre, it depicts the defeat of the Company of the Hat in 1363 outside the town of Torrita, south-west of Siena (pl. 64).[4] Although decorating a room that no longer functioned as the government's principal council chamber, this painting provides a vivid testimony of a shift in the government's priorities, away from the acquisition of territory (see pl. 50), to the defence of territory from marauding outsiders.

After four attempts to form a government in 1368, a regime known as the Riformatori was finally established. In terms of its membership, it represented the interests of various political parties – the Monti – whose loyalties were tied to past government regimes.[5] It was comprised of fifteen members, eight drawn from the 'little people', four from the supporters of the Twelve and three from those of the Nine. It was therefore proportionally more representative of the artisan class of the city than previous regimes and it is striking how often artists featured as members of this government's principal magistracies.

In 1371 the Riformatori were confronted by a serious rebellion of unskilled woolworkers who, driven by hunger, raided local warehouses and attacked the Palazzo Pubblico. Although they managed briefly to secure the appointment of seven of their members to the government, within a month the Riformatori had effected severe reprisals and the rebellion was quashed. After ruling for another fourteen years, the Riformatori were finally deposed in 1385 by a coalition of noble families headed by the Malavolti and the Salimbeni. The Riformatori were replaced by a new coalition government known as the ten Priors – four representatives from the Nine, four from the Twelve and two from the 'little people', thus reversing the trend established by the previous regime of a higher proportion of artisans participating in government. The new regime's troubled rule was marred by almost constant military confrontation, particularly against Florence for control of Montepulciano, a town in the south-east of the Sienese *contado*. The government of the Priors came to an ignominious end in 1399 when Siena submitted to the political control of Florence's sworn enemy, Gian

Galeazzo Visconti of Milan. His death in 1402 enabled Siena to regain its political independence, conclude a peace with Florence, renounce its claims to Montepulciano and, in 1404, form a new government of twelve Priors. The first two decades of the fifteenth century were similarly bedevilled by the territorial ambitions of Ladislas, King of Naples, between 1409 and 1414, and internal political factions.

Despite the social, economic and political difficulties that the Sienese faced during the this period, successive government regimes continued to support projects for extending and further embellishing the city's principal buildings. Work continued slowly on the Cappella di Piazza that reached completion in its first form around 1376 (see pl. 95), with the sculpted figures on the piers being added between 1378 and 1382 (see pl. 1). Frescoes were commissioned in these years for some of the principal rooms in the Palazzo Pubblico (see pl. 64), and in the early decades of the fifteenth century three major painted schemes were commissioned by the newly formed government of the twelve Priors (see pls 77, 79–81). The same magistrates initiated an ambitious sculptural project for the Campo. To replace an earlier fountain, erected between 1334 and 1346 on the north side of the piazza, in 1408 they contracted the Sienese sculptor Jacopo della Quercia to

65 Jacopo della Quercia, the Fonte Gaia, before its removal from the Piazza del Campo (nineteenth-century photograph).

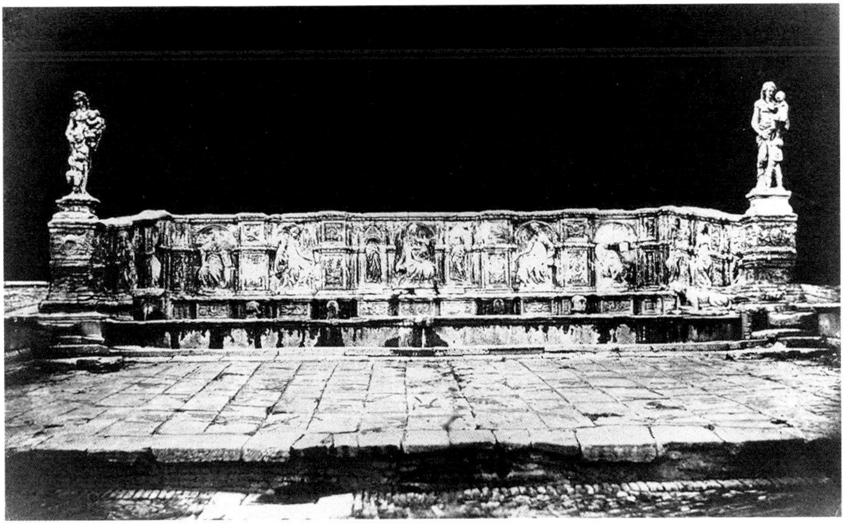

execute a monumental marble fountain incorporating both marble reliefs and statues in the round (pl. 65).[6] The 2000 gold florins paid to the sculptor for this commission is a measure of the government's commitment to this ambitious civic monument.

The project took ten years to complete but resulted in a fountain that was self-consciously Sienese and civic in content.[7] It also skilfully combined Christian imagery with the imagery of antiquity. An image of the Virgin, the patron of Siena, and her son acted as its centrepiece. Surrounded by seated figures representing the Christian Virtues, her role as the mother of God and the second Eve was highlighted by two narrative reliefs of the creation of Adam and the expulsion of Adam and Eve from paradise. Framing the entire complex were two statues representing Acca Laurentia, the mother of Romulus and Remus and thus grandmother to Senus and Aschius, the legendary founders of Siena itself, and Rhea Silvia, the foster-mother of Romulus and Remus. The message was clear: just as these two women of antiquity gave birth and nourishment to Romulus and Remus, so the Virgin would continue to protect and nurture the Sienese – provided they espoused the Christian Virtues portrayed on either side of her.

In respect of the cathedral, the pattern of government support for artistic projects appears, if anything, to have become even more consistent throughout the difficult decades of the second half of the fourteenth century. As already indicated, structural difficulties had led to the decision in June 1357 to abandon the Duomo Nuovo project, tear down the already completed vaults and proceed instead to complete the newly extended east end of the existing cathedral (see pl. 34). The next thirty-three years were devoted to completing the new chancel over the baptistery and adding a new clerestorey and vaulting to the whole length of the cathedral.[8] The re-fashioning of the east end of the cathedral included moving the high altar and the altars dedicated to the four patron saints of the city further east, together with their altarpieces, and commissioning a large number of choirstalls from local woodworkers to be placed both behind and in front of the high altar.[9] Further altarpieces were commissioned for side altars (see pls 73, 74), at least two of which were under the patronage of the city guilds, thus reflecting the more popular tone of the city's government during that time.[10]

As with the Palazzo Pubblico, a sustained campaign of artistic work took place in the cathedral during the first two decades of the fifteenth century. The walls of the chancel were decorated with frescoes, the chapels of the four patron saints were supplied with choirstalls and fresco paintings and a new sacristy was built onto the north-east corner of the building (see pl.

34).[11] As a result of the steeply sloping terrain, this extension to the cathedral had to be built out across an arch spanning the Via dei Fusari – an impressive feat of structural engineering. It, too, was embellished with frescoes and painted furnishing (see pls 75–6).

The Spedale and its Patronage of Art

As the city's principal charitable institution, the Spedale di Santa Maria della Scala faced new challenges in the decades when the Sienese were constantly confronted with outbreaks of plague and famine. It was also, however, the recipient of a large number of testamentary bequests from individuals who left part or all of their inheritance to the Spedale. The scale of the Spedale's newly acquired wealth can be judged by its purchase in 1359 of a collection of valuable relics from Constantinople for the astounding price of 3000 gold florins (pl. 66).[12] Enthusiastically supported by the government of the Twelve, the hospital authorities placed these relics in an especially created chapel on the ground floor of the rector's palace (see pl. 96). They also inaugurated an annual festival on the feast of the Annunciation at which both the Sienese and visiting pilgrims were given the opportunity to view and venerate these relics from a specially built pulpit on the façade of the hospital church (pl. 67). Probably as a direct result of this new focus upon the hospital and its church, in the 1370s the hospital authorities began to enlarge their church by moving the thirteenth-century orphanage for girls to another part of the building.[13]

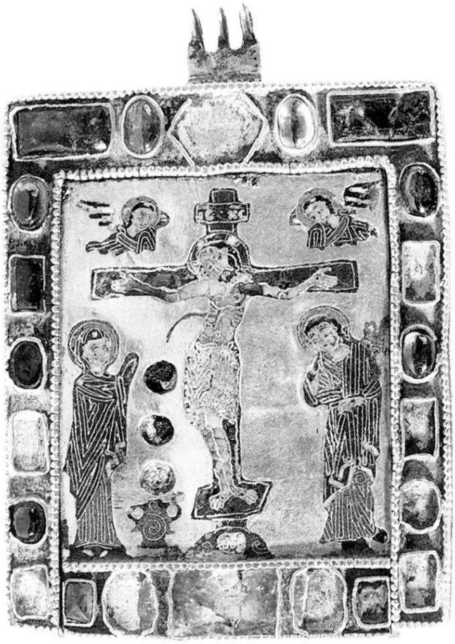

66 Byzantine reliquary containing a fragment of the Cross of the Crucifixion (twelfth century). Siena, Spedale di Santa Maria della Scala.

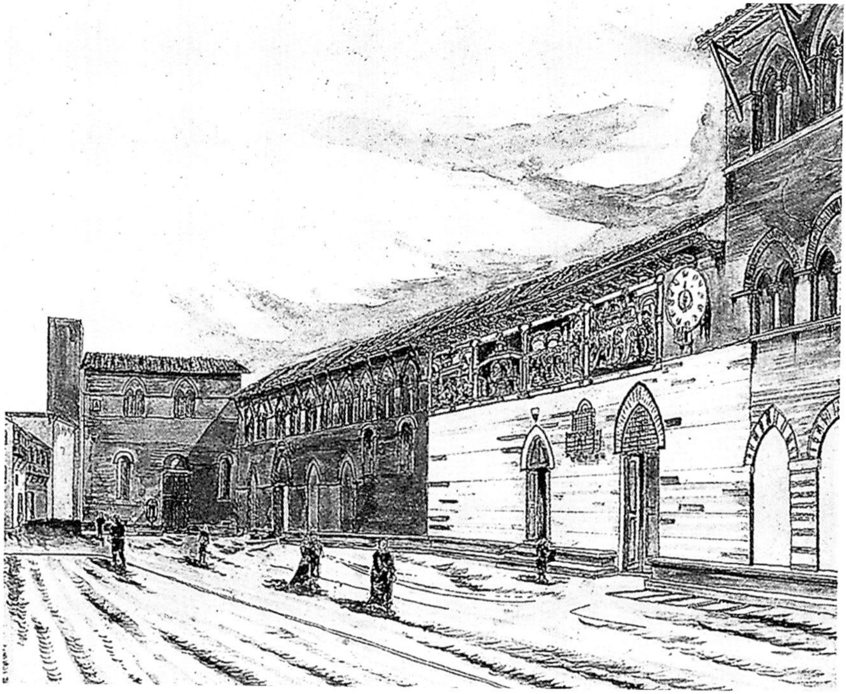

67 Reconstruction of the façade of the Spedale di Santa Maria della Scala in the fourteenth century (by Marco Parenti).

One of the most valuable relics that the Spedale acquired in 1359 was a piece of the Virgin's girdle, which she was alleged to have dropped to the apostle Thomas at the moment of her assumption into heaven.[14] Given that the feast of the Assumption was celebrated annually in the cathedral with great ceremony, this relic held huge significance both for the Spedale and for the Sienese in general. Moreover, the incident of Saint Thomas receiving the girdle became a common feature of Sienese paintings of the Assumption in the second half of the fourteenth century, as in the *Virgin of the Assumption* now in the Pinacoteca (pl. 68). Attributed to Bartolommeo Bulgarini – the painter responsible for the central panel of the cathedral altarpiece of Saint Victor (see pl. 60) – it was probably the centre of an altarpiece for the principal altar in the newly founded chapel of the relics within the Spedale (see pl. 96). On grounds of style it has been dated to the

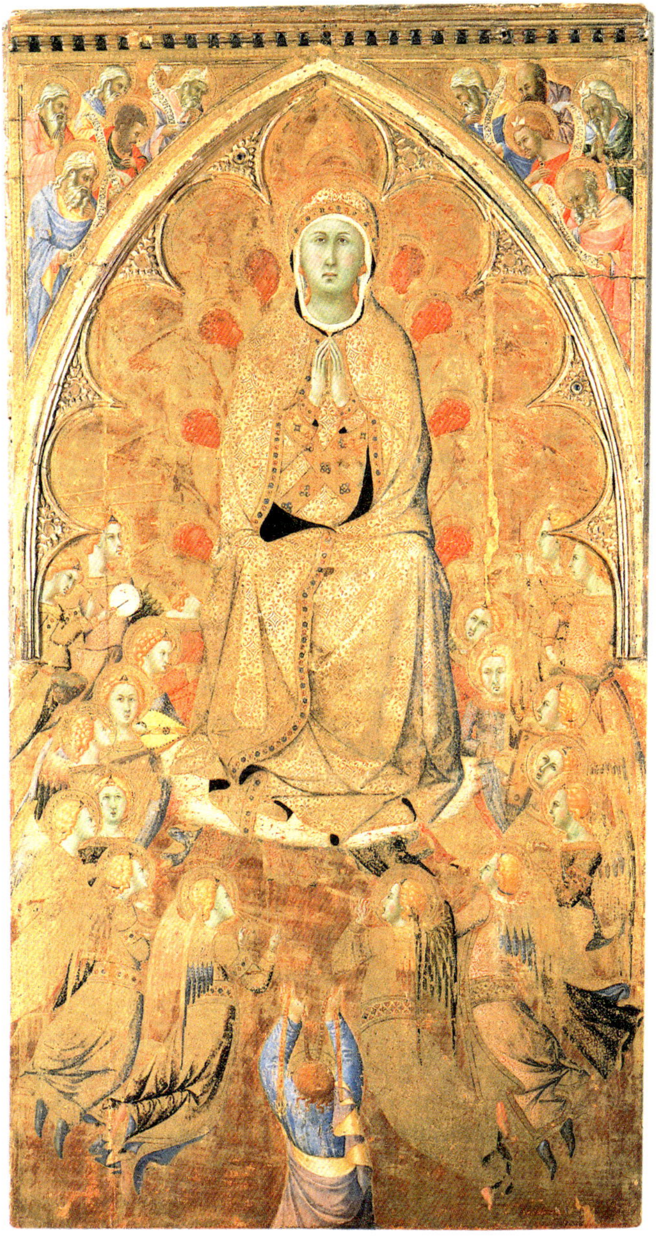

68 Bulgarini, *The Virgin of the Assumption with Saint Thomas receiving the Girdle* (1360s). Tempera on panel, 205 × 112 cm. Siena, Pinacoteca Nazionale.

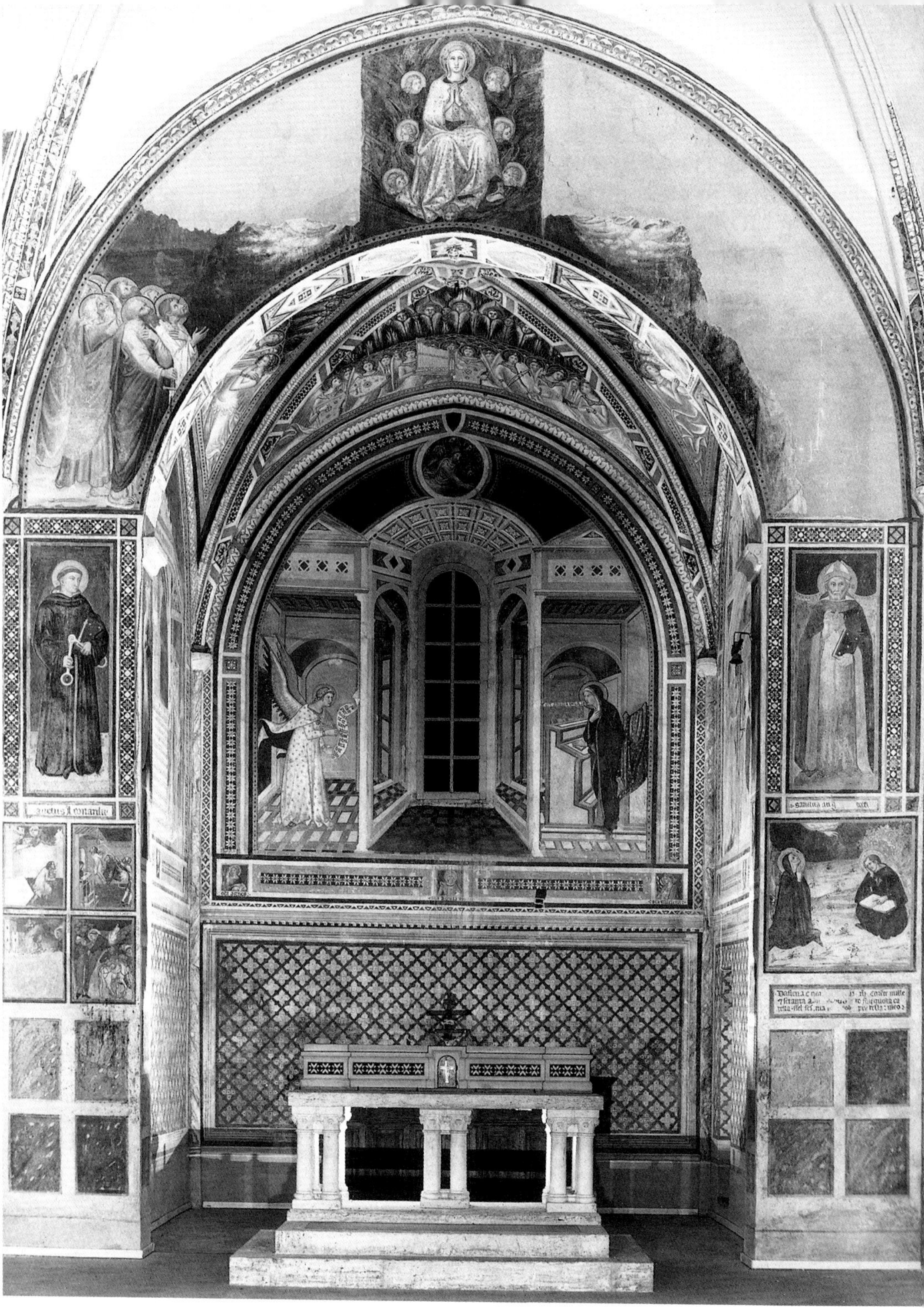

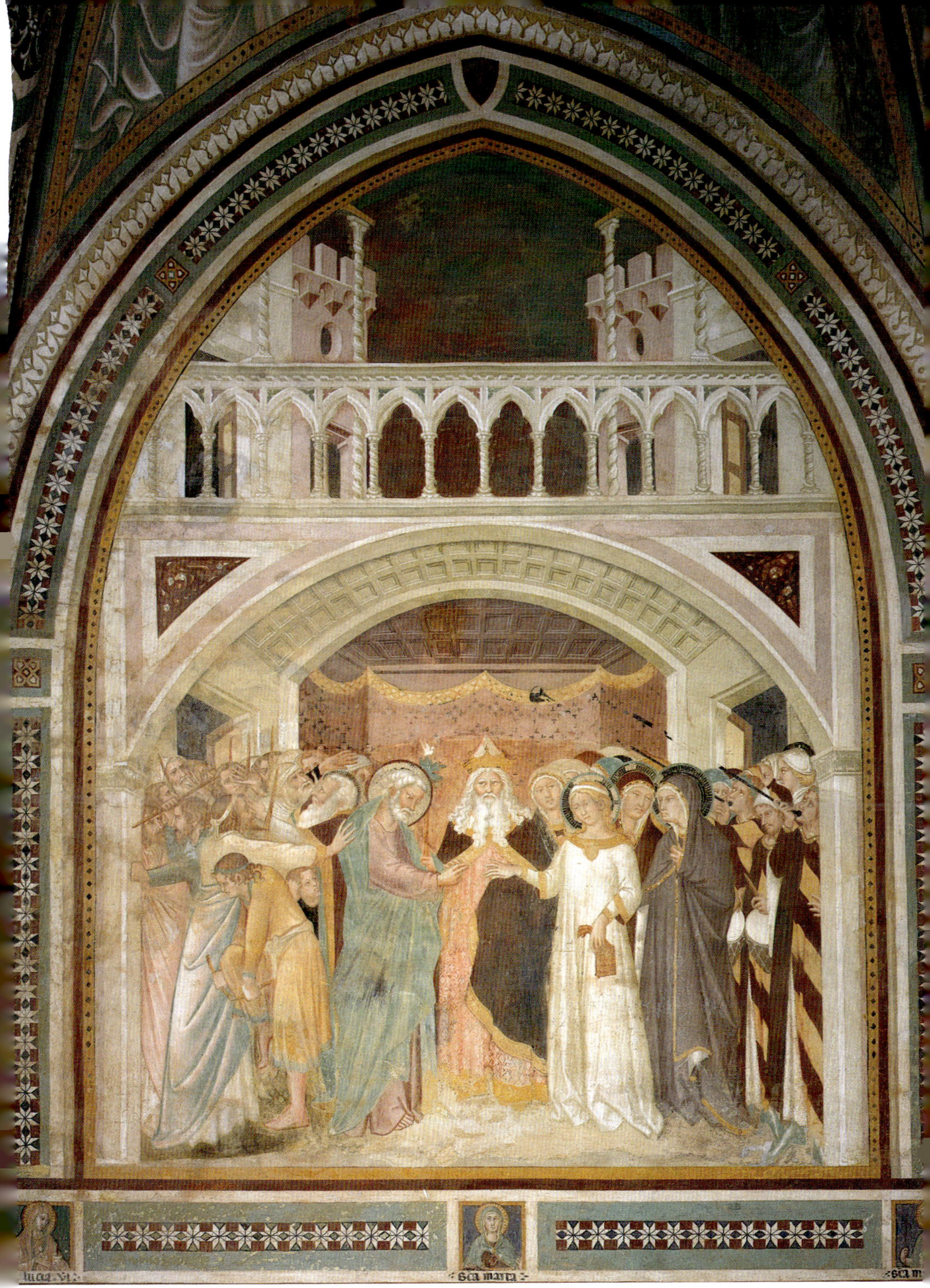

Sca marta

produce illuminations for choir books (see pl. 15).[19] The lay community that served the hospital followed the rule of the Augustinian Hermits and venerated the memory of the Blessed Agostino Novello (see pl. 54), who had died at San Leonardo al Lago. The area in which the hermitage was located – known as the Selva del Lago (the wood of the lake) – provided the hospital with vital commodities, such as straw. An early nineteenth-century description of the hermitage referred to paintings commissioned in 1360 by a rector of the Spedale. Although locating these in the cloister, rather than the church, of the hermitage, later scholars have assumed that this was in fact a reference to Lippo Vanni's fresco scheme. In addition, one of the votive figures on the inner face of the arch appears in the distinctive costume worn by the rectors of the Spedale.

The most compelling evidence, however, of the Spedale's influence over this commission occurs in the three large narrative paintings within the chancel itself and in the *Assumption of the Virgin* over the chancel arch. As indicated earlier, during the 1360s and 1370s the Spedale authorities increased the veneration of the Virgin in Siena by obtaining a collection of relics that included a piece of her girdle and by establishing a festival in her honour on the feast of the Annunciation. Thus, two of the scenes chosen for the San Leonardo scheme – the *Annunciation* and the *Assumption* – would have been especially relevant to the Spedale authorities at this particular point in the institution's history.

In addition, in the mid-1330s, Giovanni di Tese Tolomei, in his capacity as rector of the Spedale, had commissioned a series of frescoes depicting the early life of the Virgin from the city's leading painters.[20] These were located on the façade of the hospital church and therefore just to the left of the pulpit constructed in the early 1360s to display the relics on the feast of the Annunciation (see pl. 67). Early sources clearly indicate that this scheme included paintings of the presentation of the Virgin in the Temple and the betrothal of the Virgin to Joseph – two subjects that also feature prominently at San Leonardo (see pl. 70). Although it cannot be proved that a person or persons from the Spedale commissioned Lippo Vanni, it is clear that his patrons wanted him to emulate paintings executed some thirty years earlier for this civic institution. This painted scheme within a small rural church thus strongly suggests the enduring popularity of paintings of such images of the Virgin in Siena, and of the powerful influence exercised by the early fourteenth-century scheme of narrative paintings prominently displayed on the façade of one of the city's most prestigious buildings.

Since the Spedale façade frescoes are totally lost, it can only be a matter

70 (*previous page*) Lippo Vanni, *The Betrothal of the Virgin* (*c.* 1360–70). Fresco. South wall of the chancel, San Leonardo al Lago.

of informed speculation how closely Lippo Vanni might have copied them at San Leonardo. What is clear from the paintings at San Leonardo, however, is that he dealt with these traditional Marian subjects in a lively and imaginative manner. Probably inspired by a painting of the same subject by Ambrogio Lorenzetti for another *contado* church,[21] Lippo Vanni boldly incorporated the window frame of the chapel itself into the architectural setting for his painting of the *Annunciation* (see pl. 69). The grouping of the figures in the *Betrothal of the Virgin* is perhaps somewhat incoherent, but the characterisation of the figures is extremely expressive, while the treatment of the architectural setting is again assured (see pl. 70). The delicacy of the entire colour scheme, meanwhile, with its subtle range of apple greens, golden yellows, pinks and mauves is both effective and striking.

Bartolo di Fredi at Montalcino

The lost paintings of the early life of the Virgin on the façade of the Spedale of Santa Maria della Scala (see pl. 67) appear to have influenced another important painting commissioned for a church in the Sienese *contado*. In this instance, the outcome was an ambitiously conceived polyptych of the *Coronation of the Virgin* (pl. 71). Signed and dated 1388 by Bartolo di Fredi, it was executed for a chapel in the church of San Francesco in the town of Montalcino to the south of Siena.[22] In 1361 the authorities of Montalcino agreed the terms of a new set of legal obligations towards Siena and its government. Siena's political control over Montalcino was underlined by the construction of a fortress on the south side of the town. One of the signatories to the agreement was a lawyer, Griffo di Ser Paolo, who served a term as the prior of the confraternity of Saint Peter that commissioned the altarpiece from Bartolo di Fredi in 1383. The painter, meanwhile, appears to have had a number of other connections with Montalcino, both as an agent for the Sienese government (in 1375 and 1376) and as a painter – securing at least four major commissions in the 1380s and 1390s.[23]

The *Coronation of the Virgin* polyptych now forms one of the most eye-catching exhibits of the newly created civic museum in Montalcino and – apart from missing two predella panels and two pinnacle panels[24] – gives a strong sense of its original appearance, size and programme. The two wooden statues that presently stand on either side of it, although commissioned some ten years earlier, were also probably part of the original ensem-

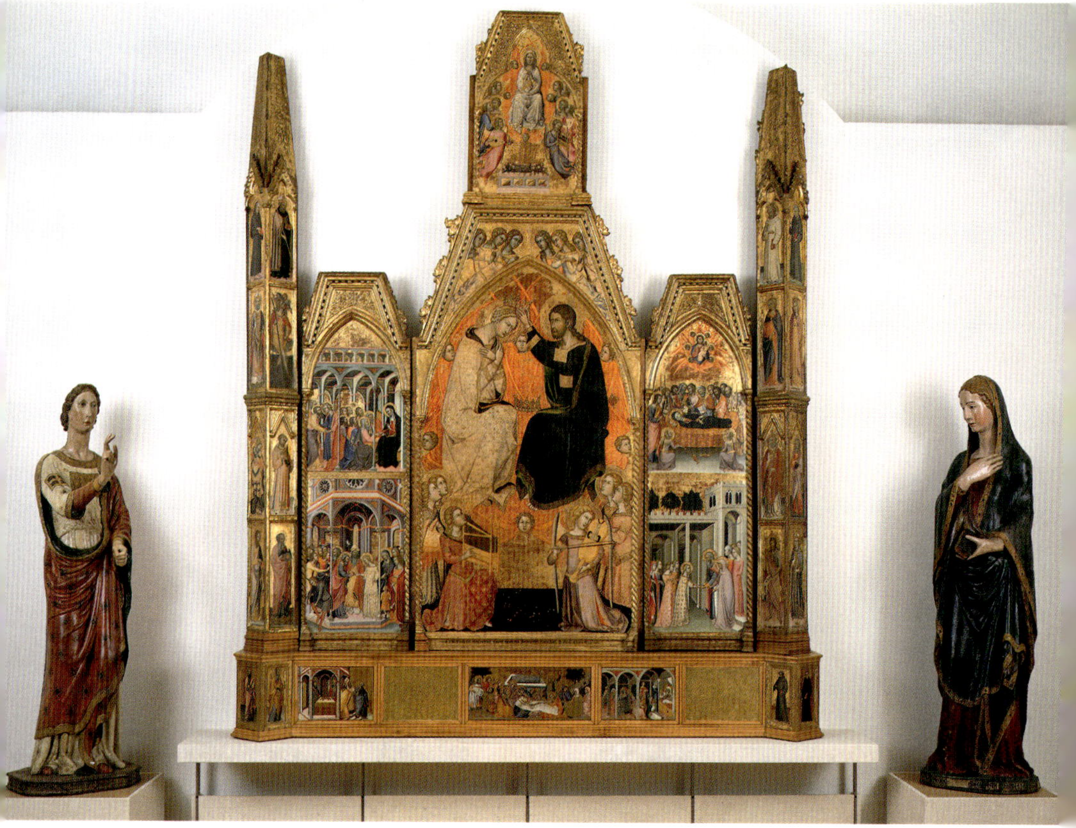

71 Bartolo di Fredi, *The Coronation of the Virgin* (1388). Tempera on panel, 332 × 279 cm. Domenico di Agostino (attrib.), *The Virgin of the Annunciation* (1369) and Angelo di Nalduccio (attrib.), *The Archangel Gabriel* (1370). Polychrome wood, 181 cm and 176 cm. Montalcino, Museo Civico e Diocesano d'Arte Sacra.

ble in the confraternity chapel.[25] This altarpiece, which approaches the scale and complexity of the front face of Duccio's *Maestà* (see pl. 35) and of Pietro Lorenzetti's Carmelite altarpiece (pl. 44), offers a compelling example of the ambition of Sienese altarpiece design in the 1380s. The central panel displays an elegant representation of the Virgin at the moment of her coronation as queen of heaven. Above this arresting image is a smaller painting of the *Virgin of the Assumption*, a subject with strong political overtones for the Sienese and their subjects. The remaining panels

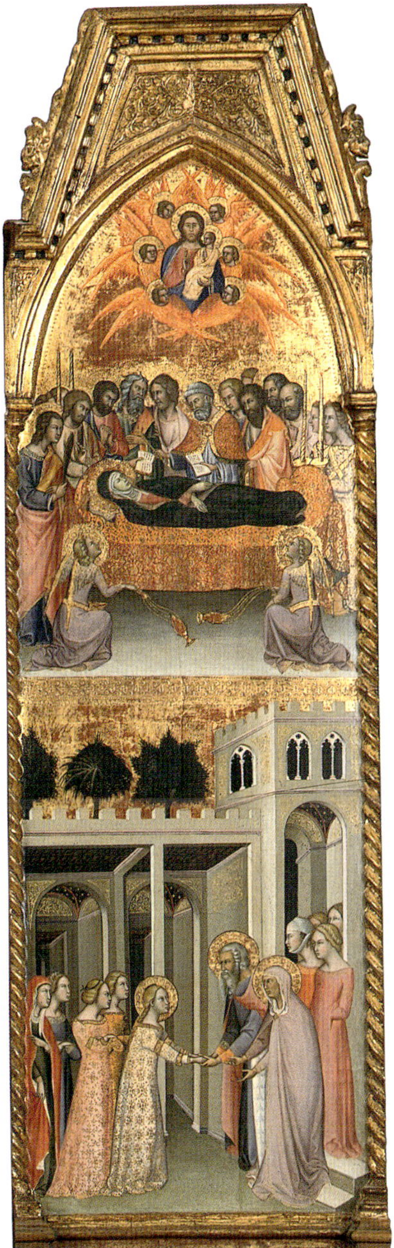

72 Bartolo di Fredi, *Scenes from the Life of the Virgin* (detail of pl. 71).

are devoted to scenes from the early life of the Virgin and the events surrounding her death and assumption (pls 71, 72). The narrative follows a sequence that begins on the left-hand side of the predella, progresses from left to right across the predella and then proceeds from the lower left to lower right of the side panels, ending with the upper left and upper right side panels.

As on other early fourteenth-century altarpieces devoted principally to the glorification of the Virgin, the polyptych includes other kinds of religious imagery. At the centre of the predella – close to where mass would be celebrated at the altar – there is an image of the dead Christ being mourned by the Virgin and other saints. On the massive architectural piers, meanwhile, appear small-scale paintings representing various saints, all of whom had a special relevance for members of the confraternity and the Franciscan Order.[26]

The *Coronation of the Virgin* polyptych is remarkable in that it was commissioned by provincial patrons from a leading Sienese painter and closely emulated the scale and imagery of earlier altarpieces designed for high altars within Siena's major churches. Undoubtedly much of the altarpiece's imagery was chosen to reflect the concerns and preoccupations of the members of the confraternity of Saint Peter and the Franciscans in whose church they met. Yet it is striking how much of its imagery also seems to reflect major iconographical themes derived from earlier Sienese art. Nowhere is this more obvious than in the inclusion of a seldom depicted scene of the return of the Virgin to the house of her parents – an event that, yet again, once formed part of the frescoes for the façade of the Spedale di Santa Maria della Scala (see pl. 67).

As with the frescoes at San Leonardo al Lago, there are a number of historical factors to account for this further example of the copying of an earlier scheme of painting. Firstly, Griffo di Ser Paolo, prior of the confraternity of Saint Peter during the 1360s, had also been a member of a Sienese confraternity that met in the vaults of the Spedale di Santa Maria della Scala. Secondly, in 1385 Bartolo di Fredi had himself received a commission from another confraternity based in the Spedale. Thirdly, there appear to have been close links between the hospitals of the Misericordia and Santa Maria della Croce in Montalcino and members of the confraternity of Saint Peter. Like their Sienese counterpart, one of the principal charitable functions of these two hospitals was to provide dowries for young women to marry. The subjects of the *Betrothal of the Virgin* and the *Return of the Virgin to the House of her Parents*, with their focus upon the Virgin's marriage, would therefore have been of special relevance to the hospital authorities, and possibly to the members of the confraternity of Saint Peter as well.[27] In short, what might on first impression appear to be a lack of originality on the part of the painter was much more probably the result of Bartolo di Fredi responding in a concrete and specific manner to the wishes and concerns of his confraternity patrons. They in turn wanted their altarpiece to reflect and emulate the scale and magnificence of paintings produced earlier in the century for major civic sites in Siena itself.

More Altarpieces for the Cathedral

The pattern of indebtedness to the work of earlier fourteenth-century Sienese painters also occurs in the city's cathedral. As noted before, during the second half of the fourteenth century the interior of the cathedral was extensively remodelled, particularly at the east end of the building. By the 1380s, however, it appears that the high altar and its double-sided altarpiece and the altars of the four patron saints with their narrative altarpieces had all been relocated in the newly extended and remodelled east end (see pl. 57). At this point, attention turned to commissioning altarpieces for the altars in the aisles and transepts of the cathedral.

In the early fifteenth-century inventories of the cathedral the dedications of these altars are systematically listed, with brief indications of the subject matter of their painted or sculpted images.[28] Unfortunately, it is by no means clear when these images were placed over the altars, but two paintings have been identified as altarpieces commissioned for the cathedral during the 1380s and 1390s. The earlier of these is a large-scale narrative painting of the *Adoration of the Magi*, first recorded in the collection of the Siena Pinacoteca in 1816 (pl. 73). Since 1842, it has been attributed to Bartolo di Fredi and dated on grounds of style to about 1385–8.[29] It would thus have been painted at approximately the same time as the *Coronation of the Virgin* polyptych for Montalcino.

The cathedral inventory of 1420 names the third altar (from the west) in the north aisle as the altar and panel of the Magi. A more descriptive entry in the inventory of 1423 refers to the chapel of the Magi and a panel painting of the 'story' of the Magi with Saint Catherine and Saint Leonard on either side of it.[30] The subject matter of the painting in the Pinacoteca obviously fits such a description. At first sight it also appears from the 1423 entry that the altarpiece of the Magi corresponded in its basic format to that of the four earlier altarpieces for the altars of the four patron saints (see pls 58, 60). The earlier altarpieces, however, all had panel paintings as

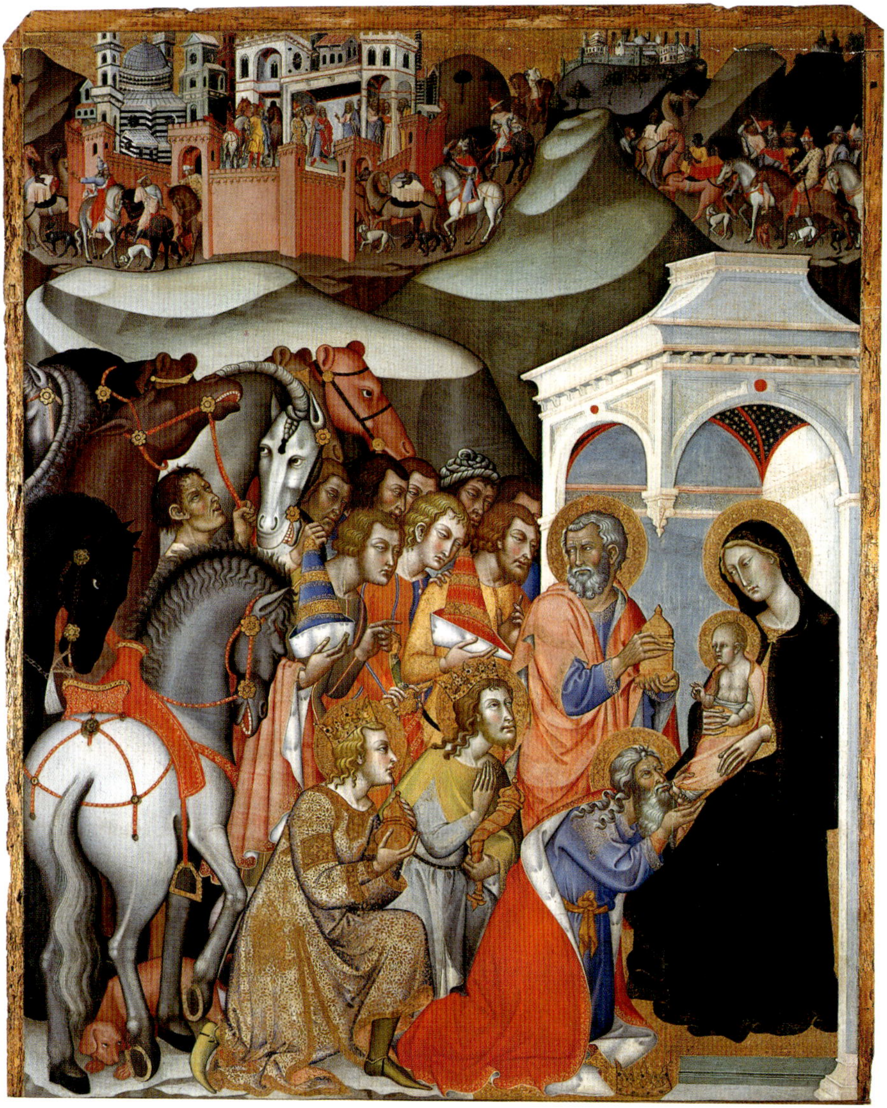

73 Bartolo di Fredi, *The Adoration of the Magi* (*c.* 1385–8). Tempera on panel, 195 × 163 cm. Siena, Pinacoteca Nazionale.

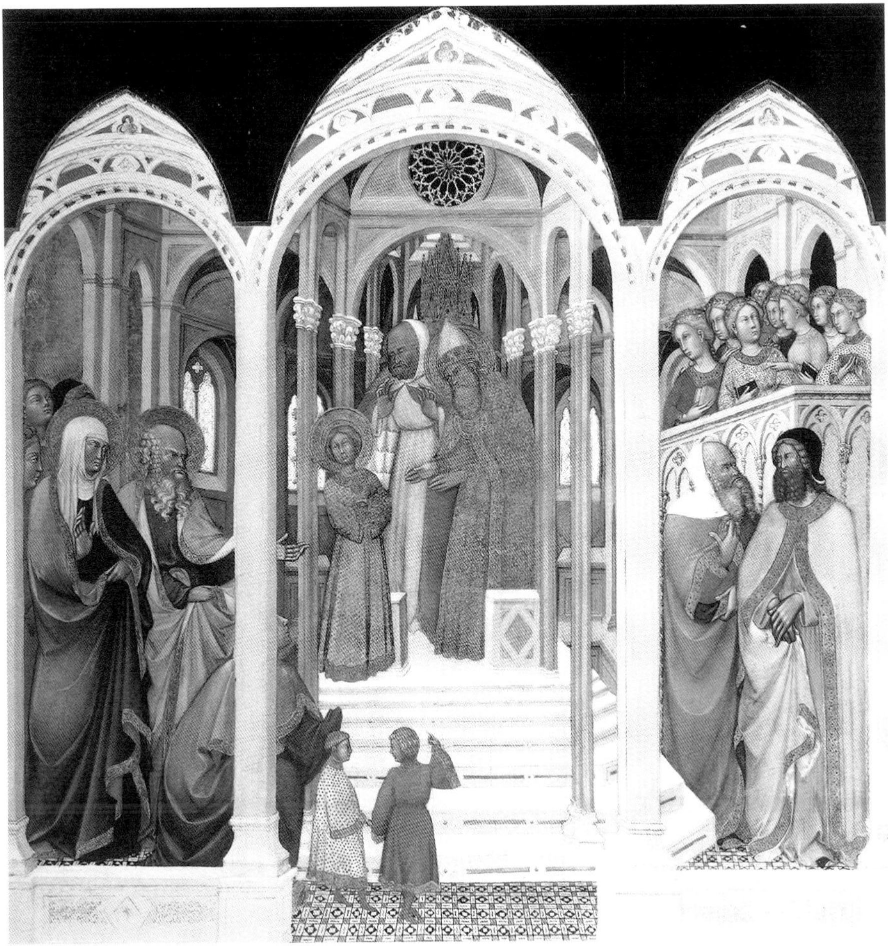

74 Paolo di Giovanni Fei, *The Presentation of the Virgin in the Temple* (*c.* 1390). Tempera on panel, 147 × 140 cm. Washington, National Gallery of Art.

their side paintings, whereas in the case of the later altarpiece it apparently combined a central painting on panel with fresco paintings on either side. Thus, on the wall behind the present sixteenth-century altarpiece, there are remains of what seem to be fourteenth-century frescoes of two standing figures of saints. These have been identified as Saint Anthony Abbot (who as an elderly hermit saint could easily have been confused with

Leonard by the compiler of the 1423 inventory) and Saint Catherine of Alexandria.[31]

The surviving panel itself suggests that Bartolo di Fredi was required to produce a painting that represented a well-known biblical event in a lively and engaging way and at the same time to fulfil the traditional devotional requirements of an altarpiece. In terms of the former, the painting offers an animated pageant of the three kings – each figure rendered distinctive in terms of age, physiognomy and rich apparel – together with their attendants. These in turn present a range of types of people – the three pages holding the swords and elegant hats of the kings and appearing in richer clothes and with fairer complexions than the servants holding the horses behind them. The horses, while not wholly realistic, present a bold pattern of curving necks and contours on the left-hand side of the composition.

There appears in the background a detailed depiction of the journey of the kings and their retinue, first to Jerusalem to meet Herod and then to Bethlehem. Just as Ambrogio Lorenzetti's representation of the Temple in the *Presentation* altarpiece deliberately evoked the architecture of the cathedral (see pl. 61), so Bartolo's depiction of Jerusalem includes a strikingly well-observed view of the exterior of the cathedral, thus once again reiterating the cherished civic myth of Siena as a second Jerusalem.

In terms of the painting as a suitable adjunct to the celebration of mass on the altar below, it is significant that the kings' act of veneration takes place in the immediate foreground, the part of the painting that would have been closest to the priest celebrating mass at the altar. The Christ Child, who embodies the eucharist, is similarly located in the lower part of the painting. The entire composition of the lower half has been arranged in such a way as to give a strong impetus to read the narrative from left to right, therefore towards the east end of the cathedral where the sanctuary and high altar lay (see pl. 57). Thus, although Bartolo's altarpiece perhaps lacks both the compositional coherence and the gravity and monumentality of Pietro and Ambrogio Lorenzetti's altarpieces, it nevertheless must once have represented a highly colourful and engaging addition to the fourteenth-century altarpieces in the cathedral.

Bartolo di Fredi with his son Andrea and another Sienese painter, Luca di Tommè, were commissioned in 1389 by the guild of shoemakers to paint an altarpiece for their altar in the cathedral. The work has since been lost, but entries in the cathedral inventories indicate that its subject was the assumption of the Virgin – a popular enough subject in contemporary Sienese painting.[32] Since the altar of the guild is named in the inventories as the fourth altar in the north aisle, it would have been to the immediate right of the Magi (see pl. 57). Some nine years later, it appears that the altar to the left of the Magi altar also received a narrative altarpiece. Described in the inventory of 1423 as the 'chapel' of Saint Peter and as embellished with a panel painting of 'Saint Peter and Paul with the offering of our lady in the middle',[33] the central painting of this altarpiece has been identified as the *Presentation of the Virgin in the Temple* (pl. 74). This painting has convincingly been attributed to Paolo di Giovanni Fei, a Sienese painter who in 1398 received payment from the cathedral Opera for work on the 'panel of Saint Peter'.[34]

In 1392 and 1393 Bartolo di Fredi too was paid for work on the 'panel of Saint Peter' and it has therefore been suggested that, like the 1389 shoemakers' altarpiece, this was a joint commission given to both Bartolo di Fredi and Paolo di Giovanni Fei. Whether the lapse of some five to six years was the result of Bartolo di Fredi failing to complete his part of the work or just a case of a drawn-out project – as with the earlier altarpieces of the patron saints – is now impossible to determine. It seems likely, however, that Bartolo di Fredi was responsible for the side panels depicting Saints Peter and Paul described in the cathedral inventories. Although these no longer survive, their probable appearance can be judged from two paintings of these saints by Bartolo di Fredi for another altarpiece.[35]

The original state of the altarpiece of Saint Peter would therefore have borne a clear similarity to the earlier altarpieces of the patron saints. Like them, its centrepiece would have been a narrative painting surmounted by three pointed arches (see pls 58–61). On either side would have been a relatively narrow side panel containing a single figure of a standing saint. In terms of its composition and painted architecture, moreover, this version of the *Presentation of the Virgin in the Temple* adopted many of the features of the Lorenzetti altarpieces. Thus, the ambitious portrayal of the exterior façade and the interior of the Temple, with its polygonal apse and vaulted chapels, owed much to Ambrogio Lorenzetti's earlier altarpiece of the *Presentation in the Temple* (see pl. 61). While appreciation of the full extent of Paolo di Giovanni Fei's pictorial illusionism is hampered by the fact that the painting has lost its original frame and been cut down at the top, it remains clear that the painter borrowed ideas from Pietro Lorenzetti's *Birth of the Virgin* (see pl. 59).[36] Like Pietro Lorenzetti, Paolo di Giovanni Fei divided his scene by means of two cream-coloured piers and portrayed these as if they supported the pointed arches of the now lost frame. He also adopted the convention of placing one of the protagonists of the painting partly behind the painted pier on the left.

By dividing the panel in this way, the painter could place the principal cult figure of the Virgin in the centre of the painting, yet convey a strong sense of the sanctuary being the most sacred part of the Temple. In the side sections, meanwhile, he was able to depict figures who are either presenting the young girl to the High Priest or who are destined to be her companions in the Temple. The pose of the Virgin, with her crossed arms, closely resembles the young boy in Pietro Lorenzetti's *Birth of the Virgin* bringing the news of the Virgin's birth to Joachim and his companion (see pl. 59). The solemnity of the event is lightened by human touches such as the young Virgin turning her head towards her parents and the curiosity of the young girls enclosed in an upper choir on the right-hand side of the painting. Although such features were common in fourteenth-century depictions of this subject, the frequency and similarity of their appearance in contemporary Sienese paintings suggest the impact of a powerful model. This is most likely, once again, to have been Ambrogio Lorenzetti's painting of the *Presentation of the Virgin* on the façade of the Spedale di Santa Maria della Scala (see pl. 67).

By 1400, therefore, it appears that a sequence of side altars in the cathedral had been embellished with altarpieces that shared a number of features. Although subtly different in terms of their overall design, they all showed as their central image a narrative scene devoted to the life of the Virgin. On either side of this central narrative painting appeared two further images, either painted on panel as part of the altarpiece or as fresco on the walls next to the altarpiece. These represented, on the left, the titular saint of the altar and, on the right, an appropriate companion saint. In their original state, all these altarpieces would have had elaborately carved wooden frames and predellas, the latter probably painted with narrative scenes. Beginning with Pietro Lorenzetti's *Birth of the Virgin* (see pl. 59) for the altar of Saint Savino and ending with the lost *Assumption of the Virgin* for the shoemakers' guild, all the major feasts of the Virgin were therefore commemorated over the cathedral altars. The fact that this had been achieved by the cathedral authorities with the co-operation of other corporate patrons, such as the guild of shoemakers, is a further testimony to the enduring strength of devotion felt by the Sienese towards their principal patron saint, the Virgin.

* * *

The Cathedral Sacristy: Frescoes and Furnishings

This continuing commitment to celebrating the Virgin through the medium of painted imagery was also expressed in the interior embellishment of the new cathedral sacristy. Built under the leadership of a particularly active cathedral *operaio*, Caterino Corsini, the sacristy comprises a large room covered by a wooden roof with three vaulted chapels at its east end. The fifteenth-century inventories make it clear that the right-hand chapel, designated 'the chapel of the books', housed the cathedral's library of liturgical and theological books, and that the left-hand chapel contained its valuable collection of relics. In the principal space were stored vestments for the cathedral clergy and all the furnishings used for the liturgy. It was in this room that the cathedral clergy put on their vestments and prepared for the celebration of mass.

After the painting of the sacristy roof and vaults by a team led by the Pisan Gualtieri di Giovanni, work began on the walls of the three chapels in about 1411 and continued to 1413. It seems that the Sienese painter Benedetto di Bindo was in charge of this stage of the commission – receiving an annual salary from the Opera for his work. The same painter was entrusted with the painted decoration of two pieces of elaborate woodwork executed by the talented woodworker Domenico di Niccolò.[37]

Dedicated to the Virgin as the titular saint of the cathedral and patron saint of the city, the central chapel was painted with four scenes of the Virgin's early life. They illustrated precisely the same four subjects that had been chosen for the façade of the Spedale di Santa Maria della Scala some seventy years earlier (see pl. 67). On the upper part of the north wall appears the *Birth of the Virgin*, on the upper part of the south wall, the *Presentation of the Virgin in the Temple*, on the lower part of the north wall, the *Betrothal of the Virgin*, and on the lower part of the south wall, the *Return of the Virgin to the House of her Parents*. Indeed, despite their now fragmentary state, these four paintings have been used by art historians as evidence of what the early fourteenth-century hospital frescoes might once have looked like.[38] Thus, for example, in the *Betrothal of the Virgin* (pl. 75), the unusual loggia, seen at a sharp angle, and the distinctive musicians on the right-hand side of the painting, have been identified as typical of the work of Simone Martini (see pl. 55) – the presumed painter of this scene in the hospital series. The inclusion of such 'copies' of this famous early fourteenth-century fresco cycle in the early fifteenth-century painted decoration of the cathedral sacristy demonstrates not only the enduring value placed on work of Simone Martini and the Lorenzetti brothers by the

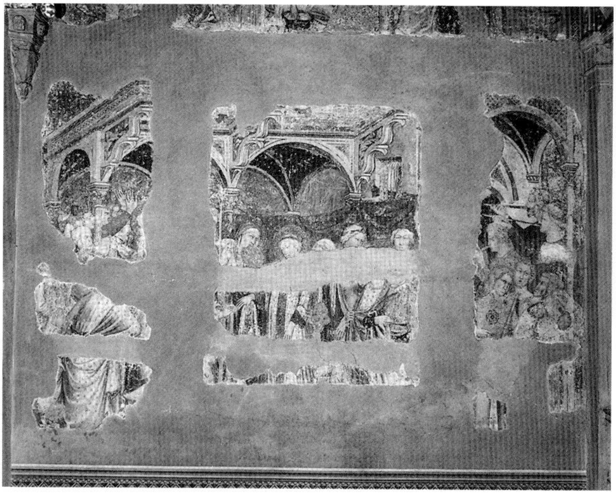

75 Benedetto di Bindo (attrib.), *The Betrothal of the Virgin* (*c.* 1411–13). Remains of a fresco in the central chapel of the sacristy, Siena cathedral.

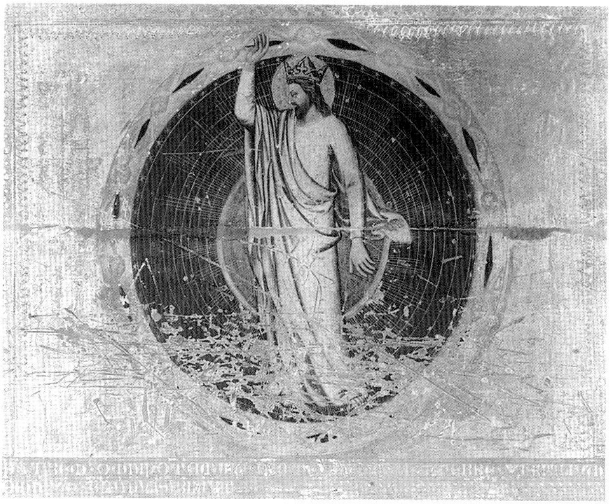

76 Benedetto di Bindo (attrib.), *The Second Article of the Creed* ('I believe in God the Father, maker of heaven and earth'), (*c.* 1411–13). Tempera on panel, Siena, Museo dell'Opera del Duomo.

cathedral authorities but also the high regard for continuity and tradition in Sienese culture.

The other two chapels were similarly decorated with frescoes that have survived in only a fragmentary state. In the 'chapel of the books', the subject matter of the surviving fresco on each wall complements the chapel's function as a repository for the cathedral library. They accordingly depict the Virgin, Christ and Saint Augustine, the last in the company of other exponents of Christian learning. It has plausibly been suggested that this choice of subject reflected current concerns about the threat posed to the faithful by the effects of both the papal schism – in which no less than three individuals were claiming to be pope – and of the allegedly heretical beliefs of men like John Wyclif and John Hus.[39]

Two paintings decorated the chapel of the relics whose subject matter again reflected the chapel's role. One of the paintings – now badly damaged – shows the Virgin appealing to the Christ Child on behalf of a group of people located in an urban setting. The other shows a procession, led by Pope Gregory the Great, making its way to Castel Sant'Angelo in Rome and witnessing a vision of the Archangel Michael on the castle battlements. Since the latter event was supposed to have taken place during an outbreak of plague in the city, it seems likely that both frescoes relate to such concerns.[40] Between 1410 and 1411, Siena had once more experienced a particularly severe outbreak of plague, causing the government to order a penitential procession through the city as a means of appealing to God and the Virgin to alleviate the suffering of the Sienese. It is likely that some of the cathedral relics were carried in this procession as a further way of encouraging a miracle of this sort.

The cathedral relics were housed in a large wooden cupboard, the doors of which were painted on both the back and the front by Benedetto di Bindo and his assistants. Now housed in the cathedral museum, the painted scheme of the cupboard is fairly straightforward, showing sixteen half-length angels on the exterior of the doors, each carrying a scroll on which is written the name of the relic that was once housed behind that particular panel. The inner surfaces, meanwhile, display a series of lively narrative scenes illustrating the history of the Cross of the Crucifixion.[41] One of the most prized relics belonging to the cathedral was a fragment of this revered object.

Benedetto di Bindo was also responsible for the painted decoration of another important piece of wooden furniture for the sacristy. Now disassembled and surviving only as separate panel paintings in the cathedral museum, it originally took the form of a series of cupboards that ran along the entire length of the south wall of the sacristy proper. These were used as storage for vestments and other liturgical objects. Above the cupboards would have been two tiers of painted wood panels acting as a kind of ornate backboard. The lower tier would have consisted of twelve paintings, each illustrating, in visual and written form, one of the articles of the Creed, the Church's principal statement of belief. The upper tier would then have shown a series of thirty-six standing figures arranged in groups of three, each comprised of a prophet, an apostle and an angel. Surmounting the entire ensemble would have been a star-spangled canopy.[42]

In their original location, placed at eye-level on the south wall of the sacristy, Benedetto di Bindo's paintings of the Creed would have provided the priests preparing for mass with a powerful reminder of the central tenets of Christian belief. The painter once again probably had a model in the series of paintings executed by Ambrogio Lorenzetti in about 1338 for the chapterhouse of the Augustinian priory of Sant'Agostino in Siena. According to Vasari, these paintings showed the apostles, each carrying a scroll on which was written one of the articles of the Creed.[43] Benedetto di Bindo elaborated on this original design by representing the apostles as more minor features of the scheme, portraying them with prophets and angels, while representing each statement of the Creed as a larger painted image. Focussing upon God the Father, God the Son and God the Holy Ghost, the painter relied on the impact of one or two figures silhouetted against an abstract background of gold leaf to convey the substance and significance of the painted text below. Thus, in the panel illustrating the article of the Creed that declares 'I believe in God the Father Almighty, maker of heaven and earth', the lyrical figure of God is portrayed in profile, blessing his new creation of the world, which appears as a series of spheres painted in delicate shades of blue and framed by an aureole of red-faced cherubim (pl. 76). Such was the apparent success of this series of paintings that its subject was subsequently used again in two later painted schemes, one in the sacristy of the hospital church of Santa Maria della Scala and the other in the cathedral baptistery (see pls 102, 103).[44]

Frescoes in the Palazzo Pubblico

In the opening years of the fifteenth century following the short but ignominious period of Visconti rule in Siena, the new government commissioned several large artistic projects for the Palazzo Pubblico.

THE CAPPELLA DEI SIGNORI

The earliest of these projects was for a chapel that was constructed in about 1404–5 on the first floor, next to the still important Sala del Mappamondo (see pls 46, 48). As soon as the Cappella dei Signori was finished, the government commissioned Taddeo di Bartolo to paint its walls and vaulting, paying him for the work at regular intervals between 1406 and 1408.

A painted inscription at the entrance of the chapel informs the visitor that it was painted in 1407.[45]

As the records of the payments make clear, the frescoes were commissioned by the government's principal magistracy, a fact that is made apparent by the imagery itself. First and foremost the paintings honour the Virgin, as in the slightly later scheme for the central chapel of the cathedral sacristy. Thus, the north wall of the chapel is embellished with four large mural paintings depicting events surrounding the death of the Virgin – the arrival of the apostles at her death bed, Christ receiving her soul at the moment of her death, the funeral procession to her burial site and Christ raising the body of the Virgin from her tomb (pl. 77). *The Funeral of the Virgin* in particular offers a sense of Taddeo di Bartolo's considerable abilities as a painter of narrative: the foreground is occupied by an impressive procession of monumentally conceived figures of different ages, genders and ethnic types (pl. 78). In the background, meanwhile, appears an assured view of a walled city, the buildings of which resemble those of Siena itself, yet again making an implicit parallel between the holy city of Jerusalem and Siena.

On the east or altar wall, Taddeo di Bartolo's frescoes probably once framed a polyptych by Simone Martini depicting the Virgin and Christ Child with saints – another indication that the early fifteenth-century Sienese civic authorities still greatly valued the work of this early fourteenth-century painter.[46] Directly above the altarpiece would have been a *Coronation of the Virgin* (now lost) executed by Taddeo di Bartolo as a replacement for an earlier painting of the same subject. This celebratory theme is continued in Taddeo's paintings of angels dancing and making music in the vaults. Finally, at the top of the altar wall, there remain frescoes by him of the Archangel Gabriel and the Virgin of the Annunciation. The painted imagery of the altar wall would therefore have focussed on the intercessory role of the Virgin as the mother of God and queen of heaven.

In the painted borders of the frescoes appear numerous depictions of Siena's civic emblems of the *balzana* and the lion of the Popolo. On the remaining surfaces of the walls painted figures depict the four Evangelists, each in the company of one of the doctors of the Church, four of the Old Testament prophets, the seven Christian Virtues and nine figures of male saints. The placing of these figures is carefully planned in relation to the chapel's function as the principal place of worship in the Palazzo Pubblico. Thus, the roundels depicting the four civic Virtues of Fortitude, Prudence, Justice and Temperance are most visible to the visitor leaving the chapel – as they would have been to the city magistrates as they left the chapel to

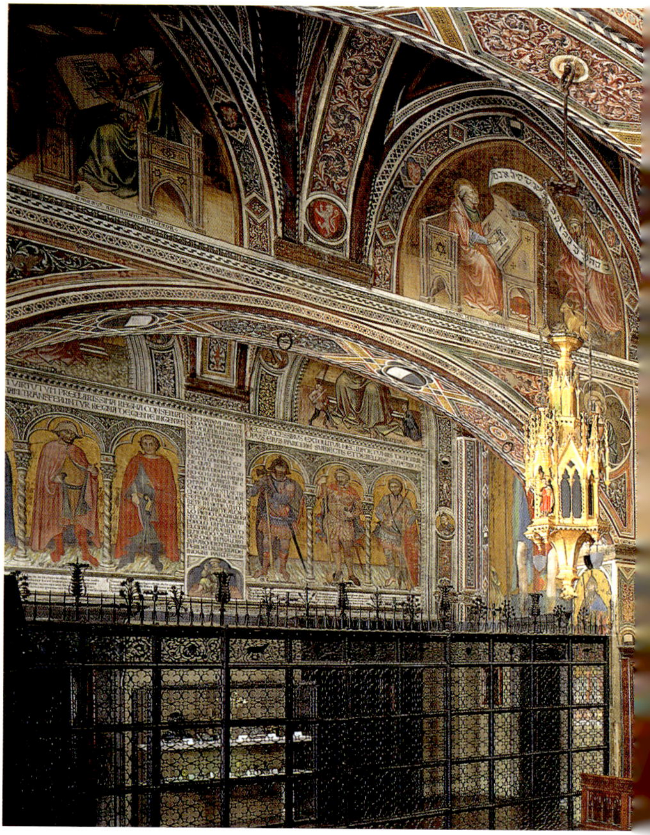

77 The Cappella dei Signori with frescoes by Taddeo di Bartolo. Siena, Palazzo Pubblico.

resume their official duties. Depicted on the piers supporting the chapel vaults is a series of saints each of whom either founded one of the principal mendicant orders in the city or who enjoyed particular veneration in Siena. An eighteenth-century source reports that mass was celebrated in the chapel by a cleric from each of the mendicant orders in turn, which suggests that the inclusion of these saints can appropriately be interpreted as a further demonstration of the intricately civic nature of this painted scheme.[47]

Four further paintings in the chapel allude to more specific political concerns of the Sienese government at the time the scheme was commissioned. In one of the chapel lunettes is a painting of a relatively obscure saint, Peter of Alexandria, holding in his left hand two flags carrying the civic emblems

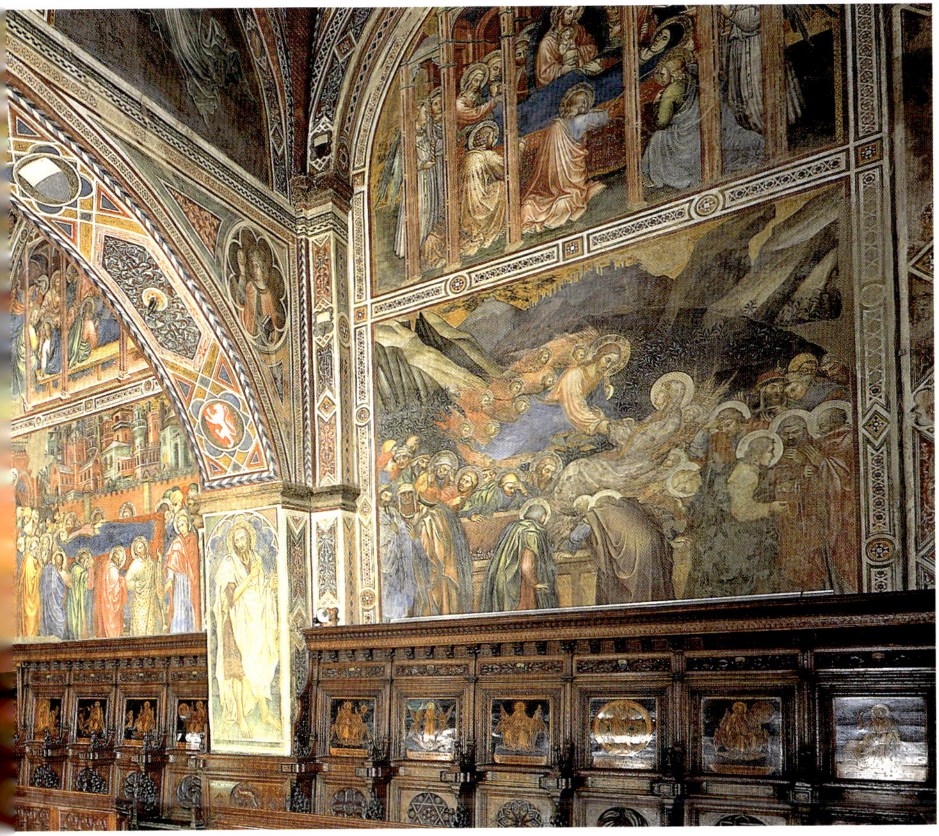

of the *balzana* and the lion. It was on this saint's feast day that the government of the twelve Priors came into power and it was therefore highly appropriate that he should be included in the painted imagery of their new chapel. Moreover, the saint is represented as a pope, a fact that carried further political connotations because, during the years in which the chapel was being painted, the twelve Priors played a minor but important role in events surrounding the resolution of a papal schism. Between September 1407 and January 1408, and again in September 1408, they played host to one of the contenders for the papal throne, the Venetian Gregory XII. Although the paintings for the chapel were commissioned in 1406 – and therefore before Gregory's visit – and were primarily intended to celebrate the Virgin and the city of Siena, it appears that part at least of the painted

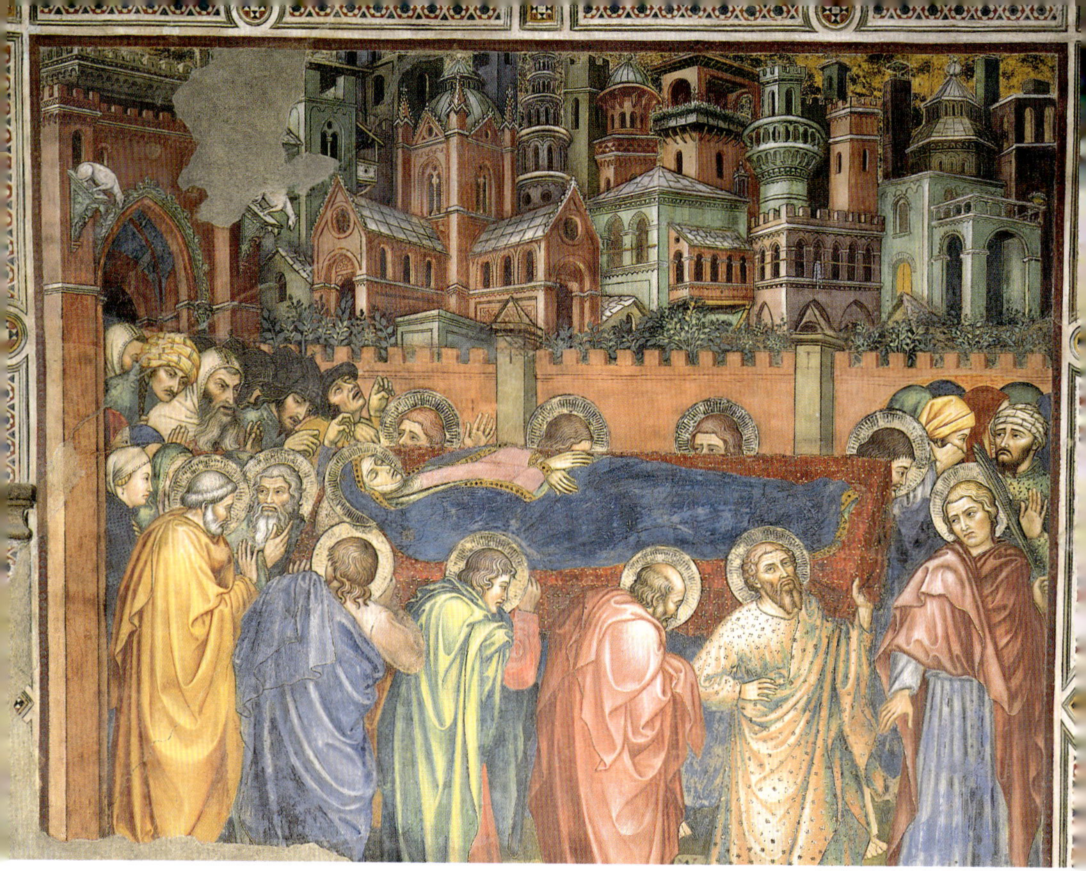

78 Taddeo di Bartolo, *The Funeral of the Virgin* (1409). Fresco, 320 × 345 cm. North wall of the Cappella dei Signori. Siena, Palazzo Pubblico.

chapel scheme was intended also as a means of celebrating Siena's support for Gregory XII during these years. The images on the altar wall of Saints Peter and Paul – both closely associated with the papacy – together with the Blessed Ambrogio Sansedoni at the entrance to the chapel, were probably included in honour of Gregory XII. The particular relevance of Ambrogio Sansedoni was that in 1273 he had pleaded successfully with another pope, Gregory X, to have a papal interdict lifted from Siena. The close identification between Ambrogio Sansedoni and Siena is emphasised by the fact that he is shown holding a detailed model of the city.[48]

* * *

THE SALA DI BALÌA

The presence of Gregory XII in Siena appears to have influenced also the choice of subject for another extensive scheme of painting in the Palazzo Pubblico. The construction of the north wall of the chapel decorated by Taddeo di Bartolo provided the opportunity to create another meeting room on the first floor of the building. Now known as the Sala di Balìa after a magistracy set up in 1455 (see pl. 48), it was originally known as the Saletta Nuova ('the new little room'). Commissioned a few months before the pope's arrival in Siena, the paintings were actually begun in April 1408 by Spinello Aretino, a painter from Arezzo who had worked extensively in Florence.[49] The entire scheme was devoted to portraying events in the life of a twelfth-century pope, Alexander III, whose papacy had been marked by fierce political struggle against the Holy Roman Emperor Frederick Barbarossa and a number of schismatic popes (pl. 79). Such a subject would have appealed to the traditional Guelph sympathies of successive Sienese regimes since the Nine and would have been relevant to the more recent traumatic experience of being subject to Visconti Milan, which was traditionally loyal to the Ghibelline cause. It would have been particularly relevant to the papal schism then affecting Siena and the rest of Italy.

More significantly for the Sienese, Alexander III had himself come from Siena and remained, at that time, the only Sienese cleric to have been elected pope. The Sienese government may therefore have been hoping that one of the outcomes of the Church councils summoned to debate the current schism would be the election of a Sienese cleric as pope. It is more likely, however, that the subject was chosen simply as a straightforward compliment to their guest, Pope Gregory XII. Gregory XII was from Venice, a city that also celebrated the defeat of Frederick Barbarossa at the hands of Alexander III because of the role it had played in those events. In 1365 the Venetian government had accordingly commissioned paintings of the subject for the walls of their principal council hall; its seems likely that the paintings for the Sala di Balìa were envisaged as a Sienese reworking of this earlier Venetian scheme.[50]

THE ANTE-CHAMBER TO THE SALA DEL CONCISTORO

After the completion of the chapel paintings, the Sienese government turned their attention to the decoration of the space that lay immediately in front of the chapel (see pl. 48). In 1408 Taddeo di Bartolo was commissioned to

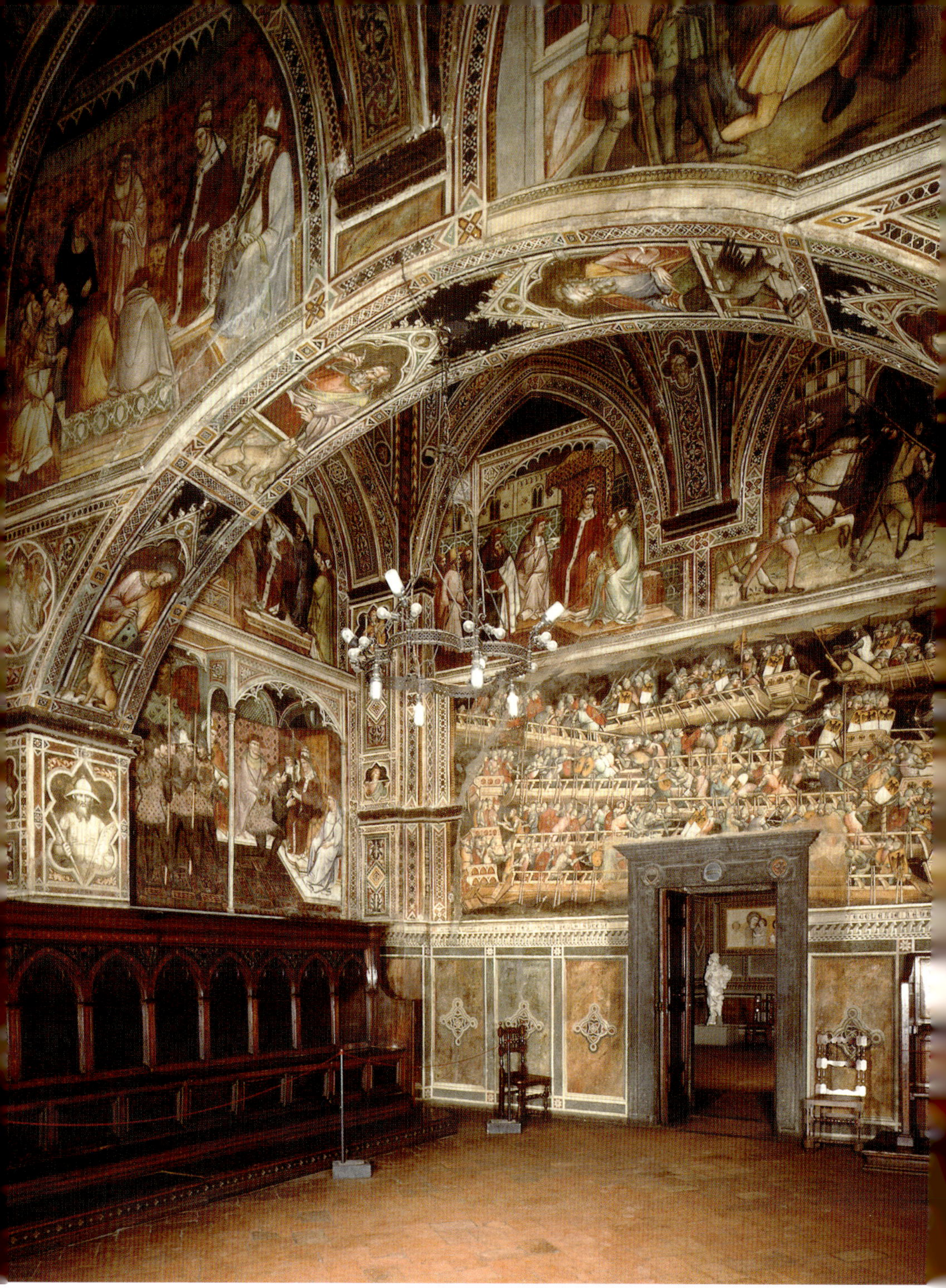

paint a large *Saint Christopher carrying the Christ Child* on the north wall of this passageway.[51] As patron saint of travellers, Saint Christopher was a fairly common subject for the painted embellishment of civic palaces in Italy: this fresco was located over an archway through which government officials and visitors would leave the principal meeting rooms on this floor of the Palazzo Pubblico. Five years later, Taddeo di Bartolo was again commissioned to paint the remainder of this part of the building. For this project, however, he was instructed to follow the directions of two prominent Sienese citizens, Pietro de' Pecci, a doctor of law and letters at Siena's university, and Ser Cristoforo d'Andrea, the chancellor of the city.[52] The erudite nature of the subject matter of the resulting painted scheme, and the presence of a large number of long painted Latin and Italian texts within it, indicate why such instruction was necessary. The painted text at the entrance of the chapel gives the date of completion as 1414.

Owing to later alterations to this part of the building, the painted passageway now appears to act as the vestibule to the chapel – hence its popular designation as the 'ante-chapel' of the Palazzo Pubblico. At the date of the commission, however, it functioned as the entrance vestibule to a meeting room that no longer exists.[53] Its painted scheme was therefore intended to reflect the political activities that took place within the one-time Sala del Concistoro rather than the religious functions of the chapel. As in earlier painted schemes for the Palazzo Pubblico, however, so-called secular imagery was in fact mixed with religious imagery, since politics was believed to be the business of God as well as man.[54] The upper lunettes of the corridor are decorated with paintings of five Christian personifications, Religion, Justice, Magnimanity, Fortitude and Prudence. Within the broad painted frames of these paintings, and in two spandrels on the wall leading into the chapel, appear a series of busts portraying famous men from antiquity. This theme is then continued on the surfaces of the broad arch that separates the ante-chamber from the Sala del Mappamondo (pl. 80). Here, four classical deities – Jupiter, Mars, Apollo and Pallas (Minerva) – appear against a gold background, each carrying an object associating him or her with either war or peace – a political theme that had earlier been explored by Ambrogio Lorenzetti in his paintings for the nearby Sala della Pace (see pl. 51). At the centre of the archway appears a circular map of Rome with its major monuments clearly displayed. Probably based on fourteenth-century descriptions of the ancient city, this painting was certainly also intended to complement Ambrogio Lorenzetti's now lost *mappamondo* on the

79 The Sala di Balìa with frescoes by Spinello Aretino and Martino di Bartolommeo (1407–8). Siena, Palazzo Pubblico.

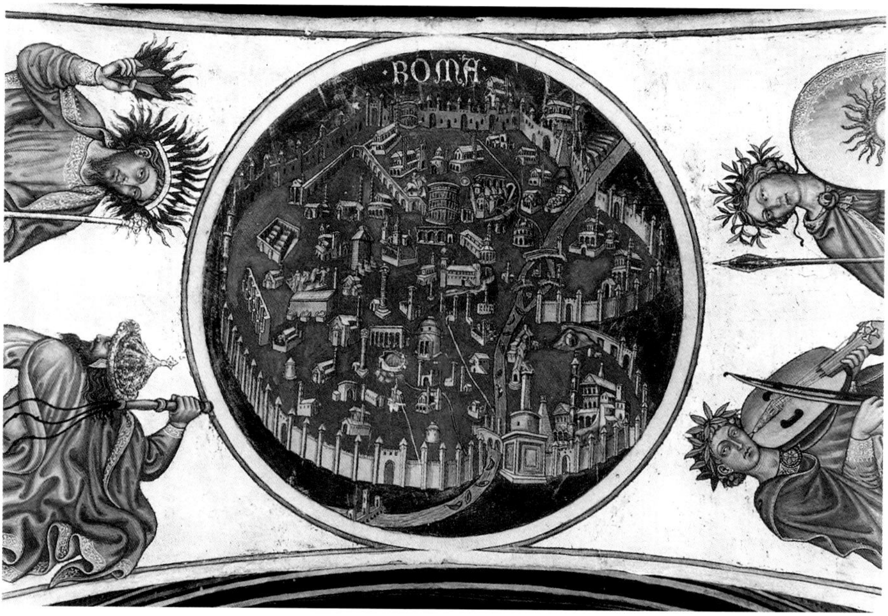

80 Taddeo di Bartolo, *The City of Rome and Four Pagan Deities* (1415). Fresco on inner archway between the Sala del Mappamondo and the former ante-chamber. Siena, Palazzo Pubblico.

west wall of the adjacent Sala del Mappamondo and to underline Siena's belief in its close links with Rome and its past glories.[55]

The sides of the archway are decorated with paintings of famous figures from antiquity. To the right (as one faces the Sala del Mappamondo) is an imposing representation of the Greek philosopher Aristotle, portrayed however in the robes of an early fifteenth-century scholar. As the painted text below him confirms, he is the teacher of civic virtue who presents the entire series to the spectator and enjoins the city of Siena to follow the examples shown in the other paintings. Opposite him, to the left of the archway, are figures of Caesar and Pompey, accompanied by written warnings about the ambition and discord that caused these two ancient heroes to engage in civil war and, as a result, to perish (see pl. 46).

This theme of using figures from ancient history as exemplars for the kinds of behaviour that Siena's governors should adopt is continued in the principal painting of the ante-chamber which takes up the entire surface of

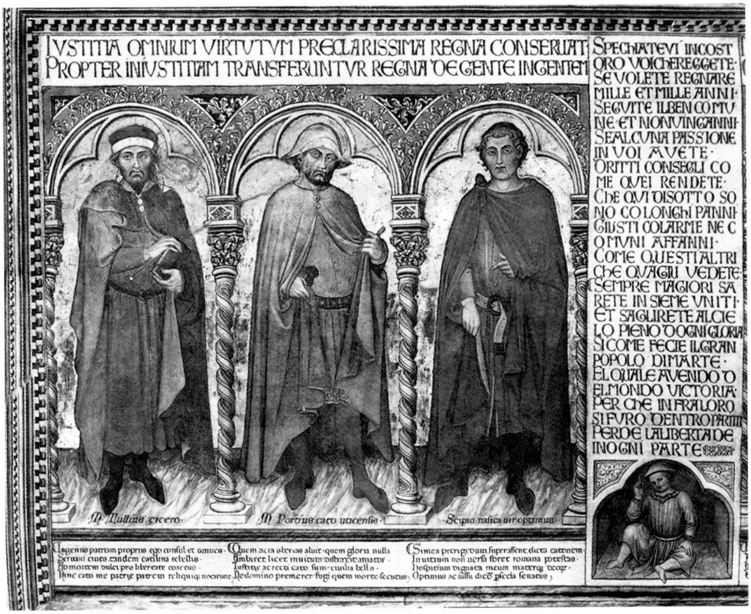

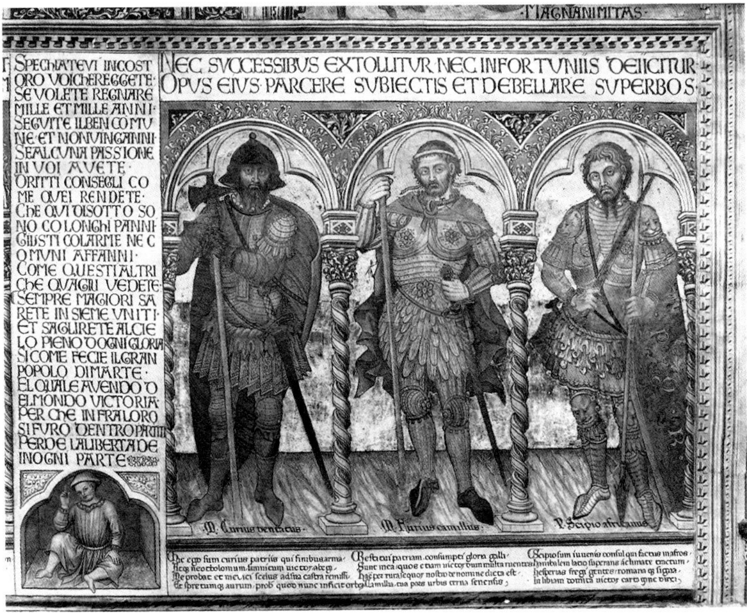

81 Taddeo di Bartolo, *Roman Republican Heroes* (1415). Fresco on west wall of the former ante-chamber. Siena, Palazzo Pubblico.

what would once have been the entrance wall to the Sala del Concistoro. It shows six heroes of antiquity divided into two groups: to the left, three dressed in civilian clothes, to the right, three dressed in armour and carrying swords or other weapons (pl. 81). As a group they present a striking unity. With his resolute stance and fiercely serious facial expression, each hero acts as a powerful presence in the relatively confined space of the ante-chamber. Each appears as if lit from the left and thus from the direction of the windows in the south wall of the Sala del Mappamondo. The optimum viewing point for this series of figures is just outside the entrance to the chapel and thus directly opposite the door that would once have led into the Sala del Concistoro.

Dividing these two groups is a long painted text in Italian, elaborating on the message of the shorter text beneath the figure of Aristotle – perhaps for the benefit of those magistrates who found the Latin of this text beyond them.[56] A small boy – possibly representing the youthful Sienese republic at the time that these heroes lived – points to the Italian text. At least three of the heroes appear to have been chosen with such a theme in mind. Thus, among the group of soldiers appears Curius Dentatus, during whose consulate the Roman colony of Senae was believed to have been founded, and Furius Camillus, who was credited with the founding of the *terzo* of Camollia within the city. The text below Scipio Africanus, meanwhile, admonishes the Sienese to rule wisely lest their liberty be replaced by tyranny.

It is significant that many of the themes that first appeared in the fourteenth-century scheme for the Sala della Pace (see pls 51–3) appeared once again in this early fifteenth-century painted scheme. Like its earlier counterpart, the complex programme of the ante-chamber relies heavily on the imagery working in concert with lengthy written texts. Both schemes appeal to political sentiments such as the need to rule wisely, by both peaceful and warlike means, and never to allow the common good to be subordinated to individual ambition and pride – because this will inevitably lead to tyranny and the loss of liberty. Like the Sala della Pace frescoes, the prominent presence of the Christian Virtues in the later scheme again suggests that the practice of such values will assist the achievement of these ideals.

Taddeo di Bartolo's scheme, however, represents the heroes and gods of antiquity, whereas Ambrogio Lorenzetti's scheme relied on more generalised allegorical personifications. Clearly, by the early fifteenth century, it was important to the Sienese government that they had in their civic palace a painted scheme that demonstrated their knowledge and respect of the history and culture of antiquity.[57] They also clearly wanted to proclaim the city's long-established connections with Rome, an ambition that undoubtedly influenced the choice of imagery for the Fonte Gaia, another contemporary civic project (see pl. 65).

In short, the first two decades of the fifteenth century were marked by a considerable number of artistic projects initiated by the new regime and their close associates such as the cathedral Opera. Like the Nine, the government of early fifteenth-century Siena sought to use painted imagery as a means of advertising their perception of the nature of 'good government' and of validating their current policies and political preoccupations. But as they did so, they apparently encouraged their painters to echo self-consciously and emulate a number of themes from the work of earlier painters such as Simone Martini and the Lorenzetti brothers.

Diversity and Versatility

Notwithstanding the active patronage of art by the city's principal institutions during this period, Sienese painters nevertheless had to negotiate a very different set of circumstances from that of their early fourteenth-century counterparts.[58] The Black Death ended the lives of a number of highly experienced and talented painters – Ambrogio Lorenzetti among them[59] – whose technical expertise was thus no longer available to younger Sienese painters. Facing an uncertain economic climate, painters were sometimes obliged to share workshop premises in order to cover their costs. For example, in 1353 Bartolo di Fredi agreed with another Sienese painter, Andrea Vanni, to rent a workshop together for a year. There are also instances of well-established master-painters collaborating on single commissions – the altarpiece commission given in 1389 to Bartolo di Fredi, Luca di Tommè and Andrea di Bartolo by the guild of shoemakers being but one example. Such collaboration had taken place in the first half of the fourteenth century – the signed *Annunciation* by Simone Martini and Lippo Memmi is a case in point (see pl. 58) – but it appears more typical of the second half of the century.[60] It may be that the development was precipitated by the fact that there was not much work to go round and it had to be shared among different painters. But it seems more likely that the reverse was the case and that too much was being demanded of fewer specialist craftworkers.[61]

The large altarpiece signed on its lower edge by both Niccolò di Ser Sozzo and Luca di Tommè in 1362 (pl. 82) provides a striking example of such collaboration. Now divested of its original piers, pinnacle panels and

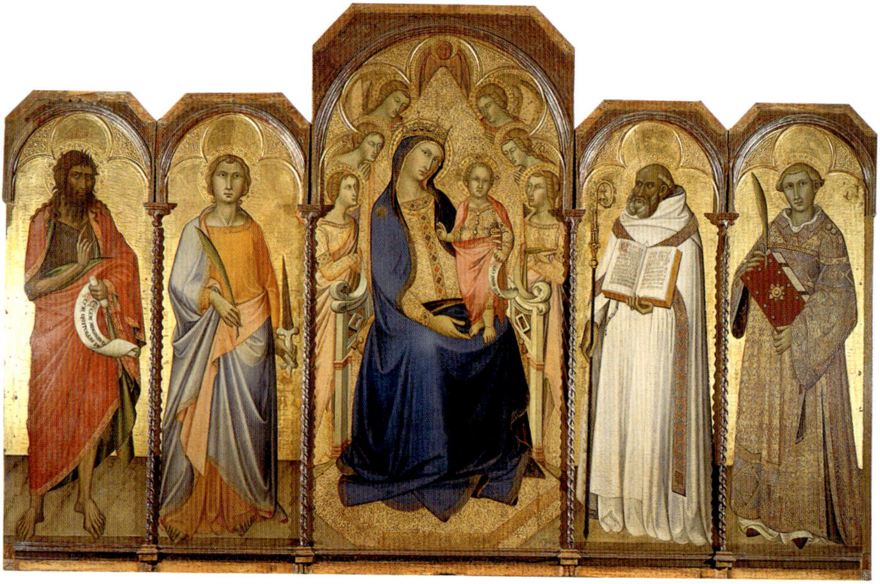

82 Niccolò di Ser Sozzo and Luca di Tommè, *Virgin and Christ Child with Saints John the Baptist, Thomas, Benedict and Stephen* (1362). Tempera on panel, 191 × 297 cm. Siena, Pinacoteca Nazionale.

predella, the altarpiece was painted probably for the high altar of San Tommaso, a church under the care of the religious order known as the Humiliati.[62] Accordingly, the apostle Thomas is portrayed on the Virgin's right-hand side, a position conventionally understood as that of greatest honour. To his right appears Saint John the Baptist, while Saints Benedict and Stephen appear to the left of the Virgin. The general consensus among art historians is that Niccolò di Ser Sozzo painted the Virgin and Christ Child, Saint Benedict and Saint Stephen while Luca di Tommè painted Saints John the Baptist and Thomas.[63] It is possible, however, that modern critical opinion has underestimated the extent and subtlety of this collaborative enterprise. Comparison with other signed paintings by Luca di Tommè indicate that he could easily vary his style of painting in order to portray, on the one hand, the features of women and young men (such as the Virgin, Saints Thomas and Stephen on this altarpiece) and, on the other, the austere, weather-beaten features of a figure such as Saint John the Baptist. In other words, he could well have executed all the figures on this altarpiece.

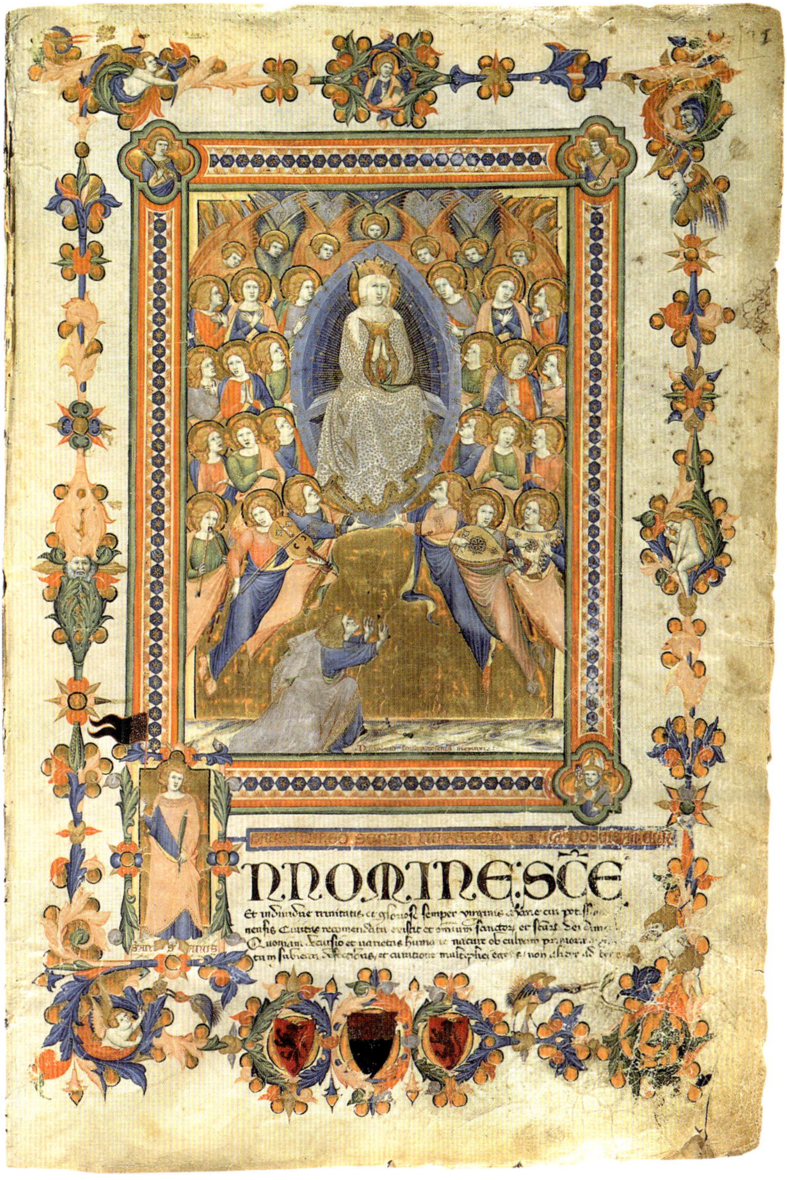

83 Niccolò di Ser Sozzo, *The Virgin of the Assumption with Saint Thomas receiving the Girdle*, and *Saints Crescenzio, Victor, Savino and Ansano* (*c.* 1336–8). Illuminated page of the *Caleffo dell'Assunta*, 43.6 × 30.5 cm. Siena, Archivio di Stato, Palazzo Piccolomini.

The altarpiece is striking also for the large amount of intricate patterning used on the robes of all the figures in the central panel and on the dalmatic worn by Saint Stephen on the right. The technique of delicately removing a layer of paint to reveal the underlying gold leaf in order to achieve this effect would have demanded an immense amount of both skill and time.[64] The fine lettering on the open book held by Saint Benedict and on the scroll of Saint John the Baptist would similarly have required highly specialised expertise. Such skills – although not unknown in the field of fourteenth-century panel painting – were more usually associated with the production of manuscripts, and it was precisely in this field that the work of Niccolò di Ser Sozzo is best known (pl. 83).[65] It may well be, therefore, that this altarpiece was produced collaboratively not merely by the allocation of single figures to one or other painter, but by exploiting their particular technical skills for different details of the figures in the painting.

Notwithstanding the difficulties and challenges facing Sienese painters in the second half of the fourteenth century, they proved responsive to a wide variety of types of commission, in addition to the major projects and schemes discussed so far in this chapter. One of the most important of these was the painting of altarpieces designed specifically for the requirements of private patrons who founded their own family, funerary chapels in Sienese churches. At some time between 1360 and 1370 Lippo Vanni painted an altarpiece for one such chapel in the south transept of the church of San Francesco in Siena (pl. 84).[66] Intriguingly – and unusually – he executed it in fresco, rather than on the customary wooden panels, possibly to enable his patrons to avoid the additional cost of employing a skilled woodworker. Instead they relied entirely on Lippo Vanni's skill as a painter to represent the ornate monumental framework customarily used on altarpieces of this date.

The central section of the painting portrays the Virgin, in the guise of both mother and advocate, but also depicts Christ, both in triumph and in his tomb – the latter image being located directly above the altar at which requiem masses would have been celebrated on behalf of the family who owned the chapel. On either side of these central images appear saints whose identities combine the religious concerns of both the patrons and the Franciscan Order in whose church the chapel lay. To the left appears Saint Francis, the founder of the Franciscan Order, in the company of another major saint, Saint John the Baptist. To the right appear two martyrs, the early Christian saint Catherine of Alexandria and the Blessed Pietro, a local Franciscan friar, who was put to death in India in 1321. As mentioned in the previous chapter, the martyrdom of the Blessed Pietro and his compan-

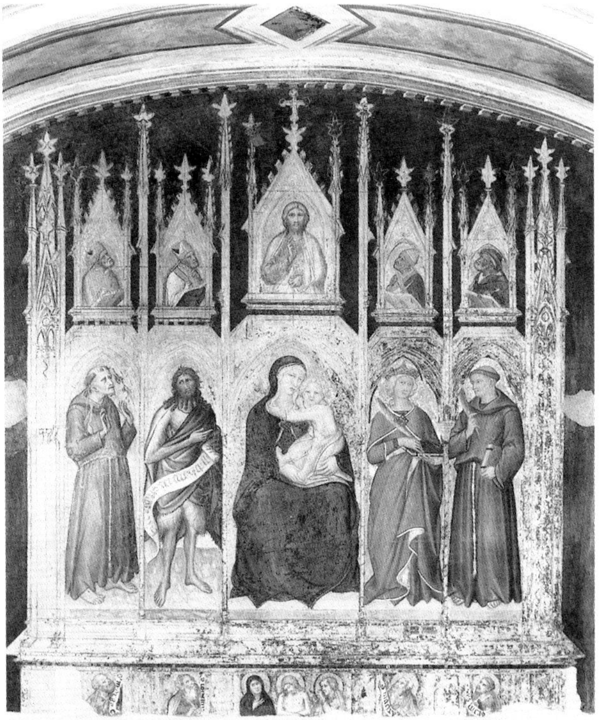

84 Lippo Vanni, *Virgin and Christ Child with Saints Francis, John the Baptist, Catherine of Alexandria and the Blessed Pietro da Siena* (1360s). Fresco. Siena, San Francesco, Martinozzi Chapel.

ions had already been commemorated in a series of frescoes painted by Ambrogio Lorenzetti for the walls of the friary cloister.[67] This cloister and its painted scheme lay directly adjacent to the chapel where the altarpiece is located. The Blessed Pietro also belonged to the Martinozzi family who are known – at least from the mid-fifteenth century – to have been patrons of the chapel.[68] It seems, therefore, that they wished their chapel to have an altarpiece that celebrated the memory of this illustrious member of their family.

Sienese painters of this period were also commissioned to paint religious objects other than altarpieces. Thus, in 1380 Francesco di Vannuccio placed the date and his name at the base of a small but ornate painting of the crucified Christ witnessed by the Virgin, Saint John the Evangelist, Saint Augustine and an Augustinian friar – the latter holding a written text on a scroll. On the reverse of this painting is a rare example of painted glass rep-

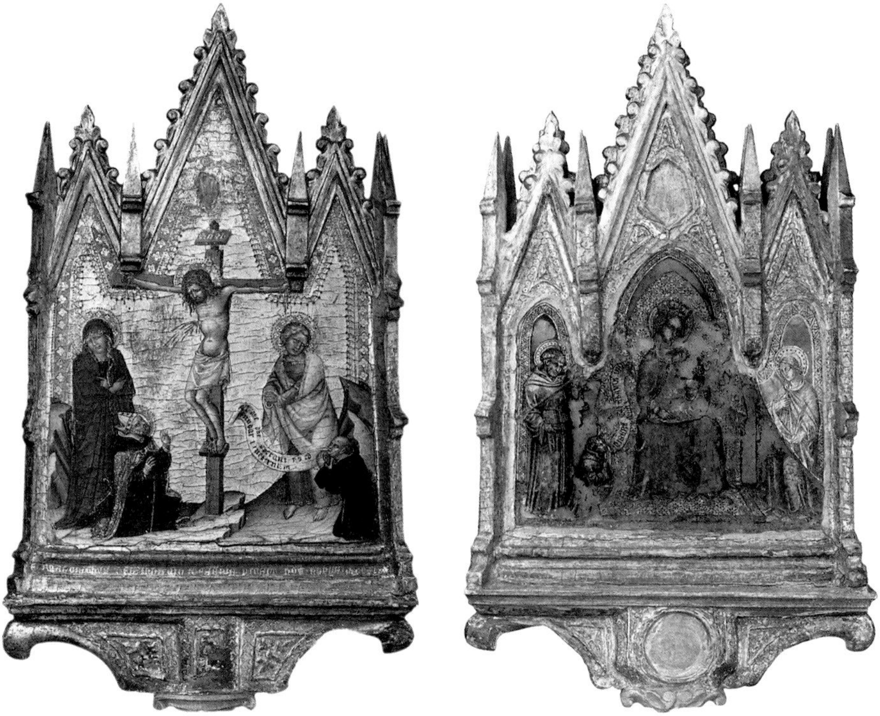

85a and b Francesco di Vannuccio, *Crucified Christ with the Virgin, Saint John the Evangelist, Saint Augustine and a Devotee* (1370s). Tempera on panel, 24 × 18 cm. *The Virgin and Christ Child with Saints and a Devotee* (1370s). Painted glass, 16 × 17 cm. Processional standard. Berlin Dahlem, Staatliche Museen, Gemäldegalerie.

resenting the Virgin and Christ Child with Saint Francis and a female saint, together with a kneeling figure again presenting a written text to the Virgin (pl. 85a and b). In a technique known as *verre églomisé*, these figures have been scratched through the gold leaf, applied to the glass, and then painted in one or more colours.[69] While the precise circumstances of its commissioning are not known, this double-sided painting was incorporated at some stage in its history into a processional standard. It would thus have acted as a visual accompaniment to the elaborate religious processions that took place within churches and throughout the streets of Siena at times of crisis (see pl. 2). Here too was a late fourteenth-century painter working on

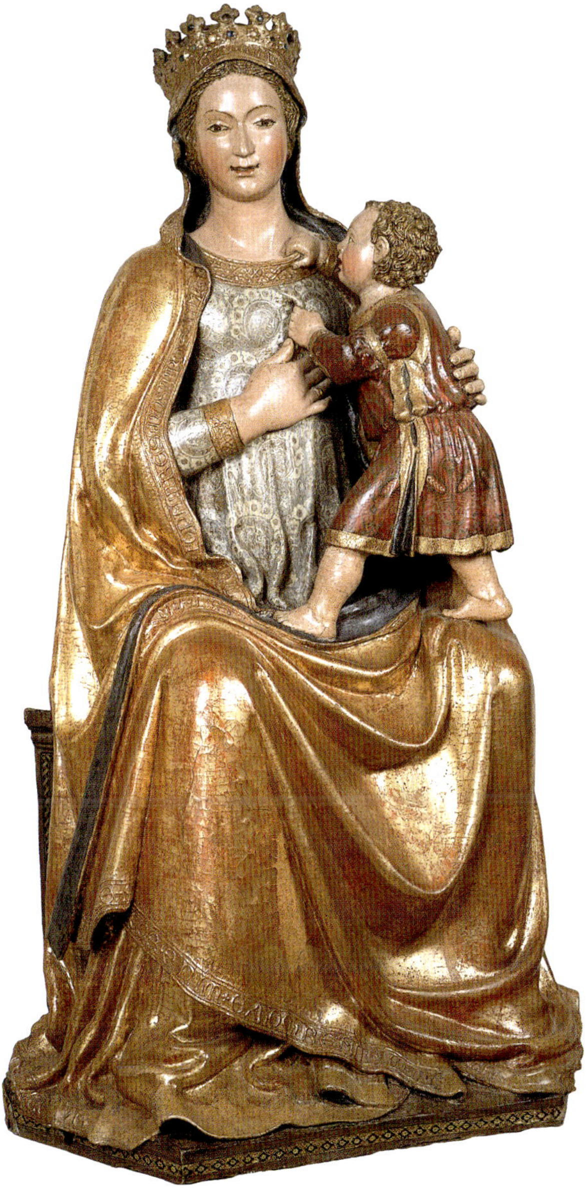

86 Giovanni di Turino (attrib.), *The Madonna of the Magnificat* (1420). Polychrome wood sculpture probably painted by Taddeo di Bartolo and Gregorio di Cecco, 133 cm. Siena, Sant'Agostino.

a miniature scale and using techniques normally associated with work in gold or on glass.

Actual collaboration between painters and other craftworkers occurred also in the production of a sculpted group of the Virgin and Christ Child (pl. 86). Known as the *Madonna of the Magnificat* – because the verses of this song of praise attributed to the Virgin are carved along the hem of the Virgin's mantle – this wooden sculpture is particularly remarkable for its rich and extensive polychromy and gilding. It was probably carved by the sculptor Giovanni di Turino as the centrepiece to a painted altarpiece by Taddeo di Bartolo and Gregorio di Cecco, for an altar under the patronage of the Marescotti family in the church of Sant'Agostino; they probably painted it as well as the altarpiece.[70] Although this is an early fifteenth-century example of such collaboration between different kinds of artist, there are numerous examples of fourteenth-century painters being commissioned to paint such sculptures – Bartolo di Fredi undertook several projects of this kind.[71] Painters gave such sculpted figures an enhanced degree of lifelikeness through the painting of flesh and of details such as the eyes and mouth, and through the use of a sumptuous range of colours and patterns on the surfaces of the carved draperies. This undoubtedly increased the emotional impact of these sacred figures, many of which figured in the staging of religious liturgies and processions.

Saint Catherine of Siena

In concluding this account of Sienese painting during the turbulent period between 1355 and 1420, it is appropriate to consider two paintings that commemorate Caterina Benincasa, now better known as Saint Catherine of Siena. Living between 1347 and 1380, she had first-hand experience of many of the events described in this chapter. For example, she not only travelled to Avignon in 1376 to plead with Pope Gregory XI to return the papal court to Rome but also was reputed to have nursed victims of the plague in Siena. In her religious life, she epitomised the highly personal and emotionally charged spirituality encouraged by the pious activities of many of Siena's lay confraternities and sororities. One of her special characteristics as a religious mystic was that she claimed to experience visions of Christ, the most famous of which took place before a twelfth-century painted crucifix in the church of Santa Cristina in Pisa.

Possibly even during her lifetime, or at the latest shortly after her death in 1380, a Sienese artist painted a frescoed image of Catherine with a female devotee kneeling before her (pl. 87). Originally located on an exterior wall adjacent to a corner of the church of San Domenico (see pl. 7), in 1667 it was moved to a fourteenth-century chapel situated at the west end of the church.[72] The painting shows the future saint dressed in the robes of the Mantellate, the group of lay women who, like Catherine herself, observed the religious rule of the Dominican Order while still remaining active members of society outside the convent walls. She also holds a lily, symbolising the vow of chastity that she had taken. On the back of her hands appear the stigmata, the wounds of the Passion of Christ that she was believed to have experienced in 1375. Since the first report of this image occurs in 1399,[73] it is unclear precisely when it was painted, but it is certain that Andrea Vanni – the painter to whom it is generally attributed – knew Catherine since he was the recipient of three letters addressed to him by the future saint.[74] When he came to portray her, however, he decided to represent her in an entirely idealised and conventional style, probably because this would have been the safest way to ensure proper respect and devotion for her reputation and memory.

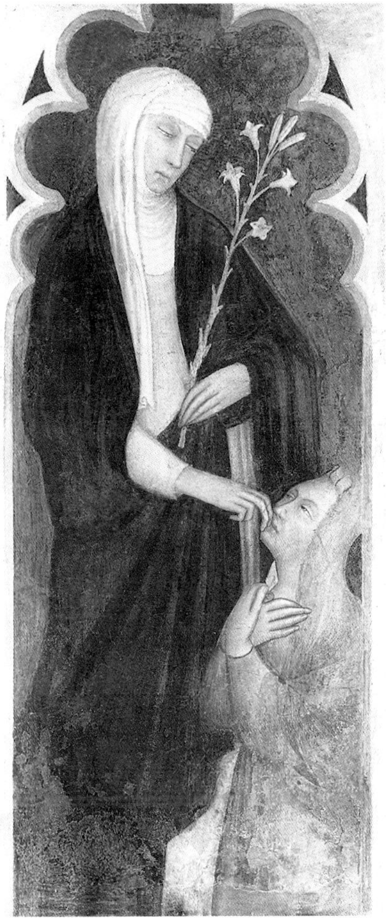

87 Andrea Vanni (attrib.), *Saint Catherine of Siena and a Devotee* (*c.* 1375–98). Fresco, 139 × 61.5 cm. Siena, San Domenico, Cappella delle Volte.

In the mid-1390s, Andrea di Bartolo produced another early representation of Catherine.[75] She is depicted in the centre of a panel painting, accompanied by four other Domincian Mantellate (pl. 88). In the predella below, each of the five women is seen experiencing a vision as the result of prayer – the three central figures specifically experiencing the stigmata. Painted in Siena, but probably always intended for the Dominican convent of Corpus Christi in Venice, this commission was undoubtedly

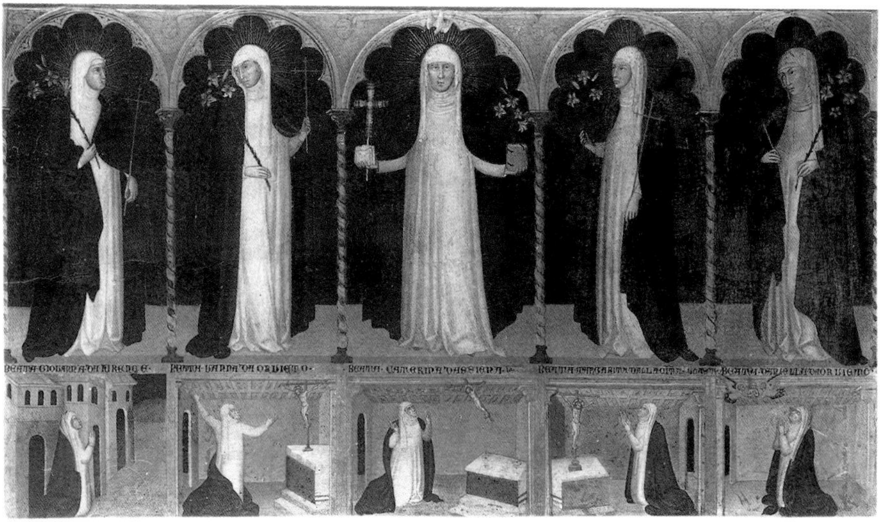

88 Andrea di Bartolo, *Saint Catherine of Siena with the Blessed Giovanna of Florence, Vanna of Orvieto, Margarita of Città di Castello and Daniella of Orvieto* (*c*. 1394–8) Tempera on panel, 56 × 97 cm. Murano, Museo Vetrario.

awarded to Andrea di Bartolo because of the long association between his family and the church and priory of San Domenico in Siena. His father, Bartolo di Fredi, was buried in the cemetery there, as were a number of Andrea's brothers and sisters who had died in infancy. Bartolo di Fredi had worked on at least one major commission for an altarpiece in San Domenico.[76] The commissioner of Andrea's Venetian altarpiece is most likely to have been Fra Tommaso d'Antonio Caffarini, at one time prior of San Domenico in Siena, who took up residence in Venice in 1394.[77] As a Dominican who played a key role in the early stages of the process of securing Catherine's canonisation as saint, he would clearly have wished to commission paintings that would assist in commemorating her identity and sanctity. Later painters were similarly employed by a variety of Sienese patrons to propagate and advance her cult (see pls 100, 106, 108, 110, 122, 138–9).

The second half of the fourteenth century, therefore, was a complex and difficult period for the Sienese. Marked by frequent changes in government and repeated visitations of plague, famine and mercenary companies, in

1399 they suffered the humiliation of handing over their political independence to the Visconti of Milan. The years immediately following the brief period of Visconti rule, moreover, witnessed a flurry of artistic commissions inaugurated by a government determined to initiate and commemorate a new chapter in the city's history. Thus a number of ambitious programmes of painted and sculpted imagery continued the already well-established tradition of celebrating the Virgin as the city's patron saint and protector, while at the same time providing a potent means of advertising the city's legendary Roman origins and the civic virtues to which Siena's governors and citizens aspired. This auspicious start to Sienese painting in the fifteenth century was fulfilled as in the ensuing decades Sienese painters and their patrons began to absorb the techniques and artistic conventions belonging to the emerging culture of renaissance Italy.

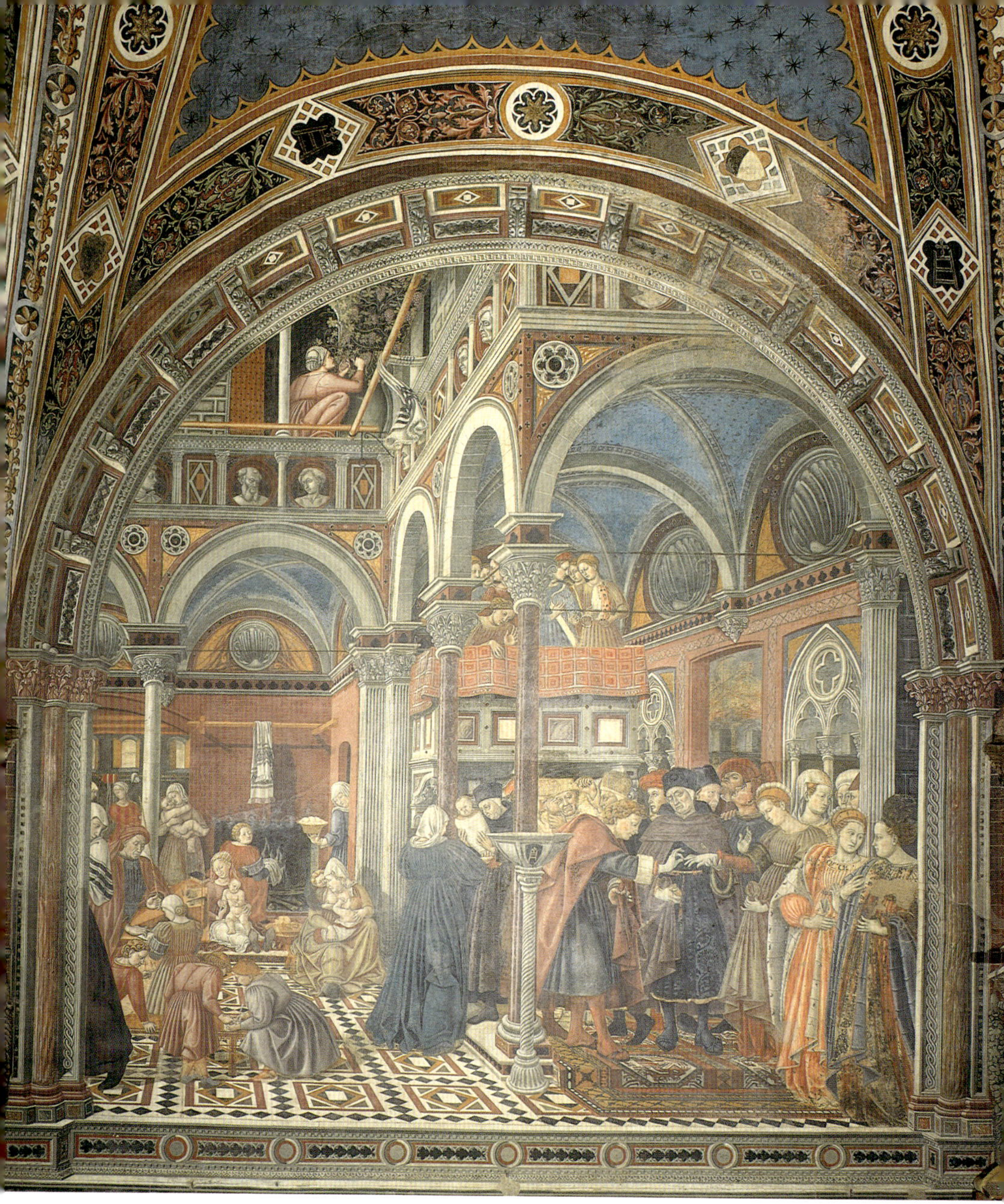

89 Domenico di Bartolo, *The Rearing and Marriage of Female Foundlings* (1441–2). Fresco on the west wall of the Pellegrinaio. Siena, Spedale di Santa Maria dell Scala.

4

Renaissance Painting in Siena (1420–1480)

The fifteenth century represented a period of relative political stability for Siena, although rivalries between various factions disrupted this from time to time. Members of the Monti of the Nine, the Riformatori and the Popolo continued to be recruited to the city's principal magistracies. Some historians detect an increasing drift towards elitism in Sienese government while others are more cautious on this point.[1] What is clear is that Siena was steadily obliged to play an increasingly subsidiary role in political processes orchestrated by other political powers – principally Florence and Rome.

At the beginning of the fifteenth century, Florence was already extending and consolidating its political control over Tuscany, acquiring in succession Arezzo (1384), Montepulciano (1399) and Pisa (1406). In 1404, the Sienese government formally accepted Florence's control over their former subject town of Montepulciano but when, between 1429 and 1433, Florence attempted to conquer Lucca, Sienese troops led by Antonio Petrucci, a prominent member of the Monte of the Nine, fought against their traditional enemy. Although this incident ended in a truce between the two cities, Petrucci later attempted to continue hostilities against Florence, resulting in exile for himself and his followers in 1456.[2]

The Sienese government was also involved in the politics surrounding the resolution of the papal schism in the early decades of the fifteenth century. As noted in the previous chapter, they allied themselves to Gregory XII but later they backed Alexander V (1409–10), John XXIII (1410–15) and finally Martin V (1417–31), supporting his decision to return the papacy to Rome. During 1423–4 Siena was chosen as the location of a council summoned by Martin V to debate the future government of the Church. Then between July 1432 and April 1433 Siena became the residence of the emperor elect, Sigismund of Luxemburg, and in 1443 Martin's successor,

Pope Eugenius IV (1431–47), also visited the city.[3] Both visits resulted in imperial and papal privileges being granted to the Sienese.

The reign of the next pope, Nicholas V (1447–55) was significant for Siena principally because in 1450 he made the famous Sienese Franciscan friar Bernardino a saint and a few months later appointed Aeneas Silvius Piccolomini as Bishop of Siena. A member of a minor branch of an important Sienese family, Aeneas's subsequent accession to the papal throne as Pius II (1458–64) cemented relations between Siena and Rome. In 1459, while visiting Siena, the new pope prompted a reform of government that allowed the Monti of the Twelve and of the Nobles (both of whom had been out of power since 1404) to participate in government once again, and the Petrucci exiles of 1456 were allowed to return to Siena. On the same visit, Pius II presented the Sienese government with an exquisitely worked golden rose and elevated the see of Siena to the status of an archbishopric. He again visited Siena in 1460 and on this occasion made his nephew, Francesco Todeschini Piccolomini, archbishop and cardinal of Siena. A year later he announced the canonisation of Saint Catherine of Siena (see pl. 122), and in 1464 gave the precious relic of the arm of Saint John the Baptist to the cathedral.[4]

In the war that followed the failed attempt on the part of the Pazzi family to assassinate Lorenzo dei Medici in 1478, Siena sided with Pope Sixtus IV (1471–84) and King Ferrante of Naples against Florence. This alliance was initially successful for the Sienese who, with the assistance of papal and Neapolitan troops, won the battle of Poggio Imperiale in 1479 and captured the town of Colle Val d'Elsa, between Florence and Siena.[5] In 1480, however, Florence made peace with the pope, and, meanwhile, the king of Naples. Ferrante's son, Alfonso of Calabria, tried to introduce a more narrowly based government in Siena. The Monte of the Riformatori were banished and the Monte of the Nine were temporarily in the ascendancy. Then in 1482 adherents of the Monti of the Nine and of the Nobles were exiled in their turn, with the banned Riformatori returning in triumph to the city.

The painted wooden cover for the accounts of the Gabella for 1483 commemorates the solemn event that took place that year in the cathedral, at the entrance of the chapel that then housed the celebrated thirteenth-century painting of the *Virgin and Christ Child*, known as the *Madonna del Voto* (see pl. 3). Presided over by Cardinal Francesco Todeschini Piccolomini, the governors of Siena symbolically rededicated the city to the Virgin by placing the keys of the city upon the altar of the chapel. This ceremony – which self-consciously echoed the dedication of the city to the Virgin in 1260 – was meant to symbolise the newly acquired unity between the adherents of the various Monti. The exiles, however, continued to foment unrest in the southern *contado*, trying to enlist assistance first from Pope Sixtus IV and then his successor, Innocent VIII (1484–92). In 1487, conditions were propitious for the return of the Nine to Siena.[6] On 22 July, the feast of Saint Mary Magdalen, the exiles led by Pandolfo Petrucci (the son of a cousin of Antonio Petrucci) entered Siena and re-asserted their political control of the city. Thereafter, the city entered a new phase in its political history.

As in earlier centuries, the artistic embellishment of the cathedral, Palazzo Pubblico and Spedale di Santa Maria della Scala continued throughout the fifteenth century as those in charge of their upkeep sought to decorate them according to the latest artistic fashion. One of the early projects was the monumental sculpted font for the fourteenth-century baptistery (pl. 90), which was initiated in 1416 by the cathedral *operiao*, Caterino Corsini. Begun by the Florentine sculptor Ghiberti and two Sienese sculptors, Jacopo della Quercia and Giovanni di Turino, and later joined by the Florentine Donatello, the font was eventually completed in 1434.[7] In its final form, it represents an impressive monument whose function is clearly signalled by the elegant gilded bronze relief of Christ's baptism, sculpted by Ghiberti, and set directly opposite the entrance to the baptistery. The narrative sequence begins, however, on the other side of the hexagonal font, directly opposite the high altar. Beginning with Jacopo della Quercia's *Annunciation to Zacharias of the Birth of Saint John the Baptist*, it follows, in anti-clockwise order, six scenes of the life of John the Baptist, the titular saint of the baptistery, ending with the arresting narrative of the head of the saint being presented to Herod. Executed by Donatello, this relief demonstrated to the Sienese the expressive power of this Florentine sculptor and his awareness of the single-point perspective construction invented by his friend the architect Brunelleschi.[8]

Within the cathedral, meanwhile, work continued on the lengthy process of completing and updating the interior decoration of the building. One project that lasted throughout the fifteenth century and well into the sixteenth was the execution of the marble pavement that still covers the entire floor of this huge building (see pl. 116). Following a complex programme devoted to the theme of Christian salvation, groups of specialists in the art of marble inlay were employed over many years to complete the ambitious project. Well-known fifteenth century painters such as Sassetta, Domenico di Bartolo and Matteo di Giovanni were also recruited to produce designs for the numerous and complex narrative scenes that make up the magnificently ornate pictorial scheme.[9]

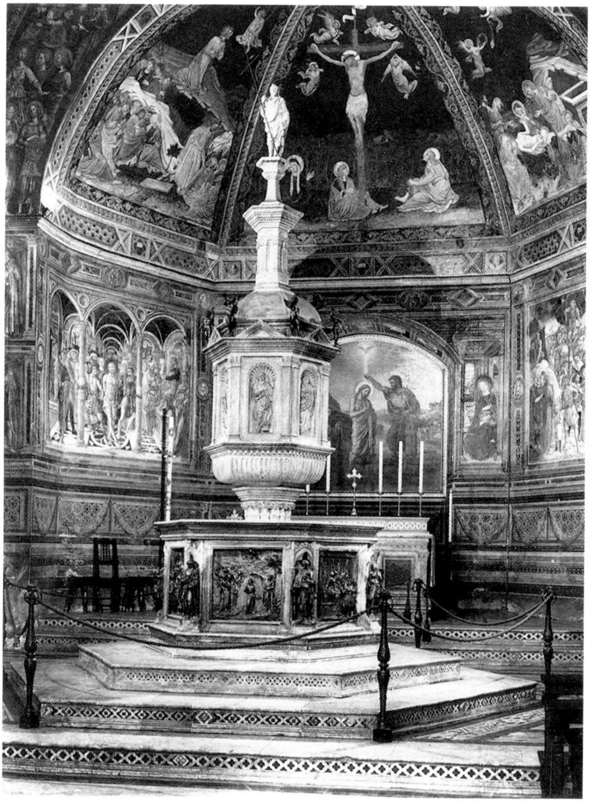

90 Donatello, Ghiberti, Jacopo della Quercia and others, the font (1416–34). Gilt bronze reliefs in a marble frame. Siena, baptistery.

Many of the cathedral altars retained both their original dedications and their fourteenth-century paintings but several altars and chapels were updated by the addition of sculpted decoration. This was particularly striking in the case of the altar in the south aisle that housed the revered thirteenth-century painting of the *Madonna del Voto* (see pl. 57). Such was the continuing devotion to this image that between 1451 and 1454 the entrance to its chapel was embellished with marble reliefs depicting scenes from the life of the Virgin. It is this elaborate framework that can be seen in the image of 1483 that records one of the many civic events that took place before this site in the cathedral (see pl. 3).[10]

A number of further artistic projects to improve and extend the fabric of the Spedale di Santa Maria della Scala likewise took place in the fifteenth century. Thus, as will be discussed later in this chapter, several major schemes of painting were executed in various parts of the building during the 1440s. Between 1466 and 1470 the hospital church was considerably enlarged in length and height (see pl. 96). Incorporating what previously had been the female orphanage, it was turned into a large and imposing space, covered by a wooden coffered roof and lit by a series of tall lunette windows closely resembling those of the most recent buildings in Florence.[11]

The emergence of a taste for architecture that was both renaissance and Florentine in style can be attributed to the direct influence of the Piccolomini pope Pius II. Between 1459 and 1464, Pius II employed the Florentine architect Bernardo Rossellino to transform his birthplace of Corsignano into a miniature renaissance city, renamed Pienza in honour of its patron and creator. Not content to confine his activities to Pienza, Pius II introduced a number of renaissance buildings to the late medieval fabric of Siena. Thus in 1462 the first column of the monumental loggia at the heart of the Piccolomini enclave of residences in the city was put into place by the Sienese architect and sculptor Antonio Federighi (see pl. 13). Through its massive columns with ornate Corinthian capitals and the Roman lettering on the upper part of the building, the loggia displays the characteristic stylistic repertoire of renaissance architecture. It is also embellished with coats-of-arms and a monumental inscription in gilded bronze letters identifying Pius II and his family.[12] Several years earlier, in about 1460, the building of another renaissance palace in Siena for Pius II's family was begun. Facing onto one of the city's principal streets leading up to the cathedral, work was still taking place in the late 1470s (pl. 91). Designed as the residence of the pope's sister, Caterina Piccolomini, the varied stonework of the three floors on the principal façade and the elegant design of the windows on the first and second floors are both thoroughly renaissance and strongly reminiscent of other palaces designed by Bernardino Rossellino. A similar kind of intention was apparent in the design and embellishment of other fifteenth-century palaces built in Siena at this time – the most notable examples are a second palace constructed for the Piccolomini family, on the basis of Bernardo Rossellino's designs, between 1469 and 1510, and the palace built between 1473 and 1476 by the Florentine architect Giuliano da Maiano for the banker Ambrogio Spannocchi, who acted as papal treasurer to Pius II (see pl. 6).[13]

Precisely at the time when Pius II's taste for renaissance architecture was beginning to make an impact on the urban fabric of Siena, the city government decided to renovate one of the city's principal monuments in a similar fashion. Between 1461 and 1468 the architect of Pius II's loggia,

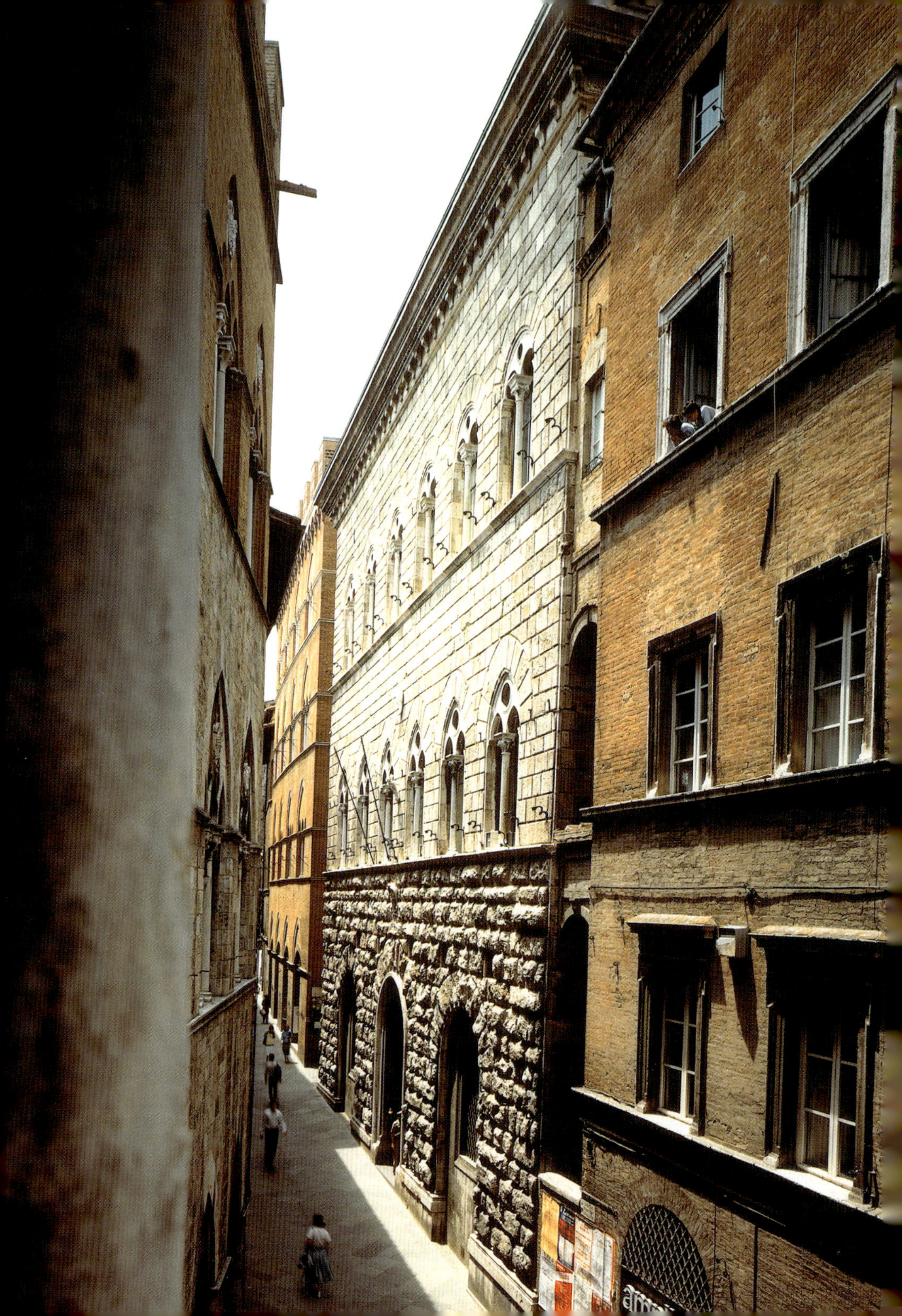

Antonio Federighi, transformed the Cappella di Piazza from a modest open-sided structure (see pl. 95) to a much more imposing edifice (see pl. 1). While respecting the profile of the fourteenth-century piers and their shallow sculpted niches, Federighi crowned his new additions to the chapel with an ornate classicising frieze, typical of the new renaissance architectural style.[14] In a similar fashion, the marble benches commissioned in the early 1460s from Federighi and another sculptor by the magistracy of the Mercanzia for their newly completed loggia displayed an awareness of the style and imagery of Roman sarcophagi. These benches were displayed, however, with other, more conventional, sculptures of saints set in niches and facing out onto the principal street on which the Loggia della Mercanzia stood (see pl. 11). Commissioned between 1457 and 1464 from Federighi and the painter-sculptor Vecchietta, they represented three of the patron saints of the city, Savino, Ansano and Victor, with Saints Peter and Paul.[15] It seems that, although Sienese patrons and their artists were by no means indifferent to the formal and expressive possibilities of the new renaissance style, they were determined to utilise these in particularly 'Sienese' ways in order to continue to reflect local concerns and priorities.

New Ways of Honouring the Virgin

Awareness of new stylistic directions in art among Sienese painters can be seen most clearly in an altarpiece painted by Sassetta for the cathedral of Siena. This is a particularly instructive example because once again it demonstrates how Sienese painters applied the new developments in a distinctively Sienese manner. Known from its subject as the *Madonna delle Nevi* (the 'Madonna of the Snows', pl. 92), the painting was originally commissioned for one of the oldest and most venerable altars in the cathedral. It stood immediately left of the doorway known as the Porta del Perdono – the side entrance to the cathedral that provided most immediate access to both the baptistery and to the civic centre of the Palazzo Pubblico and the Campo (see pls 6, 57). The earliest surviving cathedral inventories name the altar as the altar of the *Madonna delle Grazie* ('Our Lady of Thanks', in the sense of favours received), and describe it as next to a counter where votive candles were sold. The reason for its title appears to have been the fact that it then housed an ancient image of the Virgin and Child, which was probably the early thirteenth-century *Madonna degli occhi grossi* (see pl. 18), in

91 The Palazzo Piccolomini, known as the Palazzo delle Papesse. Siena, via di Città.

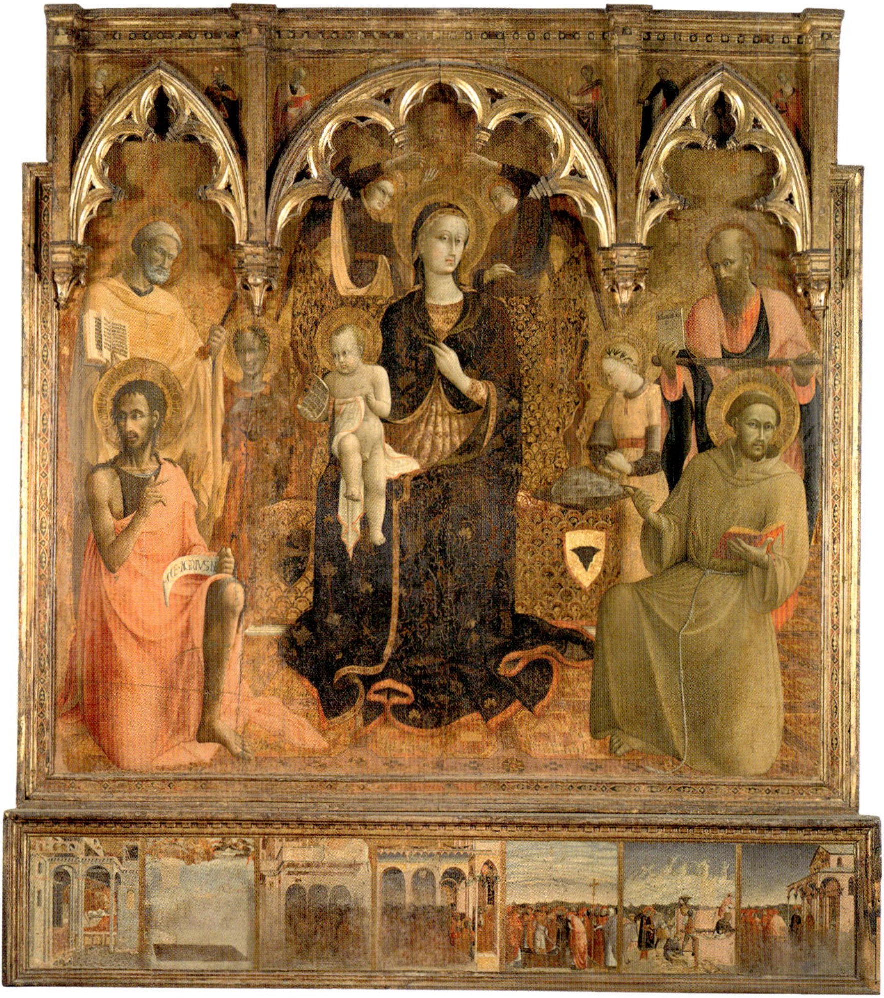

92 Sassetta, *The Virgin and Christ Child with Saints Peter, Paul, John the Baptist and Francis*, known as *The Madonna of the Snows* (1430–32). Tempera on panel, 240 × 216 cm. Florence, Collezione Contini Bonacossi.

front of which the Sienese authorities had probably dedicated Siena to the Virgin in 1260.[16] The site for the new altarpiece therefore carried with it a number of prestigious historic associations.

Sassetta received the commission in 1430 from Ludovica Bertini, the widow of Turino di Matteo (the cathedral *operaio* who had succeeded Caterino Corsini, the man responsible for both the cathedral sacristy and the baptismal font).[17] According to one local chronicler, Turino had died in 1423 and been buried in front of the Porta del Perdono.[18] In the contract for the altarpiece, Ludovica makes it clear that she is commissioning the work both in memory of her husband and also in her own right as a pious Franciscan tertiary, so the coat-of-arms of her own family as well as that of her husband appear prominently displayed on the richly ornamented fabric covering the Virgin's throne. Her commitment to the Franciscan Order is clearly demonstrated by the inclusion of Saint Francis in the right foreground of the main panel of the altarpiece. The imagery chosen for the rest of the altarpiece, however, was entirely Sienese and civic in intention. It depicts the familiar subject of the enthroned Virgin with the Christ Child on her lap and surrounded by angels and saints. The altarpiece therefore echoes the imagery of two of Siena's most revered civic icons – the front face of Duccio's high altarpiece for the cathedral (see pls 35, 36) and Simone Martini's mural in the council hall of the Palazzo Pubblico (see pl. 47). That such an association was explicitly intended is shown by the inscription engraved on the Virgin's halo: 'If you trust me, Siena, you will be full of favour'. This message of reciprocity closely follows that of the inscriptions in both Duccio's and Simone Martini's early fourteenth-century paintings.[19] It would, moreover, have acted as a reminder to the Sienese of the dedication of their city to the Virgin on the eve of Montaperti and the traditions surrounding the ancient image of the *Virgin and Christ Child* that had previously stood over the altar.

The imagery of the altarpiece was elaborated in order to honour two more of the Virgin's titles – 'Queen of Heaven' and 'Our Lady of the Snows'. Two angels behind the throne hold a crown over the Virgin's head. The angel on the left of the throne, meanwhile, carries a dish filled with snow and the angel on the right makes a snowball. The seven narrative scenes of the predella describe in detail the legend of Our Lady of the Snows. They show how, in the reign of Pope Liberius (352–66), the Virgin caused snow to fall miraculously in the heat of August on the Esquiline Hill in Rome. Furthermore, the snow fell precisely in the pattern of the ground plan of a church. The Virgin then instructed a wealthy layman and his wife, and Pope Liberius, to build a church in her honour on this site – a church that became Santa Maria Maggiore, one of Rome's major basilicas. As *operaio*, Turino di Matteo would have been closely involved with building work in Siena cathedral and therefore the subject matter of the predella would have had personal associations for him.[20] Since the miraculous event was held to have taken place on the feast of the Assumption, the subject would also have appealed to the Sienese, who had long celebrated this feast as the high point of the civil and religious calendar. At the same time, however, the choice of subject undoubtedly had a more specific and immediate political dimension to it. In 1430 when the altarpiece was commissioned, the pope was Martin V, who some years earlier had summoned a Church council in Siena cathedral, as noted at the beginning of this chapter. Martin V, as a member of the noble Roman family of the Colonna, had a particular fondness for the church of Santa Maria Maggiore. This association was commemorated in a double-sided altarpiece executed around 1428–30 by the Florentine painters Masaccio and Masolino for this church. This painting included a depiction of the miraculous fall of snow and a number of visual references to Martin himself.[21] It is probable, therefore, that one of the reasons for choosing this novel subject for the altarpiece for Siena cathedral – and indeed for changing the title of the altar on which it stood – was to commemorate and honour Siena's recent connections with Rome and the papacy.

It appears from careful physical examination of the painting that the work now in the Palazzo Pitti comprises the altarpiece in its entirety.[22] It is constructed of a single panel set over a predella and devoid of pinnacle panels and buttresses – anticipating at a relatively early date the form that later fifteenth-century altarpieces would characteristically take (see, for example, pls 109–10). However, the upper framework of the altarpiece, which emphatically divides the picture field into three parts, would have emulated the framework of the centrepieces of the fourteenth-century narrative altarpieces that stood over the nearby altars of the four patron saints in the cathedral (see pls 58–61). Even more strikingly, the broad painted frame that surrounds the sides and bottom of the painting probably directly copied the framework of Duccio's early fourteenth-century high altarpiece (see pl. 35).

This use of a single panel for the main painting allowed Sassetta to represent the subsidiary figures of the saints not as single figures set on separate panels, but as existing within the same pictorial space as the central cult figures of the Virgin and Christ Child. Sassetta thus showed himself aware of recent developments in Tuscan altarpiece design,[23] but was also undeniably paying tribute to an older Sienese tradition, demonstrated most strikingly in Duccio's *Maestà* (see pl. 36) and the main panel of Pietro Lorenzetti's Carmelite altarpiece (see pl. 43). The narrow gold bands that provide the predella with the minimum of internal framing show a similar desire to establish an illusion of continuous space, seen most obviously in the three landscape scenes on the right. The architectural and landscape settings of the seven scenes in the predella also show a marked similarity to those of Pietro Lorenzetti in the Carmelite altarpiece (see pl. 44).[24] The impression of the holy figures in the main part of the altarpiece all co-existing within a single environment was further enhanced by Sassetta representing the scene as if observed from a consistent viewing point whereby everything above the centre of the painting is seen 'from below' and everything below the centre is seen 'from above.' The illusion of an orderly, clearly defined setting for the holy figures is enhanced by the precisely delineated pattern of the carpet, the steep orthogonals of which appear to recede deep into open space. This feature suggests familiarity with Brunelleschi's invention of single-point perspective and implies that Sassetta had carefully studied Donatello's recently executed relief for the font in Siena's baptistery (see pl. 90).[25]

The poses of the major figures in the main painting also relate subtly to the original position of the altarpiece over the altar beside the Porta del Perdono (see pl. 57). Devotees entering the cathedral would first have encountered the kneeling figure of Saint John the Baptist, portrayed looking intently in the direction of the doorway. The significance of his pointing gesture towards the Christ Child is then enhanced by the text on his scroll that reads 'Ecce Agnus Domini' ('behold the lamb of God'). His status as the forerunner and baptiser of Christ is further advertised by a text taken from the gospel of Matthew (11: 11, 'Among them born of women, there is no greater than John') inscribed in his halo. The Christ Child, who also appears occupied by those approaching from the left, carries a scroll on which is written another verse from the same chapter of Matthew (11: 28, 'come to me, all you who labour and are heavy laden, and I will give you rest'). This message of comfort and welcome would have been apposite for an image placed close to one of the principal entrances of the cathedral. The poses of the remaining figures and the perspective of the pavement together act as an encouragement to the spectator to take up a position directly facing the altar and to absorb the detail of the narrative scenes in the predella illustrating the legend of the Madonna of the Snows.

Sassetta's *Madonna delle Nevi* altarpiece thus provided a worthy successor to the series of fourteenth-century altarpiece painted for the cathedral altars. Even in its present condition, it offers proof that the existing traditions of Sienese painting were eminently capable of development in the early decades of the fifteenth century. Indeed, in terms of its subtle design and novel treatment of its religious subject, Sassetta's altarpiece represented a milestone in the history of the Italian renaissance altarpiece.

Celebrating New Saints

In 1439 the officials of the Compagnia della Vergine – one of the city's most important confraternities – commissioned an altarpiece for the high altar of San Girolamo, the church of the Gesuati in Siena. The Gesuati were a new religious order with an eventful early history. Founded in 1355 by Giovanni Colombini, a member of a wealthy Sienese family, their excessive exhibition of piety on the streets of Siena led to the group's expulsion from the city in 1363. After the severe outbreak of plague in that year, however, they were summoned back to Siena and became a conventional religious order, living in the priory of San Girolamo on the south-east outskirts of the city (see pl. 6). A papal commission in 1438 then confirmed that the Gesuati could become priests, like other mendicant orders. They duly acted in this capacity for the Compagnia della Vergine and it is likely that this was one of the reasons the confraternity financed the high altarpiece for the order's church of San Girolamo.[26]

The commission resulted in a monumental polyptych that carries the name of the painter, Sano di Pietro, and the year 1444 on the lower edge of the central panel (pl. 93). Named as one of the painters who arbitrated on the price of the *Madonna delle Nevi* in 1432, Sano di Pietro was a painter who later in his career secured a succession of prestigious commissions from the Sienese government. He was also a member of the Compagnia della Vergine. The altarpiece that he executed on behalf of his confraternity was somewhat old-fashioned in design for its date. Taking the form of a Gothic polyptych, replete with pinnacle panels, pinnacles and piers, it originally stood on a predella that displayed five scenes from the life of Saint Jerome. Compared with Sassetta's *Madonna delle Nevi* altarpiece (see pl. 92), it therefore more closely resembled altarpieces that had been produced by Taddeo di Bartolo and Andrea Vanni at the turn of the century.

The apparent conservatism of the design may, however, have been deliberate. As already indicated, the Gesuati had been engaged in a campaign to establish their identity and reputation as a conventional religious order within the city. The imagery of the altarpiece would have acted as an

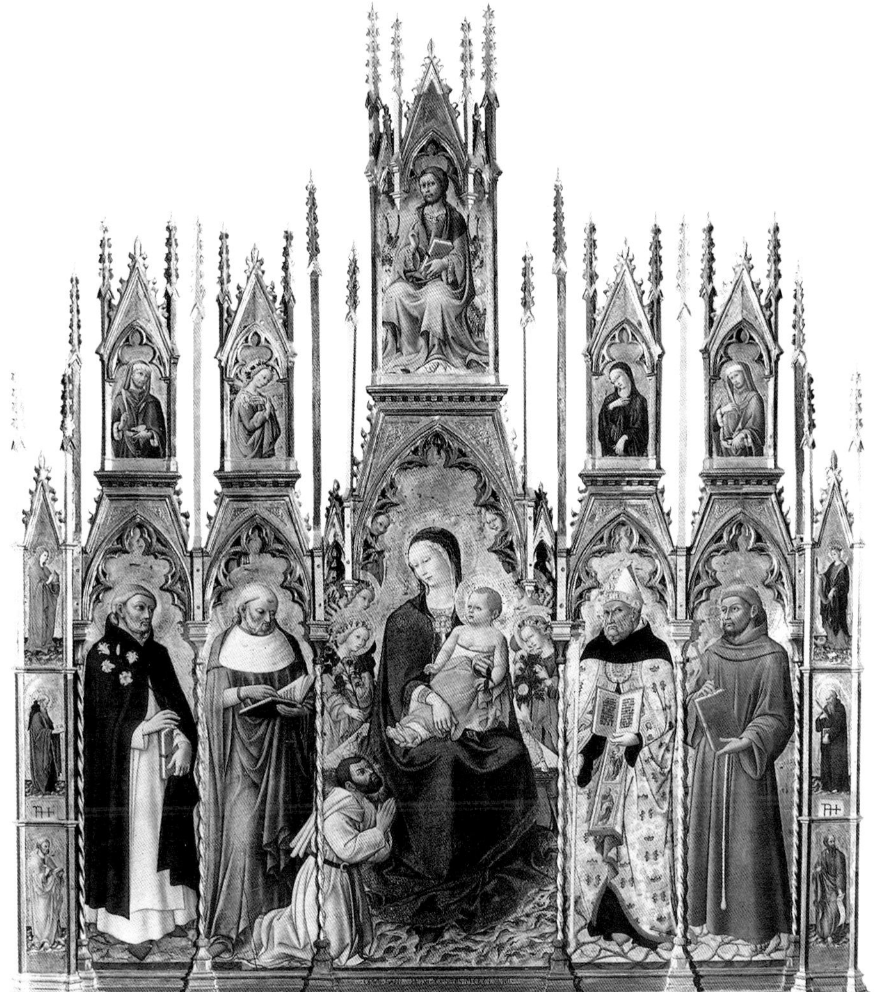

93 Sano di Pietro, *The Virgin and Christ Child with Saints Dominic, Jerome, the Blessed Giovanni Colombini, Saints Augustine and Francis* (1444). Tempera on panel, 320 × 282 cm. Siena, Pinacoteca Nazionale.

extremely effective demonstration of this. While the central part of the altarpiece is primarily directed to a celebration of the Virgin and her role in the incarnation and the redemption of humanity by Christ, the other figures on the main part of the altarpiece all had specific significance for the Gesuati. Foremost is Giovanni Colombini, the founder of the order, represented kneeling at the foot of the Virgin and Christ Child. Shown with rays of light around his head to signify his rank as a *beato* (an acknowledged holy figure but not yet a saint), Colombini is portrayed in the distinctive white habit of the Gesuati. The gracefully inclined head of the Virgin indicates that his pious act of devotion has been acknowledged.

Directly behind Giovanni Colombini stands Saint Jerome, the titular saint of the church and priory of the Gesuati. While the predella consists of a series of scenes showing Jerome as a religious ascetic and visionary, here he is portrayed as a scholar and cardinal of the Church. This appeal to the authority of the Church is further reiterated by the figure of Saint Augustine who appears in the robes of a bishop and carries a book containing a text that acknowledges Jerome's learning and eloquence. Augustine had a further significance for the Gesuati because in 1426 they had adopted the rule supposedly written by him. Finally, on the outer edges of the main part of the altarpiece appear Saints Dominic and Francis – the founders of the two mendicant orders whose religious life the Gesuati wished to emulate most closely. The focus upon the Gesuati and their identity as a religious order continued in the choice of saints for the subsidiary parts of the altarpiece. Those appearing on the outer pinnacle panels (Saints Cosmas and Damian) and the middle one of the side piers (Saints Anthony Abbot and Ephraim) were all saints associated with hospitals and the care of the sick. It is also relevant that the commission of the altarpiece was financed by a legacy given to the confraternity by a doctor, Francesco da Gubbio.[27]

In many ways, in terms of its intention and purpose Sano di Pietro's Gesuati altarpiece resembles that of Pietro Lorenzetti's high altarpiece for Santa Maria del Carmine (see pl. 44). Like that predecessor, its imposing size and rich embellishment would have been a magnificent addition to the interior of the small priory church of San Girolamo. It would also have provided the Gesuati community with a powerful statement of their newly defined identity as a 'respectable' religious order, recognised and sanctioned by the Church.

While the particular demands of this commission apparently caused Sano di Pietro to produce a conventional panel painting, another commission he received from the Compagnia della Vergine resulted in a much more innovative type of altarpiece. On 20 May 1444 the celebrated Sienese

Franciscan friar Bernardino Albizzeschi died in Aquila. Although unable to secure his physical remains, the Sienese government and the local Franciscan Observants immediately mounted an energetic campaign to have him recognised as a saint. On 7 June the prior and councillors of the Compagnia della Vergine were authorised to spend as much money as they deemed necessary for an image to celebrate the memory of Bernardino. The commission was given to Sano di Pietro on 28 May 1445. So concerned were the confraternity that the painter should achieve an accurate representation of Bernardino that they insisted that 'he will be obliged to ruin it and do it, over and over so often until the . . . [commissioners] are well pleased'.[28]

The three principal panels of this altarpiece have been identified as those now on display in the cathedral museum but for many years housed in the cathedral sacristy. They show the saint ascending into heaven, preaching outside San Francesco in Siena and preaching in the Campo (pls 94, 95). A plausible reconstruction of the altarpiece by two art historians suggests that the three paintings once formed a triptych with the two portrayals of Bernardino's power as a preacher both framing and, through the emphatic diagonals of their compositions, focussing on the central image of Bernardino himself.[29] Sano di Pietro represented the gaunt face of the saint in a particularly effective manner, with details that were almost certainly taken from Bernardino's own death mask and which appear consistently in later painted and sculpted representations of him.

Sano di Pietro's other major achievement in this altarpiece was to represent, in graphic detail, one of the principal reasons why Bernardino was revered by the Sienese. He painted two highly descriptive scenes of the saint preaching in immediately recognisable locations in Siena itself (which also show how men and women were strictly segregated at these events). Each preaching scene alludes to a particular religious cult for which Bernardino was famed. Thus in the San Francesco scene Bernardino appears in the pulpit with a crucifix, as a reminder of his devotion towards the crucified Christ. In the Campo scene, meanwhile, he holds up the IHS monogram (an abbreviation of the Greek word for Jesus), a symbol that Bernardino made famous across Italy in his preaching.

In 1448 the papal commission appointed by Nicholas V to review the case for Bernardino's canonisation arrived in Siena. On a two-day visit to the Spedale di Santa Maria della Scala – the site of a number of Bernardino's spiritual experiences and miracles – the commission celebrated mass in the oratory of the confraternity of Saints Jerome and Francis. The altar of this oratory was by then embellished with Sano di Pietro's

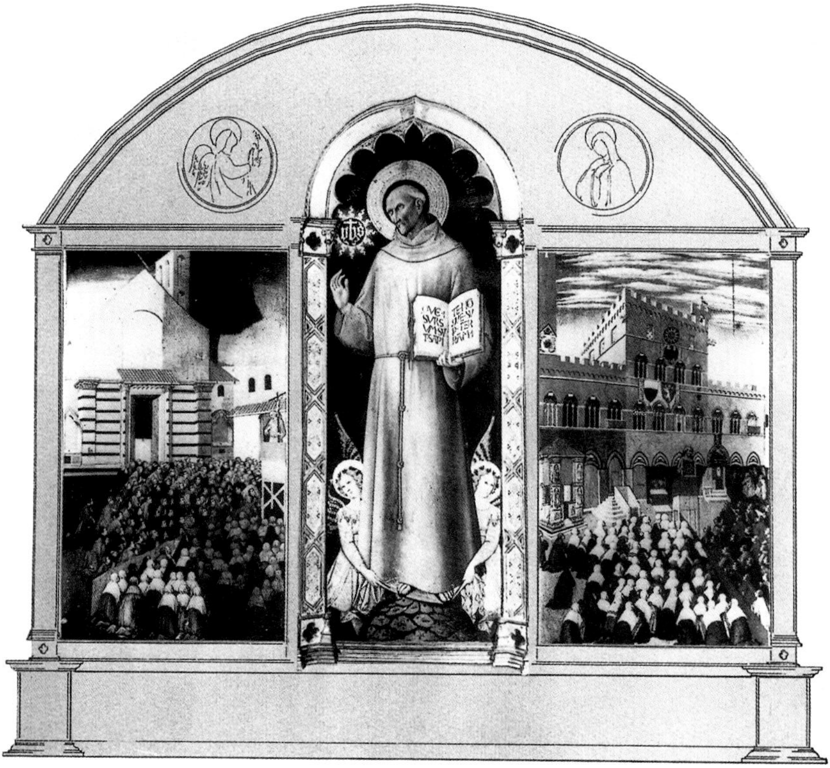

94 Reconstruction of the *Saint Bernardino Altarpiece* by Sano di Pietro (by Gaudenz Freuler and Michael Mallory).

altarpiece that had been donated to the confraternity by the Compagnia della Vergine a year earlier.[30] Two years later, on the feast of Pentecost, Bernardino was declared a saint, so achieving the highest honour that the Church could bestow in the outstandingly short period of six years. It seems likely that Sano di Pietro's novel altarpiece, with its bold promotion of Bernardino as a preacher, may have played a part in persuading the papal commission to sanction the canonisation of this revered Sienese friar.

* * *

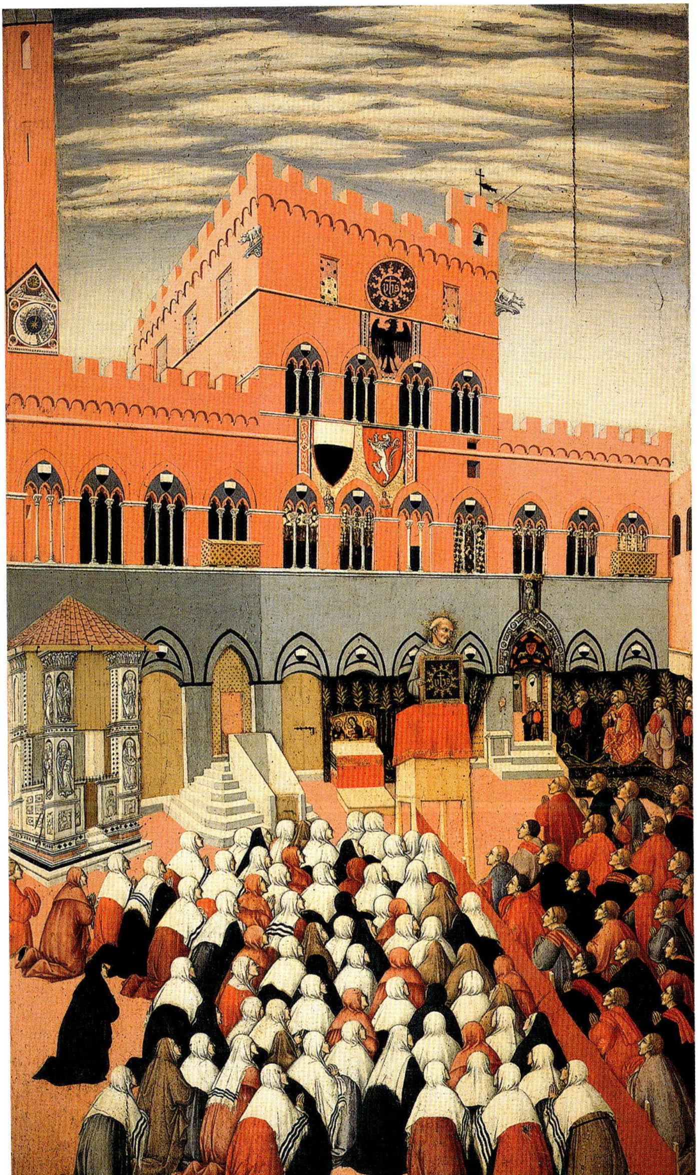

95 Sano di Pietro, *Saint Bernardino preaching in the Campo* (1445). Tempera on panel, 162 × 101.5 cm (including original frame). Siena, Museo dell'Opera del Duomo.

Paintings for the Spedale

In the years immediately before Bernardino's canonisation and the confraternity commission there had been an extraordinary number of ambitious artistic campaigns within the Spedale di Santa Maria della Scala. The earliest of these coincided with the rectorship of Giovanni di Francesco Buzzichelli, who was in charge in the Spedale between 1433 and 1444. An energetic and cultured man who had contacts with Florence and its hospitals, Buzzichelli commissioned painted covers for the hospital's administrative documents and several reliquaries in which to house the hospital's extensive collection of relics.[31] He also oversaw the execution of an impressive cycle of fresco paintings for the principal male ward of the hospital infirmary.

THE PELLEGRINAIO

Known as the Pellegrinaio, this fourteenth-century room took the form of a long vaulted hall situated on the ground floor of the hospital at right angles to what was then still part of the hospital church (pl. 96, no. 3). The project began in about 1440 with the painting of the transverse arches and the vaults with a rich array of saints and prophets by the Bolognese painter Agostino di Marsiglio (pl. 97). The religious tone of the decoration continued with a series of seven paintings illustrating the story of Tobias commissioned from Vecchietta and another painter in 1441. These are now entirely lost but were located in the first bay of the Pellegrinaio that acted as a reception area for the hospital ward beyond. In the same year another painter, Pietro d'Ambrogio, was responsible for two paintings on the window wall at the other end of the Pellegrinaio. These paintings of an unknown subject were destroyed when the Pellegrinaio was extended by one additional vaulted bay in the sixteenth century. In addition to his three paintings in the Tobias cycle, Vecchietta was also entrusted with painting the first in the series of paintings on the left-hand wall (as one faces the window wall) that illustrated scenes in the Spedale's history. This was the *Founding of the Spedale di Santa Maria della Scala* (pl. 98). Between 1441 and 1442, Domenico di Bartolo then executed three large mural paintings on the opposite right wall – the *Care of the Sick*, the *Reception of Pilgrims and the Distribution of Alms* and the *Rearing and Marriage of Female Foundlings* (see pl. 89) – all of which recorded the hospital's main activities, as clearly set out in the surviving fourteenth-century statutes. Between 1442 and 1443 Domenico di Bartolo completed two further paintings on

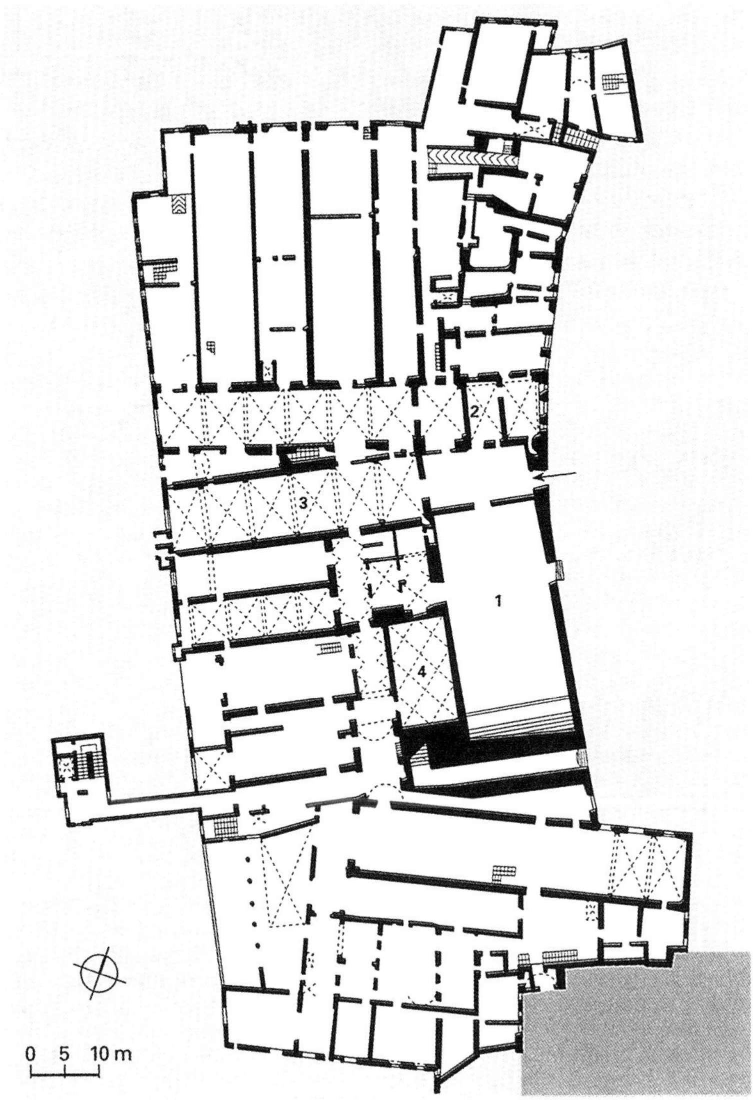

96 Plan of the ground floor of the Spedale di Santa Maria della Scala

1 Church of Santissima Annunziata
2 Chapel of the Relics
3 Pellegrinaio
4 Sacristy

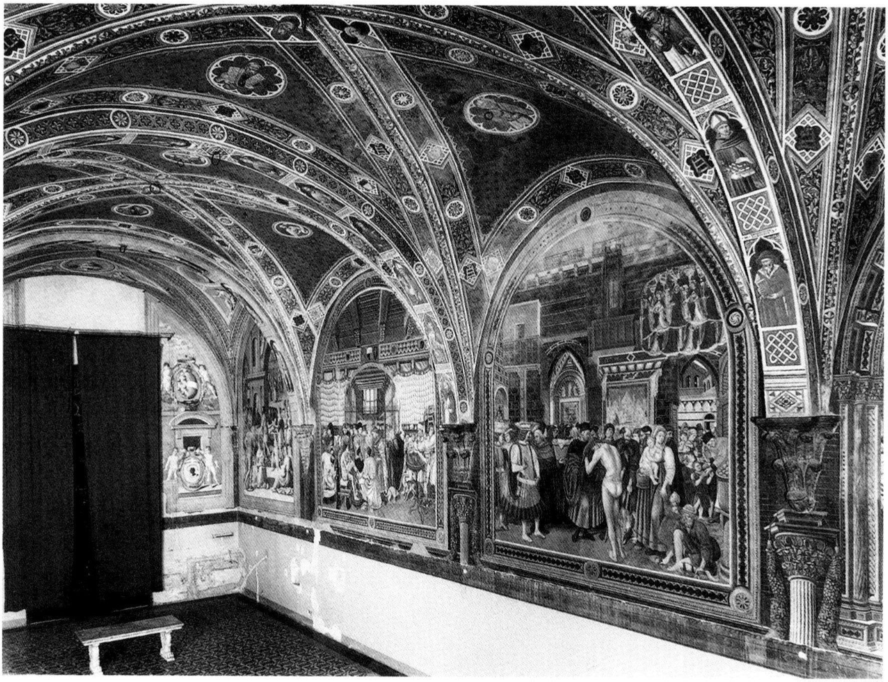

97 The Pellegrinaio with frescoes by Domenico di Bartolo and others. Siena, Spedale di Santa Maria della Scala.

98 (*facing page*) Vecchietta, *The Founding of the Spedale di Santa Maria della Scala* (1441). Fresco on the east wall of the Pellegrinaio. Siena, Spedale di Santa Maria della Scala.

the left-hand wall – the *Building of the Hospital* and *Pope Celestine III granting the Hospital Privileges* – which commemorated later stages in the Spedale's history, while Priamo della Quercia (the brother of the sculptor Jacopo), painted another scene, the *Blessed Agostino Novello assigning the Habit of the Hospital to the Rector.* Finally, in 1444 Domenico di Bartolo was paid for the painting of the *Feeding of the Poor*. Located above the door of the Pellegrinaio, this painting completed the series on the right-hand wall depicting the hospital's social and charitable activities.[32]

The painting of the walls may have proceeded in a somewhat erratic sequence but the overall scheme was nevertheless well organised. Despite

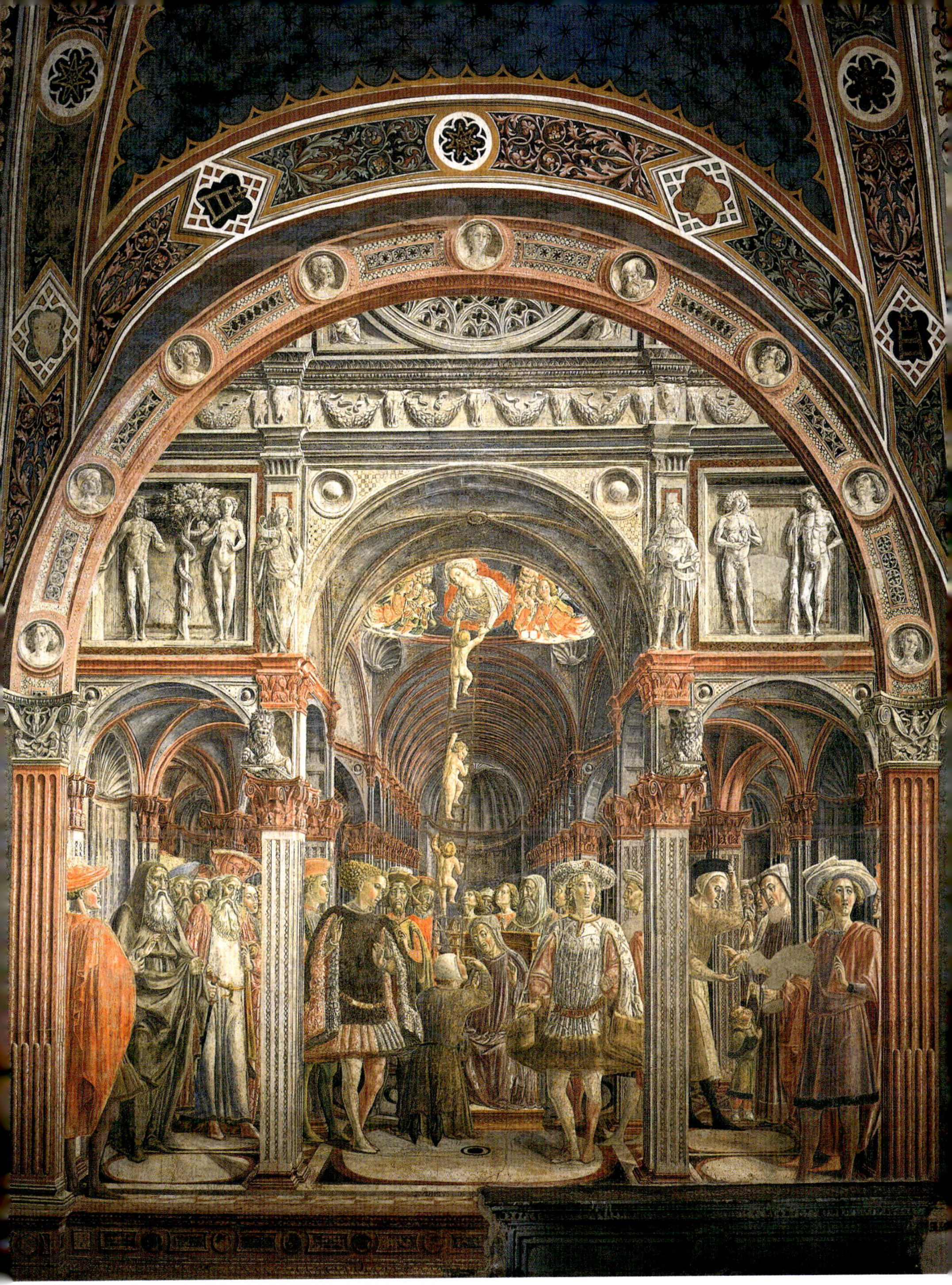

involving three different painters, all the surviving paintings share the same arched format, wide decorative borders and richly figurative compositions. The paintings of the right-hand wall – all by Domenico di Bartolo – are, however, more clearly organised and set within simpler borders. In terms of their representation, all his paintings apparently provide accurate depictions of the interior of the hospital and the people who lived and worked in it. Thus the *Care of the Sick* shows not only the appearance of one of the hospital wards next to the Pellegrinaio but also the surgical procedures of the time and a variety of types of care offered to patients by the hospital. It also appears that Domenico di Bartolo was specifically instructed to include a portrait of Bartolo di Tura Bandini, who was a celebrated surgeon working for the Spedale during this period.[33]

By contrast, the four paintings by Vecchietta, Domenico di Bartolo and Priamo della Quercia on the left-hand wall appear much more ornate, in terms of both their architectural settings and the persons depicted in these scenes. Mixing details that record the appearance of contemporary buildings and personages with others that are more fanciful, these paintings provide a compelling insight into fifteenth-century attitudes to history. The *Blessed Agostino Novello assigning the Habit*, for example, depicts an event that allegedly took place in the early decades of the fourteenth century, but Priamo della Quercia represented it as occurring in an open-sided loggia, richly embellished with sculpted figures recalling those executed by his brother. This architectural structure probably records a ceremonial loggia set up in the cathedral square in 1441 in anticipation of the visit of Pope Eugenius IV two years later. One of the bystanders, meanwhile, is shown wearing the distinctive peaked cap of the Byzantine Emperor John Paleologus who attended the Church council that met in Florence in 1439.[34] In order to glorify the Spedale and its history, therefore, events that supposedly took place more than a century earlier have been made more immediate by the inclusion of contemporary details.

The surviving paintings of the Pellegrinaio provide evidence of how receptive Buzzichelli and his painters were to the new pictorial conventions of renaissance art. For example, in his *Founding of the Spedale*, Vecchietta set the complex scene in what appears to be a vaulted church (see pl. 98). This allowed him to place the central narrative event within the nave of this church. Here the cobbler, Sorore, the mythical founder of the Spedale, is shown describing to one of the canons of the cathedral the vision that his mother was alleged to have experienced before his birth. Behind these two figures, in the space of the domed crossing, appears the vision itself – the Virgin welcoming infants who have reached heaven by climbing up the hospital's emblem of a ladder. The right-hand aisle of the church, meanwhile, acts as the setting for the first occasion when Sorore brought a foundling to one of the cathedral canons and received money for the upkeep of the child. The entire edifice is fronted by an impressive façade whose style with its antique detail of fluted piers, ornate capitals and frieze is unequivocally renaissance. Perspective has been employed to great effect, both on the pavement of the church and in the recession of the building itself. The stylishly dressed man on the right also performs the function of the 'mediator' recommended by the humanist Alberti in his influential treatise on painting written in 1435.[35]

It has been suggested that Vecchietta's familiarity with the new vocabulary of renaissance art came from his acquaintance with the work of both the Florentine painter Masolino in Rome and Castiglione d'Olona (where Vecchietta himself worked) and of the peripatetic north Italian artist Pisanello. Another painter who could have exerted an influence on his pictorial style was Domenico Veneziano who, although from the Veneto, was then working in Florence and Perugia. Buzzichelli's own contacts with Florence – particularly with the hospital of Santa Maria Nuova where Domenico Veneziano executed a scheme of frescoes – could have acted as a further incentive to Vecchietta to display his knowledge of the latest artistic trends.[36]

In spite of its modernity, the painting nevertheless remains a highly Sienese rendition of this mythical event in that it recalls Ambrogio Lorenzetti's skilful deployment of architecture and pictorial space to organise and enrich a narrative (see pl. 61). The sheer enjoyment of a crowd of figures, some dressed in the height of courtly fashion, and of ornate decorative detail is also typical of Sienese art. Although rejected by writers such as Alberti, such features continued to be favoured by Sienese painters and their patrons, thus tending to make them highly appreciative of the elegant and decorative style of north Italian painters such as Gentile da Fabriano and Pisanello, rather than of the more restrained style of the Florentine Masaccio and his followers.

THE 'OLD' CHAPEL OF THE RELICS

Once he had embellished one of the principal spaces in the hospital with an impressive series of paintings that celebrated its history and function as a major charitable institution, Giovanni Buzzichelli turned his attention to the Spedale's valuable relics and their future housing, beginning the construction of a new sacristy, next to the hospital church (see pl. 96, no. 4).

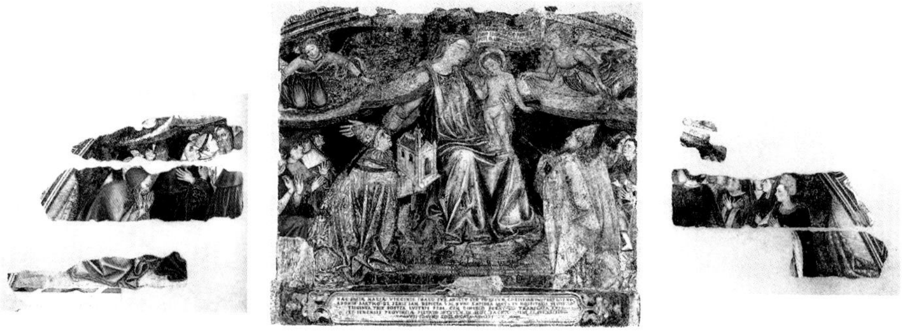

99 Reconstruction of Domenico di Bartolo, *The Madonna della Misericordia* (1444). Fresco. Siena, Spedale di Santa Maria della Scala and Pinacoteca Nazionale.

It had not been painted when he died but his role in the project is nevertheless commemorated by his coat-of-arms located – with those of the Spedale and the city – just above the capitals of the sacristy.

To give a new significance to the original fourteenth-century chapel of the relics (see pl. 96, no. 2), now divested of its precious contents, Buzzichelli commissioned Domenico di Bartolo to paint a fresco in the old chapel honouring the Virgin as the hospital's patron saint and protector.[37] Originally located over a doorway to one of the hospital's principal wards, the *Madonna della Misericordia*, as the image came to be called, became a cult object in its own right. When it was removed from this site in 1610, the central section of the fresco was taken to Buzzichelli's new sacristy and displayed within an imposing fifteenth-century tabernacle. Two other parts of the fresco, rediscovered only in 1970,[38] are now housed in the Pinacoteca. A photomontage of the three surviving pieces of Domenico di Bartolo's painting conveys something of the impact that this arresting image of the Virgin must once have made (pl. 99). It shows her in the guise of 'Our Lady of Mercy', an established iconographic type that depicts the Virgin sheltering her devotees beneath her cloak. In his version, Domenico di Bartolo has taken the unusual step of placing the Virgin and her son facing in different directions, implying that both sets of kneeling devotees are the object of their attention. This detail makes for a greater dynamism in the figurative composition, while the sense of inclusion would have been emphasised by the folds of the wide cloak that once enveloped the kneeling figures on both sides. Although it is difficult to appreciate in its present fragmentary state, the painting gives an impression of an expansive spatial setting. Thus the devotees have been portrayed as though kneeling in a semi-circle on either side of the central figures of the Virgin and Christ Child, and the Virgin's altar-like throne is set upon a series of circular steps covered by a decorative carpet.

The iconography of the painting is also distinctive in showing to the left members of the clergy, headed by a pope presenting a miniature church to the Virgin and Christ Child, and to the right members of the laity, led by an emperor. The striking figure of the man in the left-hand fragment who wears the distinctive black and white costume of the rectors of the hospital probably represents Buzzichelli himself – a reminder of Domenico di Bartolo's well-documented abilities as a painter of contemporary portraits.[39] It may also be, therefore, that the woman with a fashionable headdress on the extreme right represents Buzzichelli's wife. Similarly, the distinctive faces of the pope and the emperor may record those of Pope Eugenius IV and the Emperor Sigismund, both of whom had visited Siena in the late 1430s and early 1440s and had awarded honours to the city and its institutions. If this is so, then one of Domenico di Bartolo's achievements in painting this familiar subject was to commemorate and dignify Buzzichelli's personal devotion to the Virgin by setting it in a much wider social context, embracing both the Church and the Sienese state.

THE 'NEW' SACRISTY

The responsibility for embellishing Buzzichelli's new sacristy devolved to his successor, Urbano di Pietro del Bello, who was rector of the Spedale between 1444 and 1450. As indicated in a painted text in the sacristy itself, he chose one of the painters of the Pellegrinaio, Vecchietta, to undertake this task. Vecchietta's work in the sacristy involved three separate schemes. The earliest was the painting of the *Arliquiera*, a wooden structure designed to enclose the hospital's precious relics in a niche in the wall of the sacristy, for which the painter and two named assistants received several payments between April and December 1445.[40] When completed, on its outer face the *Arliquiera* displayed a series of saints and *beati* who were particularly revered in Siena and in the Spedale (pl. 100). Members of major religious orders were skilfully juxtaposed with members of the lay orders associated with them. Thus below the Dominican friar Ambrogio Sansedoni appeared the Dominican tertiary Catherine of Siena. Represented just above the massive metal bolts that secured the doors of the *Arliquiera* was the Blessed Agostino Novello, a figure of particular relevance to the Spedale. Believed to have written the rule for the hospital community of Augustinian

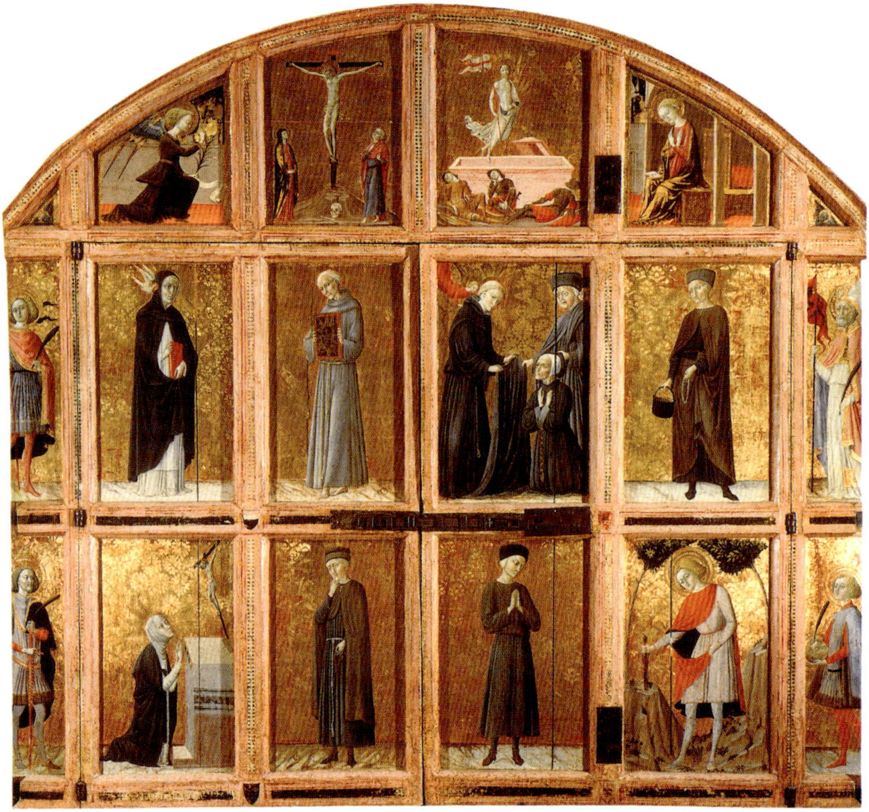

100 The outer shutters of the *Arliquiera* showing paintings by Vecchietta of the patron saints and *beati* of Siena, the *Annunciation*, the *Crucifixion* and *Resurrection of Christ* (1445). Tempera on panel, each shutter 273 × 187 cm. Siena, Pinacoteca Nazionale.

tertiaries, this Augustinian friar is accordingly shown in the act of bestowing the mantle of office on the kneeling figure of a rector – it seems reasonable to suppose that it may be intended as a portrait of Urbano himself (pl. 101).

Above this array of civic saints was placed a sequence of four paintings that portrayed in the outer compartments the Archangel Gabriel and the Virgin of the Annunciation and in the centre the Crucifixion and the Resurrection. While the first two figures alluded to the annual display of the

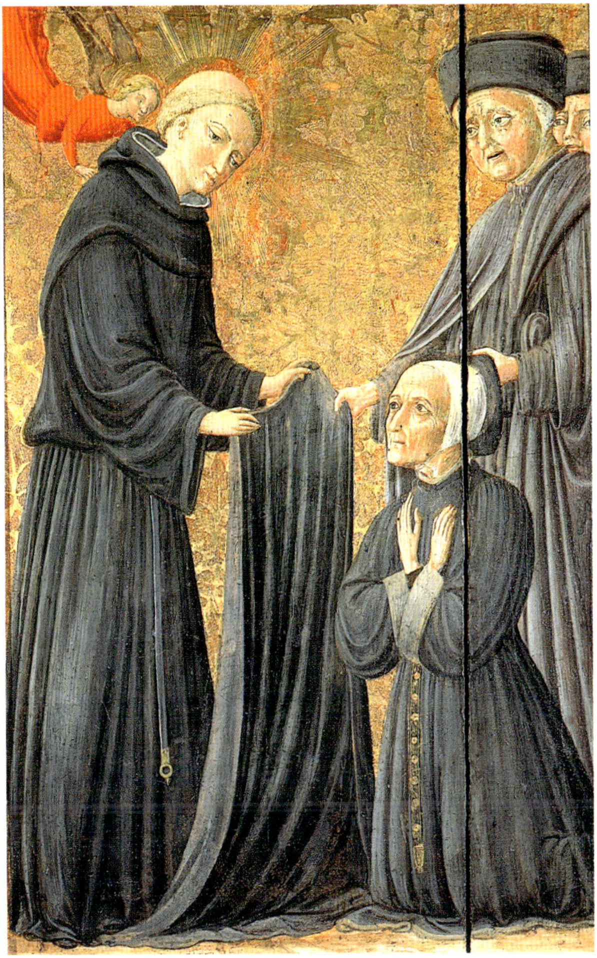

101 Vecchietta, *The Blessed Agostino Novello assigning the Habit of the Hospital to the Rector* (detail of pl. 100).

relics to the public on the feast of the Annunciation, the second two scenes acted as a reminder of a prized relic held in the *Arliquiera* – one of the nails believed to have been used at the Crucifixion. The inner surfaces of the doors were painted with eight scenes depicting the Passion. Thus, when the doors were opened, the relics would have been framed by an entire sequence of paintings illustrating the key events that led up to the Crucifixion and Resurrection. Like Benedetto di Bindo's early fifteenth-century reliquary cupboard for the cathedral sacristy, there was an explicit association between the relics and the Crucifixion. However, whereas Benedetto di Bindo's series of paintings related the relic of the Cross to the legendary history of the Cross, Vecchietta's series for the *Arliquiera* associated the relic of the nail directly to the narrative of Christ's Passion itself.

In 1446 Vecchietta also received a substantial payment for materials and work on the vaults of the sacristy. Three years later he received further payment for ten 'stories' in the sacristy. While some scholars have assumed that Vecchietta and his assistants took the whole period between 1446 and 1449 to complete the painting of the entire sacristy, others have argued for two separate campaigns of work, one for the vaults and the other for the walls.[41] As a result of the hospital church being greatly enlarged some two decades after Vecchietta's paintings were completed, the 'new' sacristy was itself replaced by another, located nearer the high altar of the new church. At an unknown date, Vecchietta's paintings were then covered with whitewash that was removed only in the middle of the nineteenth century. In the interim, they had suffered considerable damage, leaving some paintings completely obliterated and others lacking important details. Enough survives, however, to allow the judgement that in its original form this must have been a complex and erudite scheme designed to convey a powerful message of the divinely sanctioned authority of the Church.[42]

Drawing upon the earlier schemes painted for the chapterhouse of the Augustinian priory of Sant'Agostino and the sacristy of the cathedral (see pl. 76), the frescoes of the Spedale sacristy illustrated the principal tenets of the Christian faith, as embodied in the Apostles' Creed. Beginning at the extreme left-hand corner of the left wall (when facing the altar) and proceeding in a clockwise direction round the entire sacristy, the spectator is treated to a highly detailed visualisation of the principal statements of faith made when reciting the Apostles' Creed. Since the room contains only ten bays, some bays portray several articles simultaneously, while others depict only parts of particularly significant statements. Examination of one of the bays that remain in relatively good condition reveals the greater complexity of Vecchietta's scheme when compared with that of Benedetto di Bindo for the sacristy cupboards in the cathedral. Designed to illustrate the article: 'from thence [heaven] he [Christ] shall come to judge the quick and the dead', the upper lunette painting shows Christ seated in heaven surrounded by ranks of the saints (pl. 102). To the left appears the Virgin, interceding on behalf of those who have been selected to enter heaven. To the right appears Saint John the Baptist, whose pointing gesture indicates those who have been damned to the torments of hell. At the centre of the lower com-

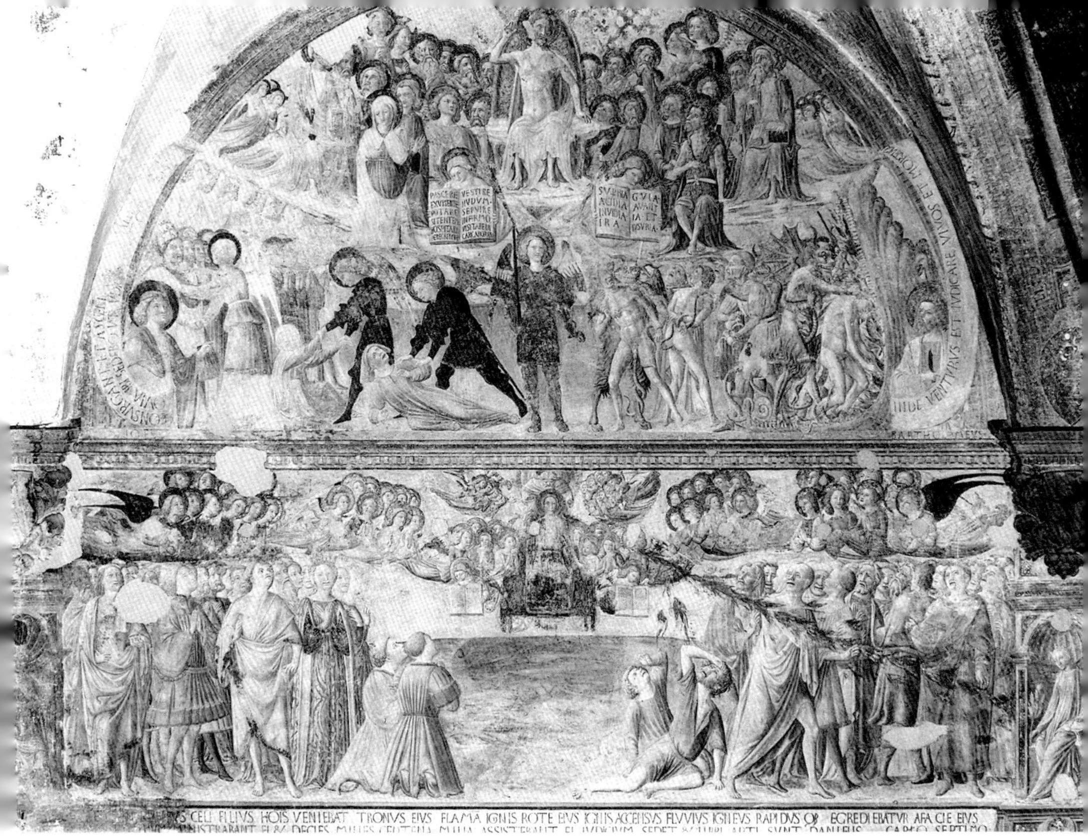

102 Vecchietta, *The Last Judgement*, and *Daniel's Vision of Heavenly Judgement* (1446–9). Fresco on the south wall of the old sacristy depicting the seventh article of the Apostles' Creed. Siena, Spedale di Santa Maria della Scala.

position appears the Archangel Michael, who was traditionally associated with this day of judgement. To reinforce the severity of his role, both he and his two companions have been represented in armour.

As in all the bays of the sacristy, the message of the painting is reinforced by the use of painted texts. Thus, directly below Christ are two angels who carry open books on which are displayed (on the left, and over the blessed) the names of the seven Christian Virtues and (on the right, over the damned) the names of the seven Vices. In the right-hand corner of the painting appears a three-quarter-length figure of the apostle Bartholomew, holding a scroll on which is written the relevant article of the Creed. The entire scheme would have cleverly reinforced the traditional belief that at Pentecost each one of the apostles received divine inspiration to recite one article of the Creed. In the left-hand corner appears the Old Testament prophet Joel, carrying a scroll on which is written the text: 'let the people be wakened, and come up to the valley of Jehosaphat: for there will I sit to judge all the people around' (Joel 3:12) – which provided written justification for later Christian belief in the Last Judgement. The message was made even more effective by the portrayal on the lower part of the wall of an event drawn from the Old Testament and believed to have been relevant to the subject of the upper painting. This was Daniel's vision of heavenly judgement as recounted in the Book of Daniel. The relevant verses are written out in the lower border of the painting (Daniel 7:9–13). As a vision that involved a fiery stream issuing from before God, seated in judgement, this subject formed a particularly apt parallel for the painting above it.

Vecchietta's paintings on the walls of the sacristy therefore provided a detailed visualisation of the articles of the Creed, as appropriate for the room in which the priest would prepare for the celebration of mass. With its emphasis on the redemptive power of Christ's death upon the Cross, the Creed was a highly appropriate subject for a room that contained relics that included a nail of the Crucifixion. The originality of the sacristy scheme also lay in the inclusion of ten large-scale paintings of narrative scenes drawn from the Old Testament – many of which had not previously been portrayed in Sienese art. The powerful message of these paintings – that the entire history of the Christian Church was planned and sanctioned by divine authority – was reinforced in the paintings on the vault of the sacristy. Subdivided into numerous compartments, the focus is on the figure of Christ seated in glory and surrounded by cherubim and angels. Around him appear representations of the four evangelists, the four doctors of the Church and a number of Old Testament prophets. Their role as purveyors of sacred wisdom is further conveyed by the biblical texts they display or are shown writing.

While thus profoundly religious in subject, the painted embellishment of the sacristy included several broadly civic references. Above the capitals of each bay were once emblems of the city, the Spedale and the rector, Buzzichelli. Directly below the capitals, there appear to have been a series of seated allegorical figures representing various civic virtues similar to those portrayed by Ambrogio Lorenzetti in the *Good Government* in the Sala della Pace (see pl. 52). In a number of paintings the participants appear in contemporary dress – as seen clearly in the left-hand foreground of *Daniel's Vision* (see pl. 102). A badly damaged painting on the lower wall beneath the penultimate scene of the Creed series also shows the rector and brothers of the Spedale distributing alms. Just as the decoration of the sacristy marked an important development in the Sienese tradition of representing the Creed, so it reflected the particular nature of its location in one of the city's principal civic institutions.

Paintings for the Cathedral Baptistery

A substantial payment to Vecchietta in 1450 by the Opera del Duomo for painting the vaults and walls of the baptistery indicates that by that time he was involved in another major fresco scheme. Other payments, dated between 1447 and 1453, indicate that this was a complex and long project involving painters from as far afield as Bologna, Forli and Borgo San Sepolchro.[43] The result of their collaborative endeavours is a programme of fresco decoration that covers all six vaults of the baptistery (pl. 103) and the shallow apse behind the high altar (see pl. 90). The three vaults of the entrance or western bays of the building are decorated with the figures of the twelve apostles posed against a starry blue background. The borders and corners of the vaults and the surfaces of the arches are further covered with a varied repertoire of figures representing prophets, sibyls, saints and Virtues. The three vaults of the eastern bays are decorated with twelve paintings, each representing an article of the Apostles' Creed, together with broad bands of painted decoration showing a series of heads of men and women in contemporary dress and classical putti housed in architectural niches (pl. 104). On the apse wall is a series of large-scale narrative paintings illustrating five scenes from Christ's Passion, beginning with the Agony in the Garden and ending with the Lamentation over his dead body (see pl. 90). On either side of the niche housing the high altar are paintings of the Archangel Gabriel and the Virgin of the Annunciation – a Marian dimension to the programme that is continued by a painting of the Assumption of the Virgin on the outer surface of the arch framing the apse. On the inner surfaces of the altar niche are figures portraying saints and *beati* particularly venerated by the Sienese.

Nineteenth-century restoration has now made it difficult to assign specific paintings to particular artists but it seems likely that Agostino di Marsiglio (the Bolognese painter responsible for the painted vaults of the Pellegrinaio) painted the side vaults of the three western bays, while his fellow Bolognese, Michele di Matteo di Lambertini, painted the three upper Passion scenes in the altar apse. Vecchietta joined the project at a later date – probably around 1449, while in the last stages of painting the hospital sacristy. He and his assistants painted the central vault of the entry bays, all

104 (*facing page*) Vecchietta, *The Last Judgement* (*c.* 1450–53). Fresco in a central vault depicting the seventh article of the Apostles' Creed. Siena, baptistery.

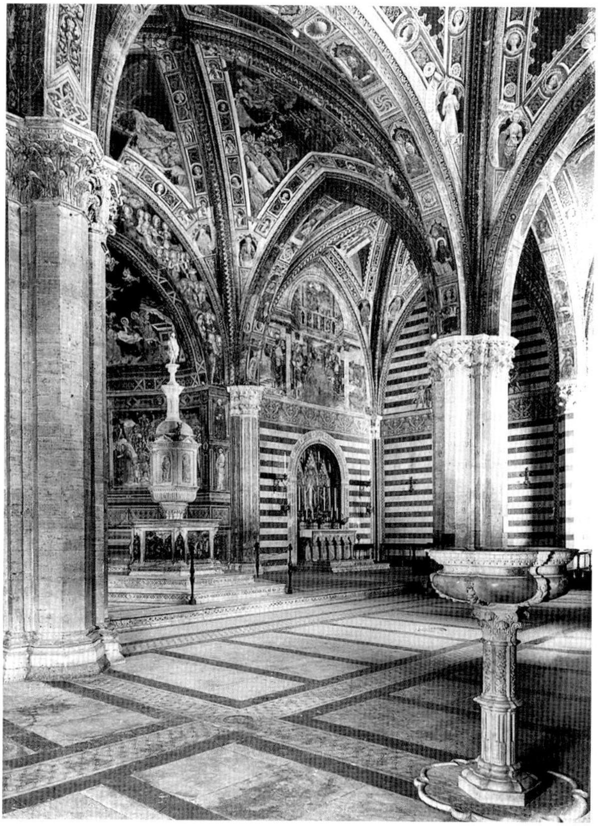

103 The interior of the baptistery, Siena.

three vaults of the eastern bays and the remaining paintings in the lower part of the apse and high altar niche.

The choice of imagery was particularly apt for its location. As the church where all Sienese were baptised, the baptistery already housed the magnificent sculpted font executed by a variety of sculptors in the early decades of the fifteenth century. The presence of a series of paintings directly above and adjacent to the baptismal font that illustrated the principle beliefs of the Christian faith was thus highly appropriate. The inclusion in the lower left-hand corner of each painting of the kneeling figure of a man with the word 'Credo' ('I believe') issuing from his mouth makes the didactic intention of this series inescapable. As in the hospital sacristy scheme, the paint-

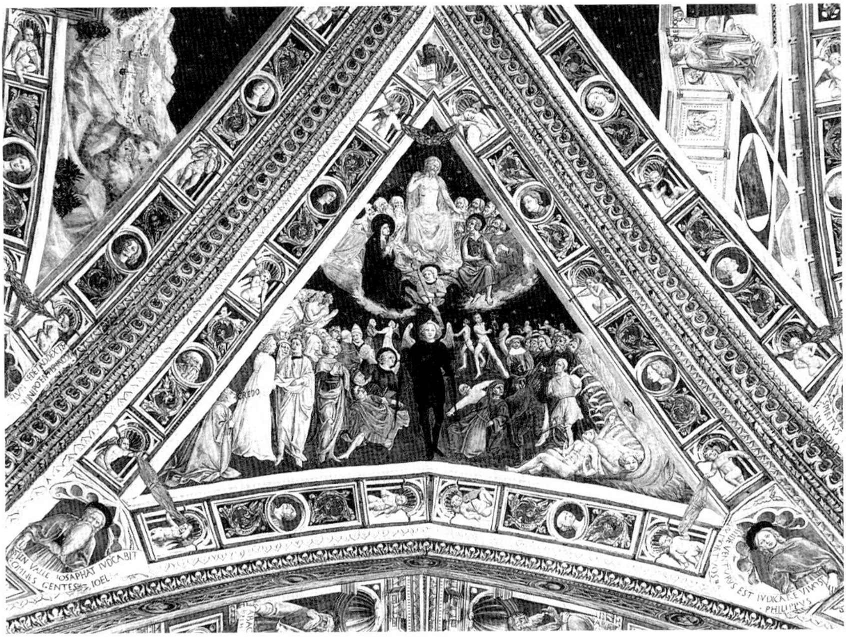

ings in the baptistery illustrate the widely held belief that the Creed was invented by the twelve apostles and endorsed by the words of the prophets, sibyls and later saints. The exemplary nature of the Creed is further highlighted by the presence in the painted borders of figures whose texts allude to key Christian virtues.

The wall behind the high altar and directly opposite the baptismal font is devoted to paintings that represent the events that led to Christ's incarnation and his death on the Cross to redeem humanity. They therefore provide a suitable pictorial context for both the high altar and the baptismal font. The *Assumption of the Virgin* and the series of saints and *beati* introduce a more civic note into the scheme, reminding worshippers of the cathedral's dedication to the Virgin of the Assumption and of the holy men and women most revered by the Sienese. Such is the subtlety of the overall organisation of the scheme that a number of significant juxtapositions occur between its various parts. For example, the painting in the series of the Articles of the Creed depicting the ascension of Christ into heaven appears directly above the painting of the assumption of the Virgin on the arch of the apse.

In his translation of the abstract concepts of the Creed into visual form, it is clear that Vecchietta used his recent experience of painting a similar scheme on the walls of the hospital sacristy. Here, however, he was able to paint a single article on each of the twelve pictorial fields available to him. But – owing to lack of space – he also had to simplify his compositions to a considerable extent. Thus, in the *Last Judgement* he retained many of the details of the painting of the same subject in the sacristy but had to compress the number of figures appearing in the scene, eliminating the Archangel Michael's two companions completely(see pl. 102). In some cases the imagery approaches the austerity of Benedetto di Bindo's earlier panels for the cathedral sacristy (see pl. 76), but in others Vecchietta introduced embellishments that reflected the location of the paintings within the city's baptismal church. In the final painting of the series, illustrating the twelfth article of the Creed – 'I believe in the life everlasting' – he included in the foreground, below the crowned figures of Christ and the Virgin, the four patron saints of Siena, Ansano, Savino, Crescenzio and Victor, together with the recently canonised Bernardino.

Paintings for the Palazzo Pubblico

During this period of considerable artistic activity in the Spedale and the baptistery, the civic authorities also turned their attention to further programmes in the Palazzo Pubblico. These focussed principally on two parts of the building – the rooms on the first floor that had already received extensive painted decoration in the fourteenth and early fifteenth centuries, and the rooms on the ground floor of the palace. In the case of the former, there appears to have been a concern to reiterate the subject matter and imagery of existing schemes. Between 1424 and 1431 Mattia di Nanni made a wooden bench to be placed below Simone Martini's *Maestà* (see pls 46, 47). The back of this bench was decorated with intarsia wood panels on which were represented Roman heroes – closely emulating the subject and ethos of Taddeo di Bartolo's earlier paintings for the ante-chamber of the Sala di Concistoro (see pl. 81).[44] In 1447 a French craftworker, Giachetto di Benedetto, similarly received a commission to weave three tapestries of *Good Government, Peace* and *War* that apparently copied Ambrogio Lorenzetti's paintings in the Sala della Pace (see pls 33, 51–3).[45]

In 1446, meanwhile, Sano di Pietro was paid to repaint one of the early fifteenth-century paintings in the Sala di Balìa (see pl. 79) and then in 1448 to collaborate with the woodworker Giovanni di Magno to refashion an early fourteenth-century altarpiece by Simone Martini which then stood, in a state of evident disrepair, over the altar of the Cappella dei Signori (see pl. 77).[46] Apart from setting this altarpiece in an elaborate wooden frame that reflected the style of the surrounding fifteenth-century choirstalls, Sano di Pietro was also commissioned to paint a new predella for the altarpiece. He was expressly requested to copy the paintings of the life of the Virgin executed by Simone Martini and the Lorenzetti brothers in the mid-1330s on the façade of the Spedale (see pl. 67). The surviving paintings from this predella therefore offer valuable evidence of the appearance of those lost paintings.[47] They also show how determined fifteenth-century Sienese patrons and painters were to preserve their earlier artistic heritage.

During this period, however, a number of new themes were introduced to the Sala del Mappamondo. No longer functioning as a meeting place for the city's principal legislative council, the hall had become a place where foreign delegations were received with pomp and ceremony. The new paintings were thus designed as a form of pictorial propaganda for Siena and its government's current concerns. On the faces of the broad piers that frame the entrance between this room and the vestibule in front of the Cappella dei Signori (see pls 46, 48), two new figures were introduced. These were Saint Bernardino, painted by Sano di Pietro, and Saint Catherine of Siena, painted by Vecchietta.[48] Both are represented like painted statues, standing in niches, and with haloes to denote their status as saints. The painted inscriptions below them refer specifically to the date of their canonisation in 1450 and 1461, respectively. For this reason, it is generally assumed that the two painters were commissioned to execute these figures in anticipation of Catherine's canonisation on 29 June 1461.[49] Since the government had played a major role in securing the canonisation of both Bernardino and Catherine, it was highly appropriate that they should be commemorated in a state room visited by foreign embassies and delegations. In a similar spirit, they later commissioned two painters, Giovanni di Cristofano Ghisi and Francesco d'Andrea, to decorate the north-east arcade of the room with a painting commemorating the Sienese victory over the Florentines at Poggio Imperiale on 8 September 1479.[50] Despite its topicality, the painting was executed in a similar manner to that of the mid-fourteenth-century *Battle in the Val di Chiana* located beside it (see pls 46, 64).

The preference for traditional subject matter and imagery was continued in the paintings on the ground floor of the Palazzo Pubblico, which housed the offices of the city's most important magistracies, including that of the treasury (the Biccherna) and of provisions for the city (the Biado). In one of the rooms allocated to the Biccherna on the south side of the building, fac-

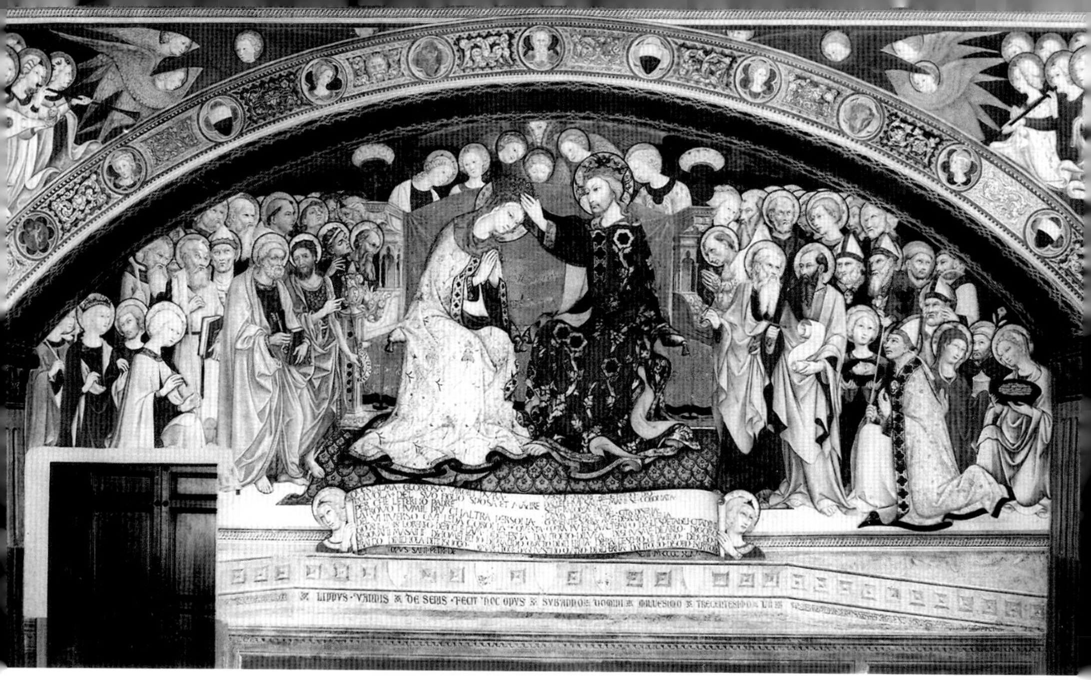

105 Sano di Pietro and Domenico di Bartolo, *The Coronation of the Virgin with Saints* (1445), repainting an earlier painting by Lippo Vanni. Fresco, 230 × 620 cm. East wall of the Sala della Biccherna. Siena, Palazzo Pubblico.

ing onto the market place that lay behind the Palazzo Pubblico, Sano di Pietro was once again commissioned to repaint extensively and 'modernise' an earlier fresco painting. According to two painted inscriptions on the lower border, this *Coronation of the Virgin* had originally been painted by Lippo Vanni in 1352 and was then repainted by Sano di Pietro in 1445 (pl. 105). Comparison with other mid-fourteenth-century Sienese paintings of this subject suggests that Sano di Pietro faithfully preserved aspects of Lippo Vanni's treatment of the subject – particularly in the detail of Christ, himself already crowned, placing the Virgin's crown on her head with both his hands. Sano di Pietro also, however, retained his own distinctive style for the portrayal of the saints gathered round the throne. Some of these figures bear such a strong resemblance to those of Domenico di Bartolo that it has been suggested that this painter too was involved in the commission.[51]

What is clear from this episode is that the magistrates responsible for commissioning the repainting were determined that the image should retain its original civic character. The inscription on the large scroll held by two angels in the lower part of the composition refers unequivocally to the 'faithful' city of Siena being 'recommended' to the Virgin, recalling the patriotic sentiment of earlier *Maestà* paintings (see pls 36, 47). Prominent among the saints on either side of the throne are, on the left, the kneeling figure of Saint Ansano carrying the black and white banner of Siena; and on the right, Saint Savino carrying the red and gold lion of the Popolo. These two civic emblems appear again in the upper border of the painting.[52]

Three years later Sano di Pietro was paid for another fresco painting for the magistracy of the Biccherna. Again located on the ground floor, it depicts three more civic saints – Saint Peter of Alexandria (holding a model of the city of Siena in his lap), the Blessed Ambrogio Sansedoni and the Blessed Andrea Gallerani.[53] This evident concern to commemorate holy figures who were held in particularly high esteem by the Sienese was expressed even more forcefully in a fresco executed by Vecchietta between 1453 and 1457. Painted on the wall of the office of the magistracy of the Biado, on the north side of the building facing onto the Campo, it depicts the Virgin as the *Madonna della Misericordia* ('Our Lady of Mercy', pl. 106).[54] Like the earlier painting of this subject for the Spedale by Domenico di Bartolo (see pl. 99), it shows angels holding the Virgin's outstretched cloak over a group of clergy on the left and lay people on the right. Men, women and children have been included as a demonstration of the inclusiveness of the Virgin's mercy towards the Sienese. This message was made even more explicit by the decoration of the edge of the Virgin's mantle with the opening words of a popular prayer that addresses the Virgin as queen and mother of mercy. Above and to the right of the principal painting appears another painted image of an act of mercy – that of Saint Martin dividing his cloak in order to give half of it to a ragged beggar. Since the magistrates of the Biado were responsible for the distribution of grain at times of need and other kinds of charitable activity, such a subject was highly appropriate for the embellishment of their office.

A further striking feature of the painted decoration on this wall is the sheer number of 'Sienese' saints portrayed: in the main painting Saints Ansano, Savino and Catherine of Siena are given particular prominence. Indeed, Catherine is shown holding the edge of the Virgin's mantle over the Sienese citizens and officials grouped on the left. On the wide inner surface of the arch above the main painting, meanwhile, there appears an extraordinary series of eighteen half-length figures set against gold backgrounds. Considerably extending the repertoire of saints and *beati* represented on the exterior of the *Arliquiera* for the Spedale (see pl. 100) and in the altar niche

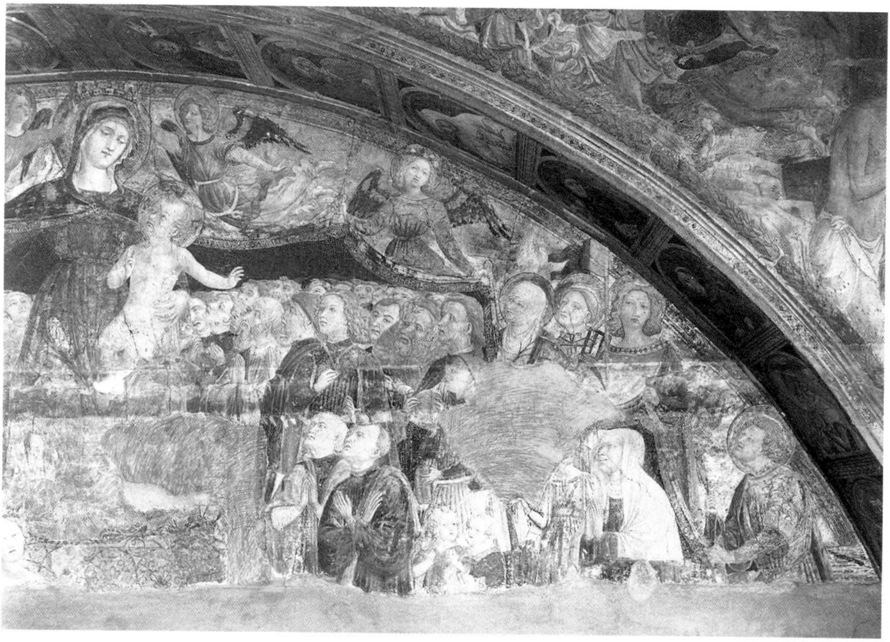

106 Vecchietta, *The Madonna della Misericordia* (*c.* 1453–7; detail). Fresco, 115 × 510 cm. West wall of the Sala del Biado. Siena, Palazzo Pubblico.

of the baptistery (see pl. 90), Vecchietta depicted a yet wider range of individuals who for their piety and devotion to the city were particularly venerated by the Sienese.

In 1456 – around the time that Vecchietta was painting his mural in the office of the Biado – Sano di Pietro signed and dated a panel painting commissioned by the five magistrates then in charge of this magistracy. An eighteenth-century source reports the panel in the same room as Vecchietta's *Madonna della Misericordia*, thus suggesting that this panel too was intended to celebrate the identity and concerns of the Biado itself.[55] It shows a striking image of the current pope, Calixtus III (1455–8), in dialogue with the Virgin, who appears on clouds over the city of Siena, portrayed on the right (pl. 107). The text below the Virgin records her assignment of Siena to the pastoral care of the Pope. The text beside Calixtus records his response: 'Virgin Mother, beloved consort of God, if your Calixtus is worthy of such a gift, I will not turn from Siena, other than

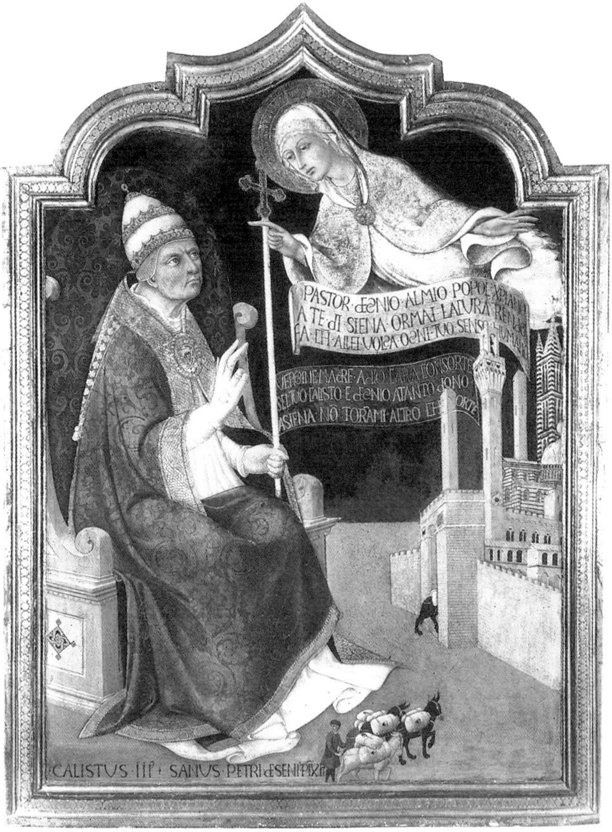

107 Sano di Pietro, *Pope Calixtus III with the Virgin blessing Siena* (1456). Tempera on panel, 158 × 115 cm. Siena, Pinacoteca Nazionale.

when dead'.[56] In 1456 Calixtus III had been instrumental in sending military assistance to the Sienese in their efforts to contain the threat posed by the mercenary leader Niccolò Piccinino. More vitally, the Pope had sent supplies of grain to Siena which was then experiencing food shortages.[57] This act must have greatly assisted the magistracy of the Biado who were primarily responsible for ensuring that the Sienese had adequate supplies of grain in times of famine. They duly commissioned Sano di Pietro – who by that date appears to have enjoyed something of the status of an official painter to the government – to execute a painting commemorating and celebrating what was perceived to be another sign of the Virgin's protection of Siena and the Sienese. In the resulting painting, Sano di Pietro showed his ability to record both the strong features of the Borgia pope as well as the distinctive appearance of Siena's principal ecclesiastical and secular buildings. A further precise detail – which would have been of particular relevance to his patrons – is the motif of the civic emblem of the *balzana* represented on the bales of grain carried on the backs of the mules being driven towards the city gate.

Renaissance Altarpieces

Those in charge of Siena's principal civic institutions in the fifteenth century, like their fourteenth-century predecessors, continued to commission paintings to decorate these religious and secular buildings, as previously shown. In so doing, they chose subjects that not only supported the designated functions of these buildings but also reflected well on themselves. During the same period individual Sienese patrons adopted similar patterns and attitudes towards the commissioning of art. Nowhere was this more striking than in Pius II's commissions for four altarpieces in the mid-1460s for his newly completed cathedral in Pienza. Built by the Florentine architect Bernardo Rossellino according to the patron's taste for both Italian renaissance architecture and the tall, luminous interiors of north European churches, it was furnished entirely according to his preferences and wishes. As he describes in his own account of his life and achievements, the east end of the cathedral comprised five chapels, the central one of which housed the bishop's throne and stalls for the canons. In the chapel next to the bishop's throne was 'the repository for the host' – a reference to the handsome marble tabernacle carved by Bernardino Rossellino. Pius II describes four other chapels adorned with 'paintings by illustrious Sienese painters'. Two further altars 'to serve the people' were located in the main part of the church.[58]

Although his account of the interior furnishings of his cathedral has given rise to speculation about the exact layout of the altarpieces,[59] what is clear is that the Piccolomini pope did indeed commission four of Siena's leading painters to execute altarpieces for his new church. These were the two slightly older painters Sano di Pietro and Giovanni di Paolo, the tried and tested Vecchietta, and a younger painter, Matteo di Giovanni who, although originating from the Tuscan town of Borgo San Sepolchro, established himself as a successful and prolific painter in Siena during the second half of the fifteenth century.

Each of the four painters executed an altarpiece whose form and subject matter appears to have been closely controlled by their humanist patron. Vecchietta's (pl. 108) takes the distinctive form of a kind of unified triptych, depicting the Virgin of the Assumption in the centre and pairs of saints on either side. These are Agatha, Pius, Calixtus and Catherine of Siena. Destined to be placed over the altar in the chapel to the left of the central chapel (when facing towards it), its subject honoured the dedication of the cathedral to the Virgin of the Assumption; the identities of the patron, Pius II, and his own patron and papal predecessor, Pope Calixtus III; and the Sienese saint whom Pius had canonised in 1461. While recalling the original design and gilded magnificence of the patronal altarpieces for Siena cathedral (see pls 58, 60), this altarpiece was rendered in a notably contemporary manner, the framework adopting the repertoire of renaissance architecture – simple, rectangular mouldings and a round (not pointed) arch, surmounted by a triangular pediment. The central image of the Virgin of the Assumption also demonstrates Vecchietta's confident handling of pictorial spaces, both in terms of the angels grouped in a circle below the seated figure of the Virgin and in the lyrical landscape behind the figure of Saint Thomas in the lower foreground. The pairs of saints on either side of this image stand on a pavement embellished with circles, likewise seen in depth. These saints too are portrayed as substantial figures who relate to one another.

The other three altarpieces offer further strong evidence of how the paintings for the new cathedral were conceived as an ensemble. Each of them comprises a single panel on which is depicted the Virgin and Christ Child enthroned in the company of four saints. As in the case of Vecchietta Assumption altarpiece, Pius II chose the saints with great care. To the right of the Virgin in Matteo di Giovanni's altarpiece appears Saint Matthew, the patron saint of Pienza. Similarly, on the altarpieces by Giovanni di Paolo (pl. 109) and Sano di Pietro there appear the name saints of Pius II's nephews and principal heirs, Antonio, Francesco and Giacomo Todeschini-Piccolomini.[60] As in Vecchietta's altarpiece, these three are set on predellas embellished with painted roundels of figures – relating to the Annunciation or the Passion of Christ – and the coat-of-arms of Pius II himself. On either side of each altarpiece appear fluted Corinthian columns carrying a classical entablature. Over these appears either a low triangular gable or a narrow lunette. These house narrative paintings, all of which relate to aspects of Christ's Passion.

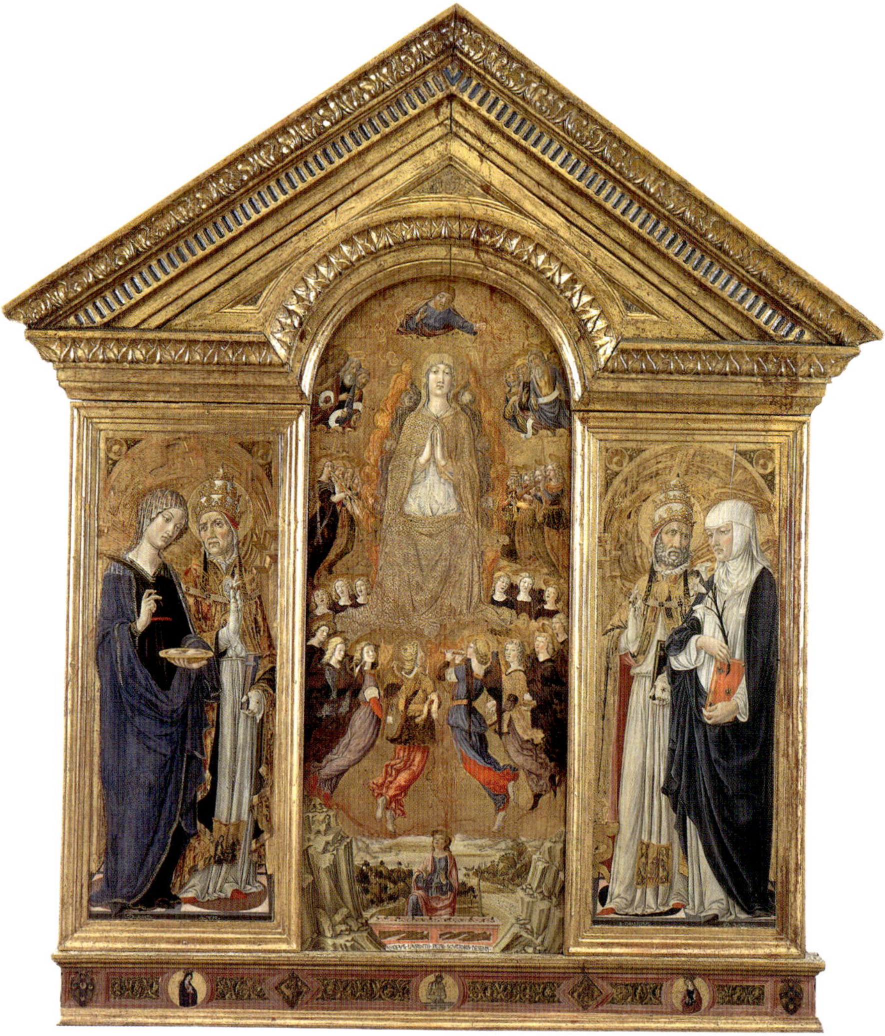

108 Vecchietta, *The Virgin of the Assumption with Saints Agatha, Pius, Calixtus and Catherine of Siena* (*c.* 1462–3). Tempera on panel, 280 × 225 cm. Pienza, cathedral.

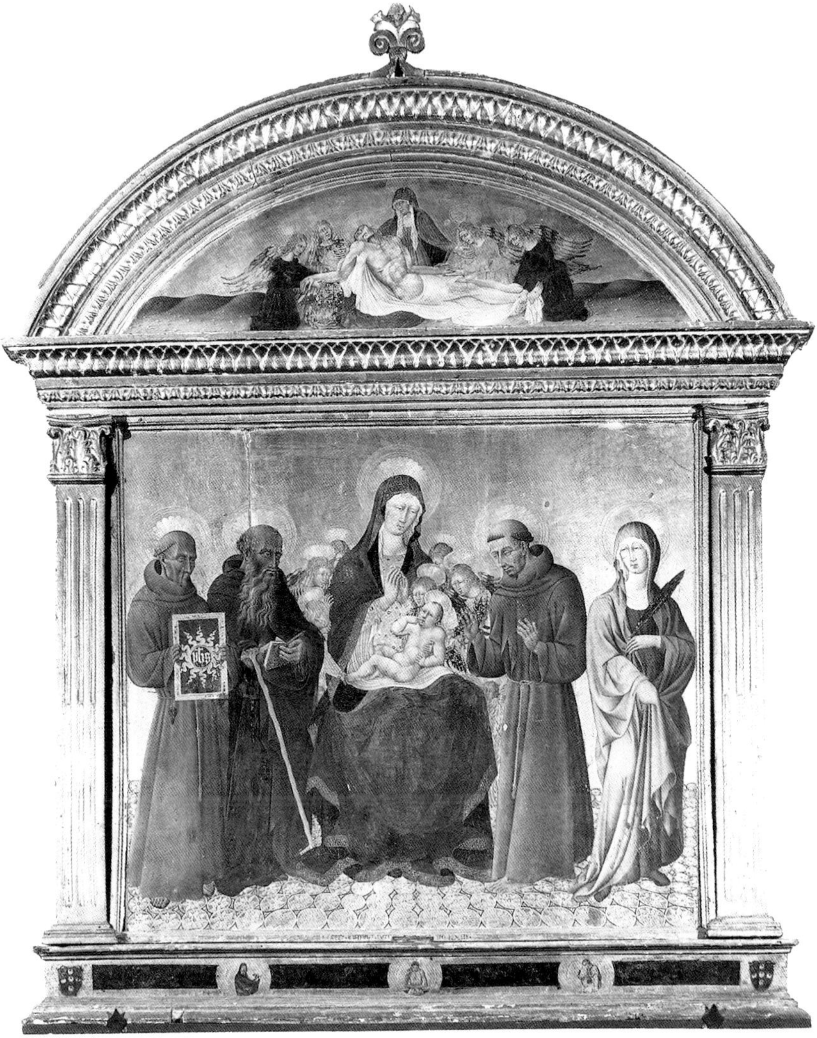

109 Giovanni di Paolo, *The Virgin and Christ Child with Saints Bernardino, Anthony Abbot, Francis and Sabina*, and (above) *The Lamentation over the Dead Christ*, (*c.* 1462–3). Tempera on panel, 304 × 234 cm. Pienza, cathedral.

What is most remarkable about the four altarpieces is that they provide the first example of Sienese painters adopting the form of the 'square panel painting' for altarpieces – yet more striking testimony of Pius II's role in introducing his fellow Sienese to the new renaissance culture. Already well-established in Florence, this style of altarpiece enabled painters to present their religious subject as a company of holy figures gathered in a unified spatial setting. The new type of renaissance frames acted as a further means of achieving this end by appearing as a kind of elaborate window through which the holy figures can be seen. While the younger painter Matteo di Giovanni appears to have been more successful in fully exploiting the pictorial possibilities of this new type of altarpiece, the older Giovanni di Paolo seems to have been more reluctant to turn his back on older Sienese pictorial traditions. Consequently, there is no great sense of spatial depth in the latter's square panel painting (see pl. 109). The decorative carpet on which the holy figures stand appears to tilt upwards and merge with the gold background of the painting. What solidity there is about the figures is achieved by their strongly stated outlines and the complex pattern of the folds of their draperies. Despite this apparent reluctance to adopt the latest developments in renaissance painting, Giovanni di Paolo nevertheless supplied his patron with other qualities, notably in the painting of the *Lamentation*. Here the foreshortened body of the dead Christ strikes the viewer forcibly and with the maximum of emotion – showing why this painter and his distinctive style was still valued by a determinedly humanist pope.

Such were the power and influence of Pius II that he was able to build a cathedral to the glory of himself and his family and furnish it with an entire set of renaissance altarpieces. In the early 1470s, however, a close associate of his commissioned a similar family monument within Siena itself – albeit on a considerably more modest scale. Giovanni Cinughi, a member of a prominent Sienese family belonging to the Monte of the Nine, had been a close friend of Pius II, who appointed him Bishop of Pienza. In his will Cinughi, concerned that Siena had only one church (the cathedral) actually dedicated to the Virgin, instructed his heirs to build a church dedicated to the Madonna delle Nevi ('Our Lady of the Snows').[61] After his death in 1470, the new church was duly built, opposite the family palace and facing onto the street that marked the route of pilgrims through the northern part of the city (see pl. 6). Small in scale and simple in design, the new church was given an elegant and thoroughly renaissance façade. The austere lines of its interior, meanwhile, functioned as a suitable setting for the altarpiece commissioned by the Cinughi family for the high altar.[62]

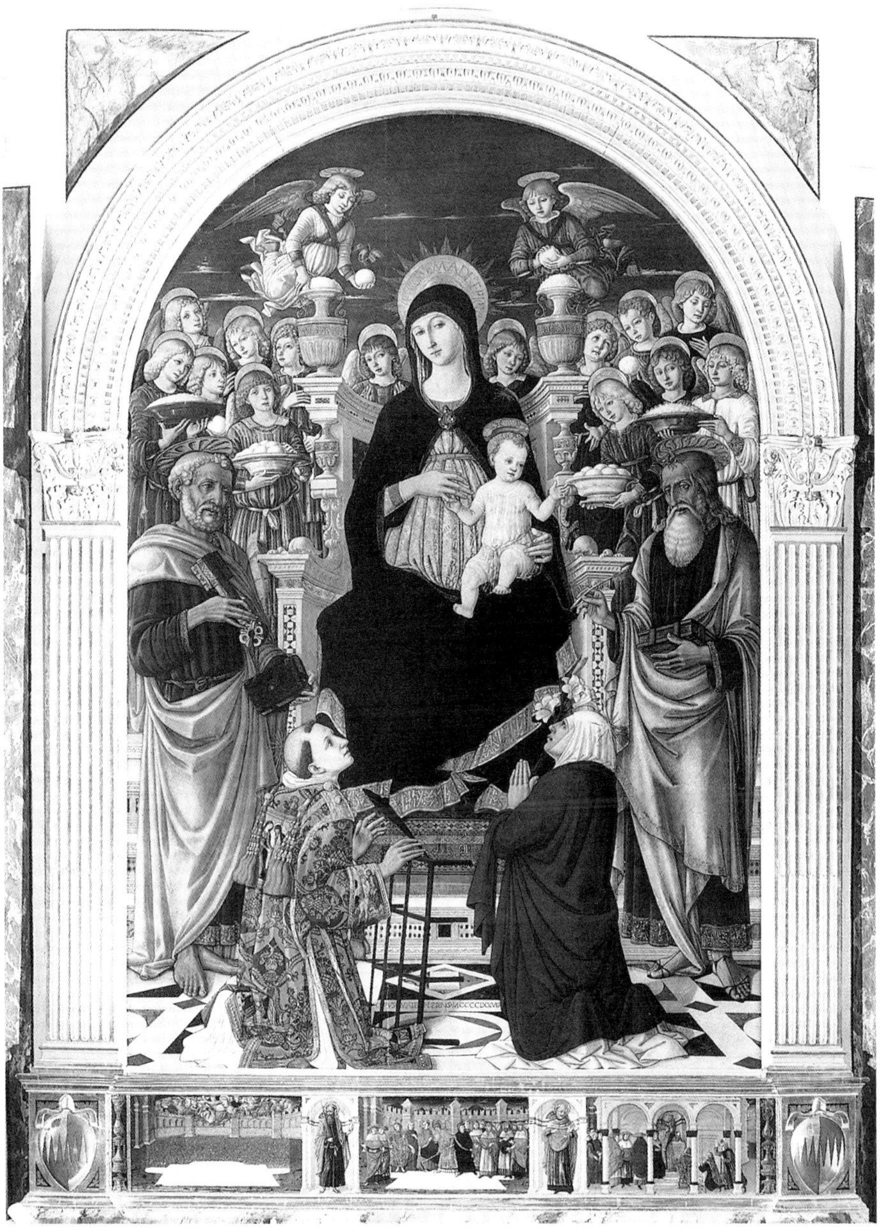

110 Matteo di Giovanni, *The Virgin and Christ Child with Saints Peter, John the Evangelist, Lawrence and Catherine of Siena*, known as *The Madonna of the Snows* (*c.* 1470–72). Tempera on panel, 327 × 224 cm. Siena, Santa Maria delle Nevi.

As appropriate to the style of the church itself, this took the form of an imposing renaissance altarpiece executed by one of Pius II's painters, Matteo di Giovanni (pl. 110). Set on a predella and within a renaissance frame, it graphically demonstrates Matteo's abilities as a painter who could handle perspective with extreme confidence and portray the holy figures as statuesque, three-dimensional entities.

As in Sassetta's earlier cathedral altarpiece (see pl. 92), the subject matter reflects the original location of the painting. It portrays the Virgin and Christ Child enthroned, in the company of four saints and a throng of angels carrying either bowls filled with snow or snowballs. Like Sassetta, Matteo di Giovanni included the well-observed detail of one of the angels actually shaping the snow into one of these. The choice of the four saints was probably intended to refer to Giovanni Cinughi himself and his ecclesiastical status: on the right appear his name saint, John the Evangelist, and Saint Catherine of Siena, recently canonised by his patron and friend Pius II. On the left appear Saint Peter, the first pope, and the deacon saint Lawrence, treasurer to another pope. The predella shows a sequence of three narrative paintings of the miraculous foundation of Santa Maria Maggiore in Rome. The first scene provides a vivid portrayal of snow falling beneath a heavenly apparition of the Virgin accompanied by angels. The plan of the church, picked out in gleaming white snow, appears on the ground below her. The third scene represents the ceremonial that customarily marked the consecration of a church at that time. Such details would have had particular relevance for those members of the Cinughi family responsible for planning the design and construction of Santa Maria delle Nevi. Bishop Giovanni Cinughi's role as founder of the church is clearly signalled by the presence of his personal coat-of-arms at either end of the altarpiece's predella.

Paintings for the Private 'Chamber'

Such altarpieces provide evidence of individual Sienese patrons using religious painting to advertise the piety, reputation and cultured taste of themselves and their families. A modest collection of fifteenth-century secular painting also demonstrates similar kinds of aspiration. However, whereas it is relatively easy to envisage the original settings of Sienese altarpieces (see pl. 14), it is more difficult to do so for secular painting of the same period. By studying inventories and written descriptions of the interiors of domestic residences owned by wealthy Italian families, together with other kinds of visual evidence, it is possible to gain some insight into this elusive subject. The principal location for most of the secular paintings commissioned at this time was the 'chamber' that belonged to the suite of rooms designed for the owner's private use, as opposed to the larger hall used for dining and public family events.[63] The standard furnishings for a chamber were a large bed, often set on a platform made of chests for seating and storage (see pl. 59), a day bed, storage chests, strong-boxes and a pair of painted wedding chests. Every chamber was also likely to have had a religious image, generally a small-scale painting of the Virgin and Christ Child.

Wooden furniture for the 'chamber', despite its ostensibly utilitarian function, became more elaborate during the fifteenth century. The chests or *cassoni* in particular were embellished with paintings whose choice of subject matter tended to reflect the recreational functions of the rooms for which they were intended. Because of the elaborate work and skill that went into their execution, *cassoni* became luxury items that reflected the wealth and status of their owners. They therefore frequently featured in the list of items gathered by a fifteenth-century bride's family as part of her dowry that would accompany her to her marital home.[64] As pieces of furniture, however, *cassoni* were particularly vulnerable to being dismantled and used for other purposes. In modern collections of renaissance art it is thus relatively unusual to find *cassoni* in their original state. What do survive in relatively large numbers, however, are rectangular painted panels that have been removed from *cassoni* and are now exhibited as paintings in their own right.

One such example is a painting that shows the biblical hero David returning in triumph to Jerusalem after his defeat of the Philistine Goliath (pl. 111). Found in the nineteenth century as part of a cupboard in the sacristy of San Francesco, its original secular function as the front face of a marriage chest is clearly indicated by the figures, worked in gilded relief, at either end of the panel. Although now lacking their heads, their emblems of the club and distaff identify them clearly as the classical hero Hercules and his lover Iole. The coats-of-arms on the shield that each of these classical figures support are those of the Buoninsegni and Piccolomini families. During the short pontificate of Pius II (1459–64), Lorenzo di Tommaso Buoninsegni married Montanina di Nanni Todeschini Piccolomini, who was the pope's niece and the sister of the three nephews who influenced the choice of subject matter for two of the Pienza altarpieces. It seems likely, therefore, that this *cassone* painting was once part of Montanina's dowry and that it was returned to the Piccolomini family after her death in 1464,

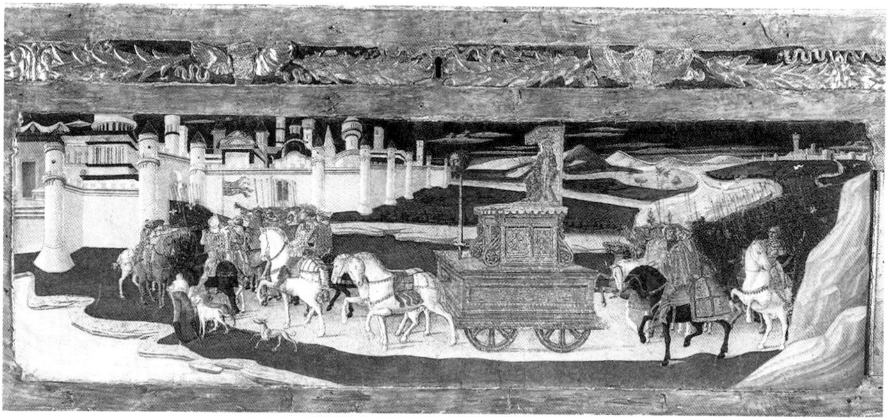

111 Benvenuto di Giovanni, *The Triumph of David* (*c.* 1459–60). Tempera on panel and gilded stucco, 56.5 × 182.5 cm. Siena, Pinacoteca Nazionale.

subsequently finding its way into the sacristy of San Francesco, a church in which in the late fifteenth century Montanina's brothers, Antonio and Giacomo, founded a funerary chapel.[65]

On grounds of style, the painting has been attributed to the Sienese Benvenuto di Giovanni. The ostensibly religious subject of the painting included a nuptial theme – since David's return to Jerusalem laid the foundations for his future marriage to Michal, the daughter of King Saul (1 Samuel, 17: 53, 18: 27). As was typical of *cassoni* paintings of this date, Benvenuto also translated the religious subject of the painting into a thoroughly secular form. David appears in gold parade armour and seated on an elaborately decorated chariot. In front of the chariot appears a group of mounted horsemen in similarly resplendent armour. All these details owe their inspiration to the costume and paraphernalia customarily used at that date for the staging of tournaments, jousts and processions that accompanied celebrations such as important dynastic marriages. On the right appears the distant city of Jerusalem. Unlike Bartolo di Fredi's earlier representation of the city in his altarpiece of the *Adoration of the Magi*, this city does not appear as a Tuscan town with a strong similarity to Siena (see pl. 73). Instead, it is depicted as a city with buildings that bear a resemblance – if somewhat fancifully – to those of ancient Rome. The owners of this *cassone* could indulge their taste for antiquarian erudition while taking pride in the fact that their families and their strategic marriage alliances were being likened to those of the famous biblical hero David and the equally celebrated mythological hero Hercules – both of whom were believed to have embodied the virtue of fortitude.

Siena and Renaissance Italy

A new development in the history of Sienese art took place in the fifteenth century. Whereas in the thirteenth and fourteenth centuries Sienese artists seem to have monopolised the most important commissions in Siena itself, in the fifteenth they had to compete with artists from other Italian towns and cities. Partly this can be accounted for by the enormous success that Florentine artists enjoyed in this period because of their reputation for skill and artistic innovation. Thus, apart from his work on the baptistery font, Donatello was also employed to produce other bronze and marble sculptures for the cathedral in the 1420s and 1450s. The Florentine painter Filippo Lippi was likewise a resident in the city between 1428 and 1429, serving as the sub-prior of the Carmelite community of San Niccolò.[66]

In addition to their awareness of the new art being produced in Florence, Sienese painters appreciated the distinctive qualities of north Italian art, with its partiality for richly worked materials and ornate decoration, which corresponded more directly to their own artistic traditions. Between 1425 and 1426 the talented north Italian painter Gentile da Fabriano spent some time in Siena, executing a painting of an enthroned Virgin and Christ Child on the exterior of the palace of the notaries, facing onto the Campo. Although now lost, Gentile's graceful style of execution of this very traditional subject apparently had a marked impact on the work of local Sienese painters, particularly that of Giovanni di Paolo.[67] Another north Italian painter, Pisanello, appears to have been similarly influential for Vecchietta in his *Founding of the Spedale* in the Pellegrinaio (See pl. 98). Vecchietta could have viewed Pisanello's work in Verona and Mantua during his period working at Castiglione d'Olona. Sienese patrons also had a number of contacts with the princely courts of northern Italy –for example, the mother of Borso d'Este, the ruler of Ferrara, belonged to the Sienese family of the Tolomei and Borso himself visited Siena in 1439 on his way to Petriolo and the famous hot-water springs to the south of Siena.[68]

Such cultural connections between Siena and northern Italy were made more substantial in the second half of the fifteenth century by the presence in Siena of Liberale da Verona and Girolamo da Cremona, two highly talented manuscript illuminators who worked on a large number of liturgi-

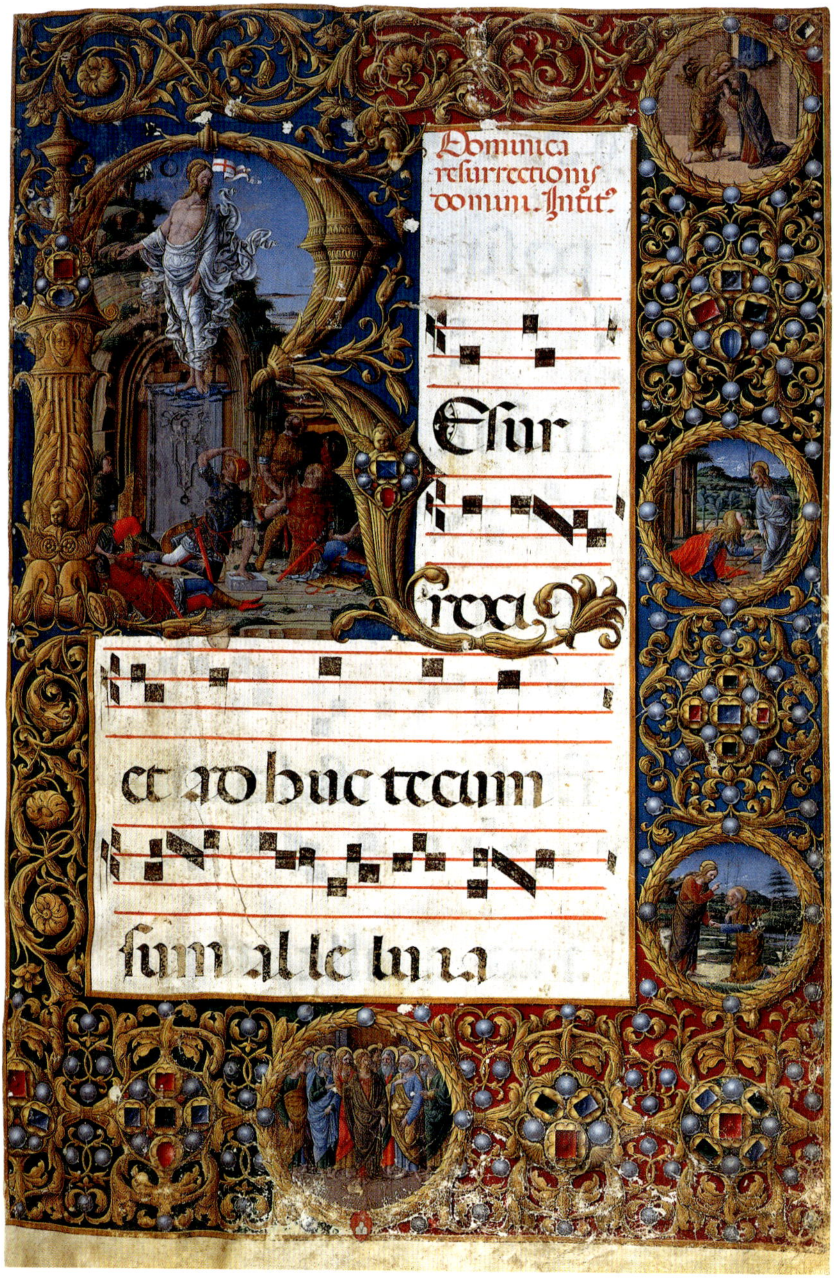
Dominica
resurrectionis
domini. Introit.
Esur
rexi
et adhuc tecum
sum al le lu ia

cal books for the Opera del Duomo during the 1460s and 1470s.[69] Their work provided a graphic demonstration of the daring feats of pictorial illusionism and decorative ornamentation that were characteristic of north Italian art at that period. They also introduced Sienese painters to the luminous effects common in the work of such painters as Andrea Mantegna, as seen in the gleaming pearls and inset jewels that decorate a page of a choirbook depicting the *Resurrection of Christ* (pl. 112).

This process of cross-fertilisation was not entirely one-sided. As in the previous century, fifteenth-century Sienese artists still secured commissions in other Italian cities. Thus, from 1437 until 1444 Sassetta executed a large, double-sided altarpiece for the high altar of the principal Franciscan church in Borgo San Sepolchro. Although it was actually produced in Siena, the painter supervised its installation in Borgo San Sepolchro in 1444.[70] Between 1435 and 1439 Vecchietta worked on frescoes for Cardinal Branda Castiglione in the cardinal's home town of Castiglione d'Olona.[71] And, according to Vasari, Domenico di Bartolo was commissioned in 1436 to execute the high altarpiece for the Carmelite church of Santa Maria del Carmine in Florence. This would have brought the Sienese painter into close contact not only with Masaccio and Masolino's recently completed frescoes for the Brancacci chapel in that church, but also with Filippo Lippi's frescoes for the cloister of this Carmelite priory.[72] It continued a long-established tradition of Sienese painters being commissioned to supply Florentine churches with altarpieces.

The election of the Sienese humanist Aeneas Silvius Piccolomini as pope in 1458 accelerated this process of cultural cross-fertilisation. As seen earlier, Pius II introduced the theory and practice of Florentine renaissance architecture not only into the Sienese *contado* at Pienza but also into Siena itself. The altarpieces for his cathedral in Pienza similarly established a taste for the new type of renaissance altarpiece among Sienese patrons. Moreover, his discriminating style of patronage continued into the sixteenth century with members of wealthy Sienese families seeking to employ painters both from Siena itself and from other parts of Italy and requiring them to produce paintings that demonstrated the latest artistic fashions.

112 Girolamo da Cremona and Liberale da Verona, *The Resurrection of Christ*, and four roundels depicting events after the Resurrection, (*c.* 1472–3). Illuminated page of a choirbook, 84 × 58 cm. Siena, cathedral, Piccolomini Library, codex no. 23.8, fol. 2r.

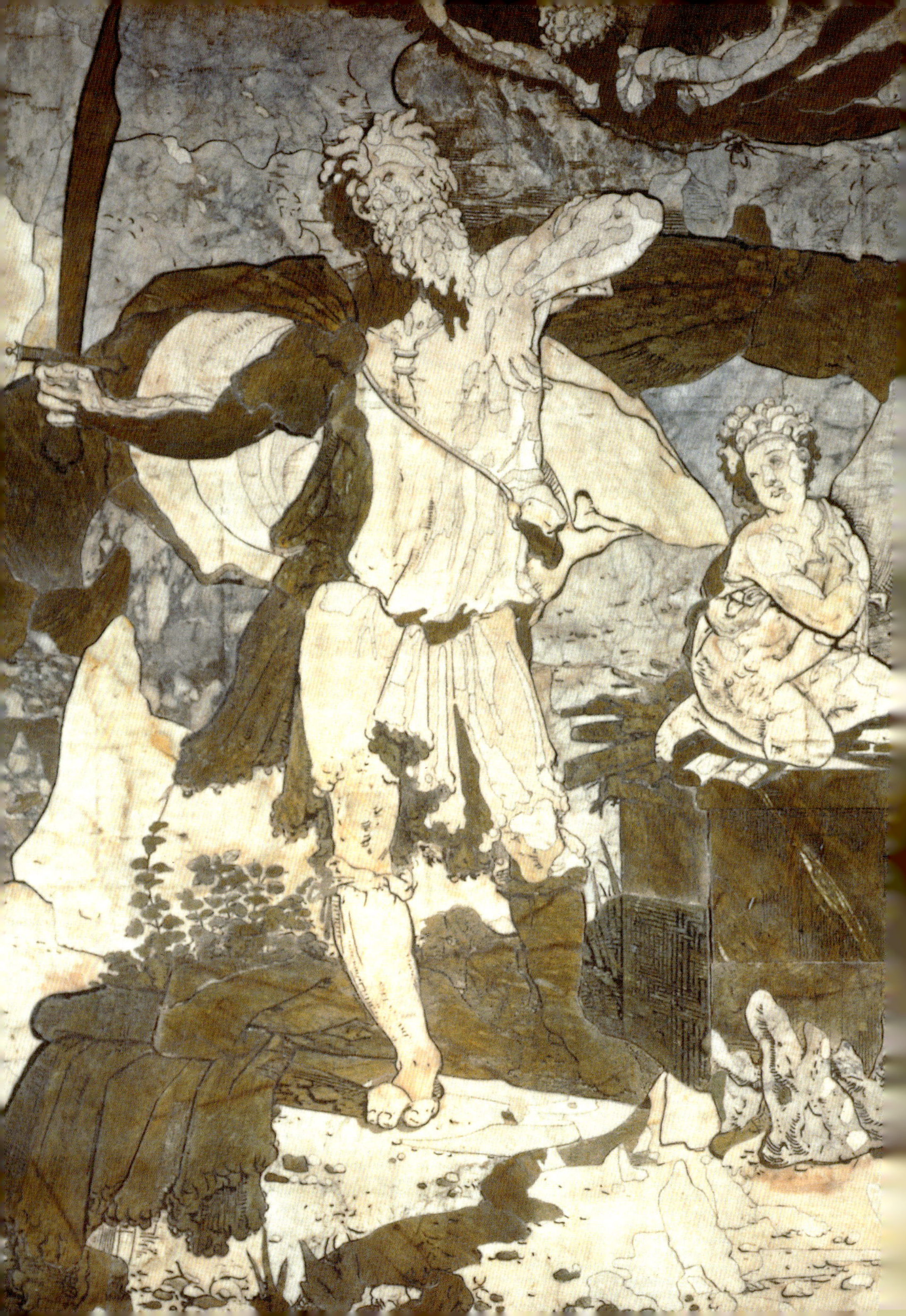

5

The Late Renaissance in Siena (1480–1555)

The years between 1480 and 1555 were tumultuous ones for the Sienese Republic. From 1487 until 1524, the city was under the political control of a single family, the Petrucci. Thereafter, although nominally an independent city state, Siena became a pawn in a game of international politics played out among the Hapsburg rulers of Spain, the kings of France and the Medici rulers of Florence. Marked by battles and sieges of the city, the period between 1525 and 1555 constitutes a heroic but eventually tragic chapter in the city's history. Indeed, in many ways the events of these years cast a long shadow back over the fifteenth century, leaving the impression that it was merely a prelude to Siena's final loss of political independence.[1]

In 1487, an armed force of exiles led by Pandolfo Petrucci entered Siena by the Porta Fontebranda, changing the existing balance of political influence between the various Monti. After the death of his brother and principal political rival, Giacomo, in 1497, Pandolfo skilfully consolidated his political authority by the manipulation of key magistracies and astute alliances with foreign powers.[2] Apart from a short period of exile in 1503, he became virtual lord (*signore*) of Siena, receiving important diplomatic guests and visitors in his own palace (see pl. 6) and securing favourable marriages for his children with members of the city's most eminent families.

After his death in 1512, the Petrucci family maintained a precarious pre-eminence in the city until 1524, when Pandolfo's son Fabio was expelled from Siena, having made himself unpopular by marrying a Medici and allying himself with Florence and the Medici pope Clement VII (1523–34). A year later, a popular revolt against the Monte of the Nine (to which the Petrucci belonged) led to the assassination of a prominent member of the Nine, Alessandro Bichi. A cross-party alliance which called itself the 'Libertini' then took power and allied itself with Clement VII's principal

113 *The Sacrifice of Isaiah* (detail of pl. 117).

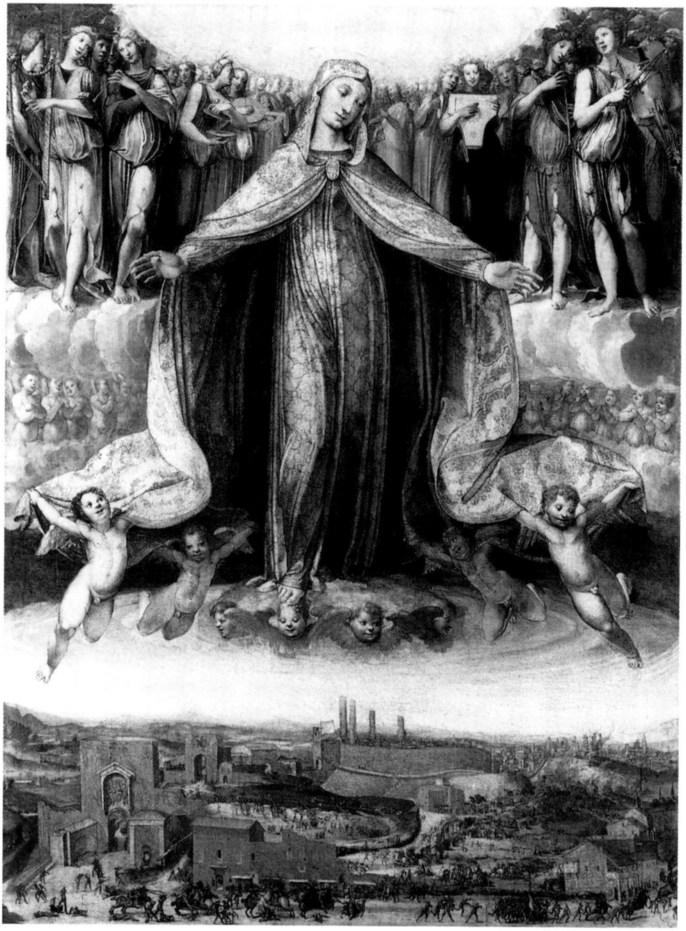

114 Giovanni di Lorenzo Cini, *The Virgin of the Immaculate Conception protects the Sienese at the Battle of Camollia* (1528). Tempera on panel, 239.5 × 174 cm. Siena, San Martino.

enemy, the Hapsburg emperor, Charles V (1515–56). In 1526, the pope therefore sent troops to occupy Siena, but the enterprise failed when the Sienese repulsed the papal forces in July at the battle of Camollia. In honour of this victory, a painting was commissioned from Giovanni di Lorenzo Cini (pl. 114).[3] Now in the church of San Martino, it graphically represents the moment when, as the Sienese believed, with the assistance of the Virgin[4] the besieged citizens defeated the enemy troops between the Antiporto and the Porta Camollia on the north side of the city.

Following the victory of Camollia, many members of the Nine were exiled and the Sienese governing regime pursued policies that allied the city even more closely to Emperor Charles V. At the Peace of Cambrai (1529) – a treaty that effectively acknowledged Hapsburg pre-eminence in Italy – Siena's political autonomy was confirmed. The city was obliged, however, to accept an imperial garrison. A year later, the Emperor's chief representative in Siena instigated a reform of the government that allowed the re-admittance of members of the Nine. In 1541, the imperial chancellor, Granvelle, was given the task of examining Siena and its incessant political infighting. He proposed a more radical reform resulting in the appointment of a new magistracy known as the Balìa of the Forty. Rumours that the imperial representative was favouring the Nine at the expense of the other Monti led to a revolt in 1545, the expulsion of the imperial garrison and the institution of a more select governing group – the Balìa of the Ten – whose membership excluded the Nine.

Two years later imperial troops re-entered the city and occupied the priory of San Domenico, while a new and unpopular fortress was built at the expense of the Sienese on the north-west outskirts of the city. The new imperial representative, Don Diego Hurtado da Mendoza, recalled the Nine, controlled the membership of the Balìa and constantly intervened in Siena's affairs. Encouraged by the arrival of French and Italian troops under the leadership of Aeneas Piccolomini, a popular uprising in 1552 led to the imperial garrison being expelled once again and the fortress being partially demolished.[5]

After this act of defiance against the Emperor, the Sienese government made a treaty with the Florentine ruler Cosimo I de' Medici and Henry II, King of France. Cosimo, however, realised that he might gain possession of Siena and its territories and therefore gave the Emperor assistance in his two campaigns to re-establish military control over the city. In 1553, imperial troops duly entered Sienese territory, capturing a number of villages and laying siege to Montalcino. But the garrison there held out so the imperial forces were obliged to withdraw. In 1554, a formidably large army of Florentine, German and Spanish troops, led by Gian Giacomo de' Medici, Marquis of Marignano, then besieged Siena itself. A force under the leadership of Piero Strozzi, a Florentine exile who had been appointed by Henry II of France as his vicar general in Siena, engaged the enemy in the Val di Chiana, but was defeated.

Inside the city, meanwhile, the Sienese held out valiantly under the leadership of the French general, Blaise de Montluc. Having endured great privation and witnessed such harrowing events as the massacre by the enemy of women and children sent out of the city for lack of food, Siena surrendered on 17 April 1555. Six hundred and fifty families escaped to Montalcino where they kept the ideal of the republic of Siena alive in exile for four more years. In 1559, however, with the treaty of Cateau-Cambrésis, Siena and its territories were formally incorporated into those of Florence. Although it maintained many of its civic institutions, laws and traditions, Siena was no longer an independent city state. Instead, it was one subject city among many within the dukedom of Tuscany.

During this period also a dramatic shift in the style of artistic patronage Siena took place. As part of his strategy for asserting his political pre-eminence, Pandolfo Petrucci was an active patron of art, particularly during the later years of his life.[6] In about 1504 he bought a complex of houses at the foot of the steep flight of steps leading from the baptistery to the cathedral and converted them into an imposing palace. Here he commissioned craftworkers and painters to furnish a number of rooms with decorative schemes that drew attention to the dynastic and intellectual concerns of himself and his family (see pls 123–6). From the late 1490s onwards, he had in addition been a patron of a number of Sienese churches – funding the construction of the convent of Santa Maria Maddalena outside the Porta Tufi and the enlargement of both the Dominican church of Santo Spirito (see pl. 8) and the Franciscan church of the Osservanza just outside the city. He also chose the last as the site for his family mausoleum, for which he commissioned a fine terracotta sculpted group of the *Lamentation* by the Sienese artist Giacomo Cozzarelli.

As *operiao* of the cathedral, Pandolfo was responsible for the decision made in 1506 to remove Duccio's *Maestà* from the high altar and replace it with a bronze ciborium executed by Vecchietta between 1467 and 1472.[7] He also took an interest in other civic projects creating, as early as 1488, a committee of experts to work on supplying the city with water and in 1508 supporting a proposed but never actually attempted scheme by the Sienese architect Baldassare Peruzzi to provide a series of porticoes round the Campo.

Pandolfo Petrucci was by no means unique in his energetic patronage of art. Other eminent Sienese families were equally active in this respect. An instructive example is the Chigi family, who was united to the Petrucci by marriage. The Chigi owed their status and extraordinary wealth to their highly successful banking activities on behalf of the papacy in Rome. In about 1505 Sigismondo Chigi built his city residence on the Via del Casato just beyond the Campo (see pl. 6) and, like his father-in-law Pandolfo Petrucci, had its rooms painted, on this occasion by the talented Lombard painter Sodoma. He also continued the building of a villa outside the city begun by his father, Mariano (pl. 115). The design of this elegant rural retreat – symbolic of the leisured and aristocratic life that wealthy Sienese such as the Chigi were now pursuing – probably provided a prototype for the famous suburban villa built on the south bank of the river Tiber in Rome by the architect Baldassare Peruzzi for Sigismondo's brother, Agostino Chigi. Now known as the Farnesina (after the name of a later owner), this villa was decorated during the 1510s with intricate schemes of fresco painting commissioned from Raphael, Peruzzi and Sodoma – the last two being known to Agostino Chigi from his home town of Siena.[8]

These striking examples of familial patronage provide persuasive evidence that the balance was now tipping away from the predominance of corporate, public art in Siena towards private and elitist art. Nevertheless,

115 Villa Chigi at Alte Volte, near Siena.

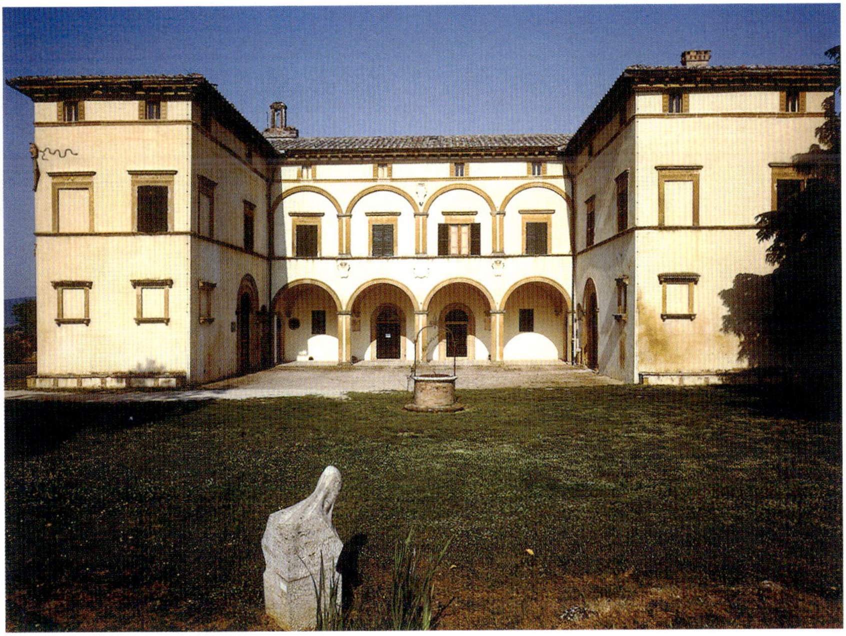

it is worth noting that some of Pandolfo's activities as a patron were addressed precisely to projects that had public, utilitarian functions, such as the supply of water to the city or the embellishment of the Campo. The history of the management of the Opera del Duomo under the *operaio* Alberto Aringhieri similarly illustrates the complexity of the emerging balance between private and public patronage of art.[9] Between 1483 and 1506, Aringhieri constructed a new chapel at the corner of the north aisle and transept of the cathedral (see pl. 34). Designed as a chapel to house the relic of the arm of Saint John the Baptist presented to the cathedral by Pius II in 1464, it was also the location of a sculpted font used as part of the Easter liturgy. This new chapel therefore played a major role in the religious life of the cathedral. Nevertheless, prominent among the fresco paintings of scenes from the life of Saint John the Baptist, commissioned from Pintoricchio for the walls of the chapel, are two votive portraits of Aringhieri himself, one as a young man and the other as an older man dressed in the robes of a Knight of Rhodes. Positioned on either side of the chapel entrance, these paintings assertively celebrate the identity, status and achievements of the man who had caused that chapel to be made.

During Aringhieri's energetic period of office, work on the cathedral pavement reached new levels of momentum, incorporating panels designed by both local painters such as Neroccio dei Landi and eminent artists from other cities such as Pintoricchio (pl. 116). Such activity continued throughout the 1520s and 1530s and became part of Baldassare Peruzzi's general refurbishment of the cathedral, which included the installation of a new high altar in 1532. As early as 1519, the cathedral Opera had enlisted the talent of Beccafumi to provide dramatic and daring designs for the pavement to be installed beneath the crossing. In 1524, he prepared further designs for the east side of the crossing, which were completed some five years later in anticipation of the Emperor Charles V's planned – though never realised – visit to the city in 1530. Beccafumi supplied his final designs in the 1540s for the panels around the high altar (pl. 117) and the series of bronze angels placed in front of the piers of the re-arranged chancel area.[10]

Art commissioned during the last decades of the Sienese republic thus presents an unusual combination of the popular and the esoteric. The foundation of two cultural institutions in the city at that time provides an interesting parallel to this intriguing paradox. In 1524 two Sienese intellectuals, one of whom was a member of the Piccolomini family, founded the Accademia degli Intronati. The erotic symbol of a slit pumpkin surmounted by two crossed pestles and the motto from Ovid – 'the best things are

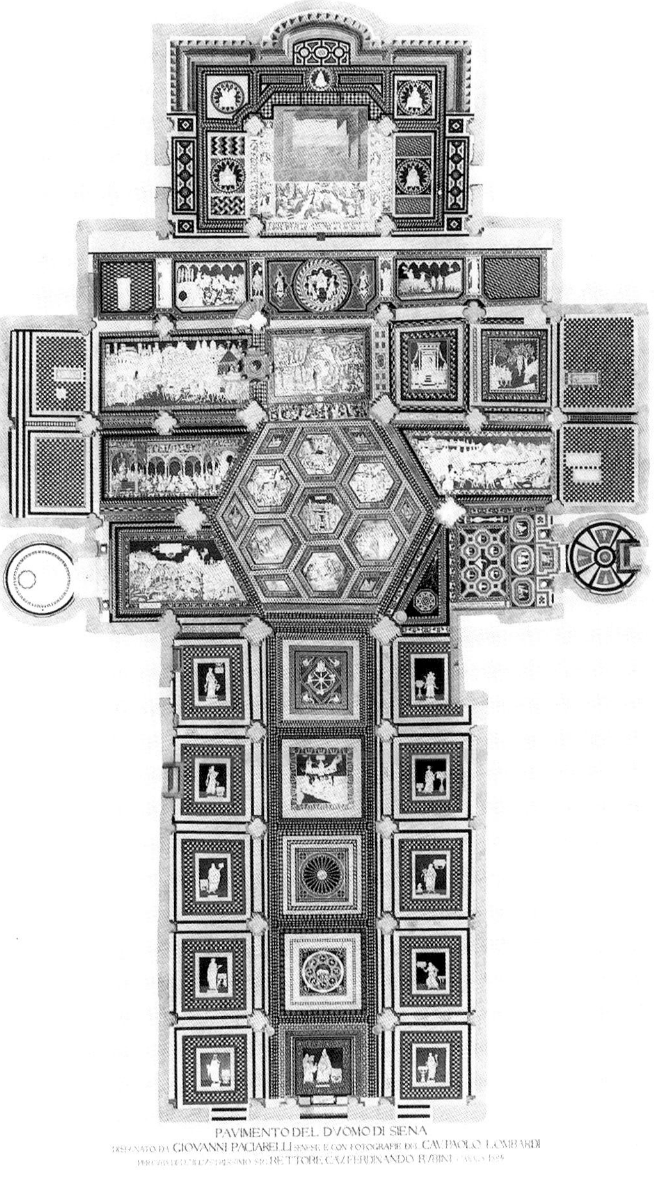

116 Giovanni Paciarelli, *The Cathedral Pavement* (1884). Siena, Museo dell'Opera del Duomo.

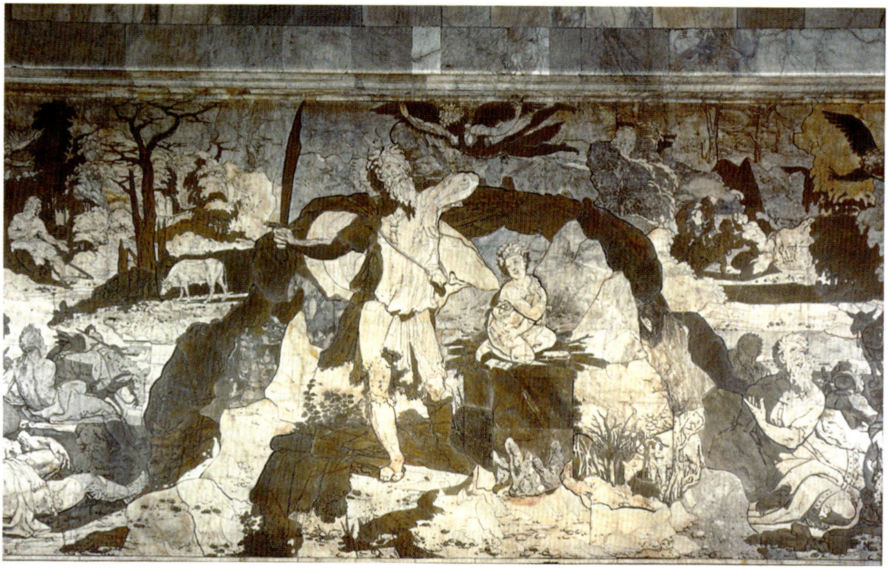

117 *The Sacrifice of Isaiah*, inlaid marble pavement panel designed by Beccafumi (1544–7). Siena, cathedral.

hidden' – adopted by the new academy indicate the elitist and esoteric nature of many of its intellectual activities. By contrast, in 1531 the Congrega dei Rozzi was founded. Catering for more robust and popular tastes, this body devoted itself principally to the performance of comic plays.[11]

As indicated in the previous chapter, one of the characteristic features of renaissance painting in Siena was the employment of painters from elsewhere in Italy. In part this was owing to the changing tastes of Sienese patrons who – through their own social and professional contacts – were increasingly aware of the skills and achievements of painters from other cities. At the same time painters, particularly from Umbria and Lombardy, were also attracted to Siena, a city that offered prospects of lucrative work. Once in Siena, they frequently worked alongside local Sienese artists. Two commissions – one from the end of the fifteenth century and the other from the beginning of the sixteenth century – illustrate this process particularly well.

* * *

Collaboration in the Bichi Chapel

Among the adherents of the Nine who returned to Siena with Pandolfo Petrucci in July 1487 was Antonio Bichi. A few months later, on 15 October, he and his daughter Eustochia obtained the rights of patronage over a chapel situated in the south transept of the church of Sant'Agostino: they dedicated it to Saint Christopher, in memory of Eustochia's deceased husband, Cristoforo Bellanti. In 1488 they commissioned local craftworkers to execute the frame of an altarpiece for the chapel and a handsome maiolica pavement incorporating the heraldic devices of both families. Five years later the family acquired special spiritual concessions from Pope Alexander VI for those who visited the chapel on designated feast days, and in 1494 secured an agreement with the Augustinian Hermits that they would fulfil various liturgical duties on their behalf. The date 1494 was placed on the entrance screen of the chapel.[12]

All that remains in the chapel today is its colourful tiled pavement and two large fresco paintings that were only rediscovered in 1977, beneath a layer of whitewash applied during the eighteenth-century remodelling of the chapel.[13] On the left or north wall appears the *Birth of the Virgin* (see pl. 119), surmounted by a lunette painting of the Tiburtine Sibyl. On the right or south wall appears the *Nativity*, surmounted by a painting of the Eritraean Sibyl. Nothing now survives of the paintings on the east wall or vault of the chapel.

Long since divided and dispersed, the chapel's altarpiece has been reconstructed by art historians (pl. 118).[14] At its centre would have been a carved wooden statue of the chapel's titular saint, Christopher (now in the Louvre, Paris). Richly painted in gold, red, blue, brown and flesh tones, and skilfully carved from a single piece of wood, the sculpture would originally have included a carved figure of the Christ Child set upon the saint's left shoulder. Attributed to the versatile Sienese artist Francesco di Giorgio, the *Saint Christopher* demonstrates both his skill as a sculptor and his appreciation of a well-established local tradition for wood carving (see pl. 86).

Behind this central sculpted group would have appeared a painting of the river across which – according to his legend – Saint Christopher carried the Christ Child. Represented on the banks of the river were a number of men disrobing to bathe (as seen from the surviving parts of this painting now in a North American collection). Probably intended as an allusion to the rite of baptism, these figures offer strikingly assured representations of the naked male form. The side panels of the altarpiece (now in Berlin) por-

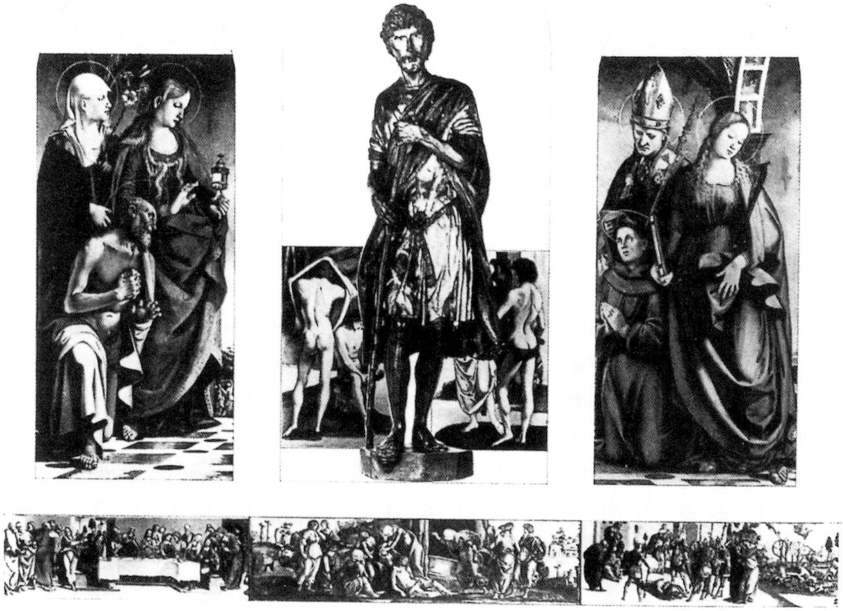

118 Reconstruction of the Bichi Altarpiece (by Max Seidel).

trayed a gathering of saints in groups of three, as if in an open-sided, vaulted loggia. On the left appear Saints Eustochia (the name saint of Eustochia Bichi) and Mary Magdalen, with Jerome kneeling in front of them. On the right appear Saints Augustine and Catherine of Alexandria, with Anthony of Padua (Antonio Bichi's name saint) kneeling between them. While the Augustinian Hermits particularly revered Saints Augustine, Jerome, Catherine of Alexandria and Mary Magdalen, Antonio Bichi had an additional personal reason for choosing Mary Magdalen for his chapel altarpiece. He and Pandolfo Petrucci had returned to Siena in 1487 on 22 July, her feast day. The foundation of the chapel and the imagery of its altarpiece thus acted as a clear statement of Antonio Bichi's re-established social status in his city.

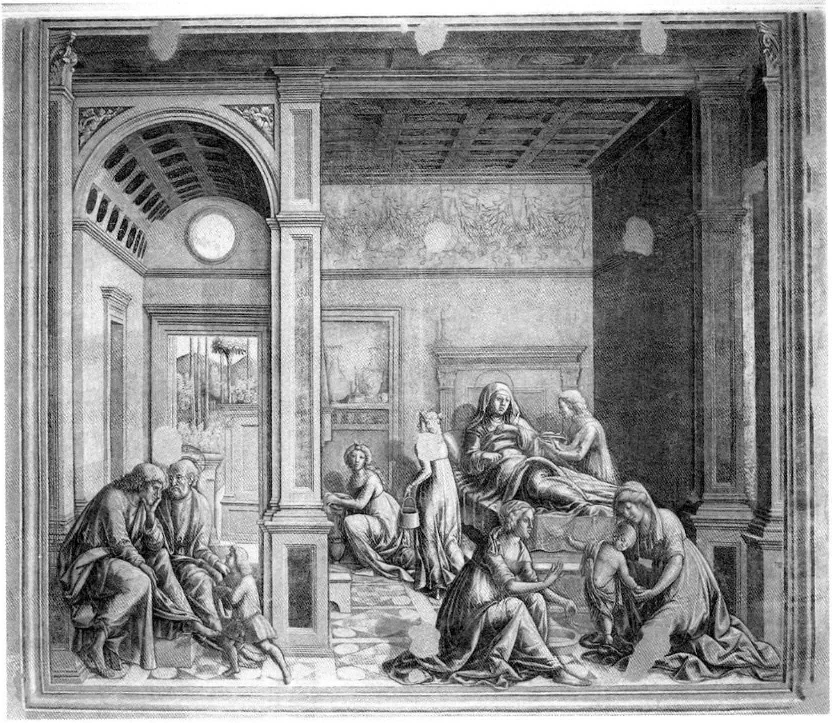

119 Close associate of Francesco di Giorgio, *The Birth of the Virgin* (*c.* 1490–94). Fresco in grisaille on north wall of the Bichi Chapel, 450 × 530 cm. Siena, Sant'Agostino.

The figures on the altarpiece – represented with clear outlines and in bold relief[15] – are characteristic of the style of Signorelli, a painter from Cortona who by that date had worked on a number of important commissions in other Italian cities, including Rome and Loreto. In 1484, three years before the foundation of the Bichi chapel, he is also documented working in Gubbio and consulting with Francesco di Giorgio on plans for a church there.[16] It may be, therefore, that Francesco di Giorgio, on his return to Siena in 1487 after working for the princely Montefeltre family in Urbino, specifically recommended Signorelli to Antonio Bichi as his collaborator on the chapel altarpiece.

Whatever the precise origins of the collaboration, the chapel frescoes were also apparently assigned to two artists – Signorelli taking responsibility for the Tiburtine and Eritraean sibyls on the upper parts of the north and south walls. Set in painted frames that take account of the viewer's position on the floor below, these figures demonstrate Signorelli's preference for multi-axial poses and voluminous drapery. They also provide evidence of his facility in depicting classicising ornamentation and lettering. The design of the *Birth of the Virgin* and the *Nativity* have been attributed to Francesco di Giorgio, although it is generally believed that their execution owed much to the skill of an unidentified painter who collaborated with him on a number of other painting projects in and around Siena.[17]

The *Birth of the Virgin* demonstrates the quality of these two paintings (pl. 119). Executed in delicate shades of grey monochrome, broken by the occasional use of gold or blue, the painting presents an orderly and balanced composition. The space of the interior of the room is carefully established through the skilful use of perspective to represent the pavement and the coffered ceiling of the bedchamber and the barrel-vaulted passageway on the left. The women attending the Virgin's mother, Saint Anne, are portrayed as graceful figures in ample draperies. On the left, meanwhile, appears the traditional scene of the small boy bringing the news of the Virgin's birth to her father Joachim and a companion. The detail of the boy's crossed arms acts as a direct quotation from the mid-fourteenth-century altarpiece by Pietro Lorenzetti over the altar of Saint Savino in the cathedral (see pl. 59) – a testimony to the enduring regard in which the Lorenzetti's work was held. Elsewhere, the painting shows the painter's skill in portraying both landscape and genre details, such as the glass vessels in the niche beside Saint Anne's bed.

The pose of the infant, supported by an attentive woman but leaning towards the right, indicates awareness on the part of the painter of the overall design of the chapel decoration. Thus, the most important cult figure in the painting is shown as if orientated towards the altar of the chapel. This is also the case in the *Nativity* on the opposite wall, where the Christ Child lying on the ground twists his head in the direction of the altar. The poses of the sibyls on the walls above are similarly aligned towards the altar where the sculpture of Saint Christopher carrying the Christ Child on his shoulder would once have stood. The texts of their prophecies, too, underline the religious significance both of the birth of Christ himself and of the Virgin's crucial role in this sacred event.

* * *

The Piccolomini Library

Whereas it now requires a substantial effort of imagination to envisage the total effect of the Bichi chapel in Sant'Agostino, the highly ornate interior of the cathedral library commissioned by Cardinal Francesco Todeschini Piccolomini at the beginning of the sixteenth century remains almost in its original state (pl. 120). Transforming parts of the canons' residence on the north side of the cathedral, Cardinal Francesco began the project in the 1490s with the construction by local stoneworkers of a sizeable rectangular room lit by two large windows set in the outer north wall. The room was intended as a library to house the rich collection of manuscript books once owned by the cardinal's maternal uncle, the humanist pope Pius II. The skilled local woodworker Antonio Barili was therefore commissioned to make a series of reading benches, executed in walnut wood. These no longer survive, but parts of them have been utilised for the display cabinets that now line the walls of the former library.

Two Sienese stoneworkers who had worked extensively on other projects in the cathedral were commissioned to execute an imposing entrance for the library, facing the north aisle of the cathedral. In terms of its classicising repertoire and rich decorative ornament, it provided a worthy successor to the renaissance architectural monuments introduced to Siena by Pius II some thirty years earlier. The entrance door itself was furnished with a pair of bronze gates executed in 1497 by the same craftworker who supplied the screen for the Bichi chapel.[18]

On 29 June 1502 in his palace in Siena Cardinal Francesco Todeschini Piccolomini signed a contract with the Umbrian painter Pintoricchio to paint the ceilings and the walls of the new library for the sum of a thousand gold ducats.[19] This extremely high fee was not only an indication of the amount of work involved but also a reflection of the lavish materials to be used in a scheme that incorporated considerable gold leaf and stuccowork as well as richly coloured pigments. The wording of the contract carefully specified that Pintoricchio should devote much of his time and artistic skill on the project – personally carrying out all the preparatory drawings for the ten paintings depicting the life of Pius II on the library walls, as well as the cartoons and frescoes themselves. The concern that Pintoricchio himself should be personally involved in his project is an indication of the value then placed on the work of this Umbrian painter. Although currently working in Perugia, during the 1480s and 90s he had been involved in a number of highly prestigious projects in Rome, including painting the private apartments of Pope Alexander VI in the Vatican and Castel Sant'Angelo.[20] In

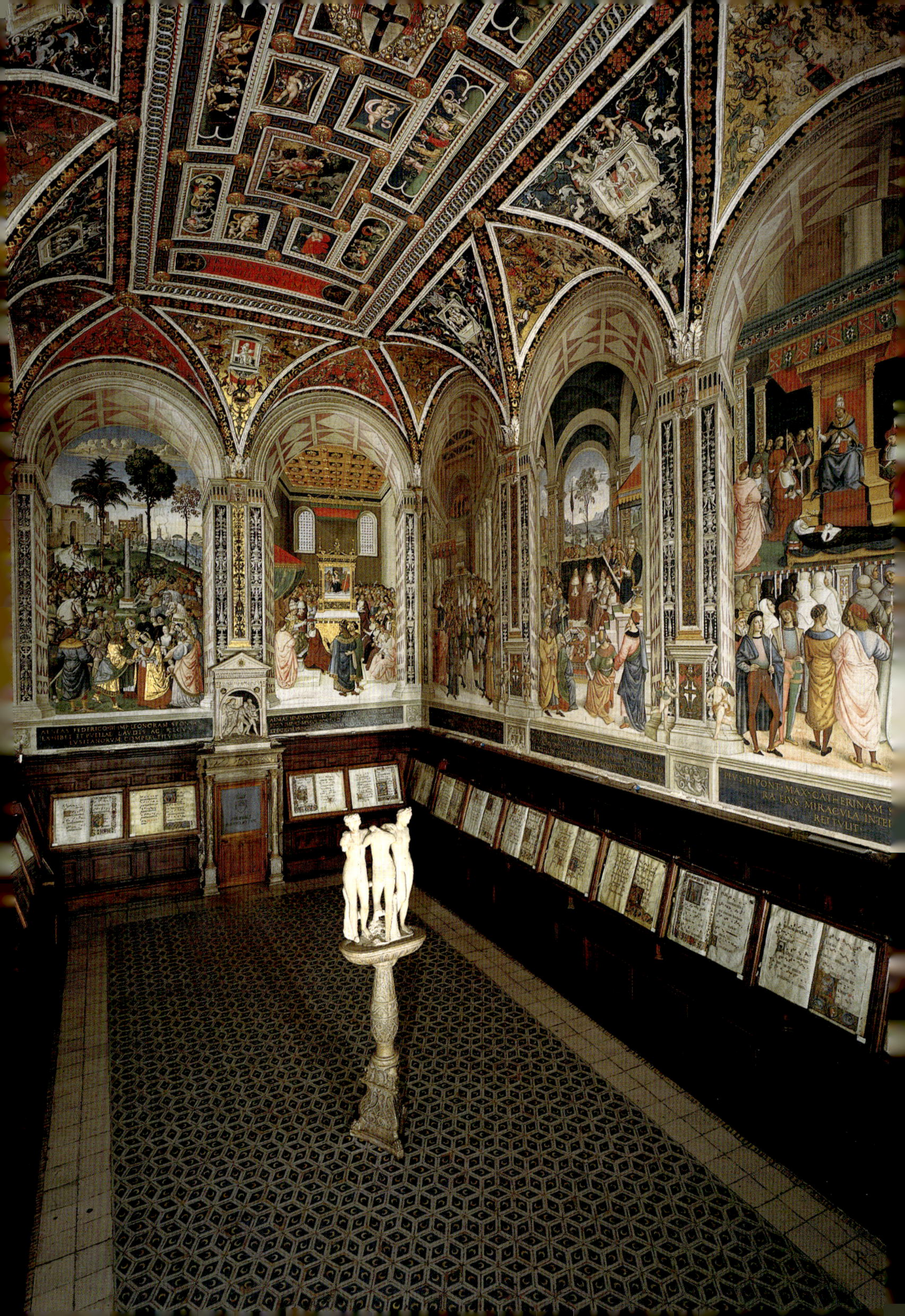

these commissions he had demonstrated his abilities as a painter who could represent narrative in a lively manner while embellishing it with rich decorative detail. He had also demonstrated a flair for replicating a particular kind of classical ornament that had recently been discovered in Rome, in the underground vaults of the Golden House of Nero near the Colosseum. Known as 'grotesques' from the fact that they were discovered in underground grottoes, this style of decoration had become fashionable with both patrons and artists in late fifteenth-century Rome.

Despite the Cardinal's insistence that Pintoricchio work on the library to the exclusion of all other projects, the painting of the library took several years to complete. Indeed, it was not until 18 January 1509 that Pintoricchio received the final payment from the Piccolomini family for this work and for other projects undertaken on their behalf. The length can partly be accounted for by the work's complexity and by the fact that in October 1503, a month after being crowned Pope Pius III, Francesco Todeschini Piccolomini died. His brothers Andrea and Giacomo Piccolomini took over responsibility for the library, drawing up a further contract with the painter to execute a large fresco over the entrance of the library representing the coronation of their brother as Pius III. It also appears that from 1503 onwards Pintoricchio, now resident in Siena, was in fact allowed to work on a number of other projects within the cathedral, as well as painting an altarpiece for the Piccolomini chapel in San Francesco.[21]

The paintings on the ceiling of the library were probably completed first, some time before 22 September 1503 – the date of Pius III's accession – since the coat-of-arms at the centre of the ceiling is still that of Cardinal Francesco Todeschini Piccolomini.[22] A number of panels contain either narrative incidents from classical mythology or figures derived from sarcophagi and the paintings discovered in the Golden House of Nero. While the entire scheme displays a brilliant range of colours and lavish use of gold, the rather clumsy representation of some of the figurative scenes suggests that Pintoricchio delegated much of the work on the ceiling to assistants. It is possible, therefore, that at this early stage of the project the master-painter remained in Perugia, working on the preparatory drawings for the narrative paintings of the library.

When Cardinal Francesco made his will in April 1503, it is clear that work on the main paintings of the library had barely begun. Five years later, on 19 and 22 April 1508, porters were paid for removing the scaffolding for the painting of the 'story of Pius in the cathedral' and for transporting it to the painter's workshop.[23] This in all likelihood marked the completion

120 The Piccolomini Library with frescoes by Pintoricchio. Siena, cathedral.

of the *Coronation of Pius III* scene located outside the library. It is generally agreed, therefore, that the ten wall paintings inside the library were executed by Pintoricchio and his assistants between about 1503 and 1507.

The ten paintings in the library devoted to portraying key events in the life of Pius II are arranged on the two long walls and the entrance wall. Framed by fictive architecture that displays both 'grotesque' decoration and the Piccolomini coat-of-arms, the overall impression is of events opening outwards beyond a series of coffered arches. The narrative sequence begins on the east wall, to the right of the window when facing it, and proceeds clockwise round the room. The visitor to the library receives instruction about the subject of each of the paintings from the Latin text in the panel below it.[24] Based on Pius II's own detailed autobiography – the *Commentaries* – and on another contemporary biography, the scenes were carefully selected to celebrate the abilities and achievements of Aeneas Silvius Piccolomini. The four scenes on the east wall demonstrate his youthful achievements as a lay diplomat and humanist. They then continue with two scenes on the entrance wall that commemorate one of his major diplomatic achievements as Bishop of Siena and his subsequent elevation to the College of Cardinals. Finally, the four scenes on the west wall graphically illustrate his coronation as pope, his sanctification of Catherine of Siena and his efforts to mount a crusade against the Turks.

As in the mid-fifteenth-century paintings for the Pellegrinaio (see pls 89, 97–8), this cycle is relatively unusual in that it depicts recent historical events. It also constitutes an extraordinary assertion of the value placed on the memory and reputation of Pius II. Although the early fifteenth-century painted cycle in the Palazzo Pubblico of the life of an earlier Sienese pope, Alexander III, provided some degree of precedent for such commemoration (see pl. 79), the Piccolomini paintings represented something new in their intensity of the celebration of a near contemporary figure.

It was undoubtedly Cardinal Piccolomini's position as Bishop of Siena that enabled this remarkable and powerful visual celebration of the Piccolomini family to be introduced into the fabric of the city's cathedral, yet the subjects of two of the murals suggest that the scheme was also intended to celebrate the identity of Siena itself and the piety of the Sienese. Just to the left of the entrance is the painting of Aeneas Silvius Piccolomini as Bishop of Siena, presiding over the meeting of Frederick III and Eleanor of Portugal (pl. 121). As recounted in his *Commentaries*, Aeneas Silvius played a prominent role in securing a marriage alliance between this

121 Pintoricchio, *The Meeting of Emperor Frederick III and Eleanor of Portugal* (*c.* 1503–07). Fresco, 700 (to top of arch) × 260cm. Entrance wall of the Piccolomini Library. Siena, cathedral.

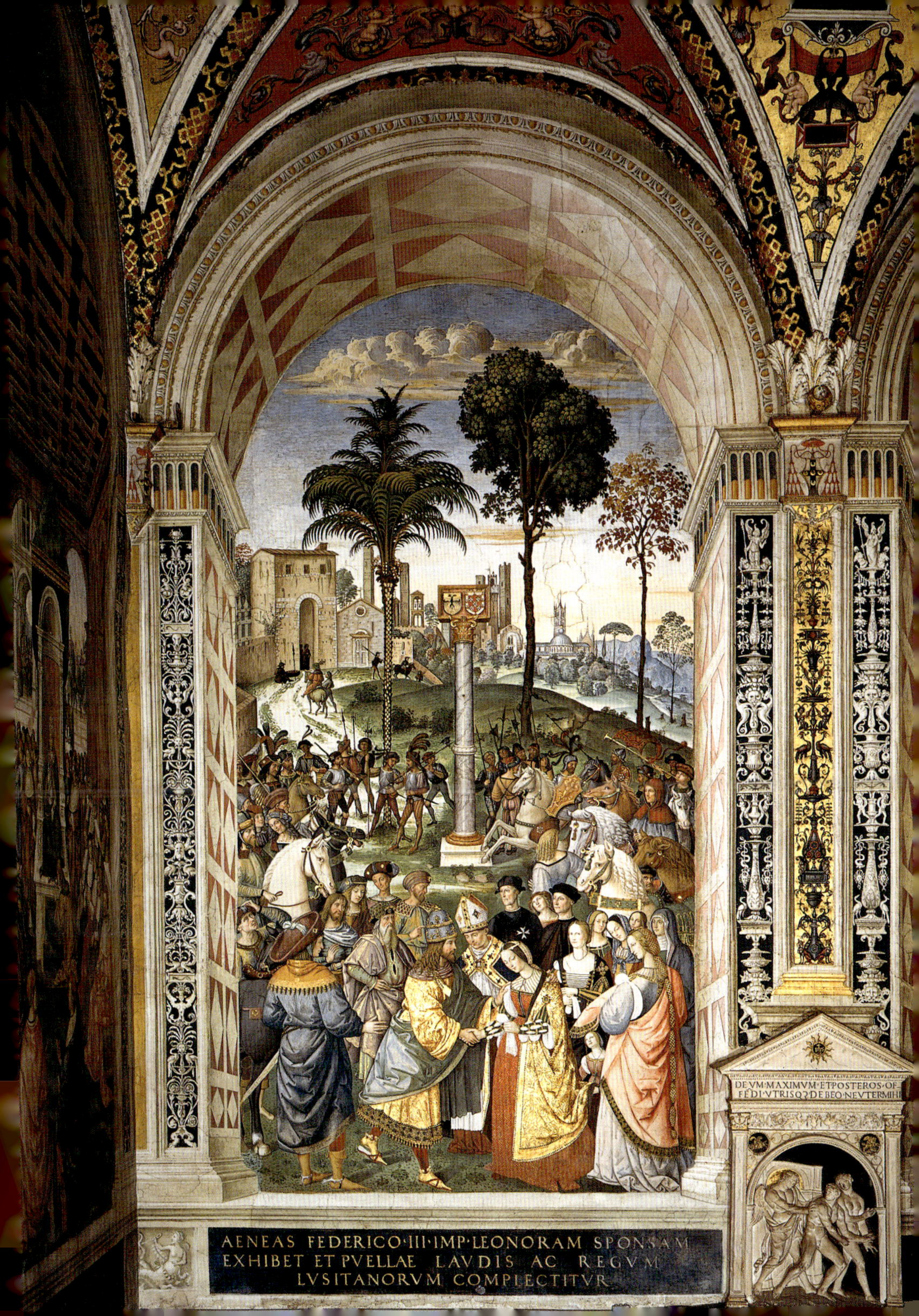
DEVM·MAXIMVM·ET·POSTEROS·OF
FEDI·VTRISQ DEBEO·NEVTER MIHI
AENEAS FEDERICO·III·IMP·LEONORAM SPONSAM
EXHIBET ET PVELLAE LAVDIS AC REGVM
LVSITANORVM COMPLECTITVR

German prince and the daughter of the king of Portugal. The painting represents their first meeting, which took place at Siena outside the Porta Camollia on 24 February 1452. It portrays also the column that was erected to commemorate this event and which still survives.[25] In addition to its detailed depiction of the magnificent costumes worn by the participants, the painting provides a graphic image of the walls and monuments of Siena, as seen from a vantage point outside the Porta Camollia. Beyond the foreground figures on the right is a distant view of the cathedral and its campanile, together with the distinctive contours of the unfinished Duomo Nuovo. Beyond that again is the Torre del Mangia of the Palazzo Pubblico.

The second painting of particular significance for the celebration of Siena appears amid the four paintings devoted to the reign of Pius II; it shows him, accompanied by his cardinals, promulgating the Church's decision on 29 June 1461 to make Catherine of Siena a saint (pl. 122). As indicated in chapter 4, this was a momentous event for the Sienese and one that resulted in paintings of the saint being placed in important locations in the city. The scene in the Piccolomini library shows Pius II seated on his ceremonial papal throne in the act of blessing the body of the saint, which allegedly remained in a perfectly preserved state in Santa Maria sopra Minerva, the principal Dominican church in Rome, the city in which Catherine died. In the foreground appears a crowd of clerics and laymen, the latter clad in the luxurious costumes favoured by Pintoricchio throughout the fresco scheme. The two figures on the left are believed to be portraits of the painter himself and the young Raphael. An arresting figure of a bearded Dominican friar on the right is likely to be a portrait of the current Master General of the Dominican Order, Vincenzo Bandello[26] – attesting once again to Pintoricchio's abilities as an observer of contemporary life.

Ironically, once completed, the library was never used for its intended purpose.[27] On the death of Pius III in 1503, his extensive collection of manuscripts remained in the family's palaces in Rome and Siena and was eventually dispersed to other libraries. Fortunately, Pintoricchio's paintings remained intact, with the result that the Piccolomini library is one of the best-preserved schemes of renaissance painting to survive today. It also provides an extraordinarily vivid example of the way in which by the beginning of the sixteenth century artistic schemes initiated by members of prominent Sienese families were beginning to take on the scale and magnificence once reserved to civic patronage of art.

* * *

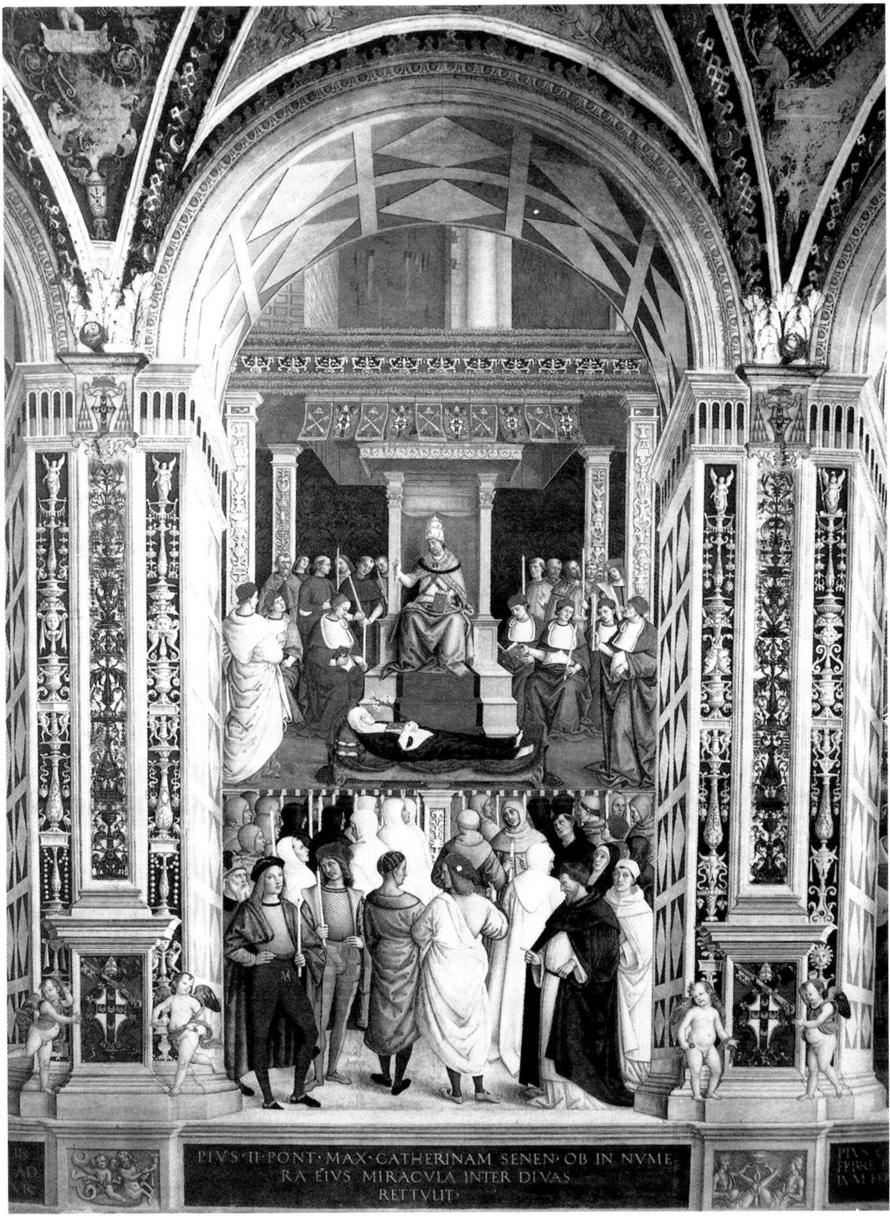

122 Pintoricchio, *The Canonisation of Saint Catherine of Siena* (*c.* 1503–7). Fresco, 700 (to top of arch) × 260 cm. West wall of the Piccolomini Library. Siena, cathedral.

The 'Magnificent Chamber' of Pandolfo Petrucci

In 1511 Vittoria Piccolomini, niece to Pius III, married Borghese Petrucci, the son of Pandolfo Petrucci.[28] This dynastic alliance was duly commemorated in one of the principal rooms in the Palazzo Petrucci (see pl. 6). Located in a medieval tower, the base of which became the principal entrance of the building, early sixteenth-century references to this third-floor room suggest that it originally functioned as an audience chamber where Pandolfo received guests and conducted official business.[29] Nothing of the sixteenth-century painted decoration remains in the room today but it is clear from two eighteenth-century descriptions that it was originally decorated with eight fresco paintings representing classical subject matter.[30]

A number of scholars have reconstructed the appearance and rich furnishings of this room.[31] Almost square in appearance, each wall would have contained either a single doorway or a window (the latter facing onto the Via dei Pellegrini, the street that leads to the square in front of the cathedral baptistery). The ceiling would have been covered by a decorative scheme of stuccowork and small paintings depicting events drawn from classical mythology. Rivalling the richness and complexity of the ceiling of the Piccolomini library (see pl. 120), it has been re-assembled almost in its totality in New York's Metropolitan Museum (pl. 123). It is generally attributed to Pintoricchio and his workshop.[32]

Beneath the ceiling would have been the eight frescoes described in the eighteenth-century sources, five of which survive today and three are lost. Following the order given in the two descriptions, their subjects would have been: the *Calumny of Apelles* (lost but generally attributed to Signorelli);[33] the *Feast of Pan* (lost but again attributed to Signorelli);[34] the *Triumph of Chastity* (National Gallery, London, signed by Signorelli); *Coriolanus persuaded by his Family to spare Rome* (pl. 126, signed by Signorelli); the *Continence of Scipio* (lost and attributed to Pintoricchio); the *Return of Ulysses* (pl. 124, attributed to Pintoricchio); *Fabius Maximus ransoming Prisoners from Hannibal* (Pinacoteca, Siena, and attributed to Genga, a painter from Urbino); and the *Flight of Aeneas from Troy* (pl. 125, also attributed to Genga).

Each of the paintings – two on each wall – would have been framed by carved wooden pilasters, some of which survive today and have been attributed to Antonio Barili, the artist who supplied the woodwork for the Piccolomini library.[35] Barili also produced a series of wooden benches, richly embellished with carvings of fruit, flowers and foliage, that were positioned round the walls below the fresco paintings in this room. Again, like

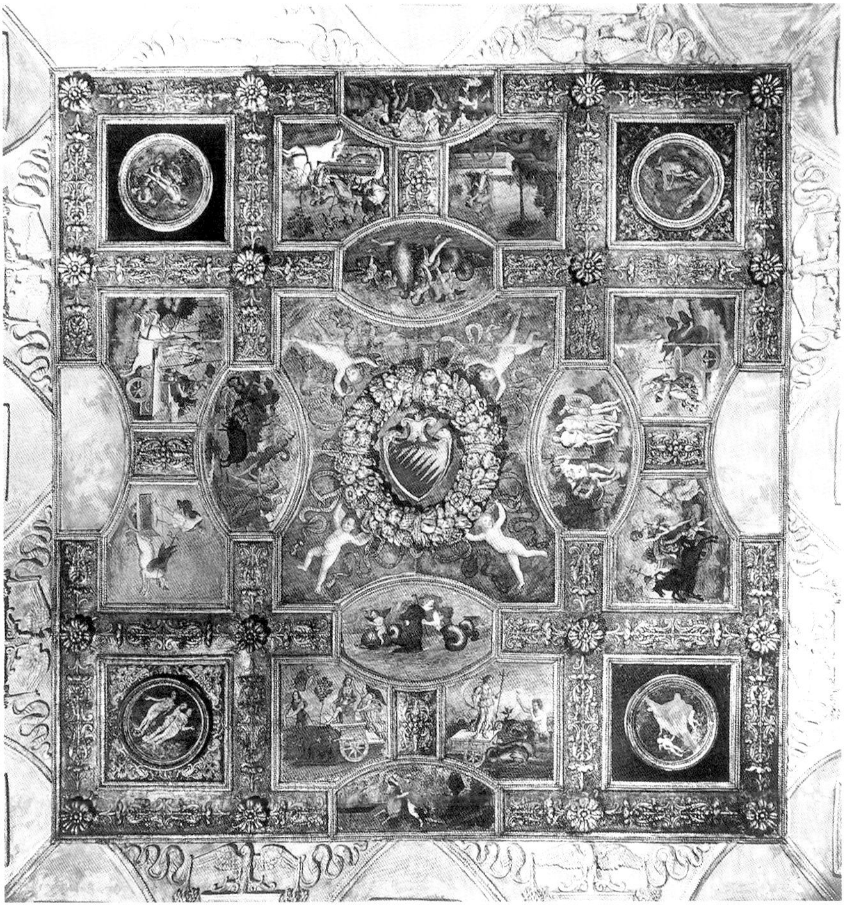

123 Pintoricchio and assistants, ceiling of the 'painted chamber' of Pandolfo Petrucci (*c.* 1507–10). New York, The Metropolitan Museum of Art, Rogers Fund, 1914. (14.114.1-22).

the library, the floor would have been covered in maiolica tiles embellished with grotesques and family coats-of-arms, some of which survive now in European museums.[36]

In its original state the *camera della torre* (the room in the tower) must have rivalled the splendour and sumptuousness of the Piccolomini library. The date of its execution is a matter of debate. The Petrucci coat-of-arms

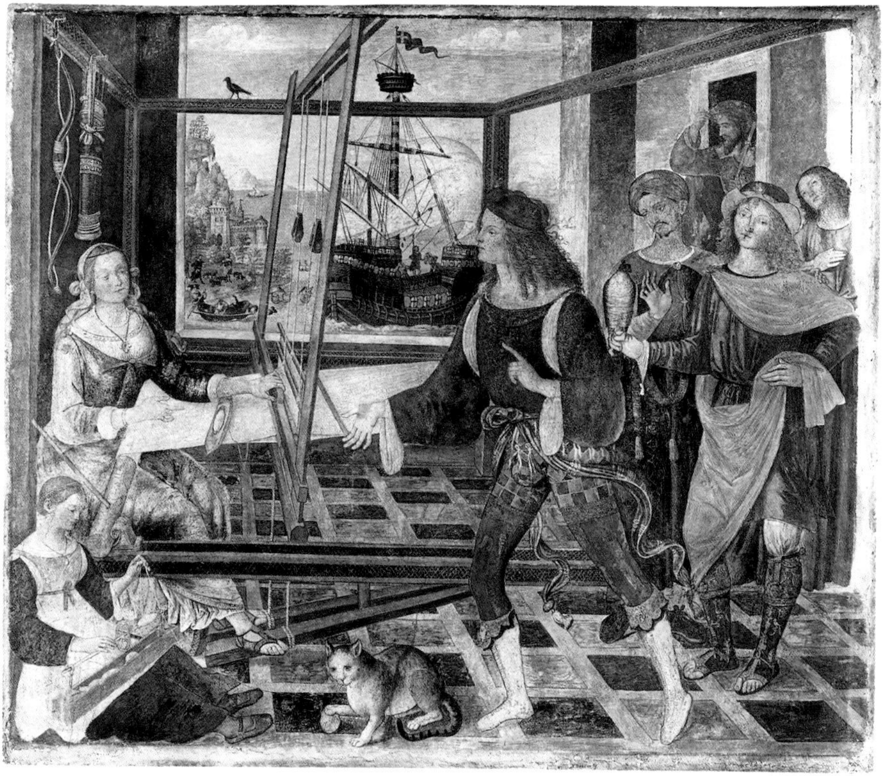

124 Pintoricchio, *The Return of Ulysses* (*c.* 1507–10). Fresco transferred to canvas, 125.5 × 152 cm. London, National Gallery.

125 (*facing page top*) Genga, *The Flight of Aeneas from Troy* (*c.* 1507–10). Fresco, 126 × 138 cm. Siena, Pinacoteca Nazionale.

126 (*facing page bottom*) Signorelli, *Coriolanus persuaded by his Family to spare Rome* (*c.* 1507–10). Fresco transferred to canvas, 125.5 × 125.5 cm. London, National Gallery.

quartered with that of the Piccolomini appear on many of the pavement tiles and in three places on the surviving woodwork from this room. This suggests that the furnishings of the room at least were executed after the marriage of Borghese Petrucci and Vittoria Piccolomini in 1511. However, only the Petrucci coat-of-arms appear at the centre of the ceiling and in the

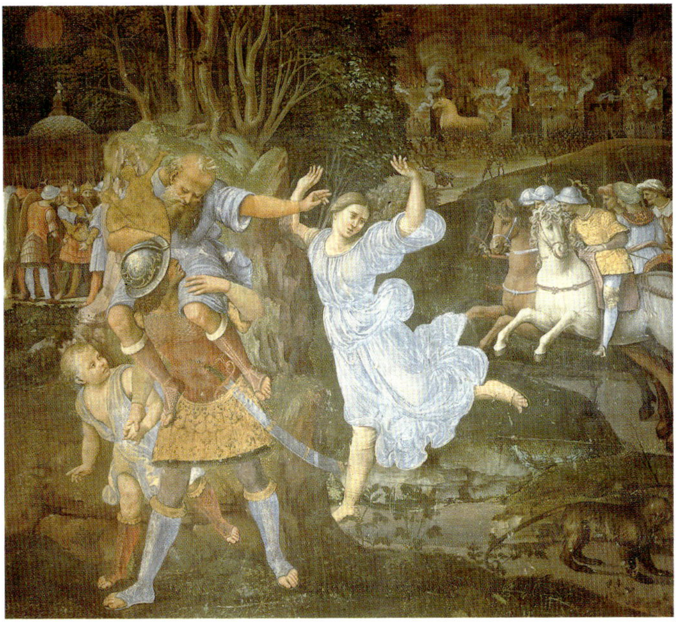

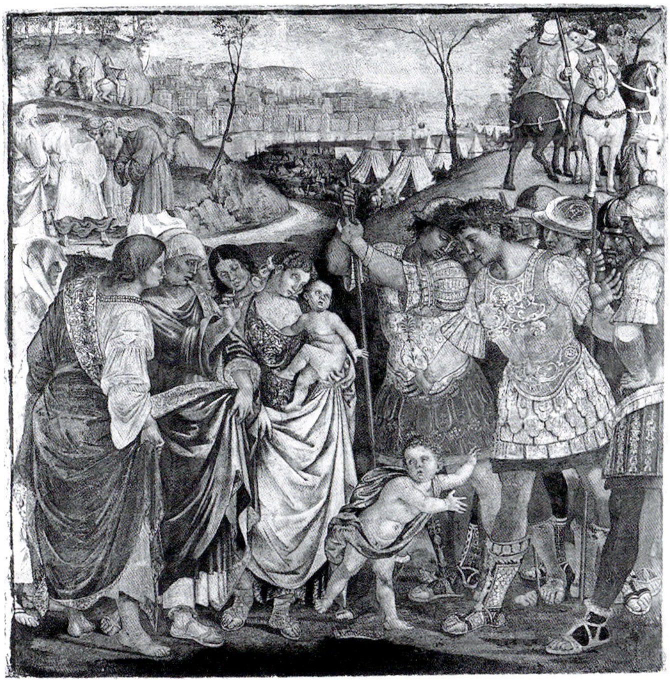

linked not to the republican government of early fourteenth-century Siena but to the political ambitions of a single powerful early sixteenth-century individual and his family.

Portraits and Painted Furnishings

From the late fifteenth and early sixteenth centuries much more painting commissioned for privately owned spaces survives than from previous centuries. This can be explained by broader social and economic trends in Italy as a whole, whereby art was increasingly sought after and valued as a luxury commodity for those who could afford it. At the same time, it can be seen as a direct result of wealthier Sienese families determinedly adopting a lifestyle similar to that of princely rulers of other Italian cities such as Urbino, Ferrara and Mantua.

Unlike other Italian cities such as Florence and Mantua, there are relatively few surviving examples of Sienese portraiture – a genre that was becoming popular elsewhere. As already noted, Sienese painters occasionally included portraits of patrons and their associates in public schemes of painting (see pls 99, 101). There is also evidence that Domenico di Bartolo made a portrait of the Holy Emperor Sigismund on his visit to Siena and that Francesco di Giorgio made both painted and sculpted portraits of Federigo da Montefeltre, his patron in Urbino. An inventory of 1483 similarly records that the famous doctor Bartolo di Tura Bandini owned a small portrait of his deceased son Tommaso.[39] However, portraits commissioned by Sienese patrons appear to be relatively rare. One of the reasons for this may be that while in a number of Italian cities there is evidence of Flemish portraits being imported and acquired by patrons, in Siena this does not appear to have been the case.

A Sienese portrait that does survive is a painting of a young woman, now in the National Gallery of Art in Washington (pl. 127). Still in a frame that is probably original, it has been attributed to Neroccio dei Landi and generally dated to the 1480s.[40] The portrait's authorship receives further confirmation in the left and right-hand corners of the painted inscription on the lower edge of the painting where the letters OP and NER appear – probably an abbreviation of 'OPUS NEROCCIO' (the work of Neroccio).[41] The identity of the sitter is unknown but the treatment of the subject is typical of portraits of young women at that date. Adopting a convention derived from Flemish portraiture, it shows her head and shoulders as if from relatively close quarters. Her physical proximity is enhanced by the distant

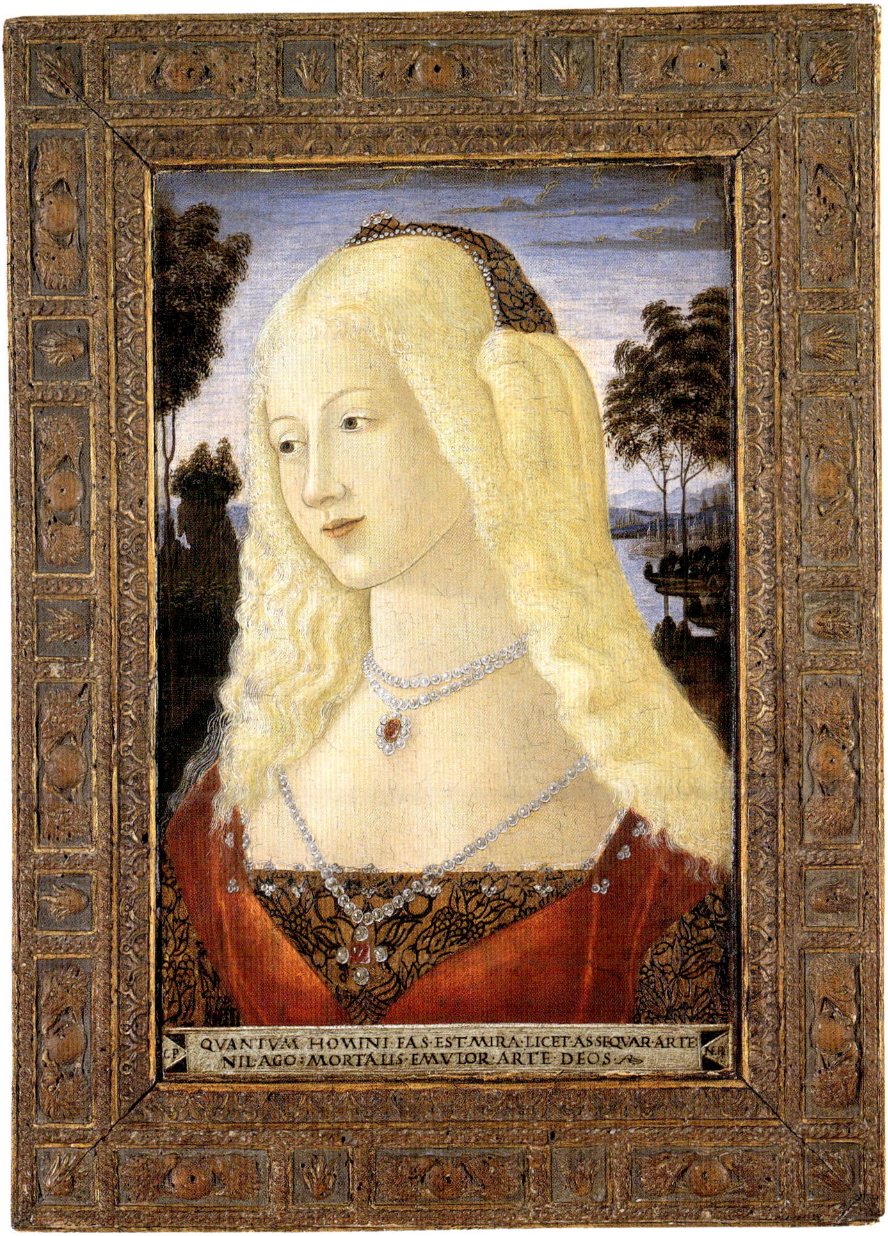

127 Neroccio dei Landi, *Portrait of a Young Woman* (*c.* 1480–90). Tempera on panel, 46.5 × 30.5 cm. Washington, National Gallery of Art.

view of a lake or river in the background and the feathery trees that frame her head. The viewer is thus encouraged to examine the features of the young woman in some detail and enjoy the texture and colour of her abundant golden hair and pale skin, the embroidery of her gown and the ropes of pearls and gems round her neck.

Given the unknown circumstances of the commission, it is impossible to determine whether Neroccio dei Landi faithfully recorded the character and individuality of his young sitter. Since she is represented with her hair loose and – apart from an embroidered cap – uncovered, it is likely that she was still unmarried at the time the portrait was painted. In terms of her comportment and dress, she also observes the social conventions recommended to well-bred, virtuous women at that time:[42] her gaze is modestly averted and her gown, although cut low, does not reveal the outline of her breasts. It is likely that the painting was commissioned as a betrothal portrait for her impending marriage to a member of the Bandini family, whose family emblem appears on the carved wooden frame.[43] The fact that her attention appears to be directed towards the left may indicate that the portrait was painted as one of a pair, the other being of her future husband.

While portraiture does not appear to have been a particularly popular form of art in renaissance Siena, another genre of secular painting definitely was. Like the portrait just discussed, this type of painting was used as a means of representing approved norms of contemporary female behaviour. It characteristically took the form of a series of panel paintings, usually three in number, each showing a single full-length figure of a woman. Originally set in a wooden framework (as seen in the series attributed to Guidoccio Cozzarelli, pl. 128), these paintings would have lined the walls of a room in the manner of painted wainscoting. Their female subject, together with the explanatory inscriptions placed upon them, would have been particularly suitable decoration for rooms used by the women of the household. Analysis of three examples provides evidence of such an intended function.

Now divested of their original framework, and having been subjected to drastic over-cleaning earlier in their history,[44] the paintings depict three famous exemplary women – one from the Old Testament and two from classical history. The landscape setting that the three paintings share suggests that their original sequence was first, the Jewish heroine Judith; second, the Carthaginian heroine Sophonisba; and third, the Egyptian queen Cleopatra. Each woman is represented with objects relating to the cause of her fame. Judith holds the head of Holofernes, the Babylonian general who threatened to conquer her city of Bethulia (Judith: 2–13) and whose head

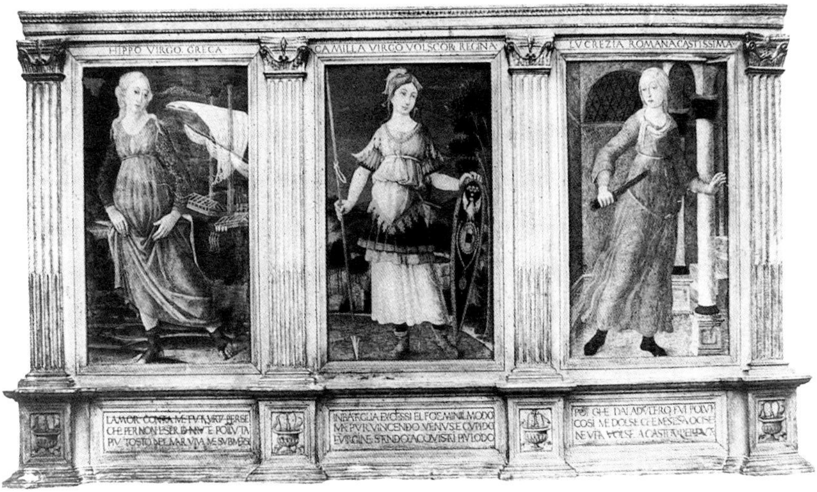

128 Guidoccio Cozzarelli, *Hippo, Camilla and Lucrezia* (*c.* 1500–10). Tempera on panel. Siena, private collection.

she struck off with the sword that she brandishes above her (pl. 129). Sophonisba holds the chalice of poison that she drank in preference to being taken to Rome as a captive of Scipio Africanus (pl. 130). Cleopatra, meanwhile, clasps the asp whose deadly bite would lead to her death after the suicide of Mark Anthony (pl. 131).

What the three women have in common is that they all exemplify the virtues of fortitude and courage in the face of adversity. This, moreover, was precisely the kind of behaviour recommended to women in treatises devoted to the subjects of the ideal family or proper moral conduct.[45] The didactic tone of this painted series would therefore have been deemed highly suitable for the education of the woman of a household – particularly, perhaps, that of a new wife arriving to take up her duties as a married woman within her husband's home. Furthermore, despite these three women's close association with the themes of death and suicide, they are treated in an elegant and decorative manner. All three appear in light diaphanous garments that sport fluttering hems, sashes and ribbons. The unknown painter portrayed them in an array of subtle pastel colours. Their faces wear expressions that belie the dramatic events that have occurred in the past or are about to unfold. The landscape background has a misty, almost poetic quality to it. In its original setting, as part of the embellish-

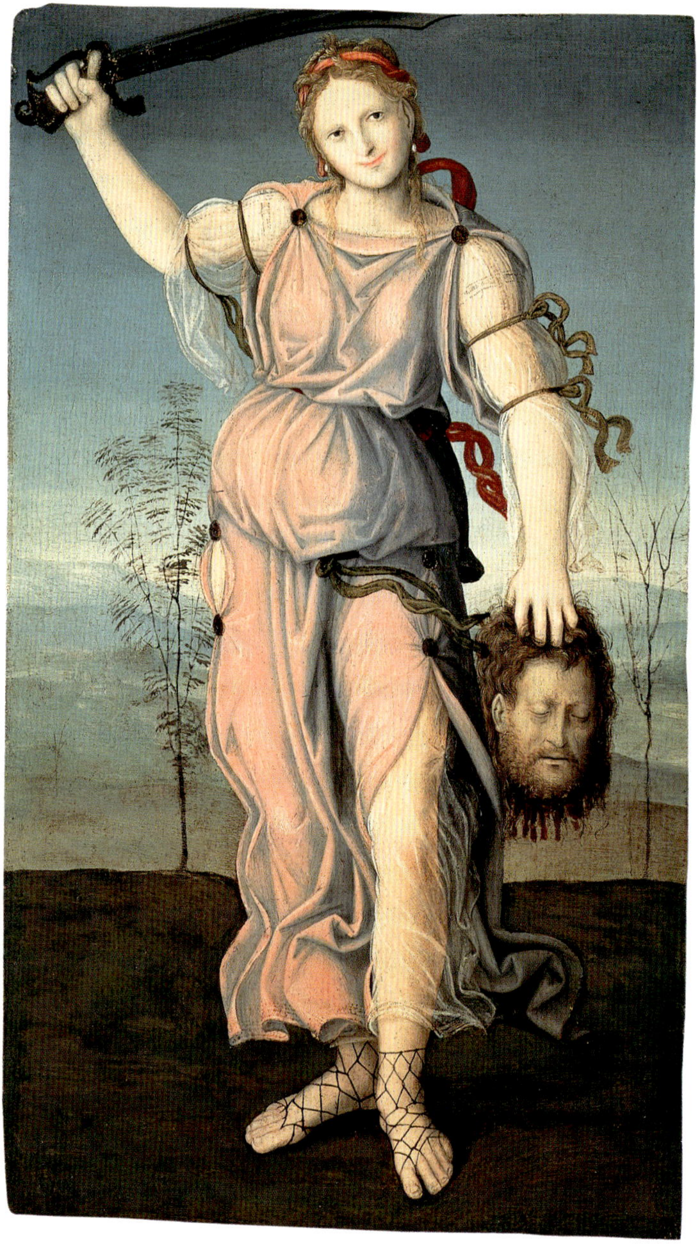

129 Master of the Chigi Saracini Heroines, *Judith* (*c.* 1500–10). Tempera on panel, 77 × 44.7 cm. Siena, Collezione Chigi Saracini.

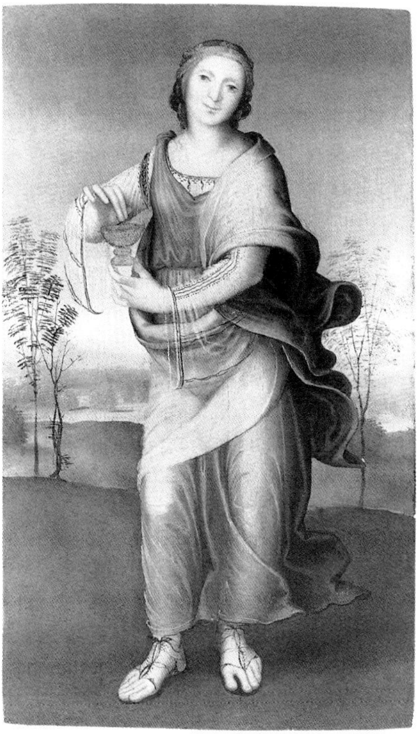

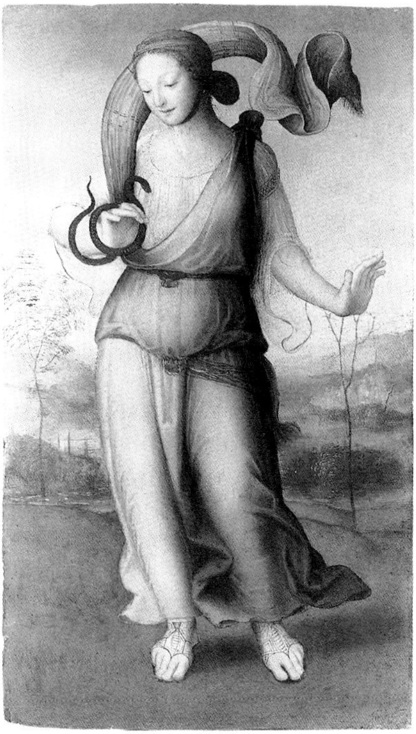

130 (*above left*) Master of the Chigi Saracini Heroines, *Sophonisba* (*c.* 1500–10). Tempera on panel, 77.1 × 43.5 cm. Siena, Collezione Chigi Saracini.

131 (*above right*) Master of the Chigi Saracini Heroines, *Cleopatra* (*c.* 1500–10). Tempera on panel, 77 × 44 cm. Siena, Collezione Chigi Saracini.

ment of a private room frequented by the women of one of Siena's wealthier families, this painted series would once have created a pleasingly decorative – as well as didactic – ambience for its owners.

* * *

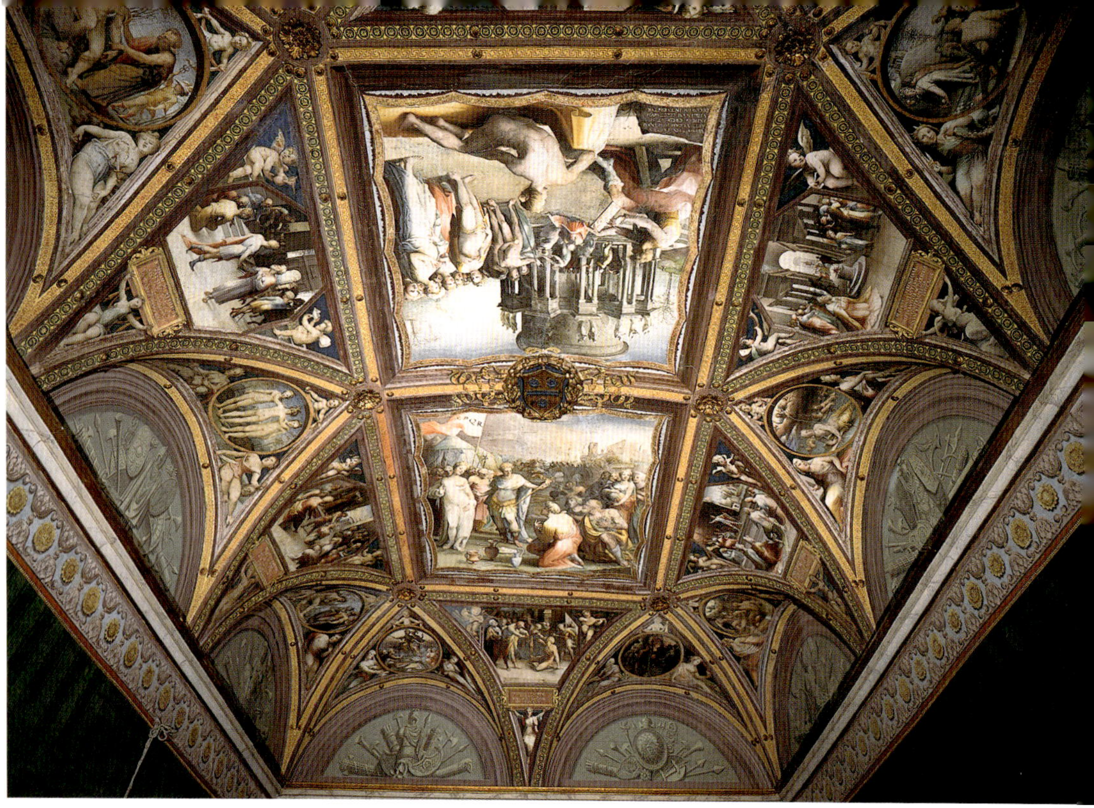

133 Beccafumi, ceiling decoration for a room on the first floor of Agostino Venturi's palace (*c.* 1519–21). Siena, Palazzo Bindi Segardi (formerly Venturi).

which appear like tapestries pegged out across the surface of the ceiling – and of six of the triangular compartments around the edges of the ceiling are all drawn from the *Memorable Deeds and Sayings* compiled by the first-century Roman author, Valerius Maximus. Widely popular in the medieval and renaissance periods, this collection of anecdotes was valued because it claimed to record the illustrious deeds of Greek and Roman worthies. It was also conveniently arranged in order to exemplify various human virtues. From the selection of subjects it appears that the patron and his scholarly advisors wanted to emphasise the qualities of religious faith, fortitude, patience, belief in one's abilities, abstinence, love of one's country, severity and justice. These were all virtues that have both a practical moral application and in certain cases – such as love of one's country – a specifically civic one.[50]

The subjects of the two large central paintings, separated by the Venturi coat-of-arms can be tied more directly to the theme of marriage. Both celebrate female beauty: one depicts the occasion when the famous Greek artist Zeuxis undertook to paint an image of Helen, a woman of renowned and outstanding beauty. Drawing inspiration not from artistic convention but from nature, Zeuxis summoned the most beautiful women of the city to act as his models, taking the best features from each. The other painting depicts a scene known popularly as the 'Continence of Scipio' that commemorates an act of generosity by the Roman general Scipio Africanus, who returned a beautiful young woman, taken prisoner by his troops, to her fiancé and his parents. He also insisted that the money and jewels brought as ransom be given to her as a wedding gift.

Beccafumi's distinctive style of painting enhanced the refined and erudite nature of this scheme commissioned for a room in a privately owned palace. Openly receptive to the grace and facility of Raphael's recent work for Agostino Chigi in Rome, he portrays the principal figures in the two paintings as elegant creatures clad in diaphanous garments or body-hugging armour, with carefully dressed hair and long tapering fingers.[51] The colours deployed here and throughout the ceiling are reminiscent of those of the heroines on the panels in the Chigi Saracini collection (see pls 129–31) and are at times startling in their combination of pale blues, pinks, mauves and apple greens. The backgrounds of the two paintings, meanwhile, show the painter's skill in evoking the imposing character of antique architecture and the smoke-laden drama of a battlefield.

The Oratory of San Bernardino

In painting the façades of the town houses of the Bardi and Borghesi families, Sodoma and Beccafumi appear to have been engaged in a competition to show who could best display knowledge of the latest artistic fashions of contemporary Rome. A few years after these commissions, the two painters were again involved in a project that brought them together. The new project was a scheme of fresco paintings to embellish the interior of a meeting room belonging to one of the city's oldest confraternities – the Confraternity of Santa Maria degli Angeli della Veste Nera (Saint Mary of the Angels and of the Black Robes). Founded in honour of the Virgin – as witnessed by its commission in 1262 of a large panel of the Virgin and Christ Child enthroned with angels (see pl. 24) – after 1450 the confra-

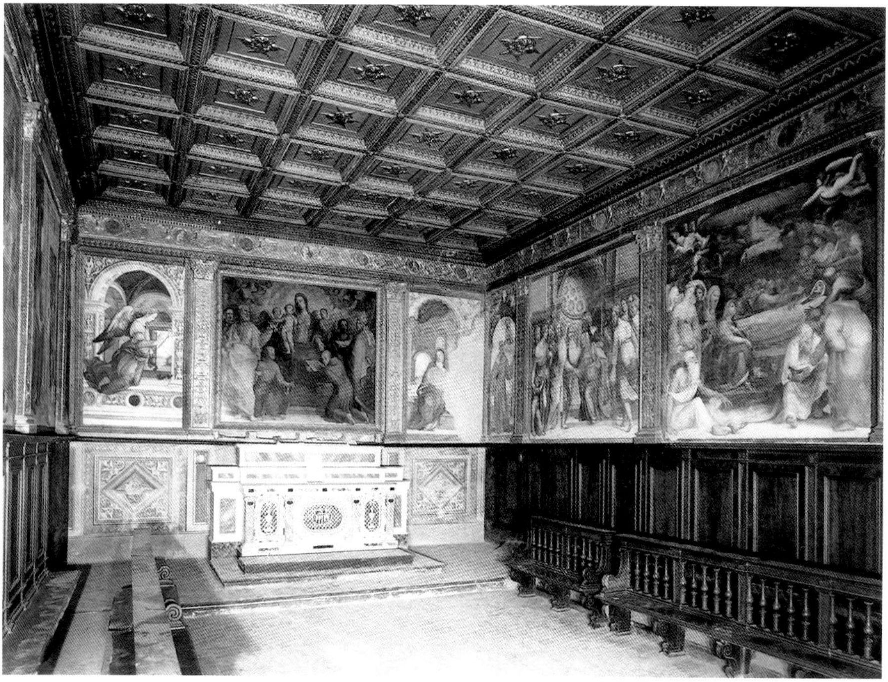

134 The interior of the Oratory of San Bernardino, Siena.

ternity also adopted Bernardino as one of their saints, adding his name to the confraternity's title.[52] For this reason the room that Sodoma and Beccafumi painted is now known as the Oratory of San Bernardino (pl. 134).

Designed as a place where the members of the confraternity would meet to conduct both their collective devotions and their administrative business, the Oratory of San Bernardino offers a rare example of an early sixteenth-century decorative ensemble that has survived in almost its original form. Entered by a single door at the west end of the south wall, it comprises a simple rectangular room lit by two windows on the short west wall and covered by a coffered ceiling richly embellished with gilded cherubim on a bright blue background. This ornamentation, executed in papier mâché, also occurs in the frieze that runs all round the room. The frieze is decorated with thirty-six figurative roundels representing the Virgin and Christ Child, Franciscan saints and the IHS monogram of Saint Bernardino.

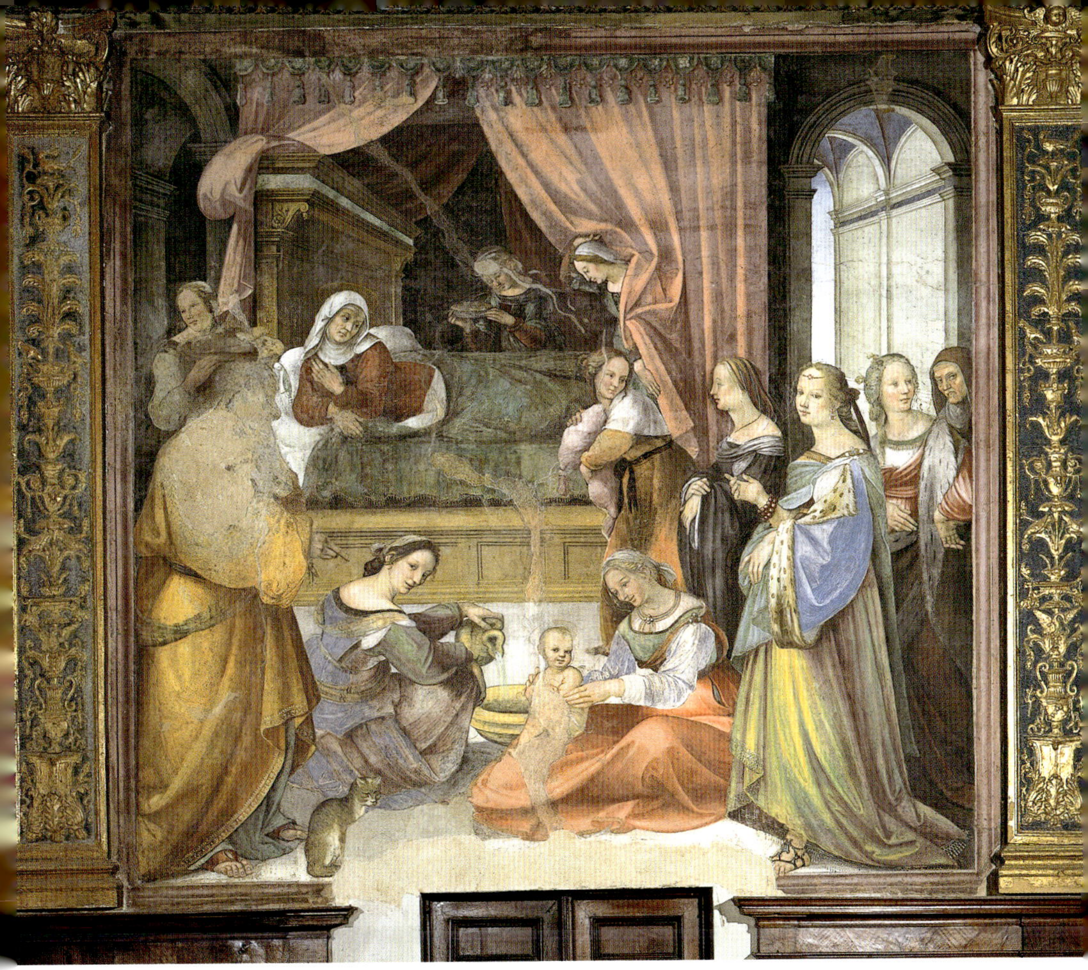

135 Girolamo del Pacchia, *The Birth of the Virgin* (1518). Fresco, 295 × 317 cm. Siena, Oratory of San Bernardino.

Below it is a series of large-scale fresco paintings separated from one another by pilasters decorated with candelabra motifs.

Beginning on the long north wall and working in a clockwise direction round the room, the paintings consist of narrative scenes from the life of the Virgin. First come the *Birth of the Virgin*, the *Presentation of the Virgin in the Temple* and the *Betrothal of the Virgin* (pls 135–7). On the short east or altar wall the frescoed figures of the Archangel Gabriel and the Virgin of the Annunciation frame an altarpiece (on panel and now missing its predella) that portrays the *Virgin and Christ Child with Saints*. On the long

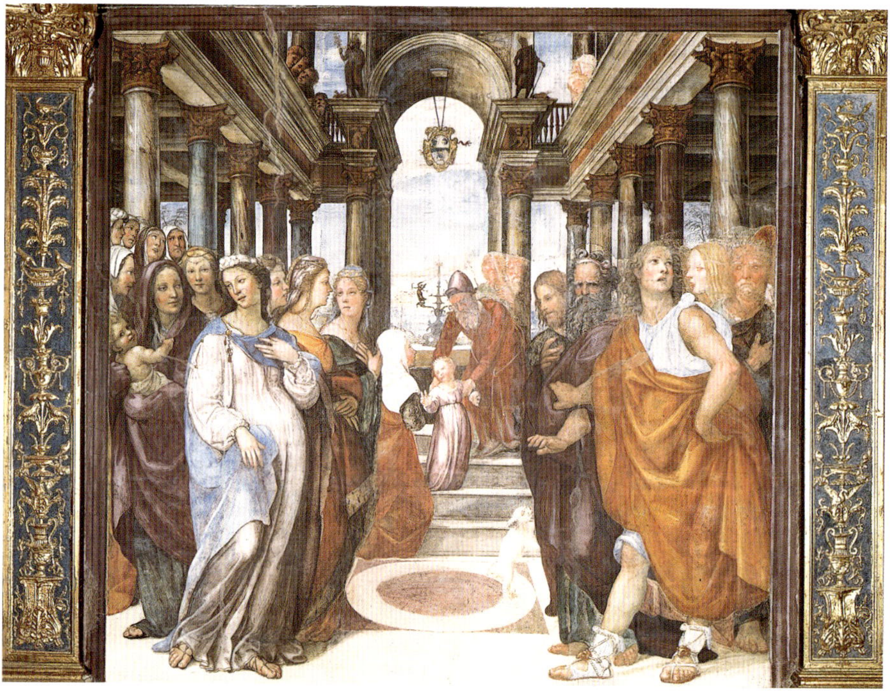

136 Sodoma, *The Presentation of the Virgin in the Temple* (1518). Fresco, 295 × 305 cm. Siena, Oratory of San Bernardino.

south wall appear the *Visitation*, the *Dormition of the Virgin* and over the doorway the *Assumption of the Virgin*. On the west wall between the two windows of the room is the *Coronation of the Virgin*. At each corner of the room appears a single figure of a major Franciscan saint standing in a painted niche. Below the fresco paintings on the north, south and west walls is wooden seating for the confraternity members.

Begun in 1496, the embellishment of the confraternity oratory was a drawn-out project involving the collaboration of several different kinds of craftworkers, including glass-manufacturers, woodworkers, painters and gilders. Payments occur in the confraternity accounts in an irregular and sporadic fashion over a period of many years – between 1496 and 1537.[53] The reason for this was probably the collective nature of the enterprise, which required the confraternity to find members willing to finance and

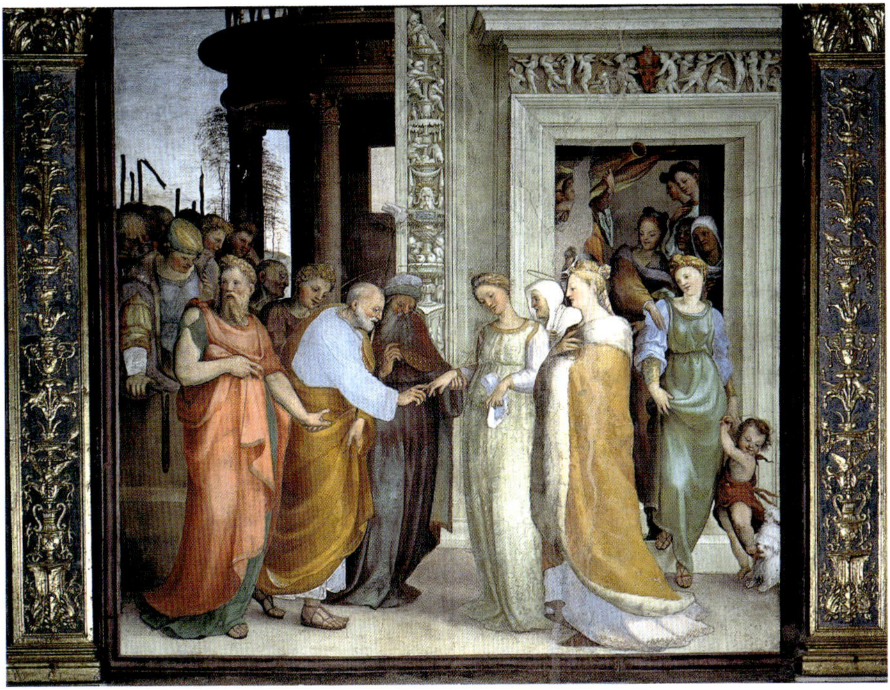

137 Beccafumi, *The Betrothal of the Virgin* (1518). Fresco, 295 × 304 cm. Siena, Oratory of San Bernardino.

organise the project. Even the execution of the principal paintings in the room apparently involved three different stages. A payment in December 1518 indicates that by this date three painters had responsibility for executing six of the eight narrative paintings (if one counts the two frescoes on the altar wall as one painting of the Annunciation).[54] Thus it appears that the Sienese painter Girolamo del Pacchia who was a member of the confraternity, had been assigned the paintings of the *Birth of the Virgin* and the *Annunciation*. He also painted one of the four Franciscan saints. Beccafumi, who two years earlier had acquired a house from the Maretti family – likewise members of the confraternity – had been entrusted with painting the *Betrothal* and the *Dormition*.[55] Sodoma, meanwhile, fresh from working in Rome, had been assigned the painting of the *Presentation* and the *Coronation* and was responsible for the three remaining Franciscan saints. It may be, therefore, that he was the master-painter in overall charge of the project.[56]

Ironically, given his possibly central role in the enterprise, Sodoma appears to have left Siena as soon as he had executed the paintings assigned to him in 1518, only returning to complete the scheme with his paintings of the *Visitation* and the *Assumption* at some time between 1525 and 1529. The execution of the altarpiece by Beccafumi took even longer: first discussed in 1533, it was finally completed in 1537.

Girolamo del Pacchia, the painter who seems to have had the closest links with the confraternity, provided his patrons with three paintings whose style reflects that of earlier altarpieces commissioned from him by patrons in and around Siena. Their stylistic idiom also demonstrates an appreciation of Sodoma's earlier Sienese work, as well as that of other contemporary painters based in Florence and Rome. In the *Birth of the Virgin*, for example, Girolamo appears to have studied Andrea del Sarto's painting of this subject in the forecourt of the church of the Santissima Annunziata in Florence, adopting the generously proportioned figures and ample draperies of the women visitors in this fresco completed some four years earlier. Similarly, the two cherubs who perch on the cornice of his figure of Saint Bernardino suggest an awareness of those in Raphael's painting of *Galatea* (*c.* 1513) in the Villa Farnesina in Rome. It is not certain that the painter had visited Rome by this date, but knowledge of Raphael's painting could have been relayed to him by Sodoma, who had just returned from Rome having completed the frescoed decoration of Agostino Chigi's bedroom in the same villa. His paintings of the *Archangel Gabriel* and the *Virgin of the Annunciation* on the altar wall of the oratory (pl. 134), meanwhile, closely reflect two painted panels of the same subjects executed by him some four years earlier for a church in the *contado* town of Sarteano.[57] Taking the elegantly convoluted pose of the seated Virgin and the lyrical landscape scenes in the backgrounds from his earlier work, he added complex drapery folds and richly embellished architectural settings to the confraternity versions.

Sodoma had first established his reputation in Siena as a painter of large-scale narrative frescoes in the extensive series of paintings that he executed between 1505 and 1508 on the walls of the cloister of the Benedictine abbey of Monteoliveto. Then in Rome he had experience on various projects of fresco painting, including the ceiling of the Stanza della Segnatura (1508) and the decoration of the Chigi room in the Farnesina (1516–17).[58] Both projects brought him in close contact with Raphael, who was then at the height of his powers, producing a magnificent series of paintings within various *Stanze* of the Vatican, as well as in Chigi's villa during the second decade of the sixteenth century.

In his painting of the *Presentation*, Sodoma once again introduced many of the lavishly attired bystanders that are characteristic of his Monteoliveto frescoes (see pl. 136). The architectural setting for the scene, however, appears to have been influenced by Raphael's fresco of the *Expulsion of Heliodorus* (1512) in the Stanza d'Eliodoro.[59] Both paintings depict two sets of marble colonnades seen in sharp recession, thus providing a framework and focus for an important event taking place at some distance from the spectator. In the case of the confraternity painting, this is the crucial encounter between the young child and the High Priest at the high altar, which forms the focal point of the story of the Virgin's presentation in the Temple.

By this date, Beccafumi had already produced a number of originally conceived altarpieces for several of Siena's churches (see pl. 139),[60] while his painting of the façade of the Borghesi palace had not only demonstrated his skill in the art of fresco painting (see pl. 132), but also provided evidence of his receptivity to ancient and contemporary Roman art. In his painting of the *Betrothal of the Virgin*, his preference for slender, elegant figurative types that are much less amply proportioned than those of Sodoma and Girolamo del Pacchia is apparent (see pls 134–7) – a style that, as already seen, continued in his later paintings for the ceiling of the Venturi palace (see pl. 133). The elaborately decorated marble doorway in the *Betrothal of the Virgin*, with its striking frieze and pilaster, together with the circular building behind it and to the left, again demonstrate the painter's interest in architecture, both ancient and contemporary, which he could have seen in Rome. Indeed, the circular building bears a strong resemblance to the martyry, known popularly as the Tempietto, that was constructed in 1502 by the architect Bramante near the Roman church of San Pietro in Montorio.[61]

By selecting these three particular artists to work on the walls of their oratory, the confraternity of Santa Maria degli Angeli secured the services of painters who were experienced in producing religious imagery on an ambitious scale and could provide paintings that reflected an awareness of the latest artistic fashions in Florence and in Rome. There is also good evidence from the paintings themselves that the three painters were concerned to work together on the scheme in a harmonious and unified fashion.

This is particularly evident on the north wall, where the first three paintings in the narrative cycle occur. Sodoma's *Presentation* provides a highly focussed and centralised composition for the middle painting on this wall (see pl. 136). The strongly stated diagonal of the headboard of Saint Anne's bed in Girolamo del Pacchia's *Birth of the Virgin*, to the left-hand side, together with the poses of Saint Anne and the maid at the foot of her bed, twisting towards the right, lead the eye of the spectator towards Sodoma's central painting (see pl. 135). More subtly, the shift in scale and tone between the brightly lit marble doorway and the dark circular building beyond it in Beccafumi's *Betrothal of the Virgin* provides a similar emphasis, from the other side, leftwards towards the centre of the wall (see pl. 137). The three paintings show a similar range of bright, resonant colours – seen most strikingly in the repeated use of various shades of white, pale blue, apple green, golden yellow and purple.

The generously proportioned figures and richly modelled draperies in the paintings by Sodoma and Girolamo del Pacchia on the walls of the oratory provide a further unifying element to the painted scheme. As already noted, Beccafumi's figurative types are distinctive in this respect. Moreover, unlike the evenly lit scenes provided by Sodoma and Girolamo del Pacchia, Beccafumi seems to have been interested in increasing the drama and emotion of the event in question by deploying a striking combination of light and dark – seen here most obviously in the jubilant figures emerging out of the darkness of the doorway on the right of the *Betrothal*, and in the broken rods of the Virgin's unsuccessful suitors appearing like blasted tree trunks silhouetted against the sky on the left.

These stylistic preferences of Beccafumi become even more obvious in his painting of the *Dormition of the Virgin* on the south wall where he employs a range of impressive pictorial devices, including the ambitious foreshortening of some of the major figures and again dramatic contrasts of dark and light.[62] His later altarpiece, however, while displaying a darker overall tonality than the framing paintings by Girolamo del Pacchia, nevertheless appears in its choice of colours and in the size of its principal figures to represent an attempt by the painter to ensure that his altarpiece blended successfully with the existing scheme (see pl. 134).

When seen with its original predella, the imagery of the altarpiece would have provided a fitting and effective culmination to the entire painted scheme. Showing the Virgin in her guise as a tender mother and attentive recipient of the prayers of the saints around her, the altarpiece complements the celebration of the most significant events in her life located on the walls of the oratory. The kneeling figures of Saint Francis on the left and Saint Bernardino on the right – the latter turning from his presentation of the famous IHS monogram to the Christ Child to look straight out at the spectator – further commemorate the other two saints to whom the confraternity had a special devotion. Once included on the predella of the altarpiece were two small paintings showing members of the confraternity, in their dark grey robes, adoring the monogram of the name of Jesus. Both altarpiece and fresco paintings thus demonstrate, in a compelling fashion, the determination and commitment of this Sienese confraternity to honour both their patron saints and their own collective identity.[63]

Continuing the Cult of Saint Catherine

While the paintings of the Oratory of San Bernardino demonstrate the continuing devotion of the sixteenth-century Sienese to the Virgin and Saint Bernardino, other artistic projects bear witness to their equally consistent devotion to the memory of Saint Catherine of Siena. After her canonisation by Pope Pius II in 1461, and her inclusion among the painted imagery of the Sala del Mappamondo in the Palazzo Pubblico (see pl. 46),[64] there appear to have been two focal points for her subsequent commemoration in fifteenth- and early sixteenth-century Siena. The first was at the site of her family home, a short distance from the Fonte Branda, one of the city's principal fountains. Responding to an appeal by the local inhabitants, in 1466 the government purchased the house and thereafter oversaw a project to transform it into a shrine to the saint (see pl. 6). A small church was built on the site of her father's workshop and a confraternity meeting room – similar in scale and function to that of the Oratory of San Bernardino – was built on the site of the former family kitchen. Both buildings were embellished with images of the saint.[65]

The second place in which the cult of Saint Catherine of Siena was assiduously developed was in the church of San Domenico (see pl. 7), the principal church of the religious order to which Catherine had belonged and where she had regularly worshipped. Since she had died in Rome and been buried there in Santa Maria sopra Minerva, the Sienese could not boast of having their saint's body in one of their churches, but in 1384 the Dominicans in Siena were able to acquire the highly esteemed relic of the saint's head. In the 1460s Niccolò Bensi, a member of a wealthy Sienese family and a scribe at the papal court, commissioned a chapel and a marble tabernacle in which to place this precious relic. Located in the south aisle of San Domenico, the entrance arch to the chapel provided a clear view of the tabernacle, set over the altar, and of the head of the saint behind a metal grille. The exquisitely carved marble of Giovanni di Stefano's tabernacle and the intricate inlay of the marble pavement of the chapel provided a suitably magnificent setting for this revered object.[66]

In the mid-1520s Sodoma was involved in two schemes of fresco painting designed to celebrate further the identity and sanctity of Saint Catherine, one for the church near Fonte Branda and the other for the reliquary chapel in San Domenico. At the first, Sodoma appears to have played only a limited role, executing the fresco of cherubs supporting a painted canopy on the altar wall. Three other painters – including Sodoma's collaborator at the Oratory of San Bernardino, Girolamo del Pacchia – executed a number of frescoes on the walls of the church depicting scenes from Saint Catherine's life.[67]

By contrast, in the reliquary chapel in San Domenico Sodoma was responsible for the entire project – painting frescoes on the altar and left walls of the chapel and on the inner façade and upper part of the entrance arch.[68] Consisting of scenes from the saint's life, the entire narrative scheme was set in a highly illusionistic painted framework similar to that of contemporary decorative schemes in Rome. The device of representing a balustrade and steps leading into the scene of the *Execution of Niccolò di Tuldo* on the left wall is strikingly similar to Sodoma's 1516–17 fresco of the *Wedding of Alexander and Roxane* in the Villa Farnesina in Rome. In terms of its illusionism and rich classical decoration, the scheme is reminiscent of Filippino Lippi's frescoes of 1488–93 for the chapel of Cardinal Oliviero Carafa in the Dominican church of Santa Maria sopra Minerva. Since Saint Catherine's body was enshrined in that Roman church such similarities were probably not merely coincidental.[69] Otherwise, in terms of their luminous colour effects (particularly evident in the robes and veils of Saint Catherine herself and her companions, pl. 138), generously proportioned figures and evocative landscape settings, the frescoes are entirely typical of Sodoma's mature style as a painter. Building on his achievements as a painter of narrative on the walls of the cloister at Monteoliveto and the Oratory of San Bernardino, he provided the Bensi family and the Dominican community at San Domenico with an impressive painted scheme that commemorated the sanctity and achievements of Saint Catherine of Siena in a highly celebratory fashion.

Some ten years before the frescoes were completed, Beccafumi produced an altarpiece depicting the saint (pl. 139). Commissioned for the abbey church of San Benedetto, situated just beyond the Porta Tufi, one of Siena's southern gates, the altarpiece may have been intended for

138 Sodoma, detail of *Saint Catherine of Siena's Vision of the Virgin and Christ Child* (1526). Fresco on the altar wall of the Cappella di Santa Caterina. Siena, San Domenico.

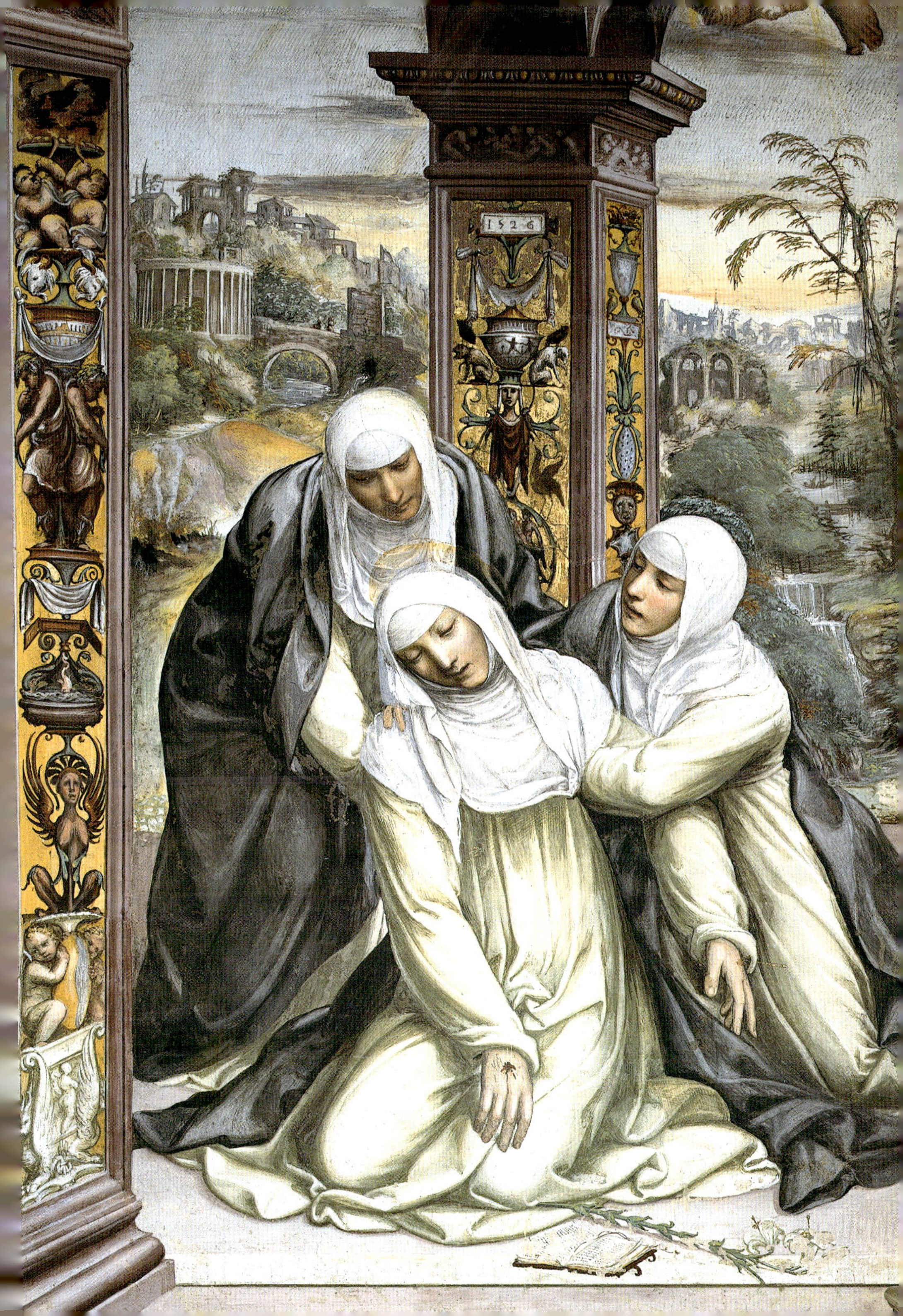
1526

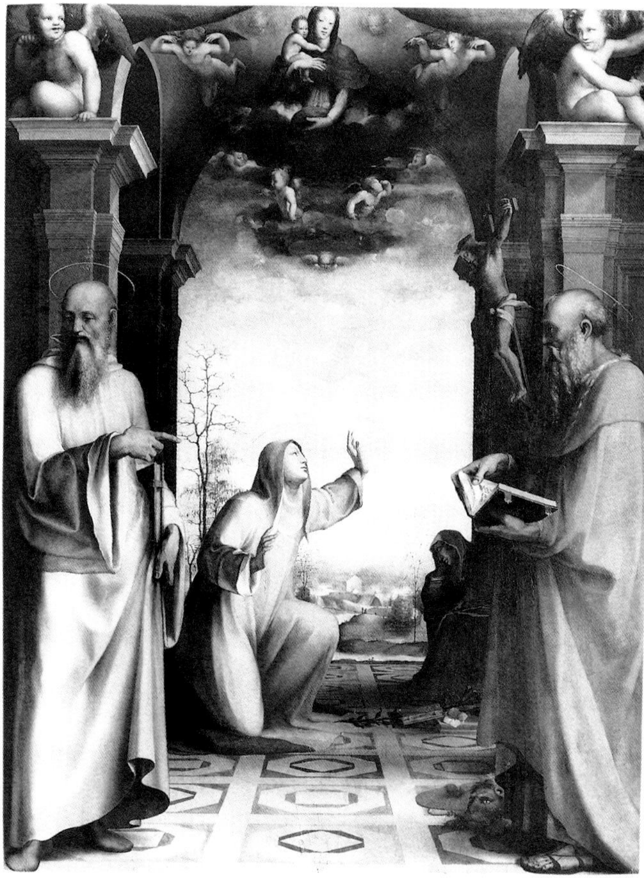

139 Beccafumi, *Saint Catherine of Siena receiving the Stigmata with Saints Bernard and Jerome* (*c.* 1514–15). Tempera and oil on panel, 212 × 162 cm. Siena, Pinacoteca Nazionale.

an altar dedicated to Saint Catherine in that church.[70] This would account for the fact that it is this saint who is the principal figure at the centre of the painting – seen kneeling in an open loggia in front of a crucifix. The saint's expression of intense emotional involvement with the crucifix indicates that – unusually for an altarpiece – the central subject of the painting is Saint Catherine receiving the stigmata, an event that was believed to have taken place before a painted crucifix in the church of Santa Cristina in Pisa and which was one of the most celebrated aspects of her sanctity.

The painting is by no means simply a straightforward narrative depiction of this event. Standing in the foreground are two dignified figures of elderly male saints. On the left appears Saint Benedict, titular saint of the church for which the altarpiece was painted, wearing the white habit of an Olivetan monk, the order to which the abbey and church belonged.[71] Opposite him and clad in the red robe of a cardinal is Saint Jerome, whose life as a hermit provided another saintly model for members of the Olivetan order. As well as signalling the provenance of this altarpiece in an Olivetan church, however, the contemplative poses of these two figures, together with the books that they prominently display, suggest a further layer of expressive meaning in this painting. For the two saints also appear as scholarly authorities meditating upon and giving their endorsement to the theological significance of the saint's experience of the stigmata.

At the top of the painting, appearing as a heavenly apparition, are the Virgin and Christ Child accompanied by a throng of jubilant angels. In terms of pictorial composition, therefore, Beccafumi thus cleverly conveyed the visionary aspect of Saint Catherine's spiritual experience before the image of the crucifix. In so doing he was probably indebted to the example of two Florentine altarpieces executed by Fra Bartolommeo in the first decade of the sixteenth century. In these – one intended for a Dominican church in Venice and the other for a church in France – the Florentine painter similarly explored the possibility of placing the central cult figures in the upper part of the painting and the remaining figures in an architectural setting that opens out onto landscape.[72] To these earlier models, however, Beccafumi added his own invention and propensity for experiment, seen most clearly in the striking juxtaposition of light against dark and in the daringly foreshortened poses of the two angels on either side of the Virgin and Christ Child.

Three Altarpiece Commissions

The apparent rivalry between Sodoma and Beccafumi, already suggested in their work in the Oratory of San Bernardino and their paintings of Saint Catherine, is likewise evident in a number of innovative altarpieces produced by the two painters for the city's principal churches. Although both painters were commissioned to execute altarpieces that represented the theme of the Virgin and Christ Child enthroned with saints, they also pro-

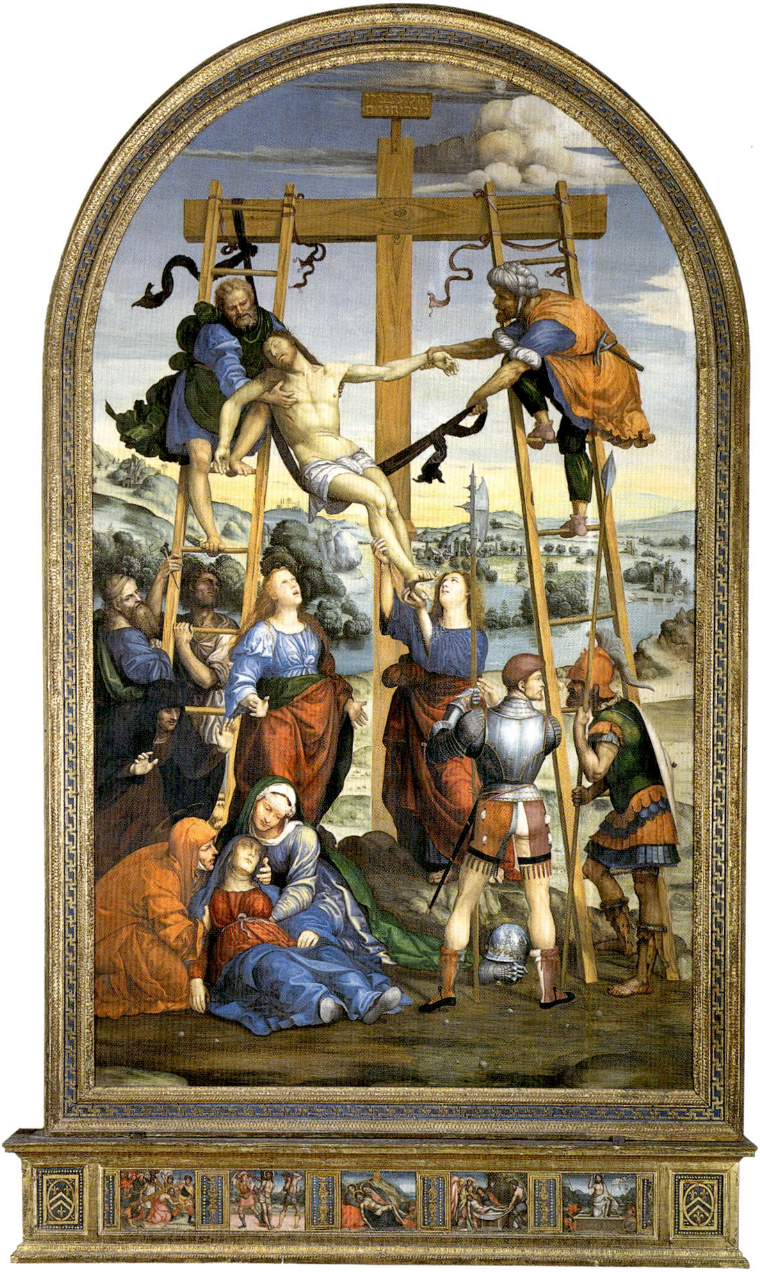

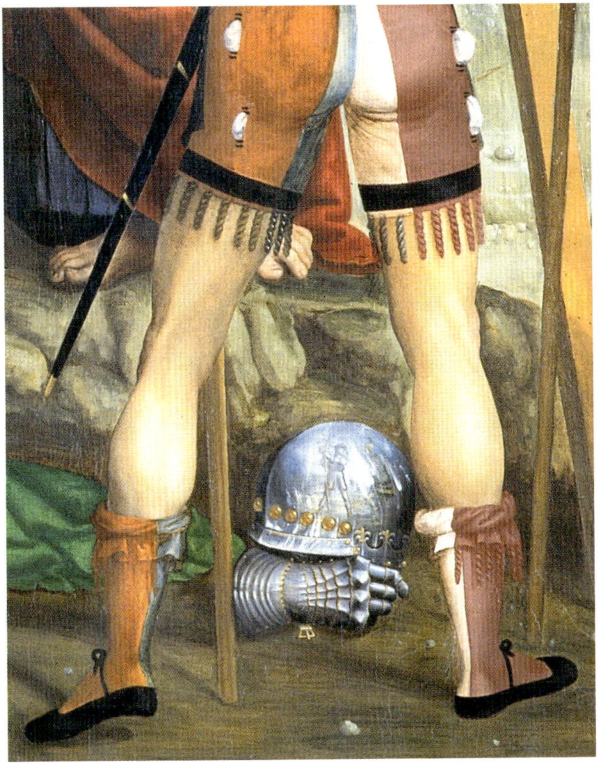

140 (*facing page*) Sodoma, *The Deposition from the Cross* (*c.* 1510–13). Oil on panel, 426 × 263 cm (main panel), 43.5 × 282 cm (predella). Siena, Pinacoteca Nazionale.

141 Reflection of a pikeman in a helmet (detail of pl. 140).

duced a series of narrative altarpieces which pushed beyond the conventional boundaries for the representation of these subjects.

The earliest of these works was Sodoma's monumental altarpiece of the *Deposition of Christ* (pl. 140). Still within its blue and gold wooden frame and with its predella,[73] this painting is now housed within Siena's Pinacoteca and is therefore divorced from the surroundings for which it was designed. From descriptions of the altarpiece in the sixteenth-century, it seems that it was commissioned for the altar of the Cinuzzi family in the church of San Francesco, and the family's coat-of-arms accordingly appears at either end of the predella.[74] Sodoma's altarpiece thus once stood over the fifth altar along the south wall of this barn-like mendicant church. By virtue of its imposing size, its bright and luminous colours and its clear, expressive figurative composition, the altarpiece would undoubtedly have been a striking sight in its setting.

Generally dated between 1510 and 1513, the altarpiece was executed after Sodoma's work at Monteoliveto and in the Vatican, but before the commission for the nearby Oratory of San Bernardino. The figurative types and light, bright colours of the altarpiece are reminiscent of his work at Monteoliveto, but they also suggest his awareness of Raphael's recent work in both Florence and in Rome. The treatment of the subject and the way the major actors in the dramatic event are portrayed indicate that Sodoma may have studied an altarpiece of the same subject in the Santissima Annunziata in Florence. Begun by Filippino Lippi in 1503, this was completed by Perugino after the painter's death in 1504.[75] In Siena, meanwhile, Sodoma probably profited from the example of a large *Crucifixion with Saints*, also by Perugino, that had been commissioned by the Chigi family for their altar in Sant'Agostino. Closely comparable in scale and format, the placing of the Cross against an expansive landscape background is very similar in both paintings.[76]

Regarding the altarpiece's original impact, it is worth noting Vasari's brief praise of it in the 1568 edition of the *Lives*.[77] Although generally critical of Sodoma and his work – because of his allegedly dissolute life-style – Vasari commented that this painting was considered to be one of the best that Sodoma produced. Specifically, Vasari singled out for praise a man seen from the back but whose face is also visible in the helmet lying on the ground (pl. 141); with his striking parti-coloured hose, gleaming cuirass and swaggering pose he is certainly an eye-catching feature of the painting. Moreover, the tiny detail of this figure, seen from the front and as if reflected on the polished surface of the metal helmet, is unquestionably a testimony to Sodoma's powers of visual observation. Indeed, within the terms of the debate then being conducted over the relative merits of painting and sculpture,[78] by simultaneously showing both the back and front of a human figure, Sodoma was making a bold claim for what painting could achieve. Although he represented this religious subject in an entirely decorous way, he also took the opportunity to fashion the altarpiece as a work of art and to display his skills as a painter in a bold and self-conscious manner.

Like the *Deposition*, Beccafumi's altarpiece of the *Nativity* was designed for a side altar in one of Siena's largest and most important churches. Unlike the *Deposition*, however, it can still be seen over the third altar on the north side of the church of San Martino, located a short distance from the Campo (see pl. 6). It is also still within its original carved marble frame (pl. 142) and thus provides a compelling example of the imposing architectural settings that were common for altarpieces of that date. The marble altar and elaborately decorated frame were commissioned on 28 January

1522 from the Sienese sculptor Lorenzo di Mariano, known as 'Il Marrina', by a wealthy widow, Anastasia di Nanni Marsili. Her act of piety was duly recorded on the altar step, and by the heraldic emblems of her own family and that of her deceased husband, Ugolino Ugolini, on the base of the altarpiece frame. Since the church of San Martino was assigned to a reformed branch of the Augustinian Hermits in 1522, it is likely that the Marsili altar was part of a general re-organisation of the altars within the church. Dedicating the altar to Saint Joseph, Anastasia gave instructions in her will of 1528 that this saint's feast should be celebrated annually there, as well as the feasts of the Conception, Nativity, Presentation and Assumption.[79]

Beccafumi's response to a commission to paint a traditional subject appears to have been characteristically novel and innovative. As in other earlier examples of Nativity paintings, he included in its design not merely the holy family and the ox and ass but also the shepherds who had been summoned by angels to venerate the new-born child (pl. 143). In the manner of Bulgarini's fourteenth-century altarpiece depicting this subject (see pl. 60), it seems that Beccafumi too was instructed to include a reference to the Trinity, in the form of a dove hovering in a golden aureole of light over the scene. And like other Sienese painters of this subject, he portrayed the stable in which Christ was born as a makeshift wooden structure, erected within the ruins of a classical triumphal arch – the latter symbolising the passing of the old religious order to make way for the new.[80]

Despite adhering to such conventions for the portrayal of this religious subject, Beccafumi nevertheless enlivened it with his own distinctive style of painting. The Virgin, arrayed in shades of pink and rose, blue and green, corresponds to the slim, elegant young women of the *Betrothal of the Virgin* in the Oratory of San Bernardino and on the ceiling of the Venturi palace (see pls 133, 137). With a gesture of great refinement, the Virgin is portrayed as lifting up the luminous pink and white cloth to reveal the brightly lit Christ Child – while the priest, at the altar below, would display the holy wafer above his head at the most solemn moment of the celebration of mass. Other eucharistic symbolism is cleverly incorporated into the painting, such as the lamb (a symbol of sacrifice) just to the left of the infant, and the vine leaves (a symbol of the communion wine) growing up the right-hand side of the ruined arch.[81] Joseph, the titular saint of the altarpiece, appears as a prominent, pensive figure in the left foreground.

While the angels, grouped round the holy family, share the elegance of the Virgin's pose and costume, the shepherds appear as dark figures, emerging from the shadows. This dramatic effect is enhanced by the portrayal of

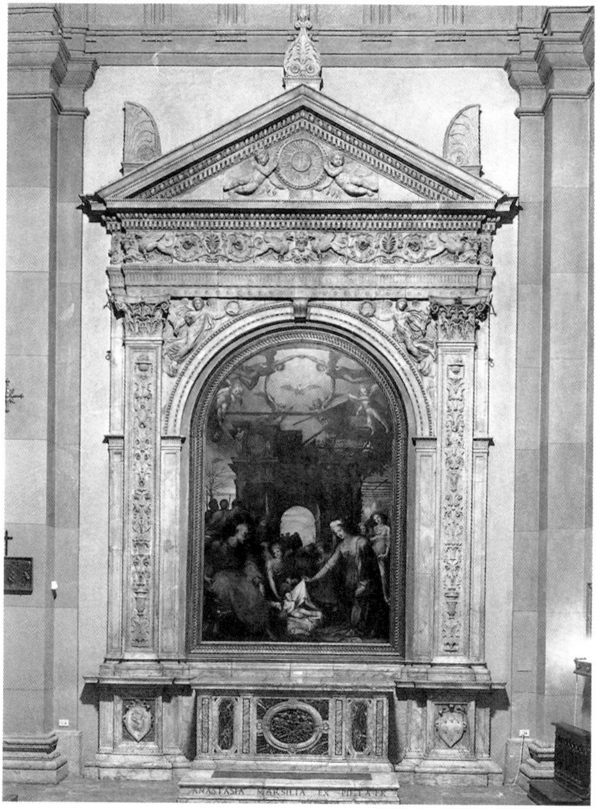

142 Lorenzo di Mariano, known as 'Il Marrina', and Beccafumi, the Marsili altar and altarpiece (*c.* 1522). Siena, San Martino.

these figures silhouetted against a sky that evokes the effect of dawn light – another apt symbol for a painting celebrating the birth of Christ. The dark barren trees on the left of the painting – a striking contrast to the leafy trees just above the Christ Child – further suggest that one of the messages of the painting is that the birth of Christ heralded a new age.

In the upper part of the painting the darkness is dissolved into an aura of golden light. Here once again Beccafumi explored a number of daring pictorial effects – not only in the representation of the four angels as if seen from below, but also the challenge of portraying two circles in depth.[82] The two chubby putti – who strongly echo those painted by Raphael for the Loggia of Psyche in Agostino Chigi's Roman villa – perform a further important role for the spectator located in front of this altarpiece. The one

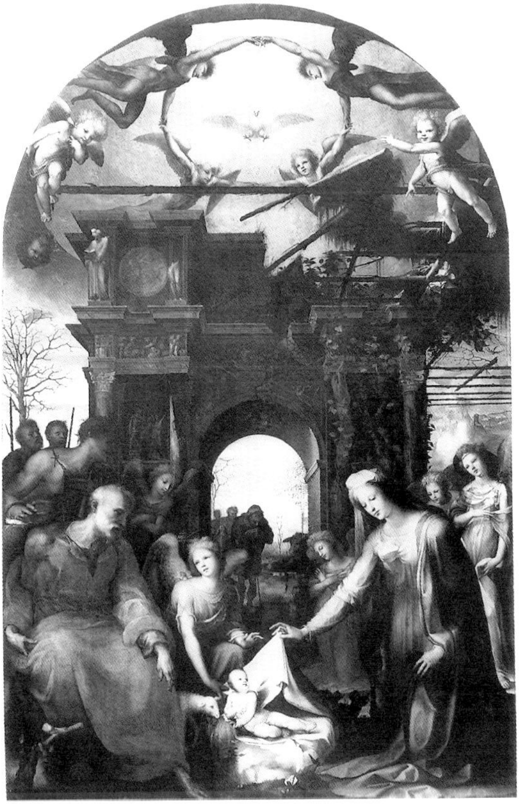

143 Beccafumi, *The Nativity and Adoration of the Shepherds* (*c.* 1522). Oil on panel, 390 × 235 cm. Siena, San Martino.

on the right, whose dark eyes and cheeky grin directly engage with the spectator, points with his left hand to the dove of the Holy Spirit beside him. His right hand, meanwhile, points in the direction of the Christ Child. The attention of his companion on the left is completely focussed on the new-born infant.

For both these altarpieces Sodoma and Beccafumi were concerned to include a range of pictorial effects that demonstrated their receptivity and awareness of the latest innovations in artistic style and fashion. In both cases, it seems also that their patrons were pleased to accept the novelty of their approach to their traditional religious subjects. In the case of a third commission, however, awarded to Beccafumi by the Carmelite friars of San Niccolò al Carmine, this appears not to have been the case. Once again, it is Vasari who acts as a witness to this incident. Writing in his biography of Beccafumi in the *Lives*, he states that the painter, having gained fame for his work in Siena, received

> a commission to do a panel for the Carmine of Saint Michael subduing Lucifer. Being a man of ideas, he thought of a new treatment of this theme to prove his ability. Thus he began a shower of nude figures, representing Lucifer and his followers driven out of heaven, though they were rather confused owing to the labour he bestowed on them. The picture remained unfinished, and after Domenico's death it was taken to a room near the high altar at the top of the stairs in the great hospital [Santa Maria della Scala], where it may still be seen. It is remarkable for some nude figures finely foreshortened. In the Carmine, where it was to have gone, another [also by Beccafumi] was placed representing God upon the clouds, surrounded by angels. In the middle is Saint Michael in armour, pointing as he flies to Lucifer, who is driven to the centre of the earth amid burning walls, falling rocks and a flaming lake, with angels in various postures and nude figures swimming about and suffering torment, the whole done with such style and grace that the place seems illuminated by the fire.[83]

The earlier of these two versions of the expulsion of the rebel angels from heaven by the Archangel Michael is now in the Pinacoteca (pl. 144). The second is still over a side altar on the south wall of the church of San Niccolò al Carmine, but without its original predella (pl. 145).[84] Comparison of the two paintings confirms how perceptive Vasari's analysis was. The earlier version is at first sight difficult to read: the lower part of the painting is dominated by the tall, elongated figures of three standing nude men. It requires some effort to discern that, within the gloom that surrounds them, other figures are shown in convoluted poses. In the upper part of the painting, encircled by a swirling mass of flying angels, is the arresting figure of Saint Michael. Clad in fanciful antique armour, he holds his sword aloft as a sign of his victory over the vanquished rebel angels. Above him in turn appears an extraordinarily daring representation of God, portrayed in extreme foreshortening. As the deity presiding over this act of heavenly vengeance, he appears as an insubstantial – but certainly visionary – phenomenon.

The second version, by comparison, is much more clearly organised. Here God appears as a monumental figure, seated in judgement. The bright red of his voluminous mantle and the golden hemisphere behind him ensure that this figure dominates the composition as a whole. The angelic company is organised into an orderly choir of seated figures surrounding God, with only a few of their companions engaged in expelling the rebel angels. Saint Michael has been placed much lower in the composition and acts as the principal agent between heaven and hell. Although still holding a sword above his head, he has been divested of armour and appears in a pale pink and golden yellow tunic, tied across the chest with pale blue ribbons. Beneath him, the fallen angels recline in a series of subterranean vaults lit by sulphurous light. The devil has been transformed into a snarling monstrous beast that has the appearance of a classical chimaera.

It is intriguing that Beccafumi painted two versions of this altarpiece. Based on a passage from the Book of Revelation (20: 1–3), which describes a vision of an angel that overthrows and imprisons Satan – in the form of a dragon – in a bottomless pit, it is certainly the case that the second version adheres more faithfully to the biblical text. In his account of the commission, Vasari suggests that the painter left the first one unfinished because he could not resolve the artistic challenge of painting the subject in a sufficiently novel way. There remains the possibility that the Carmelites at San Niccolò were unhappy with Beccafumi's treatment of this religious subject because of its nudity and its unstructured composition (see pl. 144). We know from the writings of the Dominican reformer Girolamo Savonarola that so-called indecency in religious art was a current concern for churchmen.[85] Similarly, if the seventeenth-century Venetian writer Carlo Ridolfi is to be believed, the Franciscan prior of the church of Santa Maria Gloriosa dei Frari in Venice was critical about the scale of the apostles dwarfing the figure of the Virgin in Titian's *Assumption of the Virgin* for the high altar of his church.[86] It is perhaps for these reasons that in the second version of the painting none of the fallen angels in the lower part appears completely nude and, as already noted, the entire painting is much more clearly organised with the division between heaven and hell more clearly stated and the respective roles and stature of God and Saint Michael made more obvious (see pl. 145). Nevertheless, by accepting even the second version of this altarpiece for their church, the Carmelites were apparently willing to endorse both the elegant, mannered representation of the archangel and his angelic companions and the bizarre and dramatic lighting effects favoured by Beccafumi. Therefore, as Vasari suggests, this second painting should not be seen as a compromise on the part of the painter but rather as an adjustment and reworking of his initial conception of an unusual and striking religious subject.

* * *

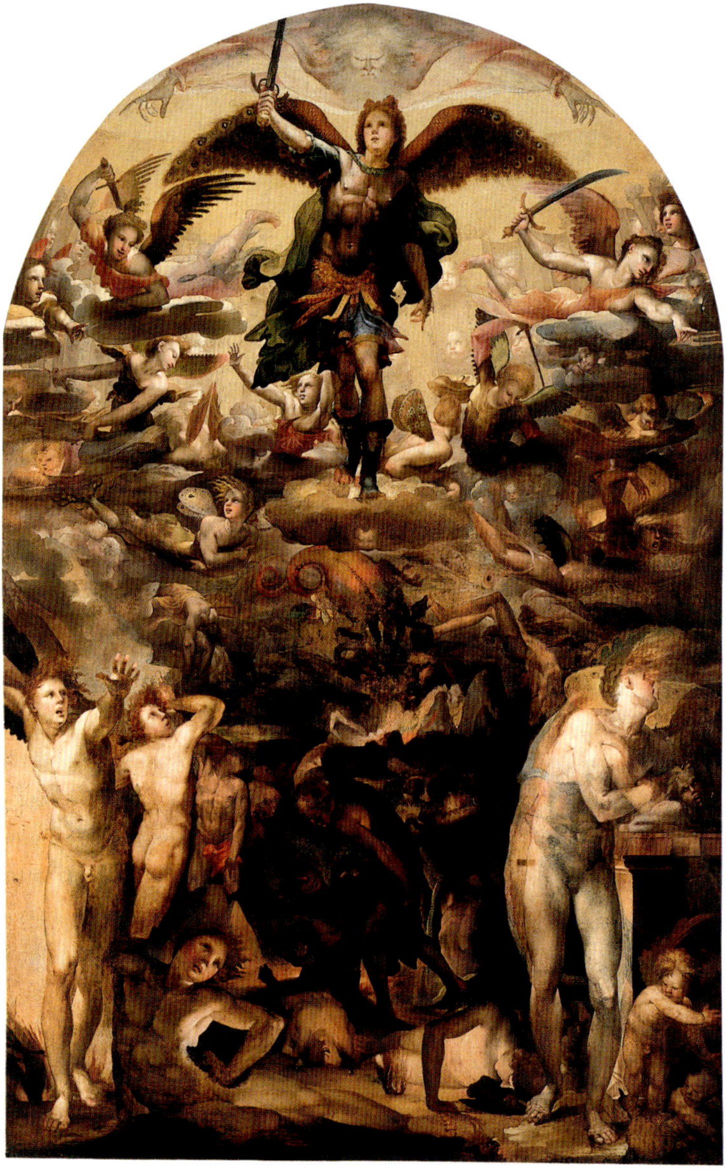

144 Beccafumi, *The Fall of the Rebel Angels* (*c.* 1524). Oil on panel, 348 × 228 cm. Siena, Pinacoteca Nazionale.

145 (*facing page*) Beccafumi, *The Fall of the Rebel Angels* (*c.* 1528). Oil on panel, 347 × 225 cm. Siena, San Niccolò al Carmine.

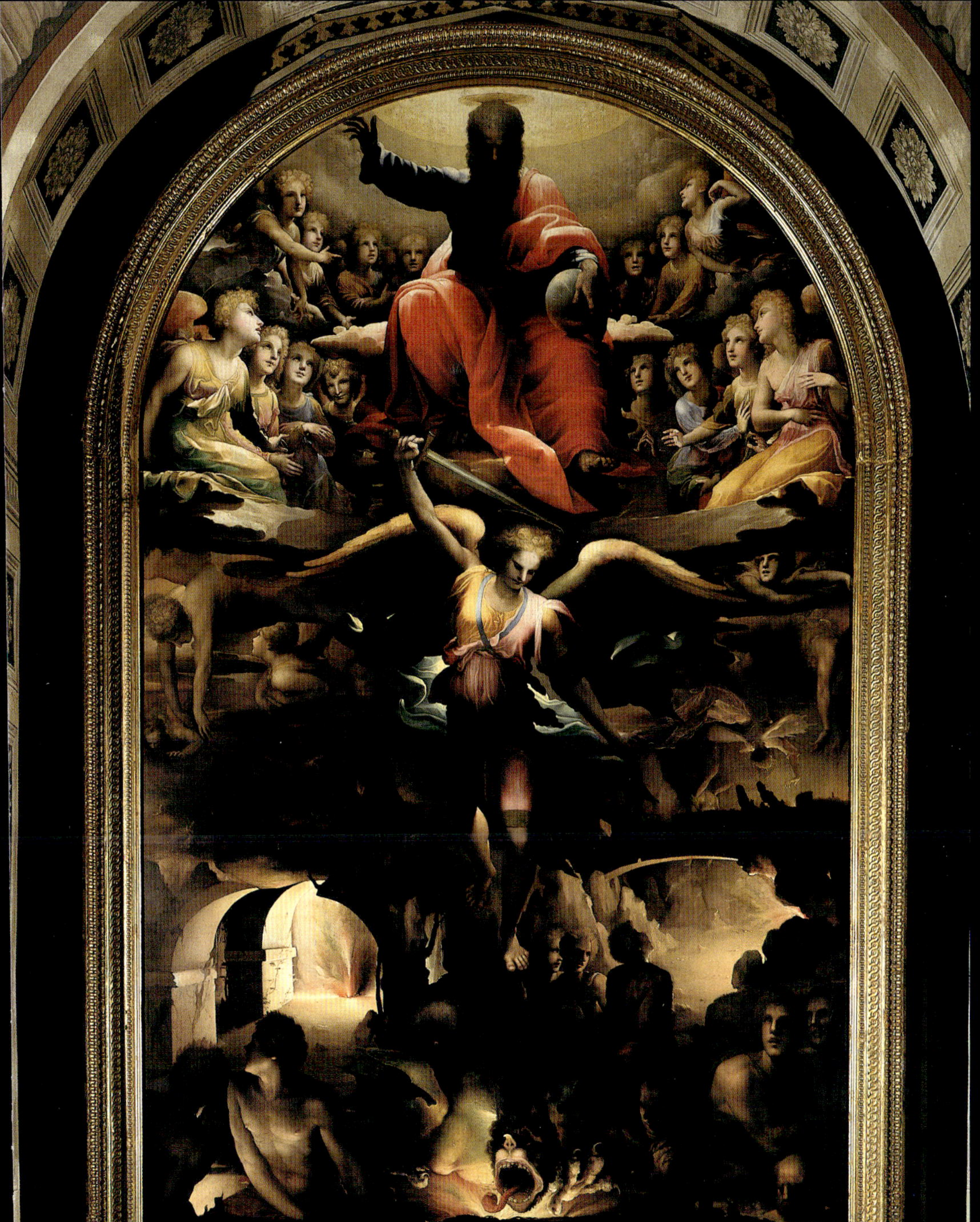

Civic Piety in the Palazzo Pubblico

Both Sodoma and Beccafumi received important public commissions from the Sienese government to execute paintings for the Palazzo Pubblico, in addition to their work for wealthy private and corporate patrons. Following the exile of Fabio Petrucci in 1524 and the victory over papal and Florentine forces in the battle of Camollia in 1526, the Sienese government were eager to project an image of republican unity and self-sufficiency. They therefore initiated several schemes of painting, the subject matter of which reiterated many of the city's most cherished political values.

On 5 April 1529 Beccafumi was commissioned to paint the ceiling of a large room on the first floor of the Palazzo Pubblico whose north wall faces onto the Campo (pl. 146). Now known as the Sala del Concistoro, it appears that it became the meeting place of this magistracy only after the remodelling of the Palazzo Pubblico in the seventeenth century (see pl. 48). Designated as the *sala dipinta* (the 'painted room') on an early seventeenth-century plan of the building,[87] it is likely that it was originally designed as a room for the reception of foreign embassies and similar ceremonial events. Despite being required to complete the work within eighteen months and receiving payments for it in May and August 1530 and October 1532, Beccafumi left this elaborate scheme of painting unfinished in order to go to work for another patron, Andrea Doria, in Genoa. He then resumed the project in 1534, receiving final payment for it on 21 April 1535.[88] Thus, a project that was meant to have taken only eighteen months in fact took six years to complete. Sodoma, meanwhile, received and executed more modest projects for the Palazzo Pubblico. The earliest of these were for the two figures of Saints Ansano and Victor, to be placed on either side of Ambrogio Lorenzetti's lost map on the west wall of the Sala del Mappamondo (see pl. 49). These were commissioned on 31 August 1529 and were completed by 1530.[89]

SODOMA'S COMMISSIONS

Continuing the series of images of Sienese saints that had been begun by Sano di Pietro and Vecchietta in the 1460s, the choice of Saints Ansano and Victor undoubtedly reflected the renewed confidence of the Sienese government after the battle of Camollia. Saint Ansano, seen on the left baptising a kneeling man and holding a banner embellished with the *balzana* in his left hand, appears as the embodiment of Siena's claim to be a republic founded on Christian precepts. On the right Saint Victor, arrayed in classical armour and with his sword held aloft in the traditional gesture of acclamation of a victorious Roman general, acts as the embodiment of Siena's claim to military virtue and honour. His shield, supported by the wreathed putto on the left, displays the traditional colour and motto of Siena's other emblem of 'Libertas' (liberty). Given the date of the paintings, the inclusion of this emblem is likely to refer specifically to the political party of the 'Libertini' who freed Siena from the 'tyranny' of Fabio Petrucci and his family.

Both paintings display Sodoma's customary assurance in the portrayal of the human figure, a skill that is particularly evident in the bronzed, muscular torsoes of the two men receiving baptism from Saint Ansano. As in the frescoes for the chapel of Saint Catherine of Siena, they again provide evidence of Sodoma's ability to create the illusion of seeing these two figures from the spectator's vantage point within the Sala del Mappamondo, yet also as though situated within a painted architectural setting that exhibits an abundance of ornament.

In 1532 Sodoma was paid for adding a third figure to the saints portrayed on the north side of the Sala del Mappamondo.[90] Painted in a broadly similar style to the figures of Saints Ansano and Victor, the painting portrays the fourteenth-century Sienese *beato* Bernardino Tolomei, who founded the abbey of Monteoliveto in the south-eastern *contado*. Both the gleaming white robes of the Olivetan habit and the lyrical landscape setting behind the figure suggest that Sodoma drew upon his experience of working at Monteoliveto some fourteen years earlier.

From a long painted inscription it appears that a contemporary member of Bernardino's family, Francesco Tolomei, promoted this particular government commission. Francesco Tolomei also seems to have been influential in the commission awarded to Sodoma in 1538 to fresco the niche behind the altar of the Cappella di Piazza facing the Campo (see pl. 1). Now barely visible, seventeenth- and eighteenth-century accounts imply that the subject of this painting was again traditional.[91] Portraying Siena's principal holy patron, the Virgin, with her son, it also once included the four other protector saints – Ansano, Savino, Crescenzio and Victor.

BECCAFUMI'S 'PAINTED ROOM'

Compared with Sodoma's paintings for the Palazzo Pubblico, Beccafumi's frescoes on the ceiling of the Sala del Concistoro are much more complex in their subject matter and imagery (pl. 146). Nevertheless, once deciphered and understood, they too reiterate the themes of earlier painted schemes in

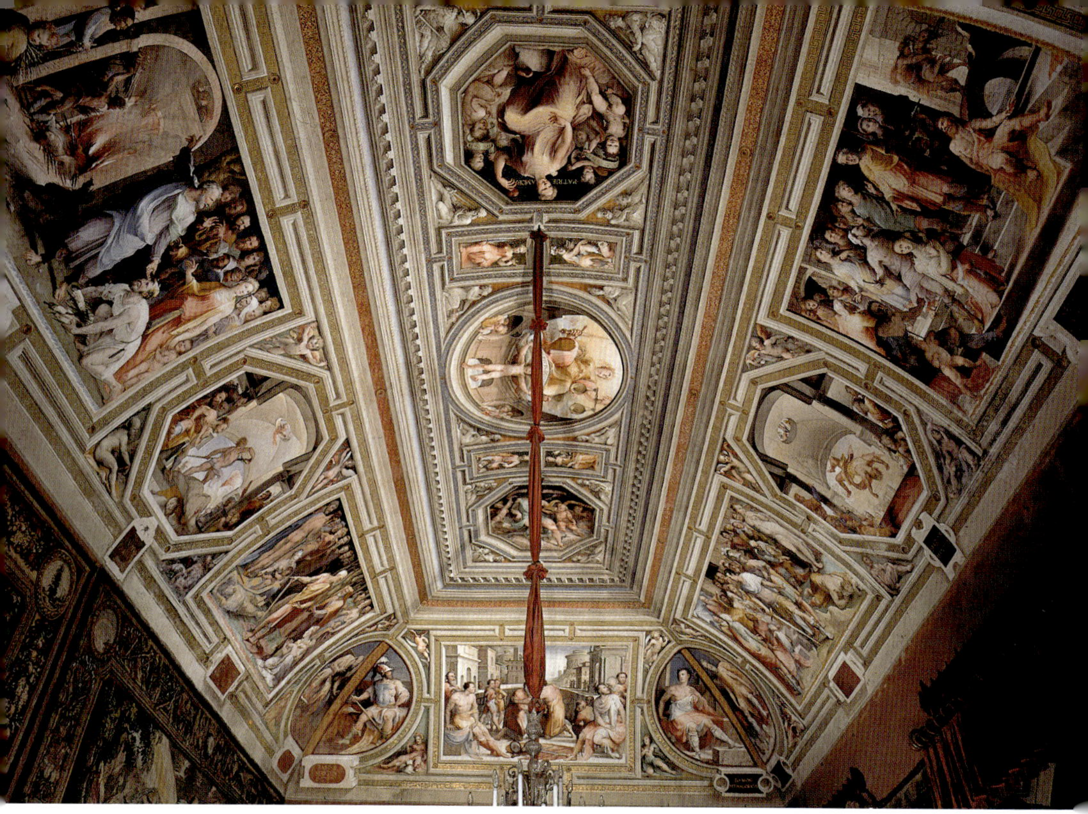

146 Beccafumi, ceiling decoration of the Sala del Concistoro (1529–32, 1535). Siena, Palazzo Pubblico.

the Palazzo Pubblico. The ceiling, which was undoubtedly constructed at the time of the commission, is comprised of a large rectangular centrepiece surrounded on all four sides by a deep cove. All the framework round the individual scenes and figures is achieved through the use of skilful painting – a tribute to Beccafumi's powers of pictorial illusion and his attentive study of other contemporary painted ceilings such as Michelangelo's in the Sistine Chapel and Perino del Vaga's in the Palazzo del Principe in Genoa.[92] Capitalising on his experience of executing a similar scheme for the ceiling of the Palazzo Venturi (see pl. 133), Beccafumi employed a framework of whites, greys and pale blues, enlivened with gold and touches of red. This cool and restrained framing enhanced the dramatic effects of backgrounds that were either pale and luminous or very dark. Within the principal paintings themselves, meanwhile, Beccafumi again exploited his preferred and highly distinctive palette of rosy pink, apple green, powder blue, golden yellow and mauve.

The scheme seems initially somewhat overwhelming in its intricacy and esoteric subject matter, but is in fact highly organised and logical in its overall political message. Like the Palazzo Venturi scheme, the source for the subjects of the paintings on the cove of the ceiling is Valerius Maximus's *Memorable Deeds and Sayings*. The key to the choice of this Roman author's narratives lies in the imagery on the central part of the ceiling. At the centre is an arresting image of Justice grasping her traditional emblems of the sword and scales. Beneath her appears a putto displaying the first part of a biblical text, from Proverbs: 8:15, that reads in its entirety: 'By me, kings reign [and princes decree justice]'. Just as Ambrogio Lorenzetti had placed great emphasis on this Christian Virtue and its divine inspiration in his painted allegory of *Good Government* in the nearby Sala della Pace (see pl. 52), so Beccafumi emphasised the ethereal quality of the figure of Justice by showing her daringly foreshortened, as if she were a heavenly apparition, transported on clouds and bathed in luminous light. In the four smaller, rectangular compartments surrounding Justice appear seated figures, two male and two female. Their attributes signify that – again like Ambrogio Lorenzetti's painting – they represent two branches of justice, one relating to criminal and the other to commercial justice. The two octagonal paintings at either end of the central section of the ceiling also portray allegorical figures of qualities deemed essential for good government. From the mottoes surrounding the figures in the compartment at the west end of the ceiling, it appears that the man dressed in a striking green and turquoise tunic is an allegory of benevolence or good will. The lettering above the head of the female figure at the east end of the ceiling similarly identifies her as a personification of the patriotic virtue of loving one's country. In her left hand this figure displays a human heart – one of the traditional pictorial symbols of Charity, particularly in respect of the love of God.[93]

On the cove around the central section of the ceiling the sixteen paintings each relate to one of the three central allegorical figures (pl. 147). In terms of format, however, they fall into three categories. Six appear as rectangular paintings – two of which are placed on each of the long north and south sides of the ceiling and one of which appears on each of the short east and west ends of the ceiling. These paintings are richly populated with figures whose sophisticated organisation and animated poses are reminiscent of Raphael's cartoons for the Sistine tapestries.[94] Two appear as octagonal

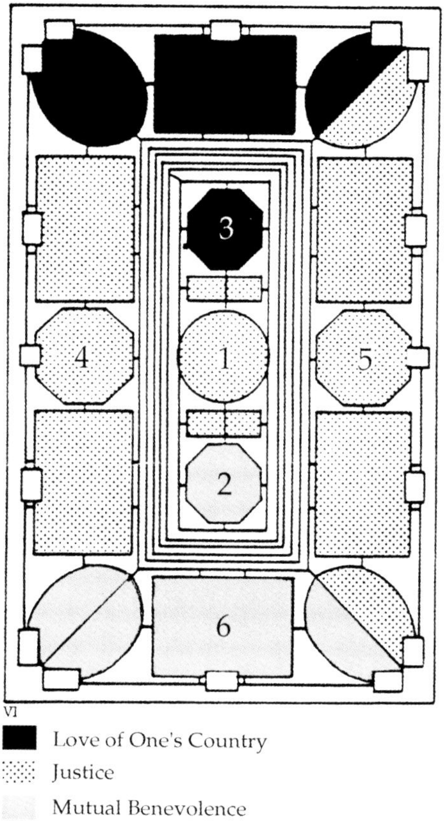

147 Diagram of the ceiling decoration of the Sala del Concistoro
1 Justice Enthroned
2 Mutual Benevolence
3 Love of One's Country
4 The Execution of Spurius Cassius
5 Marcus Manlius thrown from the Capitol
6 The Reconciliation of Marcus Emilius Lepidus and Fulvius Flaccus

paintings and act as centrepieces for the north and south sides of the ceiling. The dramatically foreshortened figures of both scenes create a spectacular illusionism similar to that of the neighbouring central painting of Justice. Finally, at the corners of the ceiling appear eight semi-circular paintings. These represent seated male figures silhouetted against a dark blue sky.

As already noted, the subjects of the paintings on the cove of the ceiling are all drawn directly from Valerius Maximus. The overall message of the elaborate scheme is therefore that the deeds and actions of men from Greek and Roman history exemplify certain civic virtues – such as justice, benevolence and love of one's country – which the governors and citizens of contemporary Siena should emulate. The aims and ideals of this painted programme were therefore like those of the paintings executed by Taddeo di Bartolo in the second decade of the fifteenth century for the nearby antechamber to the original meeting room for the Consistory (see pl. 81).[95] However, in place of Taddeo di Bartolo's series of standing figures exemplifying the heroic qualities of Roman republicanism, Beccafumi created a highly sophisticated scheme of narrative scenes, framed at the corners by pairs of seated figures. Although the identities of the various heroes and anti-heroes of Greek and Roman history are briefly indicated by the names inscribed on the deep red fictive tablets of the lower border, the interpretation of the scheme nevertheless requires a sophisticated awareness of Valerius Maximus's text and its moralising content.

For example, the central octagonal painting on the south side of the ceiling illustrates the execution of Spurius Cassius (pl. 148). Suspected of wanting to usurp political power by courting popularity with the people, Spurius was accused by his own father of aiming at tyranny and was condemned to death. Beccafumi chose to show the moment just after his execution. The decapitated body of the aspiring tyrant lies prominently in the foreground, the blood still flowing from his severed neck, with his head beneath the body. The youthful, semi-naked executioner, with his flimsy loincloth accentuating rather than covering his buttocks, appears just above the corpse in the act of sheathing his sword. The treatment of this moralising subject thus has a distinctly erotic, sado-masochistic quality to it. Beccafumi also uses this painting to demonstrate his skills in pictorial illusionism and foreshortening. Like the companion paintings of *Justice* and *Marcus Manlius thrown from the Capitol* in the central section of the ceiling, the spectator is invited to view the scene and the figures populating it as if from below – including such conceits as the glimpse of the putto, seen through the oculus at the centre of the vault of the open-sided building in which this act of justice took place.

By comparison, the painting of the *Reconciliation of Marcus Emilius Lepidus and Fulvius Flaccus* that dominates the west side of the ceiling is a more measured composition (pl. 149). Representing the peace made between a powerful consul and his principal enemy, the subject was chosen to illustrate a notable act of benevolence and good will in ancient Roman

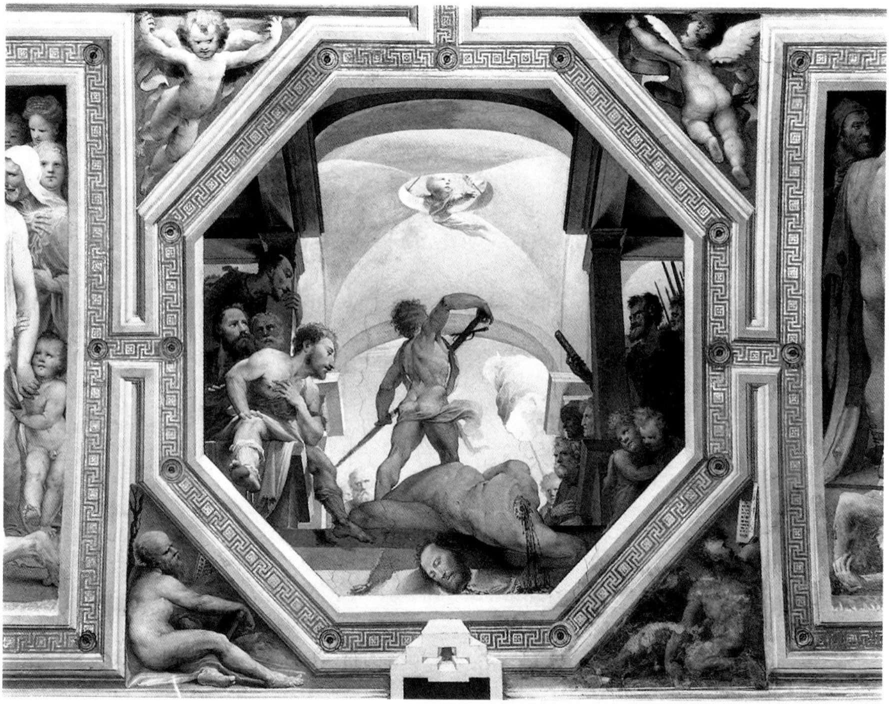

148 Beccafumi, *The Execution of Spurius Cassius* (detail of pl. 146).

history. Set in an orderly and impressive rendition of the Campo Marzio in Rome, with temples and other ancient civic buildings in the background, the two protagonists are represented embracing one another in a dignified manner. Other figures witness this scene including two animated youths to the left of the kneeling consuls. A bearded man on the extreme right looks directly out towards the spectator and may be a portrait of the painter himself.[96] If this is the case, it appears that this particular painting was of some significance for the scheme as a whole. It is the first painting to draw one's attention as one enters the room since it lies directly opposite the entrance door. In colour, perspective and luminosity, it also functions as an eye-catching painting within the generally rich embellishment of the ceiling as whole.

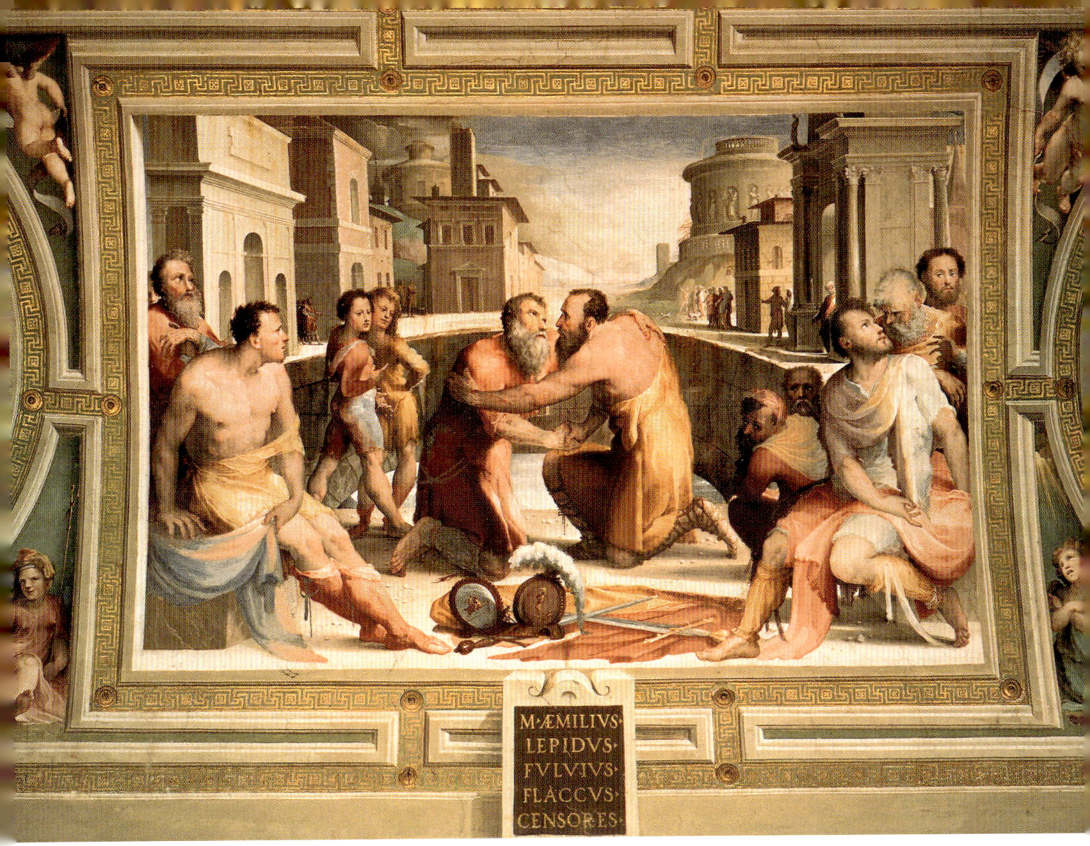

149 Beccafumi, *The Reconciliation of Marcus Emilius Lepidus and Fulvius Flaccus* (detail of pl. 146).

Its theme would, moreover, have been of special relevance to Beccafumi's government patrons at the time of the painting's execution. As seen in previous chapters, one of the endemic weaknesses of Siena's political system was the tendency towards faction among its governing classes – a tendency that sat uneasily with the ideals of communality and unity to which the republican regime aspired. That this was a continuous concern can be judged from the painted texts and imagery chosen for many of the paintings commissioned for the walls of the Palazzo Pubblico over three centuries (see pls 47, 51, 52, 81). Only recently, however, the city had experienced the 'tyranny' of Pandolfo Petrucci and his sons and the victory of the Libertini over this threat to Siena's status and liberty as an independent republic. If the ideal of liberty was to be preserved, it was essential that the members of Siena's governing families did not engage in factional disputes but instead – like Marcus Lepidus and Fulvius Flaccus – reconcile their differences and work together for the common good of the Sienese re-public. For this reason alone the choice of this subject and the prominence given to it in the scheme for the ceiling of the 'painted room' were entirely apposite.

As noted earlier, in order to maintain the city's political independence, Siena's governors had courted the Hapsburg emperor, Charles V, as the city's protector and mentor. That this was a double-edged sword was proved only too clearly by later events in the 1540s and 1550s, a decade or more after the ceiling decoration was completed. In 1529, however, when Beccafumi was awarded the commission, the city authorities were expecting a visit from this powerful prince. It thus seems likely – if ironic in the perspective of subsequent events – that the project was initiated with this visit in mind. Speculation therefore arises as to whether any aspect of the ceiling's programme might have been intended specifically for the benefit of Charles V and his officials. In general terms, the painted scheme would have suggested the presence of a political regime composed of men knowledgeable about the deeds and precepts of classical history and possessed of sophisticated tastes in contemporary art. The overall message would have been one of the virtue and benefits of a republican, not an imperial, system of government. Finally, the choice of the text from Proverbs to embellish the commanding central painting of *Justice* may have once carried a message for the Emperor himself. Stating that kings only reign according to the dictates of Justice, this motto would have acted as timely reminder to Charles V that his powers were God-given and should be exercised in a just and merciful manner.

* * *

In many ways, the ceiling of the Sala del Concistoro represents the culmination of sixteenth-century Sienese civic art. Although completed by 1535 and therefore twenty years before the fall of the Sienese republic, it provides another compelling demonstration of the traditional yet also innovatory characteristics of Sienese painting at that time. Painted in a manner comparable with the highly fashionable styles favoured by the princely courts of Rome, Florence and Mantua, its subject addresses the universal and time-honoured theme of what constitutes the best form of government for an independent city state such as Siena. It thus reiterated the central themes of a number of earlier schemes commissioned in the fourteenth and fifteenth centuries for neighbouring rooms in the Palazzo Pubblico.

As this study has sought to show, one of the most striking features of Sienese culture is the strong and self-conscious awareness of the city's history and traditions, together with an enduring capacity to devise new ways of keeping such history and traditions alive. Probably the most obvious example of this is the continuing devotion of the Sienese to the Virgin, and also to other local saints such as Ansano, Bernardino and Catherine. Painters played a crucial role in creating and sustaining the belief that the Virgin and saints were closely involved in the fortunes of the city and its inhabitants. Those responsible for commissioning their work similarly sought to ensure that such venerable traditions were sustained by specifically instructing painters to emulate older, revered images of the Virgin and saints. Even when such instructions were not apparently forthcoming, there is a strong sense that Sienese painters were themselves acutely aware of such models – Sassetta's *Madonna of the Snows* being a striking case in point (see pls 92 and 36, 43).

There is, of course, ample evidence of substantial changes in Sienese painting over the three centuries covered by this study. As has been shown, Sienese painters were by no means indifferent to trends and artistic experiments – and indeed, in the early fourteenth century, it can justifiably be claimed that Sienese painters were themselves in the forefront of such experimentation. By the sixteenth century, however, there appears to have been a distinct change in the style of artistic patronage and the types of paintings commissioned from Sienese painters. Although religious paintings continued to be popular with Sienese patrons, there was a marked increase in the amount of domestic art commissioned by them – an increase that cannot be attributed simply to better rates of survival of such works of art (see, for example, pls 111, 123–33). Paintings were recognised not merely as expressions of family piety and religious devotion but as hallmarks of social prestige and affluence. Thus they were more frequently regarded as objects to be enjoyed privately and at one's leisure. Such paintings were often erudite, demanding specialised forms of knowledge of their audiences, both in terms of their subject matter and the ways in which they had been painted (see pl. 133). Sixteenth-century painting in Siena, as elsewhere in Italy at that time, was becoming increasingly elite.

This study began with an acknowledgement of how influential the period from 1260 to 1555 has been for the characterisation of Sienese painting in general. There were, of course, many gifted Sienese painters working in later centuries and there are impressive examples of baroque art in Siena – the seventeenth-century chapel of the *Madonna del Voto* in the cathedral being a notable example (see pl. 20).[97] The seventeenth and eighteenth centuries in Siena were also remarkable for the number of Sienese scholars such as Giulio Mancini, Girolamo Gigli, Giovanni Antonio Pecci and Guglielmo della Valle who wrote extensively about the city's artistic monuments and the lives of the painters who embellished them.

The nineteenth century, in turn, with its enthusiasm and taste for medieval culture, witnessed ambitious programmes of restoration of many of the city's principal buildings and the paintings within them. At the same time scholars, such as Gaetano Milanesi and Luciano Banchi, published numerous archival documents relating to the activities of Sienese painters working between the thirteenth and sixteenth centuries. And in the twentieth century with the consolidation of art history as an academic subject, a further extensive body of literature has been produced on Sienese painting.

Among Sienese scholars, especially, there is thus a long history of writing about Sienese painting, which began after the city's loss of political independence in 1555 and took shape in the following centuries. One of the characteristic aims of many contributors to this historical narrative was to preserve the memory of Sienese art and culture during the period when Siena enjoyed its own political independence and cultural autonomy. Such writers were also concerned to demonstrate a pride in their city, its urban topography, political history, civic traditions and, above all, its enduring devotion to the Virgin as the protector and patron of the city. In this respect, they fairly reflected the painters and patrons about whom they wrote and whose art expressed a similar commitment to Siena and its culture.

Notes

Introduction

1 See e.g.: Dundes and Falassi (1983), pp. 9–10, 100–09; Parsons (1997), pp. 185–9. Please note that in the notes to this and the following chapters, references are made where possible to accessible English-language publications.
2 See Webb (1996), pp. 251–75; Norman (1999), pp. 3–4, 28–33.
3 See Hook (1979), pp. 125–7.
4 See e.g.: Gardner (1979); J. Cannon in Turner (1996), XIII, p. 817.
5 Stubblebine (1964); G. Chelazzi Dini in Chelazzi Dini, Angelini and Sani (1998), pp. 10–17.
6 See e.g.: Fehm (1986); Steinhoff-Morrison (1989); Freuler (1994a).
7 See e.g.: *Painting in Renaissance Siena 1420–1500* (1988); *Domenico Beccafumi* (1990); *Francesco di Giorgio e il Rinascimento* (1993).
8 See Nevola (2000), esp. for fifteenth-century government planning in respect of the city's main thoroughfare.
9 According to the findings of an ongoing archaeological investigation of the foundations of the cathedral. See also Brogi (1998).
10 Demolished in the seventeenth century, its replacement now stands to the north of the cathedral. Throughout this study, the orientation of churches will be described in terms of liturgical convention, whereby the chancel and high altar are located at the east end of the building.
11 Named thus because of its location opposite the flight of steps leading up to the cathedral. The Spedale also took the ladder (*scala*) as its emblem and this in turn became inextricably linked to the hospital's mythical foundation. For a comprehensive study of the history of the Spedale and its art, see Gallavotti Cavallero (1985).
12 See Southard (1980), I; C. Cunningham in Norman (1995), II, pp. 34–42.
13 Now known by its acquisition number as Polyptych 47. See Gallavotti Cavallero (1985), p. 110, fig. 73 (colour).
14 See Torriti (1998), pp. 63–5, 86–7, 216–17.
15 Under the care of respectively the Dominican, Franciscan, Servite, Augustinian Hermit and Carmelite religious orders.

16 For a detailed study of the new church and its adjacent priory: Mussolin (1997).
17 For the foundation of Santa Marta: Norman (2000), pp. 273–4, 282–5.
18 See Leoncini (1994), pp. 64–5.
19 Friedman (1998); Nevola (2000), p. 46.
20 For the Porta Romana *Coronation of the Virgin*: P. Scapecchi in *Mostra di opere d'arte restaurate* (1979–83), II, pp. 120–27, who also discusses the issue of whether Simone Martini painted images of the Virgin on both the Porta Romana and the Antiporto in the early part of the fourteenth century. See also Nevola (2000), pp. 35–6.
21 The present building was originally two *palazzi*, one belonging to Giacomo Todeschini Piccolomini and the other to his brother Andrea. See Jenkens (1999).
22 Baxandall (1972), p. 3.
23 See Norman (2000), pp. 294–9.
24 Saint Bernardino (1427; ed. 1989), II, p. 1254.
25 For a useful summary of the technique of fresco painting: Welch (2000), pp. 66–7.
26 For the form and function of altarpieces, in general: Dunkerton (1991), pp. 25–37.
27 For a detailed study of Italian Renassance *cassoni*: Baskins (1998); and of birth trays: Musacchio (1999).
28 For a representative range of such sculpted items: *Scultura dipinta* (1987).
29 For a useful discussion of fourteenth-century Sienese painters' use of drawings: Maginnis (2001), pp. 111–18.
30 For this drawing: A. De Marchi in *Francesco di Giorgio e il Rinascimento* (1993), cat. no. 59, p. 310.
31 See Martindale (1988), pp. 37–8.
32 E.g., according to the eighteenth-century historian Giovanni Antonio Pecci, Sister Giovanna Petroni (d. 1387) headed a successful workshop of manuscript illumination in the convent of Santa Marta. See Biblioteca Comunale, Siena, MS A III 3, fols 116–24.
33 These were a series of frescoes for the chapterhouse of San Francesco in Siena (see pp. 108–11 and pl. 56), probably executed in the early 1340s, and a series of frescoes for the exterior façade of the Spedale di Santa Maria della Scala, with a recorded date of 1335 (see pp. 136, 147–8 and pl. 67). It also appears that they worked together on an ambitious series of frescoes in the church of Santa Margherita in Cortona, for which see Cannon and Vauchez (1999).
34 See Skaug (1976).
35 For the 1353 agreement: Freuler (1994a), doc. 1, p. 416; for the formal dissolution of the partnership in 1475: C. Zarrilli (ed.) in *Francesco di Giorgio e il Rinascimento* (1993), doc. 23, p. 531.
36 For a detailed analysis of the techniques used on *Christ healing a Man born Blind* and *The Transfiguration* from the back predella of the *Maestà*: *Art in the Making* (1989), pp. 83–9.
37 See Martindale (1988), pp. 188–9; Norman (1999), pp. 71, 73, 223 n. 15.

38 As, e.g., *The Nativity and Adoration of the Shepherds*, hanging on the south aisle wall in San Domenico. Dated *c.* 1475–80 and originally for the altar of the Tancredi family. The main panel has been attributed to Francesco di Giorgio (*c.* 1500), the lunette panel of *Christ in the Tomb* to Matteo di Giovanni (*c.* 1493–9) and the predella (showing *The Massacre of the Innocents* and scenes from the lives of saints) to Bernardino Fungai (*c.* 1500). See M. Seidel in Riedl and Seidel (1985–), II.1.2, pp. 593–8.

39 See R. Bartalini in *Scultura dipinta* (1987), p. 102.

40 See Neri Lusanna (1981), who cautiously attributes the sculpture to Francesco di Valdambrino. Cf. L. Bellosi in *Scultura dipinta* (1987), pp. 166–8, who attributes it to Giovanni di Turino.

41 Now housed in the Archivio di Stato, Siena (Arte dei Pittori, Statuti, nos 59–60).

42 For a translation by G. Erasmi of the statutes of the painters' guild (1356–1402): Maginnis (2001), pp. 201–24. See also pp. 84–94 for an analysis of these statutes.

43 Vasari (1568; ed. 1960–), V, pp. 166, 381; Eng. trans. (1963), III, pp. 141, 285. See also E. Carli in Turner (1996), XXIX, p. 1.

44 Vasari (1568; ed. 1960–), V, p. 165; Eng. trans. (1963), III, p. 140. For discussion of the accuracy of Vasari's account: F. Sricchia Santoro in Turner (1996), III, p. 497; Dubus (1999), pp. 3–4, 15.

45 F. P. Fiore in Turner (1996), XI, p. 687.

46 Coor (1961), pp. 3, 12.

47 Cited in Starn (1987), pp. 4–5.

48 In translation this reads: 'Guido da Siena painted me in the pleasant days, whom may gentle Christ afflict with no suffering'.

49 For discussion of the relationship between Siena and its subject territories and the impact of this on fourteenth-century art: Norman (1999).

50 See the relevant documents (nos 3–8) published by Banker (1991) who also gives a detailed analysis of this important fifteenth-century commission.

1 Early Sienese Painting

1 For a detailed discussion of the historical authenticity of the 1260 vow: Webb (1996), pp. 251–75; Norman (1999), pp. 3–4; Parsons (2001), pp. 136–43.

2 An autograph copy by Niccolò di Giovanni Ventura, a minor painter and seller of artists' materials, is now in the Biblioteca Comunale, Siena, MS A IV 5. It has been published as 'La sconfitta di Montaperto' (ed. 1844).

3 Van Os (1984–90), I, pp. 11–12; Norman (1999), pp. 28–9. The provenance of this painting is the church of Sant' Ansano in Castelvecchio. A marginal annotation in the cathedral inventory of 1439 suggests, however, that it was taken to this church from the cathedral. For recently expressed doubts that the painting was ever on the cathedral high altar: Argenziano (2001), pp. 103–4; Maginnis (2001), pp. 137–8, n. 99.

4 A number of other paintings have been attributed to this anonymous early

thirteenth-century painter, dubbed the Master of Tressa, after the provenance of one of the paintings. These are: the *Christ in Majesty with Scenes from the Legend of the True Cross* (Pinacoteca, Siena); the *Virgin and Christ Child and Saints* (Chigi-Saracini Collection, Siena); and the *Virgin and Christ Child and Narrative Scenes*, originally from the parish church of Santa Maria at Tressa (Museo Diocesano, Oratory of San Bernardino, Siena).

5 For a colour illustration that shows these items clearly: Norman (1999), pl. 38, and pp. 29–33, for further discussion of the probable original form of this thirteenth-century painting.

6 In an exhibition held at the Lindenau-Museum, Altenburg, in 2001, an alternative reconstruction of the high altarpiece has been proposed, whereby the *Madonna del Voto* is framed by twelve scenes from the life of Christ. These have traditionally been attributed to Guido da Siena and are now divided between various museums. For a judicious assessment of this reconstruction: Schmidt (2001).

7 Bellosi (1991a), pp. 13–17. See also Schmidt (2001), p. 514.

8 *Cronache senesi* (ed. 1931–9), pp. 90, 314; 'La sconfitta di Montaperto' (ed. 1844), p. 46; Norman (1999), pp. 31–3. For recent views that the altarpiece was commissioned for another altar in the cathedral: Maginnis (2001), pp. 137–8, n. 99; Schmidt (2001), pp. 513–14; Israëls (2003), pp. 36–7.

9 Van der Ploeg (1993), pp. 83–95.

10 For a useful summary of Sienese Ghibellinism during this period: Waley (1991), pp. 114–25.

11 According to the city statutes of 1309–10, the Nine had to be 'of the merchants of Siena or truly of the middling sort of people'. For an authoritative analysis of the Nine and their policies: Bowsky (1981).

12 For a concise account of the complex building history of the cathedral: T. Benton in Norman (1995), II, pp. 130–35, 141–3.

13 For a recent, illuminating contribution to this debate: Gillerman (1999).

14 Gallavotti Cavallero (1985), pp. 61–4.

15 Norman (1999), p. 50.

16 For a list of payments for the new building: Brandi (1983), pp. 415–17.

17 Published in Riedl and Seidel (1985–), I.1.1, p. 457, doc. 2.

18 For further discussion of late medieval lay piety and its reliance on religious imagery: D. Norman in Norman (1995), I, pp. 179–82.

19 Recovered in a restoration campaign in 1950. For further discussion of this painting, see pp. 53–4.

20 The painting was removed from San Domenico in 1888 and for many years was located in the Sala del Mappamondo in the Palazzo Pubblico (see pl. 46). It was returned to the church in the late 1990s. For further discussion of its provenance: H. Trottmann in Riedl and Seidel (1985–), II.1.2, pp. 637–8.

21 Hoeniger (1995), pp. 22–4.

22 Cannon (1980), pp. 42, 184; Cannon (1982), p. 76, n. 55.

23 See Cannon (1980), pp. 183–8, 279, who similarly links the production and repainting of the thirteenth-century painting of Saint Dominic, now in the Fogg

Art Museum, Cambridge (Mass.), with the history of this confraternity in San Domenico.

24 See H. Teubner in Riedl and Seidel (1985–), II.1.2, pp. 503–5.

25 Van Os (1984–90), I, p. 29, and Hoeniger (1995), p. 39, assume it was painted for the high altar of San Domenico.

26 Gardner (1979), pp. 107–8; Cannon (1980), p. 433.

27 Corrie (1990). See also Corrie (1996), pp. 55–8.

28 Mina (2000), pp. 242–7.

29 Published in Brandi (1933), p. 10.

30 Until at least 1782, this painting was kept in the Oratory of Santa Maria degli Angeli, later known as the Oratory of San Bernardino, situated next to the church of San Francesco (see pl. 6).

31 Bellosi (1991a), pp. 14–16, attributes it to Dietisalvi di Speme, a painter who received payments from the city treasury between 1259 and 1291.

32 For a fuller discussion of the painting and its commission: D. Norman in Norman (1995), I, pp. 59–63; Maginnis (1997), pp. 64–78.

33 Hueck (1990), pp. 40–43.

34 Now on the altar of the Bardi Chapel in Santa Croce, Florence, and generally dated *c.* 1255. See Garrison (1949), p. 155, no. 405; Goffen (1988), pp. 29–50.

35 Placed along the lower frame, the five saints were Catherine of Alexandria, favoured by the Dominicans because of her reputation for learning; Dominic, the founder; Jerome, whose writings were particularly important for late medieval veneration of the Virgin; Augustine, whose rule the Dominicans adopted; and Peter Martyr who reputedly founded the Laudesi confraternity in Santa Maria Novella.

36 Examples of early fourteenth-century *Maestà* survive in the abbey church of Badia a Isola, just north of Siena, the Collegiata of San Giuliano at Castel Fiorentino and the Galleria Comunale, Città di Castello.

37 Torriti (1990), p. 9, fig. 2.

38 Carli and Imberciadori (1987), p. 64. According to Pecori (1853, 1975), p. 431, the convent of Santa Chiara was founded in 1261. The crucifix has generally been dated earlier than the *Madonna del Bordone* on stylistic grounds (see J. Cannon in Turner, 1996, VII, pp. 816–17), but the foundation date of the convent suggests that it may have been produced at the same time as Coppo's Sienese painting.

39 Carli (1981), p. 14; Torriti (1990), p. 11; J. Cannon in Turner (1996), XIII, p. 820.

40 The panel painting has been cut at either end – but the surviving words of the painted inscription are identical to those on Guido da Siena's *Maestà* (apart from the different dates on the two paintings).

41 For an informative summary of Church legislation on altars and their embellishment: Gardner (1994), pp. 6–12.

42 White (1979), pp. 25–6, 67–8, suggests that the two outermost figures are now missing from this panel painting. Judging from other early examples of this type of painting, however, such as the one illustrated in Van Os (1984–90), I, fig. 13, which still has its original frame, this seems unlikely.

43 Carli (1981), p. 22.

44 Bellosi (1991b), pp. 18–26. The payments occur between 1278 and 1302.

45 See the reports in: *The Daily Telegraph* 15 December 2001, p. 19; *Corriere di Siena*, 31 December, 2001, p. 27; *Toscana Oggi*, 24 February 2002, p. 21.

46 There are close similarities between the *Betrayal* and a small panel painting of the same subject, now in the Pinacoteca, Siena (see Torriti, 1990, fig. 8). On these grounds, therefore, Carli (1981), p. 14, attributes the frescoes to a collaborator of Guido da Siena. Bellosi (1991a), pp. 16–17, suggests that they might be by Dietisalvi di Speme, whom he characterises as the 'alter-ego' of Guido da Siena.

47 For a detailed catalogue of these painted covers: Borgia (1984), esp. cat. nos 1–14, pp. 42–68.

48 Bellosi (1991a), p. 14.

49 For the difficulties of finding objects produced for secular use at this date: Goldthwaite (1993), pp. 212–13. A number of maiolica jugs with bold geometric patterns, dated to the last decades of the thirteenth century and now in the civic museum in Montalcino, provide a rare example of the kinds of decorative, but strictly utilitarian, item that once furnished privately owned houses.

50 For an insight into the complex ways in which Sienese painters were influenced by and in turn influenced Byzantine artists: Belting (1982); Derbes (1989); Corrie (1996).

51 See, e.g., the illumination of the *Creation of the Fishes and the Birds*, folio 38 in the late thirteenth-century 'Treatise on the Creation of the World', now in the Biblioteca Comunale, Siena, MS H VI 31, and illustrated, in colour, in Chelazzi Dini, Angelini and Sani (1998), p. 17.

52 See Bellosi (1991a/b); G. Chelazzi Dini in Chelazzi Dini, Angelini and Sani (1998), pp. 12–17.

53 For publication and detailed study of these: Satkowski (2000).

2 'Golden Age'

1 Agazzari (1922), p. 17.

2 Most notably in Hook (1979) and Bowsky (1970 and 1981).

3 See Norman (1997), pp. 325–37.

4 Waley (1991), pp. 34–5, 206–7.

5 Bowsky (1964). Other historians give even higher estimates. See Steinhoff (2000), p. 42, n. 80.

6 *Cronache senesi* (ed. 1931–9), p. 555.

7 See Caferro (1998).

8 Cited in White (1993), p. 227.

9 Hook (1979), p. 36. See also Waley (1991), pp. 13–15; Balestracci and Piccinni (1977); Bowsky (1981), pp. 260–98.

10 For a clear summary of the history of the building of the Palazzo Pubblico: C. Cunningham in Norman (1995), II, pp. 34–52.

11 Comprising six vaulted bays, the baptistery was built between *c.* 1316 and 1325. Its elaborate entrance façade was only completed when the cathedral chancel was extended over the baptistery in the second half of the fourteenth century.

12 See chapter 3, p. 128.

13 Recorded in the *Cronache senesi* (ed. 1931–9), p. 90; trans. in White (1979), pp. 96–7.

14 For detailed analyses of the *Maestà*: Bellosi (1999); Norman (1999), pp. 21–43.

15 Such as the ninth-century mosaic in the principal apse of Santa Maria in Domnica in Rome, illustrated in Norman (1995), II, pl. 47.

16 See G. Aronow in Van Os (1984–90), II, p. 232.

17 As proposed by Van der Ploeg (1993), p. 61 and fig. 38.

18 The text reads in full: MATER S[AN]C[T]A DEISIS CAUSA SENIS REQUIEI/ SIS DUC[C]IO VITA TE QUIA PINXIT ITA (Holy mother of God, be the cause of repose for Siena and because he painted you thus, of life for Duccio).

19 At the time of writing, this magnificent example of late medieval stained-glass was undergoing restoration and was the subject of an exhibition in the Spedale di Santa Maria della Scala.

20 See n. 18 above and Introduction, n. 48.

21 In 1302 Duccio had also received a commission to paint an altarpiece for the Nine. See Satkowski (2000), p. 67, no. 36.

22 White (1993), p. 289.

23 See D. Norman in Norman (1995), II, pp. 73–4.

24 *Art in the Making* (1989), pp. 72–89; D. Norman in Norman (1995), II, pp. 63–7.

25 See Cannon (1982), pp. 79–80; (1994), p. 41.

26 See Van Os (1984–90), I, p. 64. For a colour illustration: Gallavotti Cavallero (1985), fig. 73.

27 For discussion of these three important altarpiece commissions for other cities: Van Os (1984–90), I, pp. 63–75. For good colour illustrations: *Art in the Making* (1989), pp. 98-123; Chelazzi Dini, Angelini and Sani (1998), pp. 72–3, 127.

28 Cannon (1994), pp. 56–8, who concludes that the altarpiece is a 'cautious repetition' of Ugolino's Santa Croce altarpiece by one of his assistants. The convent of Santa Chiara moved to the site shown on pl. 6 only after 1555. Before then it was situated outside the Porta Romana.

29 For details of the commission and reconstruction: Maginnis (1975); Cannon (1987).

30 For the iconography of the altarpiece and the sources on which it was probably based: Cannon (1987); Van Os (1984–90), I, pp. 91–9; Frugoni (1988), pp. 8–12.

31 See K. Christiansen in *Painting in Renaissance Siena* (1988), p. 64, citing later

evidence for this in 1370 and 1431. See also Israëls (2001), pp. 533–4, docs VII and VIII, p. 543.

32 For further discussion of these two commissions: pp. 108–11 below.

33 See Norman (forthcoming).

34 For Simone Martini's *Maestà*: Norman (1999), pp. 48–58, 63–5; Bagnoli (2000). For a range of colour details of the painting: Carli (1996).

35 See A. Martindale in Turner (1996), XX, pp. 504–5; Norman (forthcoming). For discussion on the indebtedness of Simone's treatment of the *Maestà* theme to courtly poetry and diplomacy: Campbell (1997), pp. 99–102; (1998).

36 These scrolls were probably introduced at a late stage in the execution of the *Maestà* by Simone Martini. See Bagnoli (2000), pp. 83–5, 90.

37 The painting has traditionally been linked to a payment to Simone (Martini) by the Sienese treasury for painting the castles of Montemassi and Sassoforte.

38 As suggested by Martindale (1986), pp. 267–8; (1988), pp. 40–41.

39 Moran (1977). For a judicious analysis of the ensuing controversy: Maginnis (1988a). To the publications cited there, can be added: Kupfer (1996); De Wesselow (2000); Moran and Mallory (2000).

40 For a summary of these views: D. Norman in Norman (1995), I, pp. 136–7. See also Campbell (1997), pp. 36–8, 62–3; De Wesselow (2000).

41 Notably by Kupfer (1996), who on the basis of various kinds of historical evidence suggests that the *Mappamondo* represented a map of the terrestial world with Italy and Siena at its centre. See also De Wesselow (2000), pp. 21–4. However, Moran and Mallory (2000), pp. 24–8, question that the *Mappamondo* on the west wall was necessarily the one executed by Ambrogio Lorenzetti.

42 See De Wesselow (2000), p. 22.

43 This is the general consensus among scholars who link its execution either to the 1314 decision to paint Giuncarico or to a series of payments made to the painter Simone between 1330 and 1331 for the painting of various castles in the Sienese *contado*. De Wesselow (2000), pp. 31–7, however, argues that the 'castle series' was, in point of fact, a series of small panel paintings located on the west wall below the *Submission of a Castle*.

44 See Bagnoli (2000), pp. 88–94.

45 The reconds of these payments are published in Maginnis (1988a), pp. 139–40.

46 As argued most eloquently by Polzer (1983); (1985); (1987).

47 See the perceptive remarks made by De Wesselow (2000), pp. 27–8, on this point. See also the views of a number of other art historians cited by Moran and Mallory (2000), pp. 18, 33, 38.

48 As argued by De Wesselow (2000), pp. 28–31, 38–9, who believes that the *Guidoriccio* was executed in 1352 following Guidoriccio da Fogliano's death and state funeral in Siena. In his view, therefore, the painting acted as a kind of painted adjunct to the *Mappamondo* of 1345.

49 For a detailed summary of the problematic nature of both kinds of evidence: Moran and Mallory (2000).

50 See ibid., pp. 19, 29–30.

51 For a review of the literature on the painted scheme of the Sala dei Nove: D. Norman in Norman (1995), II, pp. 145–67. To the publications cited there can be added: the detailed photographic survey of the frescoes in Castelnuovo (1995); Norman (1997); Gibbs (1999); Skinner (1999); Ben-Aryeh Debby (2001); Campbell (2001).

52 Published in Maginnis (1989), appendix nos 4–17.

53 See Frugoni (1991), p. 136. Cf. Kempers (1992), p. 137.

54 As early as 1425, e.g., the Sienese saint Bernardino referred in detail to the painting in a Lenten sermon. See Bernardino (1425; ed. 1958), II, pp. 266–9. For discussion of the significance of the saint's description of the painting: Ben-Aryeh Debby (2001).

55 White (1972), pp. 93–6; Skinner (1999), pp. 19–20.

56 For the relevance of this campaign for the frescoes in the Sala dei Nove: Norman (1997).

57 For a more detailed discussion of these points: D. Norman in Norman (1995), I, pp. 202–7.

58 For this painting: Martindale (1988), pp. 32–4, cat. no. 41, pp. 211–14.

59 For the links between San Leonardo al Lago and Sant'Agostino in Siena and their respective roles in promoting the cult of Agostino Novello: Norman (1999), pp. 138–9.

60 See H. J. B. Maginnis in Turner (1996) XIX, p. 655. For colour illustrations of this scheme: Frugoni (1988), pp. 16–31.

61 See A. Martindale in Turner (1996), XX, p. 565. For colour illustrations of this scheme: Lunghi (1996), pp. 155–83.

62 The exact date of this commission is not known. Those who wish to relate it closely to the Assisi Passion series date it to the 1320s, e.g. H. J. B. Maginnis in Turner (1996), XIX, pp. 666, 668. Those who associate it with the cloister frescoes (for which, see p. 111), date it to the late 1330s, early 1340s, e.g. Seidel (1979a); Frugoni (1988), pp. 59–62; Burke (2002).

63 Burke (2002), pp. 478–83.

64 Ghiberti (*c.* 1447–55; ed. 1947), pp. 37–8.

65 It is interesting in this context to note that in 1335 the same three painters may also have collaborated on a now lost fresco series for the exterior of the church of the hospital of Santa Maria della Scala (see pl. 67), for which see Norman (1999), pp. 87–103.

66 The evidence for this occurs in a mid-fourteenth-century drawing of a design for the Duomo Nuovo (Museo dell'Opera del Duomo, Siena, illus. in Van der Ploeg, 1993, fig. 46) where a number of altars are grouped round an ambulatory at the east end of the building. Four flank the high altar and could have been dedicated to each of the four patron saints.

67 For these altarpieces: Norman (1999), pp. 67–85. See also G. Chelazzi Dini in Chelazzi Dini, Angelini and Sani (1998), pp. 86–90, 135–7, 174.

68 As reconstructed by Beatson, Steinhoff and Muller (1986). These two paintings are now in the Statens Museum for Kunst, Copenhagen, and have been attributed to an unknown Sienese painter dubbed the Master of the Palazzo Venezia Madonna.

69 Illustrated in colour in Norman (1999), pls 80–83.

70 Reconstructed by Cannon in Cannon and Vauchez (1999), pp. 111–54, who argues that these paintings were executed by the Lorenzetti and their assistants in the mid-1330s.

71 Maginnis (1991), p. 37; (1997), pp. 113, 138–9, 203. For a highly perceptive analysis of the treatment of pictorial space in these two altarpieces: White (1972), pp. 99–100.

72 Cannon (1980), pp. 270, 315, n. 240. See also Davies/Gordon (1988), pp. 14–16; Schmidt (1996), pp. 26–9.

73 *Art in the Making* (1989), pp. 90–97.

74 See Campbell (1997), pp. 44–106; Norman (1999), pp. 58–63.

75 In 1305 workmen were paid for the construction of a wooden bed frame in the newly built communal tower. See Campbell (1997), p. 32.

76 For a detailed and illuminating discussion of the subject matter of the surviving painting in this tower room and the kinds of literary source on which they were likely to have been based: Campbell (1997), pp. 107–90.

77 See Ghiberti (*c.* 1447–55; ed. 1947), pp. 37–8.

78 Simone Martini probably left Siena for Avignon around 1336. For an account of his years in Avignon: Martindale (1988), pp. 45–54.

79 As suggested by the summary of the painter's will made on 9 June 1348, for which see Wainwright (1975).

3 Crises, Changes and Continuities

1 During this period, plague struck Siena again in 1363, 1374, 1383, 1389, 1399–1400 and 1410–11.

2 For a well-informed summary of the governments of the second half of the fourteenth century: Caferro (1998), pp. 21–4.

3 For a detailed study of the mercenaries and their impact upon Siena between 1342 and 1399, ibid.

4 Southard (1980), I, pp. 241–8; G. Borghini in Brandi (1983), pp. 224–6. For the victory of 1363 and its financial consequences for Siena: Caferro (1998), pp. 94–8.

5 For a detailed discussion of the social classes represented by the Monti: Wainwright (1980).

6 Owing to its outside location and the fact that it was carved in porous local marble, the sculptures on the Fonte Gaia became badly worn over the centuries. In 1858, the civic authorities decided to substitute the original fountain with a faithful copy of it. Executed by the city's leading nineteenth-century sculptor, Tito Sarrocchi, the new fountain was installed ten years later, slightly to the west of the original fountain. From 1904 until the 1990s, the surviving fragments of Jacopo della Quercia's fountain were on display in the upper loggia of the Palazzo Pubblico. They are now being restored and put on permanent display in the new civic museum in the Spedale di Santa Maria della Scala.

7 For a detailed analysis of the commission and the imagery of the fountain: Beck (1991), I, pp. 81–5.

8 Van der Ploeg (1993), pp. 115–17; T. Benton in Norman (1995), II, p. 137.

9 Van der Ploeg (1993), pp. 117–20. For the choirstalls and their sculptures: Carli (1978).

10 For one of these guild altarpieces, see pp. 144–5. See also Van Os (1984–90), I, p. 51; D. Norman in Norman (1995), I, p. 19.

11 The skilled woodworker Domenico di Niccolò was responsible (*c.* 1403–7) for the choirstalls in the chapels of Saints Ansano, Savino and Victor. Between 1404 and 1405, various painters were employed to paint the lives of titular saint in the chapels of Saints Ansano, Victor, Savino and Crescenzio. Between 1401 and 1406, Taddeo di Bartolo painted a series of scenes from the Old Testament in the chancel of the cathedral. See Carli (1979), pp. 83–4. For the paintings of *c.* 1411–13 in the sacristy: pp. 147–9.

12 For the acquisition of the relics: G. Derenzini in *L'Oro di Siena* (1996), pp. 67–78.

13 See G. Piccinni in *L'Oro di Siena* (1996), pp. 39–44; Norman (1999), p. 149. For the extension of the hospital church: Gallavotti Cavallero (1985), pp. 64, 79.

14 This highly-valued relic is now displayed in an elaborate eighteenth-century reliquary. See *L'Oro di Siena* (1996), cat. no. 40, p. 174.

15 For this altarpiece and its date: Steinhoff-Morrison (1989), pp. 603–13; Norman (1999), pp. 150–51. For the construction of the chapel of the relics: Gallavotti Cavallero (1985), pp. 105–7.

16 The central panels of two of these altarpieces are now in the Pinacoteca, Siena: the *Virgin and Christ Child* (no. 76), dated *c.* 1355, and the *Virgin and Christ Child* (no. 80), dated *c.* 1359–60.

17 See J. Steinhoff-Morrison in Turner (1996), V, p. 165.

18 For these frescoes and their links with the Spedale: Norman (1999), pp. 132–55.

19 Gallavotti Cavallero (1985), pp. 73–6; Norman (1999), pp. 145–6.

20 See chapter 2, n. 65.

21 In the chapel attached to the Oratory of San Galgano at Montesiepi. Although only the *sinopia* of Ambrogio Lorenzetti's original painting of the *Annunciation* (see pl. 16) survives, the later fourteenth-century reworking of the painting provides clear evidence that the painter imaginatively utilised the actual window of the chapel within his painting.

22 For a detailed account of the polyptych and its commission: Freuler (1994a), pp. 188–221, cat. nos 48–59, pp. 469–76; Norman (1999), pp. 160–75.

23 Freuler (1994a), pp. 134–259, 368–81; Norman (1999), pp. 162, 175–81.

24 These are the *Annunciation to Joachim* (Pinacoteca, Vatican), the *Presentation of the Virgin in the Temple* (Wawel Castle, Krakow), the *Archangel Gabriel* and the *Virgin of the Annunciation* (Los Angeles County Museum). Freuler (1994a) in his reconstruction of the polyptych also proposes two more paintings (the *Adoration of the Shepherds*, Pinacoteca, Vatican, and the *Adoration*

of the Magi, Polesdon Lacy, National Trust) as pinnacle panels, but their inclusion seems at odds with the characteristic design of other late fourteenth-century polyptychs.

25 The *Virgin of the Annunciation* is now attributed to the Sienese sculptor Domenico di Agostino and the *Archangel Gabriel* to Angelo di Nalduccio, a painter and sculptor with connections to both Siena and Montalcino. See Bagnoli (1997), pp. 24–5, 28–9.

26 Norman (1999), pp. 169–72.

27 Ibid., pp. 172–5. For the two payments to Bartolo di Fredi for his 1385 confraternity commission: Freuler (1994a), docs 66–7, p. 425.

28 These are now kept in Siena's state archive (hereafter ASS) and the archive of the cathedral Opera (hereafter AOMS).

29 Freuler (1994a), pp. 284–96, cat. nos 60–1, pp. 476–8.

30 ASS, inventory no. 28, fol. 14v, inventory no. 29, fol. 18r.

31 Freuler (1994a), pp. 284–300; Israëls (2003), pp. 76, 84–5. The fourteenth-century frescoes were repainted in the fifteenth-century with another figure introduced behind the so-called Saint Anthony Abbot.

32 See e.g. ASS, inventory no. 29, fol. 18r. For the records of the commission: Freuler (1994a), docs 72–7, pp. 426–7.

33 ASS, inventory no. 29, fol. 18r.

34 Shapley (1979) I, pp. 175–7; G. Chelazzi Dini in Chelazzi Dini, Angelini and Sani (1998), pp. 199–200.

35 For the records of the 1392/3 payments: Freuler (1994a), docs 80, 81, p. 428. See also cat. nos 81, 82, p. 495, for the paintings of *Saint Peter* and *Saint Paul* that probably reflect the lost paintings for the cathedral altarpiece.

36 Mallory (1976), p. 119; Van Os (1984–90), II, pp. 136–7.

37 J. Mongellaz in Turner (1996), III, 3, p. 707; Gregory (1998), pp. 207–12.

38 Gallavotti Cavallero (1987); Maginnis (1988b).

39 Gregory (1998), pp. 221–6.

40 Mongellaz (1985), pp. 84–6.

41 See Carli (1981), p. 256 and pl. 294; G. Chelazzi Dini in Chelazzi Dini, Angelini and Sani (1998), pp. 214–15.

42 This description is based on the reconstruction in Gregory (1998), pp. 214–19, fig. 9.

43 Vasari (1568; ed. 1960–), II, p. 180; Eng. trans. (1963), I, p. 123. Vasari also states that at the foot of each figure was a small narrative painting exemplifying the relevant article of the Creed.

44 It was also the subject chosen for the intarsia panels of the choirstalls of the chapel in the Palazzo Pubblico, executed by the woodworker Domenico di Niccolò between 1415 and 1428 (see pl. 77). Domenico may well have also been responsible for the cupboards and wooden framework of the sacristy Creed paintings.

45 For a detailed account of this chapel and its paintings: Norman (1999), pp. 195–207.

46 Eisenberg (1981); Christiansen (1994).

47 Gigli (1723, ed. 1974), II, p. 258.

48 Illustrated in Norman (1999), pl. 218.

49 Southard (1980), I, pp. 372–93; G. Borghini in Brandi (1983), pp. 226–8; Martindale (1995), pp. 40–45. The Sienese painter, Martino di Bartolommeo painted the sixteen Virtues on the ceiling of the room (Dec. 1407–April 1408).

50 Fortini Brown (1988), pp. 37–42, cat. no. IV, pp. 261–5.

51 Southard (1980), I, pp. 354–8; G. Borghini in Brandi (1983), pp. 241–56; G. Solberg in Turner (1996), XXX, p. 232.

52 Rubinstein (1958), p. 190.

53 As confirmed by the plan of the first floor of the Palazzo Pubblico executed *c.* 1658 before major alterations were made to the building. See Norman (1999), pl. 58.

54 For detailed discussion of this scheme and its political meaning: Rubinstein (1958), pp. 190–207; Southard (1980), I, pp. 358–71; Solberg (1991), pp. 121–2, 223–33, 883–960.

55 Significantly the map of Rome is oriented towards the Sala del Mappamondo. For the links between this painting and Ambrogio Lorenzetti's *Mappamondo*: De Wesselow (2000), pp. 21–3.

56 Rubinstein (1958), p. 193.

57 There is also some evidence for such interest in the first half of the fourteenth century. Thus in 1330 Simone Martini was paid for painting Marcus Atilius Regulus for the Sala del Concistoro, and an entry for 1330 in a contemporary chronicle also records paintings of 'Roman stories' by Ambrogio Lorenzetti on the exterior of the Palazzo Pubblico.

58 For the impact that these changed circumstances had on the quality of art in the second half of the century, see the classic case made by Meiss (1951, ed. 1978). For more recent debates on this issue, see Van Os (1981); D. Norman in Norman (1995), I, pp. 177–95; Maginnis (1997), pp. 164–91; Steinhoff (2000).

59 See H. J. B. Maginnis in Turner (1996), XIX, p. 671.

60 A number of these are listed and discussed in Steinhoff (2000).

61 For a body of contemporary evidence that suggests this: Cohn (1992), pp. 244–80.

62 For an account of this altarpiece, its commission and iconography: Van Os (1984–90) II, pp. 44–7.

63 See C. Hicks in Turner (1996), XIX, p. 753.

64 For an account of this technique known as *sgraffito*: *Art in the Making* (1989), pp. 130–34.

65 See V. Wainwright in Turner (1996), XXIII, pp. 95–6; G. Chelazzi Dini in Chelazzi Dini, Angelini, and Sani (1998), p. 185.

66 Van Os (1984–90) II, pp. 36–9.

67 See chapter 2, p. 111.

68 Borsook (1980), p. 47; C. B. Strehlke in *Painting in Renaissance Siena* (1988), pp. 261–3.

69 Carli (1981), p. 235; Bock (1986), p. 32; Boskovits (1988), pp. 35–7; Eisler (1996), p. 24; G. Chelazzi Dini in Chelazzi Dini, Angelini and Sani (1998), pp. 197–8.

70 See Neri Lusanna (1981), who cautiously proposes the name of Francesco di Valdambrino as the sculptor of the group. L. Bellosi in *Scultura dipinta* (1987), cat. no. 43, pp. 116–18, prefers to attribute it to Giovanni di Turino on the basis of stylistic similarities between the *Madonna of the Magnificat* and the sculptor's work on the baptistery font (see pl. 90).

71 See Freuler (1994a), pp. 272–4, and docs 32, 67–8, 96, pp. 420, 425, 431.

72 See the entries by H. Teubner and I. Bahr in Riedl and Seidel (1985–) II.1.2, pp. 505–6, 546–7.

73 See the document dated 12 November 1399 cited by I. Bahr in ibid., p. 545.

74 See V. Wainwright in Turner (1996), II, p. 21.

75 Freuler (1987), pp. 570–77.

76 Ibid., pp. 571–2; (1994a), pp. 341–67, and docs 68, 23, 58, 91–4, 105–6, 110, pp. 417, 419, 424, 430, 432.

77 For an account of the life of Fra Tommaso and his probable influence over the choice of imagery for the altarpiece: Freuler (1987), pp. 571–7.

4 Renaissance Painting

1 Hicks (1960); cf. Ascheri (1985), pp. 11–56, (1993), pp. 7–15; Ascheri and Pertici (1996); Catoni (2000), pp. 33–4, 43–4.

2 Ascheri (1985), pp. 14–15; (1993), pp. 12, 19.

3 See C. B. Strehlke in *Painting in Renaissance Siena* (1988), pp. 33, 40, 47, 49, 53.

4 See Hook (1979), p. 59; M. Collareta in *Francesco di Giorgio e il Rinascimento* (1993), cat. no. 11, pp. 146–7, cat. no. 15, pp. 154–5.

5 A *biccherna* cover for 1479 shows the triumphal entry of the Sienese troops and their allies into Colle Val d'Elsa. See Borgia (1984), cat. no. 70, pp. 180–81.

6 Shaw (1996/7).

7 Pope-Hennessy (1985), pp. 210–11; Torriti (1988), pp. 154–8.

8 For perceptive analyses of this relief: White (1972), pp. 149–50; Bennett and Wilkins (1984), pp. 161–5.

9 Santi (1982), pp. 5–7, 34, 36, 38.

10 Another view of this chapel and its sculpted entrance is provided by a *biccherna* panel probably executed in 1526 by Domenico Beccafumi. See Borgia (1984), cat. no. 93, pp. 226–7. Between 1450 and 1451, the chapel of Saint Ansano was also decorated with sculpted reliefs depicting scenes from the saint's life.

11 Attributed to the Sienese builder and stoneworker, Guidoccio d'Andrea, possibly with the assistance of the young Francesco di Giorgio. For an account of the construction of the new church and its principal furnishings: Gallavotti Cavallero (1985), pp. 200–7.

12 Jenkens (1997); Nevola (2000), p. 43. This renaissance monument has recently undergone extensive restoration.

13 For these renaissance palaces in Siena: Torriti (1988), pp. 79, 310, 322; Jenkens (1999), (2001); Nevola (2000), pp. 41, 43–5.
14 Southard (1980), I, pp. 127–8; Torriti (1988), p. 30.
15 Hansen (1987). See also Friedman (1998), p. 335; Nevola (2000), p. 43.
16 It appears from the inventories of 1435 and 1439 that after placing the *Madonna delle Nevi* on the altar, the older image was hung on the wall beside the altar. A marginal note in the inventory of 1439 then records its subsequent removal to the church of Sant'Ansano. It was there that the *Madonna degli occhi grossi* was subsequently identified in the mid-nineteenth century. The account given by the fifteenth-century chronicler Niccolò di Ventura broadly confirms this chain of events.
17 The contract is published in Pope-Hennessy (1939), pp. 44–6, n. 58.
18 Van Os (1984–90), II, p. 174. When the present book was in press, a detailed study of the altarpiece was published by Israëls (2003). She argues that: the idea of the altar chapel originated during Turino di Matteo's lifetime; the altar was set against the wall of the Porta del Perdono (cf. pl. 57); and the choice of imagery was owing to the advice of Cardinal Antonio Casini, Bishop of Siena (1408–27).
19 See chapter 2, pp. 76, 78, 92–3. The inscription in Latin reads: 'FIDIS IN ME SIENA ERIS GRATIA PLENA'.
20 Van Os (1984–90) II, pp. 169–74.
21 Dunkerton (1991), pp. 252–4; Israëls (2003), pp. 97–126, argues that the commissioner of this Roman altarpiece was Cardinal Antonio Casini (see note 18).
22 The painter thus apparently disregarded the instruction in the contract of 1430 that the altarpiece should also include a pinnacle panel of the Redeemer.
23 Sienese painters, such as Bartolo di Fredi and Taddeo di Bartolo, had already produced altarpieces depicting the Virgin and Christ Child with saints gathered in a common setting, but had still retained framing that separated the central group from the side figures. Altarpieces painted in the 1420s by Florentine painters, such as Masaccio and Fra Angelico, pursued similar aims. Gentile da Fabriano's greatly admired *Adoration of the Magi* altarpiece of 1423 for the Strozzi Chapel in Florence provided a striking precedent for an altarpiece comprising a single panel surmounted by three richly decorated arches. This was, however, an altarpiece with a narrative subject as its main image, a type that was already well established in Sienese art (see pls 58–61). A small painting by Sassetta of *Saint Martin dividing his Cloak for a Beggar* (Chigi Saracini Collection, Siena), which can be dated securely to 1433, provides good evidence that Sassetta had studied one of Masaccio's frescoes for the Brancacci Chapel (*c.* 1424–7) in Florence and was thus receptive to the example of Florentine painting at that time.
24 Sassetta had recently refined his skill in representing such settings in the predella of an altarpiece executed between *c.* 1423 and 1426 for the Arte della Lana (the guild of wool merchants). Plate 14 is one of the six surviving predella panels from this altarpiece. For illustration of the other predella panels: K. Christiansen in *Painting in Renaissance Siena* (1988), cat. nos 1a-f, pp.

64–79. For a detailed reconstruction of the altarpiece's original site and function: Israëls (2001).

25 The sculpted relief on the font by Donatello was completed by October 1427.

26 Van Os (1984–90), II, pp. 53–8; Freuler (1994b), pp. 90–92, docs 12–19, pp. 96–8.

27 Freuler (1994b), pp. 90–91, docs 14–18, pp. 97–8.

28 Ibid., p. 82, doc. 3, p. 94.

29 See Freuler and Mallory (1991); Freuler (1994b), pp. 84–7.

30 Freuler (1994b), pp. 88–9.

31 Gallavotti Cavallero (1985), pp. 147–73.

32 Ibid., pp. 153, 156–7; K. Christiansen and C. B. Strehlke in *Painting in Renaissance Siena* (1988), pp. 13–15, 47–51.

33 Identified by Galavotti Cavallero (1985), p. 186.

34 C. B. Strehlke in *Painting in Renaissance Siena* (1988), p. 49.

35 Alberti, 'I like to see someone who admonishes and points out to us what is happening there . . .' Alberti (1435–6), Eng. trans. (1971), p. 78. See Baxandall (1972), pp. 71–4, who relates Alberti's recommendation to the choric figures commonly used in plays at that time.

36 C. B. Strehlke in *Painting in Renaissance Siena* (1988), pp. 48, 50, 249–50.

37 Gallavotti Cavallero (1985), pp. 165, 168–72, C. B. Strehlke in *Painting in Renaissance Siena* (1988), cat. no. 42, pp. 254–7.

38 Together with a monochrome painting of the rector and brothers of the hospital serving food to patients. This had been executed by another painter, on the other side of the wall on which the *Madonna della Misericordia* had been painted.

39 In 1434 the painter was paid for his design for the pavement panel in the north transept of the cathedral depicting *Sigismund Enthroned*. See Santi (1982), pp. 38–9, illus. p. 43. This was presumably based on a portrait of the emperor made during Sigismund's stay in Siena (1432–3).

40 Van Os (1974) pp. 16–30; Gallavotti Cavallero (1985), pp. 135–41, pp. 173–9; Torriti (1990), no. 204, pp. 249–52.

41 Van Os (1974), pp. 31, 54–61, who proposes two separate phases of work. Cf. Gallavotti Cavallero (1985), p. 180, who argues for a continuous, if interrupted, campaign of work.

42 For a detailed description of the frescoes and their iconography: Van Os (1974), pp. 31–53, 62–80.

43 See ibid., pp. 65–75 (but note that the paintings he attributes to Gualtieri di Giovanni are now generally attributed to Agostino di Marsiglio). See also A. Angelini in Chelazzi Dini, Angelini and Sani (1998), pp. 264–71.

44 Christiansen (1997).

45 Southard (1980), I, pp. 268–70.

46 Eisenberg (1981); Christiansen (1994).

47 K. Christiansen in *Painting in Renaissance Siena* (1988), cat. nos 18a–c, pp. 146–51; Norman (1999), pp. 87, 93–101.

48 Southard (1980), I, pp. 249–52; G. Borghini in Brandi (1983), p. 270. As early

as 1425 the south wall of the room had been decorated with Saint Bernardino's IHS monogram.

49 A series of ten small panel paintings depicting scenes from the life of Saint Catherine also appears to have been commissioned from the Sienese painter Giovanni di Paolo at about the same date. Probably the first complete painted cycle of Catherine's life, these paintings focus on the mystical and visionary aspects of her sanctity. For detailed discussion of the series and its possible commission by the Pizzicaiuoli, the guild of candlemakers and sellers of dry goods: C. B. Strehlke in *Painting in Renaissance Siena* (1988), cat. nos 38a–m, pp. 219–42.

50 Southard (1980), I, pp. 252–7; G. Borghini in Brandi (1983), pp. 256, 265. See also p. 174 of this chapter.

51 Southard (1980), I, pp. 165–71; G. Borghini in Brandi (1983), p. 162; Van Os (1984–90), II, p. 158; K. Christiansen and C. B. Strehlke in *Painting in Renaissance Siena* (1988), pp. 27, 36–7, 141, 250.

52 Framing the *Coronation of the Virgin*, on the left is a painting of Saint Catherine of Siena (extensively repainted in the seventeenth century) and on the right Saint Bernardino of Siena holding a model of Siena. See Brandi (1983), pls 181, 182. These have been attributed to Sano di Pietro but their date of execution is not known. Thus another room in the Palazzo Pubblico was embellished with paintings of these newly canonised Sienese saints.

53 Southard (1980), I, pp. 173–6; G. Borghini in Brandi (1983), p. 167.

54 Cairola and Carli (1963), pp. 209–10; Southard (1980), I, pp. 180–7; G. Borghini in Brandi (1983), pp. 188–93.

55 Southard (1980), I, pp. 189–90; G. Borghini in Brandi (1983), p. 193; Torriti (1990), no. 241, pp. 198–200.

56 In the original the text reads: 'VERGINE MADRE A DIO CARA CONSORTE/ SEL TUO CALISTO E DEGNIO A TANTO DONO/ A SIENA NO[N] TOR[N]AMI ALTRE CHE MORTO'.

57 C. B. Strehlke in *Painting in Renaissance Siena* (1988), p. 40.

58 Piccolomini (ed. 1984), II, pp. 551–2; Eng. trans. (ed. 1951), p. 602.

59 Van Os (1987); (1984–90), II, pp. 193–214; cf. Palladino (1994). The latter's argument, based on careful reading of available documentary evidence, appears the more persuasive.

60 Thus Saints Anthony Abbot and Francis appear on Giovanni di Paolo's altarpiece while Saint James (Giacomo, in Italian) appears on Sano di Pietro's altarpiece. See also Palladino (1994), pp. 104–5.

61 Van Os (1984–90), II, pp. 184–9; B. Santi in *Mostra di opere d'arte restaurate* (1973–83), III, pp. 130–35.

62 The church remained the property of the Cinughi family until very recently. For its architecture, see M. Tafuri in *Francesco di Giorgio architetto* (1993), pp. 23, 34, who rejects the traditional attribution to Francesco di Giorgio, preferring to assign it to Antonio Federighi instead.

63 Thornton (1991), pp. 284–319; Welch (2000), pp. 296–301; P. L. Rubin in *Renaissance Florence: Art of the 1470s* (1999), pp. 314–15.

64 E. Callmann in Turner (1996), VI, pp. 4–6; Welch (2000), pp. 282–5.

65 Torriti (1990), no. 217, pp. 292–3 (attributing it to the workshop of Neroccio dei Landi and Francesco di Giorgio); C. Alessi in *Francesco di Giorgio e il Rinascimento* (1993), cat. no. 6, pp. 122–5.

66 For the relationship of Sienese to Florentine painting during this period, see K. Christiansen's introductory essay in *Painting in Renaissance Siena* (1988), pp. 30–34. For Filippo Lippi's year in Siena: Ruda (1993), pp. 13, 23, 67, 348, n.5; Holmes (1999) pp. 15, 19–20.

67 For Gentile da Fabriano's influence on Giovanni di Paolo: G. Damiani in Turner (1996), XII, pp. 715–16.

68 C. B. Strehlke in *Painting in Renaissance Siena* (1988), p. 50.

69 See H. J. Ebenhardt in Turner (1996), XII, pp. 733–4, XIX, pp. 305–7; A. Angelini in Chelazzi Dini, Angelini and Sani (1998), pp. 287–92.

70 Banker (1991); Gordon (1993); G. Chelazzi Dini in Chelazzi Dini, Angelini and Sani (1998), pp. 225–8.

71 See J. D. Draper in Turner (1996), XXXII, p. 103.

72 C. B. Strehlke in *Painting in Renaissance Siena* (1988), pp. 252–4; G. Damiani in Turner (1996), IX, p. 94; Ruda (1993), pp. 57–8.

5 Later Renaissance in Siena

1 A good summary of Sienese politics between 1487 and 1530 can be found in Jenkins (1972), pp. 431–2. For a detailed account of the fall of Siena: Hook (1979), ch. 9, pp. 172–95. For more recent accounts, but in Italian: M. L. Lenzi and E. Pellegrini in Barzanti, Catoni and De Gregorio (1995–7), I, pp. 439–68.

2 G. Chironi in Barzanti, Catoni and De Gregorio (1995–7), I, pp. 395–406; Hicks (1996).

3 See A. Bagnoli in *Domenico Beccafumi* (1990), cat. no. 67, pp. 336–9.

4 In imitation of what was believed to have occurred on the eve of the battle of Montaperti, the keys of the city were presented to the *Madonna del Voto* in the cathedral before the battle of Camollia. A *biccherna* panel, attributed to Beccafumi, records this solemn event (for which, see Borgia, 1984, cat. no. 93, p. 226). In addition, at the suggestion of the pious Margherita de' Bichi, who had a particular devotion to the Virgin of the Immaculate Conception, the Sienese hereafter observed the feast of the Immaculate Conception with particular reverence.

5 Two years earlier, in 1550, the keys of the city had again been presented to the *Madonna del Voto* with the request that the Virgin liberate the Sienese from the presence of the imperial garrison in the newly constructed fortress. The painting was then carried round the city in procession.

6 See Clough (1995); N. Adam in Turner (1996), XXIV, p. 567. Note that Duccio's cathedral high altarpiece was moved in 1506, not 1505, as stated by the latter.

7 The ciborium was originally made for the high altar of the church of the

Spedale di Santa Maria della Scala, for which see A. Bagnoli in *Francesco di Giorgio e il Rinascimento* (1993), cat. no. 9, pp. 204–5.

8 For Agostino Chigi as a patron: Rowland (1986). For Sodoma's work for the Chigi: Sricchia Santoro (1982); E. Carli in Turner (1996), XXIX, pp. 2–3. For Peruzzi's work for the Chigi: N. Adam in Turner (1996), XXIV, p. 530.

9 A. Angelini in Chelazzi Dini, Angelini and Sani (1998), pp. 310–11.

10 For the cathedral pavement: Santi (1982), pp. 34, 58–63. For Beccafumi's work on the pavement: M. Collareta in *Domenico Beccafumi* (1990), pp. 652–76; B. Santi in Torriti (1998), pp. 200–15; Dubus (1999), pp. 32–8.

11 Hook (1979), pp. 165–6, 205–6; G. Glénisson-Delanée in Barzanti, Catoni and De Gregorio (1995–7), I, pp. 407–22.

12 F. Sricchia Santoro and A. Bagnoli in *Francesco di Giorgio e il Rinascimento* (1993), pp. 420, 440, 444–5.

13 Seidel (1979b).

14 Seidel (1984); A. Bagnoli in *Francesco di Giorgio e il Rinascimento* (1993), cat. no. 95, pp. 440–43; T. Henry in Henry and Kanter (2002), cat. nos 12–16, pp. 168–72.

15 These stylistic features are also evident in the three predella panels from the altarpiece: the *Christ in the House of Simon the Pharisee* (National Gallery of Ireland, Dublin), the *Lamentation over the Dead Christ* (Pollok House, Glasgow), and the *Martyrdom of Saint Catherine of Alexandria* (Sterling and Francine Clark Art Institute, Williamstown, Mass.).

16 See C. E. Gilbert in Turner (1996), XXVIII, pp. 699–701, esp. pp. 699–700.

17 See P. Marani in Turner (1996), XI, p. 693. For the Bichi frescoes as a whole: F. Sricchia Santoro in *Francesco di Giorgio e il Rinascimento* (1993), cat. nos 96a/b, pp. 444–7; Henry and Kanter (2002), p. 21, cat. no. 11, p. 168.

18 For the library entrance façade and its embellishment: Cecchi (1982), pp. 8, 11; G. Agosti and V. Farinella in *Domenico Beccafumi* (1990), pp. 581–3; Toracca (1998), pp. 241–2.

19 Cecchi (1982), pp. 8–9; B. Sani in Chelazzi Dini, Angelini and Sani (1998), pp. 326–7; Toracca (1998), p. 243.

20 See P. Scarpellini in Turner (1996), XXIV, p. 830; Toracca (1998), pp. 219–30.

21 Cecchi (1982), pp. 9–10; Toracca (1998), p. 245.

22 Toracca (1998), p. 245, argues, however, that the coat-of-arms, executed by a local sculptor, may have been placed there before the ceiling paintings were executed. The paintings could, therefore, date to after Pius III's death in October 1503.

23 Beck (1985), p. 142, n. 5, publishes the relevant entries from the account books of the cathedral Opera.

24 Reproduced in Toracca (1998), pp. 247–52.

25 Cecchi (1982), p. 37; Torriti (1988), p. 279; Toracca (1998), p. 250.

26 Elected in 1501, Bandello remained in office until his death in 1506. For further discussion about the two supposed portraits of Perugino and Raphael, see Toracca (1998), p. 292.

27 Apart from Pintoricchio's paintings, the library was embellished with two further works of art. These were the marble sculpted group of the Three Graces that stands today at the centre of the library and the plaster copy of the *Expulsion of Adam and Eve* from the Fonte Gaia (see pl. 65) located over the inner doorway (see pl. 120). The *Three Graces*, which is a superior Roman copy of a Greek original, was acquired by the Cardinal in Rome and remained in his palace until his death in 1503. It was then brought to Siena and placed in the library on a specially carved pedestal. At about the same time, the copy of Jacopo della Quercia's sculpted relief was also installed in the library.

28 See Zarrilli (1995), p. 51, correcting earlier authors who give the date as 1509.

29 Clough (1995), p. 391. For a detailed study of the palace itself: Ferrari, Valentini and Viti (1985).

30 These are the accounts of the room given by Abbot Giovanni Girolamo Carli (1770s, published in Davies, 1961, appendix III, pp. 571–2) and Guglielmo della Valle (1782–6), III, pp. 319–22. Carli also refers to a painted frieze of 'deities and virtues etc' in a neighbouring room. This is generally assumed to be the small room next to the room under discussion. It probably functioned as Pandolfo's private study. Three fragments of this frieze survive today in the gallery of Princeton University and have been identified as paintings of Minerva, Prudence (or Dialectic) and an unknown figure. The *Minerva* is generally attributed to the Umbrian painter Girolamo Genga.

31 Davies (1961), cat. nos 910, 911, 3929, pp. 436–9, 472–9, 485–6; F. Sricchia Santoro in *Domenico Beccafumi* (1990), pp. 590–2, cat. nos 49a/b, pp. 260–62; Torriti (1990) cat. nos 333, 334, pp. 328–33; Clough (1995), pp. 392–3; Henry and Kanter (2002), pp. 72–3, cat. nos 90, 91, pp. 224–5.

32 Sricchia Santoro (1982) has, however, attributed it to Genga and Giacomo Pacchiarotto. See also Torriti (1990), pp. 330–31.

33 A painted maiolica plate of *c.* 1520, now in the Ashmolean Museum, Oxford, and illustrated in Clough (1995), pl. 110, offers an indication of what the lost painting probably looked like.

34 A pen and ink drawing, attributed to Signorelli, now in the British Museum, probably records one part of the lost painting's composition. See Popham and Pouncey (1950), I, cat. no. 236, pp. 146–7, pl. CCVIII.

35 Now located in the Pinacoteca and in the offices of the Superintendent of Art in Siena. See S. Fraschetti in *Domenico Beccafumi* (1990), cat. no. 190, pp. 552–3.

36 In London, the Victoria and Albert Museum; Paris, the Louvre; and Hamburg, Museum für Kunst und Gewerbe. One of the Hamburg tiles is illustrated in Clough (1995), pl. 111.

37 See Davies (1961), p. 475.

38 Ferrara, Valentini and Viti (1985), pp. 145–6.

39 G. Agosti in *Francesco di Giorgio e il Rinascimento* (1993), p. 490.

40 Coor (1961), 57–61, cat. no. 63, pp. 191–2. This author, on grounds of style, dates the portrait to 1475–80. Shapley (1979), I, pp. 343–4, and Campbell (1990), p. 91, however, propose a date of *c.* 1490.

41 The Latin text on the lower edge of the painting reads, in translation, in full as: 'Whatever a human being is permitted to attain, I attain through my wondrous art. [Yet] I achieve nothing, for I, a [mere] mortal compete through art with the gods.' Translation from Coor (1961), pp. 191–2.
42 For a useful summary of conduct books on the subject of women's behaviour: King (1998), pp. 20–39. See also the perceptive comments made on this subject by Simons (1988); Jacobus (1998), pp. 184–7.
43 Coor (1961), p. 59.
44 Sricchia Santoro (1988), cat. nos 14a–c, pp. 83–9, esp. p. 84.
45 For a more detailed exploration of the role of exemplary women as models of behaviour for renaissance women: Ajmar (2000).
46 A. De Marchi in *Domenico Beccafumi* (1990), cat. no. 85, pp. 426–7; P. Giannattasio in Torriti (1998), pp. 240–1.
47 Vasari (1568; ed. 1960–), V, pp. 165–6; Eng. trans (1963), III, p. 141.
48 As indicated by Vasari (1568; ed. 1960–), IV, pp. 319–20; Eng. trans (1963), II, pp. 294–6. See also Freedberg (1971), p. 65.
49 A. Angelini and A. Pinelli in *Domenico Beccafumi* (1990), pp. 126–7, 622–36; B. Sani in Chelazzi Dini, Angelini and Sani (1998), pp. 366–7.
50 A. Pinelli in *Domenico Beccafumi* (1990), pp. 630–36.
51 R. Guerrini in Torriti (1998), cat. no. P31, p. 97.
52 L. Martini in *Domenico Beccafumi* (1990), p. 600.
53 Ibid., pp. 600–06, 617.
54 Published in Cust (1906), pp. 295–6.
55 As noted by L. Martini in *Domenico Beccafumi* (1990), p. 621, n. 27, the coat-of-arms of this family appears over the doorway of the building in Beccafumi's *Betrothal* (see pl. 137).
56 As noted by Hayum (1976), p. 37, 179–80, Sodoma is the only painter who is referred to as 'master' or 'mister' in the contract of December 1518.
57 Sricchia Santoro (1988), pp. 45–52. See also B. Sani in Chelazzi Dini, Angelini and Sani (1998), pp. 359–60.
58 See Hayum (1976), pp. 4–36; E. Carli in Turner (1996), XXIX, pp. 1–3; B. Sani in Chelazzi Dini, Angelini and Sani (1998), pp. 335–40.
59 Painted between 1512 and 1514. See Freedberg (1971), pp. 34–8, esp. pp. 36–7; N. Penny in Turner (1996), XXV, p. 901.
60 See F. Sricchia Santoro in Turner (1996), III, p. 468.
61 B. Sani in Chelazzi Dini, Angelini and Sani (1998), p. 360; M. Folchi in Torriti (1998), p. 87.
62 Illustrated in *Domenico Beccafumi* (1990), fig. 23, p. 616. See also n. 82 below.
63 A similar impulse to celebrate the identity of specific confraternity members can be seen in the presence of family coats-of-arms in eight of the fresco paintings. These probably record the families of those members who took a prominent role in organising and financing the project. For the identification of three of these coats-of-arms, see L. Martini in *Domenico Beccafumi* (1990), p. 606.

64 See chapter 4, p. 207.

65 Torriti (1988), pp. 238, 240, 243; H. Stein Keck in Riedl and Seidel (1985–), II.1.1, pp. 80–84.

66 Hayum (1976), pp. 196–7; Torriti (1988), pp. 258–9; I. Bahr, S. Hansen, W. Loseries and P. A. Riedl in Riedl and Seidel (1985–) II.1.2, pp. 562–88.

67 The two other painters who probably worked on this scheme were Giacomo Pacchiarotti and Vincenzo Tamagni (a San Gimignanese painter who had worked with Raphael on the Vatican Logge). See Sricchia Santoro (1988), pp. 43, 53–4; P. A. Riedl in Riedl and Seidel (1985–) II.1.1, pp. 136–42. The scheme was finally completed by two further painters early in the 17th century.

68 He may have painted the chapel in its entirety. Hayum (1976), pp. 198–200, suggests that the oil paintings by Francesco Vanni (executed in 1593–6) on the right wall and on the lower part of the entrance arch may be late sixteenth-century replacements for frescoes by Sodoma that had rapidly deteriorated. The cupola of the chapel was completely reconstructed after an earthquake of 1798.

69 Hayum (1976), pp. 48–51, also sees evidence of Sodoma exploiting his knowledge of ancient and contemporary Roman art in his painting of the chapel frescoes. For the Carafa chapel scheme: Geiger (1986).

70 See M. Maccherini in *Domenico Beccafumi* (1990), cat. no. 9, pp. 110–15. Such a location would also account for the subject matter of the altarpiece's predella, which in its original state depicted five scenes from the life of Saint Catherine. See M. Torriti in P. Torriti (1998) cat. nos P11, P12a/b, pp. 72–5. However, in 1735 the painting was recorded as on the altar of Saint Benedict within the church.

71 For the relevance of the altarpiece's subject for the Olivetan Order: Pike Gordley (1992).

72 These are *God the Father with Saints Mary Magdalen and Catherine of Siena* now in Lucca and the *Virgin and Christ Child with Saints* in the cathedral of Besançon, France. For the former, see Humfrey (1990) and for the latter, see Chastel (1990). Beccafumi could have seen both altarpieces in Fra Bartolommeo's workshop in the Dominican Observant priory of San Marco in Florence. The Dominican Observant priory at Santo Spirito (see pl. 8) in Siena could also have been a location where Beccafumi could have familiarised himself with Fra Bartolommeo's style of painting, principally through the work of Albertinelli, a close associate of the Dominican painter. Beccafumi himself painted an altarpiece for Santo Spirito in 1528 which, in terms of its figurative composition, again shows an appreciation of Fra Bartolommeo's altarpiece designs.

73 The predella shows five other scenes from the Passion. As noted in Torriti (1990), p. 361, they are generally attributed to an assistant of Sodoma's.

74 First noted by Sigismondo Tizio in his history of Siena (1513). See also R. Bartalini in *Domenico Beccafumi* (1990), cat. no. 46, pp. 246–9; B. Sani in Chelazzi Dini, Angelini and Sani (1998), p. 339.

75 Hayum (1976), pp. 18–22.
76 Illustrated in Chelazzi Dini, Angelini and Sani (1998), p. 328.
77 Vasari (1568; ed. 1960–), V, p. 385; Eng. trans. (1963), III, p. 288.
78 Most famously exemplified in the writings of Leonardo da Vinci. See Kemp (1997), pp. 111–12.
79 A. Angelini in *Domenico Beccafumi* (1990), cat. no. 19, p. 146.
80 M. Folchi in Torriti (1998), cat. P40, p. 116.
81 The vine leaves also correspond to the vine leaves on the Marsili coat-of-arms that is also located on the right-hand side of the altar frame.
82 Beccafumi had already explored such effects in the *Dormition of the Virgin* in the Oratory of San Bernardino. Both paintings probably owed their inspiration to Rosso's *Assumption of the Virgin* in the forecourt of the Santissima Annunziata in Florence. Beccafumi, however, imaginatively reworked this Florentine model into paintings of great originality and expressiveness.
83 Vasari (1568; ed. 1960–), V, pp. 167–8; Eng. trans. (1963), III, pp. 142–3. See also A. Angelini and A. M. Guiducci in *Domenico Beccafumi* (1990), cat. nos 21 and 25, pp. 152–3, 168–71; M. Folchi in Torriti (1998), cat. nos P50, P64, pp. 126–8, 139–42; Dubus (1999), pp. 136–40.
84 Vasari in his account of the painting describes a predella of five small scenes in tempera. Two of these, depicting scenes from the legend of Saint Michael, have been identified in the Carnegie Museum of Art, Pittsburgh. See A. M. Guiducci in *Domenico Beccafumi* (1990), cat. no. 26, pp. 172–3. The present predella below the altarpiece in San Niccolò al Carmine is seventeenth century. See Torriti (1988), p. 212.
85 As demonstrated in his 1496 'Sermons on Amos', published in translation by Gilbert (1980), pp. 157–8.
86 Ridolfi (1648; ed. 1914–24), I, p. 163.
87 Illustrated in Norman (1999), pl. 58.
88 See the documents (nos 141, 143–7) published by S. Moscadelli and C. Zarrilli (eds) in *Domenico Beccafumi* (1990), pp. 690–91.
89 Hayum (1976), p. 219; see also G. Borghini in Brandi (1983), p. 270.
90 Hayum (1976), pp. 219–20; Southard (1980), I, pp. 261–3.
91 Southard (1980), I, pp. 130–32; see also G. Borghini in Brandi (1983), p. 347, n. 335.
92 The Sistine Chapel ceiling was executed between 1508 and 1512. Beccafumi could therefore have seen it on one of his earlier visits to Rome. Perino del Vaga worked on ceiling paintings for Andrea Doria in the Palazzo del Principe, Genoa, between 1527 and *c.* 1533 (see Freedberg, 1971, pp. 169–70). As indicated on p. 282, Beccafumi visited Genoa *c.* 1530–34, interrupting his work on the Palazzo Pubblico ceiling to do so.
93 Jenkins (1972); A. Pinelli in *Domenico Beccafumi* (1990), pp. 636–51; R. Guerrini in Torriti (1998), cat. no. P71, pp. 153–63.
94 Executed in 1515, the seven surviving cartoons are now in the Victoria and Albert Museum, London. See N. Penny in Turner (1996), X, p. 902.
95 A similar kind of intention appears to have motivated the commissioning in

1424 of the wooden intarsia bench for the Sala del Mappamondo. See chapter 4, p. 206.

96 Jenkins (1972), p. 448.

97 For the construction and embellishment of this chapel: M. Butzek in *Alessandro VII Chigi* (2000), pp. 409–12.

Bibliography

Agazzari, F., *Gli Assempri di Fra Filippo degli Agazzari*, ed. P. Misciattelli, Siena, 1922.

Ajmar, M., 'Exemplary women in renaissance Italy: ambivalent models of behaviour?', in *Women in Italian Renaissance Culture and Society*, ed. L. Panizza, Oxford, 2000, pp. 244–64.

Alberti, L. B., *On Painting* (1435–6), trans. J. R. Spencer, 3rd ed., New Haven and London, 1971.

Alessandro VII Chigi (1599–1667): Il Papa Senese di Roma moderna (exh. cat., Palazzo Pubblico and Palazzo Chigi Zondadori, Siena, 2000), ed. A. Angelini, M. Butzek, B. Sani, Siena, 2000.

Argenziano, R., 'Le origini e lo sviluppo dell'iconografia della Madonna a Siena', in *L'immagine del Palio*, ed. M. A. Ceppari, M. Ciampolini, P. Turrini, Florence, 2001, pp. 92–109.

Art in the Making: Italian Painting before 1400 (exh. cat., National Gallery, London, 1989–90), London, 1989.

Ascheri, M., *Siena nel Rinascimento: istituzioni e sistema politico*, Siena, 1985.

——, *Il Rinascimento in Siena (1355–1555)*, Siena, 1993.

——, 'Siena in the fourteenth century: state, territory and culture', in *The Other Tuscany*, ed. T. W. Blonquist and M. F. Mazzaoui, Kalamazoo, 1994, pp. 163–97.

——, *Siena nella storia*, Milan, 2000.

——, and Pertici, P., 'La situazione politica senese del secondo Quattrocento (1456–79)', in *La Toscana al tempo di Lorenzo il Magnifico: politica, economia, cultura, arte*, Pisa, 1996, III, pp. 995–1012.

Bagnoli, A. (ed.), *Museo civico e diocesano d'arte sacra di Montalcino*, Siena, 1997.

——, *La Maestà di Simone Martini*, Milan, 2000.

Balestracci, D., and Piccinni, G., *Siena nel trecento: Assetto urbano e strutture edilizie*, Florence, 1977.

Banker, J. R., 'The program for the Sassetta altarpiece in the church of San Francesco in Borgo S. Sepolchro', *I Tatti Studies*, IV (1991), pp. 11–58.

Barzanti, R., Catoni, G., and De Gregorio, M. (eds), *Storia di Siena*, Siena, 1995–7, 3 vols.

Baskins, C., *Cassone Painting and Gender Formation in Early Modern Italy*, Cambridge, 1998.

Baxandall, M., *Painting and Experience in Fifteenth Century Italy*, Oxford, 1972.

Beatson, E. H., Steinhoff, J. B., and Muller, N. E., 'The Saint Victor altarpiece in Siena cathedral: a reconstruction', *Art Bulletin*, LXVIII (1986), pp. 610–31.

Beck, J., 'A new date for Pinturicchio's Piccolomini Library', *Paragone*, CCCCXIX–CCCCXXI (1985), pp. 140–43.

——, *Jacopo della Quercia*, New York, 1991, 2 vols.

Bellosi, L., '"Castrum pingatur in palatio" 2: Duccio e Simone Martini pittori di castelli senesi "a l'esemplo come erano"', *Prospettiva*, XXVIII (1982), pp. 41–55.

——, 'Per un contesto cimabuesco senese: a) Guido da Siena e il probabile Dietisalvi di Speme', *Prospettiva*, LXI (1991), pp. 6–20 (1991a).

——, 'Per un contesto cimabuesco senese: b) Rinaldo da Siena e Guido di Graziano', *Prospettiva*, LXII (1991), pp. 15–28 (1991b).

——, *Duccio: The Maestà*, trans. E. Currie, London, 1999.

Belting, H., 'The "Byzantine" Madonnas: new facts about their Italian origin and some observations on Duccio', *Studies in the History of Art*, XII (1982), pp. 7–22.

Ben-Aryeh Debby, N., 'War and peace: the description of Ambrogio Lorenzetti's frescoes in Saint Bernardino's 1425 Siena sermons', *Renaissance Studies*, XV (2001), pp. 272–86.

Bennett, B. A., and Wilkins, D. G., *Donatello*, Oxford, 1984.

Bernardino, Saint, *Le prediche volgari – predicazione del 1425 in Siena*, ed. C. Cannarozzi, Florence, 1958, 2 vols.

——, *Prediche volgari sul Campo di Siena 1427*, ed. C. Delcorno, Milan, 1989, 2 vols.

Bertelli, C., 'Masolino e Vecchietta a Castiglione Olona', *Paragone*, CCCCLI (1987), pp. 25–47.

Bock, H., *et al.*, *Gemäldegalerie Berlin. Gesamtverzeichnis der Gemälde: Complete Catalogue of the Paintings*, London, 1986.

Borgia, L., *et al.*, *Le Biccherne: tavole dipinte delle magistrature senesi (secoli XIII–XVIII)*, Rome, 1984.

Borsook, E., *The Mural Painters of Tuscany*, 2nd ed., London, 1980.

——, and Superbi Gioffredi, F., *Italian Altarpieces 1250–1550*, Oxford, 1994.

Boskovits, M., *Frühe Italienische Malerei, Gemäldegalerie Berlin*, Berlin, 1988.

Bowsky, W. M., 'The impact of the Black Death upon Sienese government and society', *Speculum*, XXXIX (1964), pp. 1–34.

——, *The Finance of the Commune of Siena, 1287–1355*, Oxford, 1970.

——, *A Medieval Commune: Siena under the Nine, 1287–1355*, Berkeley and London, 1981.

Brandi, C., 'Una Madonna del 1262 ed ancora il problema di Guido da Siena del 1221', *L'Arte*, I (1933), pp. 3–13.

—— (ed.), *Il Palazzo Pubblico in Siena: vicende, costruttive e decorazione*, Milan, 1983.

Brogi, A., 'Tempo e immagine del Duomo di Siena' in *La ricerca delle origini: Leggere l'arte della Chiesa*, ed. S. Bruschelli, Siena, 1998, pp. 45–66.
Brown, P. F., *Venetian Narrative Painting in the Age of Carpaccio*, New Haven and London, 1988.
Burke, S. M., '*The Martyrdom of the Franciscans* by Ambrogio Lorenzetti', *Zeitschrift für Kunstgeschichte*, LXV (2002), pp. 460–92.
Caferro, W., *Mercenary Companies and the Decline of Siena*, Baltimore and London, 1998.
Cairola, A., and Carli, E., *Il Palazzo Pubblico di Siena*, Rome, 1963.
Campbell, C. J., *The Game of Courting and the Art of the Commune of San Gimignano*, Princeton, 1997.
——, 'The lady in the council chamber: diplomacy and poetry in Simone Martini's *Maestà*', *Word and Image*, XIV (1998), pp. 371–86.
——, 'The city's new clothes: Ambrogio Lorenzetti and the poetics of space', *Art Bulletin*, LXXXIII (2001), pp. 240–58.
Campbell, L., *Renaissance Portraits*, New Haven and London, 1990.
Cannon, J., 'Dominican Patronage of the Arts in Central Italy: The *Provincia Romana, c.* 1220–*c.* 1320', Ph. D. diss., University of London, 1980.
——, 'Simone Martini, the Dominicans and the early Sienese polyptych', *Journal of the Warburg and Courtauld Institutes*, XLV (1982), pp. 69–93.
——, 'Pietro Lorenzetti and the history of the Carmelite Order', *Journal of the Warburg and Courtauld Institutes*, L (1987), pp. 18–28.
——, 'The creation, meaning, and audience of the early Sienese polyptych: evidence from the friars', in Borsook and Superbi Gioffredi (1994), pp. 41–79.
——, and Vauchez, A., *Margherita of Cortona and the Lorenzetti*, University Park, Penn., 1999.
——, and Williamson, B., *Art, Politics, and Civic Religion in Central Italy 1261–1352*, Aldershot, 2000.
Carli, E., *L'Arte nella basilica di S. Francesco*, Siena, 1971.
——, 'Le sculture del coro del Duomo di Siena, *Antichità viva*, XVII (1978), pp. 25–39.
——, *Il Duomo di Siena*, Genoa, 1979.
——, *La Pittura Senese del Trecento*, Milan, 1981.
——, *Simone Martini: La Maestà*, Milan, 1996.
——, and Imberciadori, J. V., *San Gimignano*, trans. H. R. MacLean, Milan, 1987.
Castelnuovo, E., *et al.*, *Ambrogio Lorenzetti: Il Buon Governo*, Milan, 1995.
Catoni, G., *A Short History of Siena*, trans. A. Mazzinghi, Pisa, 2000.
Cecchi, A., *The Piccolomini Library in the Cathedral of Siena*, trans. A. McCormick, Florence, 1982.
Chastel. A., 'Fra Bartolommeo's Carondelet altarpiece and the theme of the "Virgo in nubibus" in the High Renaissance', in *The Altarpiece in the Renaissance*, ed. P. Humfrey and M. Kemp, Cambridge, 1990, pp. 129–41.
Chelazzi Dini, G., Angelini, A., and Sani, B., *Five Centuries of Sienese Painting: From Duccio to the Birth of the Baroque*, trans. C. Warr, London and New York, 1998.

Christiansen, K., 'Simone Martini's altar-piece for the commune of Siena', *Burlington Magazine*, CXXXVI (1994), pp. 148–60.
——, 'Mattia di Nanni's intarsia bench for the Palazzo Pubblico, Siena', *Burlington Magazine*, CXXXIX (1997), pp. 372–86.
Clough, C., 'Pandolfo Petrucci e il concetto di "magnificenza"', in *Arte, committenza ed economia a Roma nelle corti di Rinascimento (1420–1530)*, ed. A. Esch and C. L. Frommel, Turin, 1995, pp. 383–97.
Cohn, S. K., Jr, *The Cult of Remembrance and the Black Death*, Baltimore and London, 1992.
Coor, G., *Neroccio dei Landi: 1447–1500*, Princeton, N.J., 1961.
Corrie, R. W., 'The political meaning of Coppo di Marcovaldo's Madonna and Child in Siena', *Gesta*, XXIX (1990), pp. 61–75.
——, 'Coppo di Marcovaldo's *Madonna del bordone* and the meaning of the bare-legged Christ Child in Siena and the East', *Gesta*, XXXV (1996), pp. 43–65.
Cronache senesi, ed. A. Lisini and F. Iacometti, *Rerum Italicarum Scriptores*, n.s. 15, 6, Bologna, 1931–9.
Cust, R. H., *Giovanni Antonio Bazzi*, London, 1906.
Davies, M., *The Earlier Italian Schools*, 2nd rev. ed., National Gallery, London, 1961.
Davies, M., *The Early Italian Schools before 1400*, rev. ed., ed. D. Gordon, National Gallery, London, 1988.
Derbes, A., 'Siena and the Levant in the later Dugento', *Gesta*, XXVIII (1989), pp. 190–204.
De Wesselow, T., 'The decoration of the west wall of the Sala del Mappamondo in Siena's Palazzo Pubblico', in Cannon and Williamson (2000), pp. 19–68.
Domenico Beccafumi e il suo tempo (exh. cat., Sant'Agostino, Siena, 1990), Milan, 1990.
Donato, M. M., 'Hercules and David in the early decoration of the Palazzo Vecchio: manuscript evidence', *Journal of the Warburg and Courtauld Institutes*, LIV (1991), pp. 83–98.
Dubus, P., *Domenico Beccafumi*, trans. M. Taylor, Paris, 1999.
Dundes, A., and Falassi, A., *La Terra in Piazza: An Interpretation of the Palio of Siena*, Berkeley and London, 1983.
Dunkerton, J., *et al.*, *Giotto to Dürer: Early Renaissance Painting in the National Gallery*, New Haven and London, 1991.
Eisenberg, M., 'The first altar-piece for the "Cappella dei Signori" of the Palazzo Pubblico in Siena: "... tales figure sunt adeo pulchre ..."', *Burlington Magazine*, CXXIII (1981), pp. 134–48.
Eisler, C., *Masterworks in Berlin: A City's Paintings Reunited*, Boston, New York, Toronto, London, 1996.
Fehm, S. A., *Luca di Tommè: A Sienese Fourteenth-Century Painter*, Carbondale, Kan and Edwardsville, Ill., 1986.
Ferrari, A., Valentini, R., Viti, M., 'Il Palazzo del Magnifico a Siena', *Bollettino Senese Storia Patria,* XCII (1985), pp. 107–53.
Fortini Brown, P., *Venetian Narrative Painting in the Age of Carpaccio*, New Haven and London, 1988.

Francesco di Giorgio architetto (exh. cat., Palazzo Pubblico, Siena, 1993), ed. F. P. Fiore and M. Tafuri, Milan, 1993.
Francesco di Giorgio e il Rinascimento a Siena 1450–1500 (exh. cat., Sant'Agostino, Siena, 1993), ed. L. Bellosi, Milan, 1993.
Freedberg, S., *Painting in Italy 1500–1600*, rev. ed., Harmondsworth, 1971.
Freuler, G., 'Andrea di Bartolo, Fra Tommaso d'Antonio Caffarini and Sienese Dominicans in Venice, *Art Bulletin*, LXIX (1987), pp. 570–86.
Freuler, G., *Bartolo di Fredi Cini*, Disentis, 1994 (1994a).
Freuler, G., 'Sienese quattrocento painting in the service of spiritual propaganda', in Borsook and Superbi Gioffredi (1994), pp. 81–116 (1994b).
Freuler, G., and Mallory, M., 'Sano di Pietro's Bernardino altar-piece for the Compagnia della Vergine in Siena, *Burlington Magazine*, CXXXIII (1991), pp. 186–92.
Friedman, D., 'Monumental urban form in the late medieval Italian commune: loggias and the Mercanzie of Bologna and Siena', *Renaissance Studies*, XII (1998), pp. 325–40.
Frugoni, C., *Pietro and Ambrogio Lorenzetti*, trans. L. Pelletti, Antella (Florence) 1988.
——, *A Distant City: Images of Urban Experience in the Medieval World*, trans. W. McCuaig, Princeton, 1991.
Gallavotti Cavallero, D., *Lo Spedale di Santa Maria della Scala: vicenda di una committenza artistica*, Pisa, 1985.
——, 'Pietro, Ambrogio e Simone, 1335, una questione di affreschi perduti', *Prospettiva*, XLVIII (1987), pp. 69–74.
Gardner, J., 'Guido da Siena, 1221 and Tommaso da Modena', *Burlington Magazine*, CCXXI (1979), pp. 107–8.
Gardner, J., 'Altars, altarpieces, and art history: legislation and usage' in Borsook and Superbi Gioffredi (1994), pp. 5–39.
Garrison, E. B., *Italian Romanesque Panel Painting: An Illustrated Index*, Florence, 1949.
Geiger, G. L., *Filippino Lippi's Carafa Chapel: Renaissance Art in Rome*, Kirksville, Miss., 1986.
Ghiberti, L., *I commentari* (*c.* 1447–55), ed. O. Morisani, Naples, 1947.
Gibbs, R., 'In search of Ambrogio Lorenzetti's Allegory of Justice: Changes to the frescoes in the Palazzo Pubblico', *Apollo*, CXLIX (1999), pp. 11–16.
Gigli, G., *Diario sanese* (1723), 3 vols, Bologna, 1974.
Gilbert, C. E., *Italian Art 1400–1500: Sources and Documents*, Englewood Cliffs, N.J., 1980.
Gillerman, D. M., 'Cosmopolitanism and *campanilismo*: Gothic and Romanesque in the Siena Duomo façade', *Art Bulletin*, LXXXI (1999), pp. 437–55.
Goffen, R., *Spirituality in Conflict: Saint Francis and Giotto's Bardi Chapel*, University Park, Penn., and London, 1988.
Goldthwaite, R., *Wealth and the Demand for Art in Italy*, Baltimore and London, 1993.
Gordon, D., 'The reconstruction of Sassetta's altar-piece for S. Francesco, Borgo San Sepolchro, a postscript', *Burlington Magazine*, CXXXV (1993), pp. 620–23.

Greenstein, J. M, 'The vision of peace: meaning and representation in Ambrogio Lorenzetti's *Sala della pace* cityscapes', *Art History*, XI (1988), pp. 492–510.
Gregory, J., 'The *Credo* of the Siena Cathedral Sacristy (1411–12)', *Renaissance Studies*, XII (1998), pp. 206–27.
Hansen, S., *Die Loggia della Mercanzia in Siena*, Worms, 1987.
Hayum, A., *Giovanni Antonio Bazzi – 'Il Sodoma'*, London, 1976.
Heal, B., '"Civitas Virginis"? The significance of civic dedication to the Virgin for the development of Marian imagery in Siena before 1311', in Cannon and Williamson (2000), pp. 295–305.
Henry, T., and Kanter, L., *Luca Signorelli: The Complete Paintings*, London, 2002.
Hicks, D. L., 'Sienese society in the Renaissance', *Comparative Studies in Society and History*, II (1960), pp. 412–20.
——, 'The Sienese oligarchy and the rise of Pandolfo Petrucci, 1487–97', in *La Toscana al tempo di Lorenzo il Magnifico: politica, economia, cultura, arte*, Pisa, 1996, III, pp. 1051–72.
Hoeniger, C., *The Renovation of Paintings in Tuscany, 1250–1500*, Cambridge, 1995.
Holmes, M., *Filippo Lippi: The Carmelite Painter*, New Haven and London, 1999.
Hook, J., *Siena: A City and its History*, London, 1979.
Hueck, I., 'La tavola di Duccio e la Compagnia delle Laudi di Santa Maria Novella', in *La Maestà di Duccio restaurata*, ed. L. Berti and A. Petrioli Tofani, Florence, 1990, pp. 33–46.
Humfrey, P., 'Fra Bartolommeo, Venice and Saint Catherine of Siena', *Burlington Magazine*, CXXXII (1990), pp. 476–83.
Israëls, M., 'Sassetta's Arte della Lana altar-piece and the cult of Corpus Domini in Siena', *Burlington Magazine*, XCLIII (2001), pp. 532–43.
——, *Sassetta's Madonaa della Neve: An Image of Patronage*, Leiden, 2003.
Jacobus, L., 'Piety and propriety in the Arena Chapel', *Renaissance Studies*, XII (1998), pp. 177–205.
Jenkens, A. Lawrence, 'Pius II and his Loggia in Siena', in *Pratum Romanum: Richard Krautheimer zum 100 Geburtstag*, ed. R. L. Colella *et al.*, Weisbaden, 1997, pp. 199–214.
——, 'Pius II's nephews and the politics of architecture at the end of the fifteenth century in Siena', *Bullettino Senese di Storia Patria*, CVI (1999), pp. 68–114.
——, 'Caterina Piccolomini and the Palazzo delle Papesse in Siena', in *Beyond Isabella: Secular Women Patrons of Art in Renaissance Italy*, ed. S. E. Reiss and D. G. Wilkins, Kirksville, Miss., 2001, pp. 77–92.
Jenkins, M., 'The iconography of the Hall of the Consistory in the Palazzo Pubblico, Siena', *Art Bulletin*, LIV (1972), pp. 430–51.
Kemp, M., *Behind the Picture: Art and Evidence in the Italian Renaissance*, New Haven and London, 1997.
Kempers, B., *Painting, Power and Patronage: The Rise of the Professional Artist in Renaissance Italy*, trans. B. Jackson, London, 1992.
——, 'Icons, altarpieces and civic ritual in Siena cathedral, 1100–1530', in *City and Spectacle in Medieval Europe*, eds B. A. Hainawalt and K. L. Reyerson, Minneapolis and London, 1994, pp. 89–136.

King, C. E., *Renaissance Women Patrons: Wives and Widows in Italy c. 1300–1550*, Manchester, 1998.
Kupfer, M., 'The lost wheel map of Ambrogio Lorenzetti', *Art Bulletin*, LXXBIII (1996), pp. 286–310.
Leoncini, A., *I tabernacoli di Siena: arte e devozione popolare*, Siena, 1994.
Lunghi, E., *The Basilica of St Francis at Assisi*, trans. C. Evans, London, 1996.
Maginnis, H. B. J., 'Pietro Lorenzetti's Carmelite Madonna: a reconsideration', *Pantheon*, XXXIII (1975), pp. 10–16.
——, 'The Guidoriccio controversy: notes and observations', *Revue d'art canadienne (Canadian Art Review)*, XV (1988), pp. 137–44 (1988a).
——, 'The lost façade frescoes from Siena's Ospedale di Santa Maria della Scala', *Zeitschrift für Kunstgeschichte*, LI (1988), pp. 180–94 (1988b).
——, 'Chiarimenti documentari: Simone Martini, i Memmi e Ambrogio Lorenzetti, *Rivista d'arte*, XLI (1989), pp. 3–23.
——, 'Ambrogio Lorenzetti's *Presentation in the Temple*', *Studi di storia dell'arte*, II (1991), pp. 33–50.
——, *Painting in the Age of Giotto: A Historical Reevaluation*, University Park, Penn., 1997.
——, *The World of the Early Sienese Painter*, University Park, Penn., 2001.
Mallory, M., *The Sienese Painter Paolo di Giovanni Fei c. 1345–1411* (Ph. D. diss., University of Michigan, 1965), Ann Arbor, 1976.
——, and Freuler, G., 'Sano di Pietro's Bernardino altar-piece for the Compagnia della Vergine in Siena', *Burlington Magazine*, CXXXIII (1991), pp. 186–92.
——, and Moran, G., 'New evidence concerning Guidoriccio', *Burlington Magazine*, CXXVIII (1986), pp. 250–6.
Martindale, A., 'The problem of Guidoriccio', *Burlington Magazine*, CXXVIII (1986), pp. 259–73.
——, *Simone Martini*, Oxford, 1988.
——, 'The pope in the palace: the Alexander cycle, Siena', *History Today*, XLV (1995), pp. 40–45.
Meiss, M., *Painting in Florence and Siena after the Black Death* (1951), Princeton, 1978.
Mina, G. A., 'Coppo di Marcovaldo's Madonna del Bordone', in Cannon and Williamson (2000), pp. 237–93.
Mongellaz, J., 'Reconsidération de la distribution des rôles à l'intérieur du groupe des Maîtres de la Sacristie de la cathédrale de Sienne', *Paragone*, XXXVI (1985), pp. 73–89.
Moran, G., 'An investigation regarding the equestrian portrait of Guidoriccio da Fogliano in the Siena Palazzo Pubblico', *Paragone*, CCCXXXIII (1977), pp. 81–8.
——, and Mallory, M., *Guido Riccio: A Guide to the Controversy for Tourists, Scholars, Students and Art Librarians*, Siena, 2000.
Mostra di opere d'arte restaurate nelle province di Siena e Grosseto, 3 vols, Genoa, 1979–83.
Musacchio, J. M., *The Art and Ritual of Childbirth in Renaissance Italy*, New Haven and London, 1999.

Mussolin, M., 'Il convento di Santo Spirito di Siena e i regolari osservanti di San Domenico', *Bullettino Senese di Storia Patria*, CIV (1997), pp. 7–193.

Neri Lusanna, E., 'Un episodio di collaborazione tra scultori e pittori nella Siena del primo Quattrocento: la "Madonna del Magnificat" di Sant'Agostino', *Mitteilungen des Kunsthistorischen Institutes in Florenz*, XXV (1981), pp. 324–40.

Nevola, F., '"Per ornato della città": Siena's Strada Romana and fifteenth-century urban renewal', *Art Bulletin*, LXXXII (2000), pp. 26–50.

Norman, D. (ed.), *Siena, Florence and Padua: Art, Society and Religion 1280–1400*, 2 vols, New Haven and London, 1995.

——, 'Pisa, Siena and the Maremma: a neglected aspect of Ambrogio Lorenzetti's paintings for the Sala dei Nove', *Renaissance Studies*, XI (1997), pp. 310–57.

——, *Siena and the Virgin: Art and Politics in a Late Medieval City State*, New Haven and London, 1999.

——, 'An abbess and a painter: Emilia Pannocchieschi d'Elci and a fresco from the circle of Simone Martini', *Renaissance Studies*, XIV (2000), pp. 273–300.

——, 'Siena, Italy and Europe: a reconsideration of Simone Martini's *Maestà*' in *Making Renaissance Connections*, ed. G. Neher, Aldershot (forthcoming).

L'Oro di Siena: Il Tesoro di Santa Maria della Scala (exh. cat., Spedale di Santa Maria della Scala, Siena, 1996–9), Siena, 1996.

Painting in Renaissance Siena, 1420–1500 (exh. cat., Metropolitan Museum of Art, New York, 1988–9), New York, 1988.

Palladino, P., '"Pittura in una casa di vetro": un riesame e una proposta sul programma decorativo di Pio II per la cattedrale di Pieza', *Prospettiva*, LXXVI (1994), pp. 100–08.

Parsons, G., '"Unità nella diversità": civil religion and the palio of Siena', *The Italianist*, XVII (1997), pp. 176–203.

——, *Perspectives on Civil Religion*, Aldershot, 2001.

Pecori, L., *Storia della terra di San Gimignano* (1853), Rome, 1975.

Piccolomini, A. S. (Pius II), *Pii II Commentarii rerum memorabilium que temporibus suis contigerunt*, ed. A. van Heck, 2 vols, Vatican City, 1984. Eng. trans. F. A. Gragg and L. C. Gabel as *The Commentaries of Pius II*, Northampton, 1951.

Pike Gordley, B., 'A Dominican Saint for the Benedictines: Beccafumi's *Stigmatisation of Saint Catherine*', *Zeitschrift für Kunstgeschichte*, LV (1992), pp. 394–412.

Polzer, J., 'Simone Martini's Guidoriccio da Fogliano: a new appraisal in the light of a recent technical investigation, *Jahrbuch der Berliner Museen*, XXV (1983), pp. 103–41.

——, 'The technical evidence and the origin and meaning of Simone Martini's *Guidoriccio* fresco in Siena', *Revue d'art canadienne (Canadian Art Review)*, XII (1985), pp. 143–8.

——, 'Simone Martini's Guidoriccio fresco: the polemic concerning its origin reviewed and the fresco considered as serving the military triumph of a Tuscan

commune', *Revue d'art canadienne (Canadian Art Review)*, XIV (1987), pp. 16–69.
Pope-Hennessy, J., *Sassetta*, London, 1939.
——, *Italian Gothic Sculpture*, 3rd ed., New York, 1985.
Popham, A. E., and Pouncey, P., *Italian Drawings in the Department of Prints and Drawings in the British Museum: The Fourteenth and Fifteenth Centuries*, 2 vols, London, 1950.
Renaissance Florence: The Art of the 1470s (exh. cat., National Gallery, London, 1999–2000), London, 1999.
Richards, J., *Altichiero: An Artist and his Patrons in the Italian Trecento*, Cambridge, 2000.
Ridolfi, C. *Le maraviglie dell'arte* (1648), ed. D. F. von Hadeln, 2 vols, Berlin, 1914–24.
Riedl, P. A., and Seidel, M. (eds), *Die Kirchen von Siena*, Munich, 1985–.
Rowland, I. D., 'Render unto Caesar the things which are Caesar's: humanism and the arts in the patronage of Agostino Chigi', *Renaissance Quarterly*, XXXIX (1986), pp. 673–730.
Rubinstein, N., 'Political ideas in Sienese art: the frescoes by Ambrogio Lorenzetti and Taddeo di Bartolo in the Palazzo Pubblico', *Journal of the Warburg and Courtauld Institutes*, XXI (1958), pp. 179–207.
Ruda, J., *Fra Filippo Lippi: Life and Work with a Complete Catalogue*, London, 1993.
Santi, B., *Il pavimento del Duomo di Siena*, Florence, 1982.
Satkowski, J. I., *Duccio di Buoninsegna: The Documents and Early Sources*, ed. H.J.B. Maginnis, Athens, Ga., 2000.
Schmidt, V. M., 'Il trittico di Duccio alla National Gallery di Londra: la datazione, l'iconografia e il committente, *Prospettiva*, LXXXL (1996), pp. 19–30.
——, 'Altenburg: Thirteenth-century panel paintings from Siena', *Burlington Magazine*, CXLIII (2001), pp. 512–14.
'La sconfitta di Montaperto secondo il manoscritto di Niccolò di Giovanni di Francesco Ventura' (1442–3), in *Miscellenea storica senese*, ed. G. Porri, Siena, 1844, pp. 3–98.
Scultura dipinta: maestri di legname e pittori a Siena 1250–1450 (exh. cat., Pinacoteca Nazionale, Siena, 1987), 1987.
Seidel, M., 'Gli affreschi di Ambrogio Lorenzetti nel chiostro di San Francesco a Siena: ricostruzione e datazione', *Prospettiva*, XVIII (1979), pp. 10–20 (1979a).
——, 'Die Fresken des Francesco di Giorgio in S. Agostino in Siena, *Mitteilungen des Kunsthistorischen Institutes in Florenz*, XXXII (1979), pp. 109–26 (1979b).
——, '"Castrum pingatur in palatio" 1: Ricerche storiche e iconographiche sui castelli dipinti nel Palazzo Pubblico di Siena, *Prospettiva*, XXVIII (1982), pp. 17–41.
——, 'Signorelli um 1490', *Jahrbuch der Berliner Museen*, XXVI (1984), pp. 181–256.
Shapley, F. R., *Catalogue of the Italian Paintings*, 2 vols, National Gallery of Art, Washington, D.C., 1979.

Shaw, C., 'Politics and institutional innovation in Siena, 1480–1498', *Bullettino Senese di Storia Patria*, CIII (1996), pp. 9–102, and CIV (1997), pp. 194–307.
Simons, P., 'Women in frames: the gaze, the eye, the profile in renaissance portraiture', *History Workshop: A Journal of Socialist and Feminist Historians*, XXV (1988), pp. 4–30.
Skaug, E., 'Notes on the chronology of Ambrogio Lorenzetti and a new painting from his shop', *Mitteilungen des Kunsthistorischen Institutes in Florenz*, XX (1976), pp. 301–32.
Skinner, Q., 'Ambrogio Lorenzetti's *Buon Governo* frescoes: two old questions, two new answers', *Journal of the Warburg and Courtauld Institutes*, LXII (1999), pp. 1–28.
Solberg, G., 'Taddeo di Bartolo: his life and work', Ph.D. diss., New York University, 1991.
Southard, E. C., *The Frescoes in Siena's Palazzo Pubblico, 1289–1539: Studies in Imagery and Relations to Other Communal Places in Tuscany*, 2 vols, Ann Arbor, 1980.
Sricchia Santoro, F., 'Ricerche senesi 2: Il Palazzo del Magnifico Pandolfo Petrucci', *Prospettiva*, XXIX (1982), pp. 24–31.
—— (ed.), *Da Sodoma a Marco Pino: pittori a Siena nella prima metà del cinquecento* (vol. 3 of the catalogue of the Chigi Saracini Collection), Siena, 1988.
Starn, R., 'The republican regime of the "Room of Peace" in Siena, 1338–40', *Representations*, XVIII (1987), pp. 1–32.
Starn, R., and Partridge, L., *Arts of Power: Three Halls of State in Italy, 1300–1600*, Berkeley, 1992.
Steinhoff, J., 'Artistic working relationships after the Black Death: a Sienese *compagnia*, *c.* 1350–1363(?)', *Renaissance Studies*, XIV (2000), pp. 1–45.
Steinhoff-Morrison, J., 'Bartolommeo Bulgarini and Sienese Painting of the Mid-Fourteenth Century', Ph. D. dissertation, Princeton University, 1989.
Stubblebine, J., *Guido da Siena*, Princeton, N.J., 1964.
Thornton, P., *The Italian Renaissance Interior, 1400–1600*, London, 1991.
Toracca, D., *La Libreria Piccolomini nel Duomo di Siena: The Piccolomini Library in Siena Cathedral*, eds S. Settis and D. Toracca, trans. M. Roberts, Modena, 1998.
Torriti, P., *Tutta Siena: Contrada per Contrada*, Florence, 1988.
——, *La Pinacoteca Nazionale di Siena*, 3rd ed., Genoa, 1990.
—— (ed.), *Beccafumi*, Milan, 1998.
Turner, J. (ed.), *The Grove Dictionary of Art*, 34 vols, London, 1996.
Valle, G. della, *Lettere Sanesi*, 3 vols., Venice and Rome, 1782–6.
Van der Ploeg, K., *Art, Architecture and Liturgy: Siena Cathedral in the Middle Ages*, Groningen, 1993.
Van Os, H., *Vecchietta and the Sacristy of the Siena Hospital Church*, The Hague, 1974.
——, 'The Black Death and Sienese painting: a problem of interpretation', *Art History*, IV (1981), pp. 237–49.
——, *Sienese Altarpieces 1215–1460*, 2 vols, Groningen, 1984–90.

——, 'Painting in a house of glass: the altarpieces of Pienza', *Simiolus*, XVII (1987), pp. 23–38.
Vasari, G., *Le vite de' più eccellenti pittori, scultori e architettori nelle redazioni del 1550 e 1568*, eds R. Bettarini and P. Barocchi, Florence, 1960– . Eng. trans. A. B. Hinds as *Lives of the Painters, Sculptors and Architects*, ed. W. Gaunt, 4 vols, London and New York, rev. ed., 1963.
Wainwright, V., 'The will of Ambrogio Lorenzetti', *Burlington Magazine*, CXVII (1975), pp. 543–4.
——, 'Conflict and popular government in fourteenth-century Siena: Il Monte dei Dodici, 1355–1368', in *Atti del III Convegno di studi sulla storia dei ceti dirigenti in Toscana*, Florence, 1980, pp. 57–80.
Waley, D., *Siena and the Sienese in the Thirteenth Century*, Cambridge, 1991.
Webb, D., *Patrons and Defenders: The Saints in the Italian City States*, London and New York, 1996.
Welch, E., *Art in Renaissance Italy 1350–1500*, 2nd ed., Oxford, 2000.
White, J., *The Birth and Rebirth of Pictorial Space*, 3rd ed., London, 1972.
——, *Duccio: Tuscan Art and the Medieval Workshop*, London, 1979.
——, *Art and Architecture in Italy: 1250–1400*, 3rd ed., New Haven and London, 1993.
Zarrilli, C., 'Farnese, Agnese', in *Dizionario biografico degli italiani*, Rome, 1995, LXV, pp. 50–51.

Photograph Credits

1, 2, 3, 4, 5, 7, 8, 9, 10, 11, 12, 13, 15, 16, 18, 19, 20, 21, 22, 23, 24, 27, 28, 29, 30, 31, 32, 33, 36, 37, 38, 40, 41, 42, 43, 45, 46, 47, 49, 51, 52, 53, 54, 56, 59, 63, 64, 65, 66, 69, 70, 71, 73, 75, 76, 77, 78, 79, 80, 81, 82, 84, 86, 87, 89, 90, 91, 93, 95, 97, 98, 99, 100, 102, 103, 104, 105, 106, 107, 108, 109, 110, 111, 112, 113, 115, 116, 117, 119, 120, 121, 122, 125, 128, 129, 130, 131, 133, 134, 135, 136, 137, 138, 139, 140, 144, 145, 146, 114, 142, 143, 145, 148, 149: Lensini, Siena

17, 26, 55, 58, 61, 92: © Photo Scala, Florence

25: © Photo Scala, Florence – courtesy of the Ministero Beni e Att. Culturali

39: Copyright The Frick Collection, New York

62, 124, 126: Copyright National Gallery, London

74, 127: Photographs © Board of Trustees, National Gallery of Art, Washington (74: Samuel H. Kress Collection; 127: Widener Collection)

85a, 85b: © Bildarchiv Preussischer Kulturbesitz, Berlin, 2003; Foto: Jörg P. Anders

88: Bohm, Venice

123: All rights reserved, The Metropolitan Museum of Art (Rogers Fund, 1914. (14.114.1–22))

132: © Copyright The British Museum

Index

Page numbers in *italics* refer to illustrations. Names of works of art are listed after any other subheadings